TEXT BY HANA LOFTUS

SAVE

FOREWORD BY ELIZABETH KOLBERT

365 WAYS TO SAVE THE EARTH

EARTH

NEW & UPDATED EDITION

ABRAMS, NEW YORK

PHILIPPE BOURSEILLER

FOREWORD

The book that you are holding in your hands is based on contradiction or, if you prefer, disproportion. Each date presents a bit of advice for ordinary urban and suburban living: Dispose of leftover paint properly; check your car's exhaust; boil only as much water as you need when making tea or coffee. Paired with each proposal is one of Philippe Bourseiller's spectacular photographs of the natural world—Alaska's Denali massif, Hawaii's Kilauea volcano, or Patagonia's Cerro Torre. On the left is the quotidian, on the right the sublime.

The amazing thing about this disproportion is that it turns out to be not at all disproportionate. How we go about our daily lives—what we eat, how we get to work, where we build our houses—has a transformative effect not just on our immediate surroundings, but on places as far away as the North Pole and Antarctica. In days spent moving from underground parking garages to hermetically sealed office towers and back again to air-conditioned homes, this fact is easily overlooked, and therefore it is all the more imperative that we attend to it. The food we buy in the supermarket often comes from halfway around the world; by purchasing it, we may be supporting the destruction of distant forests and indigenous cultures. The fertilizer we apply to our lawns washes off into streams and eventually into the sea, where it contributes to algae blooms that produce eutrophic 'dead zones' where no fish can survive. The water we pump from underground aquifers cannot be replaced as quickly as it is withdrawn; what we waste running half-empty dishwashers today will be lost to future generations that surely will need it.

Global warming is perhaps the clearest example of how our ordinary, everyday actions alter the planet. One of the most astonishing places that Philippe Bourseiller photographed for this volume is Greenland, which, after Antarctica, is home to the world's largest ice sheet. Last summer, I visited Greenland to interview scientists who were studying the effects of warming on the ice. I spent a day in a village on Disko Bay watching icebergs float out to sea and while I was there I spoke with some native fishermen. They described how they have seen the icebergs in the bay steadily grow smaller in recent years; instead of towering mountains of white that drift around for weeks, the icebergs now tend to be low and more likely to break apart. They also told me that for as long as anyone could remember, the bay had remained frozen over for several months each winter. For the last few years, however, there has been open water in Disko Bay all year long. The fishermen are alarmed by the change, as we all should be.

Sea ice reflects sunlight; open water absorbs it. Great stretches of Arctic sea ice are disappearing and as they vanish the earth's reflectivity decreases. The result is a feedback mechanism that amplifies human-induced global warming and pushes us closer and closer to catastrophe. Scientists warn that if we do not take steps soon to curb our emissions of greenhouse gases, we could begin to melt not just the sea ice, but the Greenland ice sheet itself. Greenland's ice sheet holds enough water to raise global sea levels by twenty-three feet.

Americans make up only four percent of the world's population, and yet we produce nearly a quarter of the world's greenhouse gas emissions. This imposes on us a particularly heavy responsibility for the way the planet is changing. Roughly three quarters of all electricity in the United States is produced by burning fossil fuels, so every time we flip on the lights, turn on the coffee maker, or watch the news on TV, we are adding to the problem, if indirectly. We contribute to it directly whenever we go out for a drive. Probably the single-most important step any individual can take to reduce his or her emissions is to purchase a fuel-efficient car and then, as often as possible, leave it in the garage. Global warming is not a problem that can be 'solved' by individual actions; that demands a concerted international effort—one that will stretch over decades. However, unless we take steps to reduce our impact on this issue, it is hard to imagine how it can ever be addressed successfully.

One of the themes of Philippe Bourseiller's photography is the power of nature; another is nature's vulnerability. This, too, seems to be a contradiction that ultimately is not. The forces that have shaped the planet over eons — whether volcanic eruptions or tectonic shifts — remain beyond man's influence. A human figure walking across the Greenland ice sheet or scaling Trou de Fer on Réunion appears as little more than an orange or grey dot in Bourseiller's photographs. At the same time, we tiny human beings have already proved to be quite capable of, and indeed adept at, destroying species that inhabited the planet long before our own species evolved. We are now in the process of altering the chemistry of earth's atmosphere by burning fossil fuel deposits that were laid down during the age of the dinosaurs. Already we have succeeded in raising carbon-dioxide concentrations to a level higher than at any other point in the last three and a half million years. 'The lifetime of one human being is nothing on a geological scale, but the traces he leaves behind can be unbelievably destructive,' Bourseiller observed.

For all their grandeur, the photographs collected in this volume are elegiac. 'I do not change or transform reality,' Bourseiller has said about his work. 'I am content with just seizing an instant of it. I hope my photographs help people become aware and fully conscious of the fact that the extraordinary landscapes that surround us are extremely fragile and they must be protected constantly.'

— Elizabeth Kolbert

CATEGORIES

Home

January: 2, 4, 5, 7, 13, 16, 26, 28

February: 3, 6, 7, 10, 15, 17, 21, 25, 28

March: 1, 18, 23, 26, 30

April: 2, 17, 19, 22, 25, 26, 28

May: 4, 7, 14, 20, 22, 23, 25, 28, 30, 31

June: 1, 2, 5, 6, 7, 11, 13, 21, 22, 24, 26, 27, 30

July: 5, 8, 18

August: 7, 9, 21, 24

September: 5, 6, 14, 21, 24, 25, 30

October: 9, 12, 16, 17, 18, 20

November: 5, 6, 7, 10, 14, 15, 16, 18, 21

December: 5, 6, 8, 11, 14, 16, 17, 19, 28, 30

Shopping

January: 1, 8, 9, 12, 17, 20, 22, 30, 31

March: 5, 9, 11, 15, 19, 24

April: 1, 15, 18, 27, 29

May: 2, 5, 8, 9, 13, 17, 18

June: 12, 15, 16, 23, 28

July: 6, 11, 17, 23, 25, 27, 28, 29

August: 3, 10, 11, 19, 22, 23, 27, 28, 29

September: 2, 9, 23, 26, 27, 28, 29

October: 3, 5, 7, 10, 15, 19, 21, 24, 27, 29, 30

November: 4, 8, 9, 17, 19, 26, 30

December: 12, 15, 18, 21, 22, 23, 24, 27, 29

Leisure

January: 10, 11, 24

February: 2, 4, 5, 14, 26

March: 12, 13, 14, 17, 22, 27, 29

April: 6, 13, 14, 16, 21

May: 6, 12, 16, 19, 26

June: 3, 4, 8, 9, 14, 17, 19, 20, 29

July: 4, 10, 13, 14, 15, 16, 19, 20, 21, 26, 30, 31

August: 2, 6, 14, 15, 18, 20, 25, 31

September: 1, 7, 13, 19

October: 26, 31

November: 24

December: 25, 26, 31

Transport

January: 19, 25

February: 11, 16, 19, 20

March: 6, 8, 20, 31

April: 4, 11

May: 10, 21, 27

June: 18, 25

July: 2, 12, 22

August: 1, 4, 5, 8, 13

September: 3, 10, 22

October: 2, 14, 28

November: 2, 22, 27

December: 1

Health / Family

January: 15, 18, 21, 23, 27

February: 1, 13, 22, 23

March: 2, 3, 4, 10, 28

April: 3, 5, 7, 8, 10, 23, 30

June: 10

July: 3, 9, 24

August: 12, 17, 26

September: 8, 11, 18

October: 1, 4, 6, 8, 11, 23

November: 11, 12, 23, 29

December: 2, 7, 20

Office

January: 14

February: 9, 18, 27

March: 7, 16

April: 9

May: 1, 15

July: 7

August: 30

September: 4, 15, 16, 20

October: 13, 22, 25

November: 1, 3, 13, 20, 28

December: 3, 9, 10

Gardening

January: 3, 6, 29

February: 8, 12, 24

March: 21, 25

April: 12, 20, 24

May: 3, 11, 24, 29

July: 1

August: 16

September: 12, 17

November: 25

December: 4, 13

Resolve to be a conscious consumer.

Everything we buy has a direct or indirect effect on the environment. Before buying things this year, ask some questions: How and where was it made? Did this process produce pollution? Does it use too much energy? Can the packaging be recycled? Will it last a long time and can it be easily repaired? Action to protect the environment can begin at the supermarket shelf or market stall. Begin to think about the items that you can buy from local sources — food, clothing, gifts — because the closer you are to the source of the product, the lower its ecological footprint.

One of the best ways to change the world is to vote with your wallet. Buy only what you need; buy the best quality and most eco-friendly items available; and don't give in to short-lived trends that fill your life with useless things.

Niger River, Mali

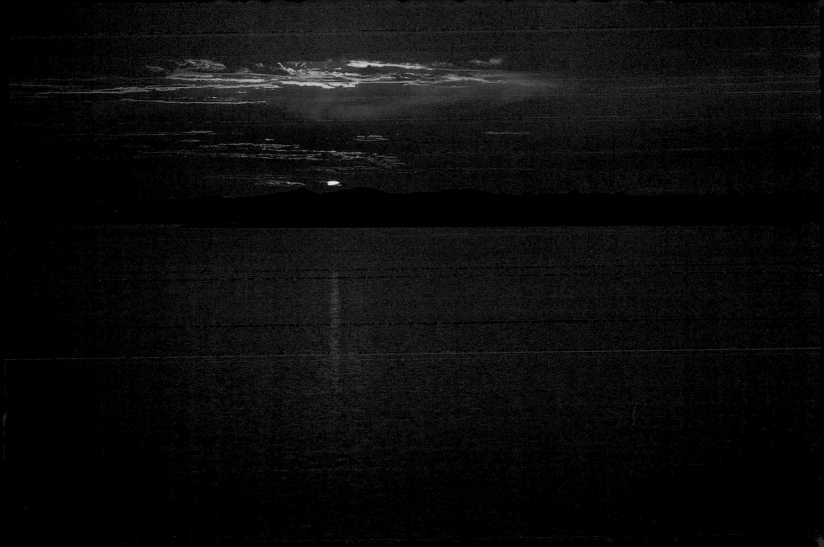

Turn down your heating by 1°C.

Our homes are a major source of the greenhouse gases responsible for climate change—responsible for around a third of carbon-dioxide emissions in the United Kingdom. Eighty percent of the energy used in the home is for heating and hot water, so carefully managing our domestic heating can make a big difference in the amount of carbon dioxide that we create.

Our homes are often overheated. The ideal living room temperature is 18 to 21°C, and bedrooms are healthier at 16°C. Turning your heating down by 1°C can save 300 kg of carbon dioxide per year and up to 10% off your bill. Use your heat wisely, and insulate well.

Whale shark, Australia

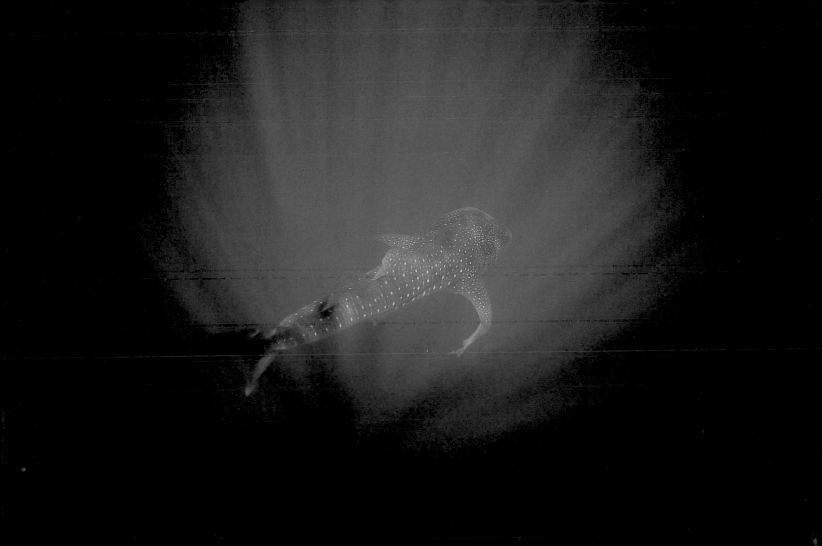

Compost your Christmas tree.

As soon as Christmas is over, trees are dumped on pavements to be picked up with the household waste and burned in incinerators. Many local authorities now collect the trees for composting or have special drop-off points for unwanted trees, so find out how the scheme for your area works. Besides providing compost or mulch, recycled trees can be used in larger environmental projects like stabilizing shorelines and eroding beachfront. Christmas cards should also be recycled.

Make sure your Christmas tree gets composted. If your local authority does not collect Christmas trees, ask if it can arrange to do so. And consider alternatives, like a potted Christmas tree that can later be planted in the garden.

Rain forest, Costa Rica

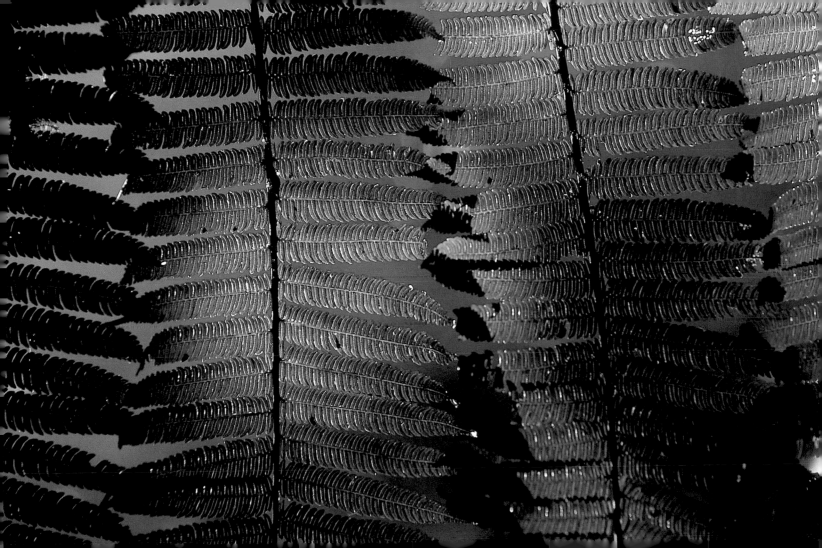

Switch to 'green' electricity.

Generating electricity for domestic consumption is very inefficient, with 80% of the energy in conventional fuels being lost in the process of converting it to grid electricity. Switching to a 'green' energy provider or tariff doesn't need to cost any more, as almost every green provider matches the price of conventional electricity. By purchasing green electricity, you are not only reducing your carbon footprint but also supporting investment in new renewable energy schemes, helping renewables replace fossil fuels and nuclear power.

Switch to a renewable energy tariff today and cut your personal carbon-dioxide emissions by over 1.5 tonnes per year.

Stream, Rocky Mountain National Park, United States

Improve the efficiency of your radiators.

The world's consumption of energy produces vast amounts of pollution and waste, especially that produced by the nuclear industry. Today there are 437 nuclear power stations in the world, an additional 30 are under construction, and 74 more are in the planning stages. Among them they produce 16% of the world's electricity, and 10,000 tonnes of nuclear waste per year, in addition to the 200,000 tonnes already in existence.

To reduce your domestic energy consumption, make your radiators more efficient by placing reflective panels behind them that will bounce the heat back into the room. Bleed trapped air out of water-filled radiators several times each season; the less air in the system, the more heat it will emit.

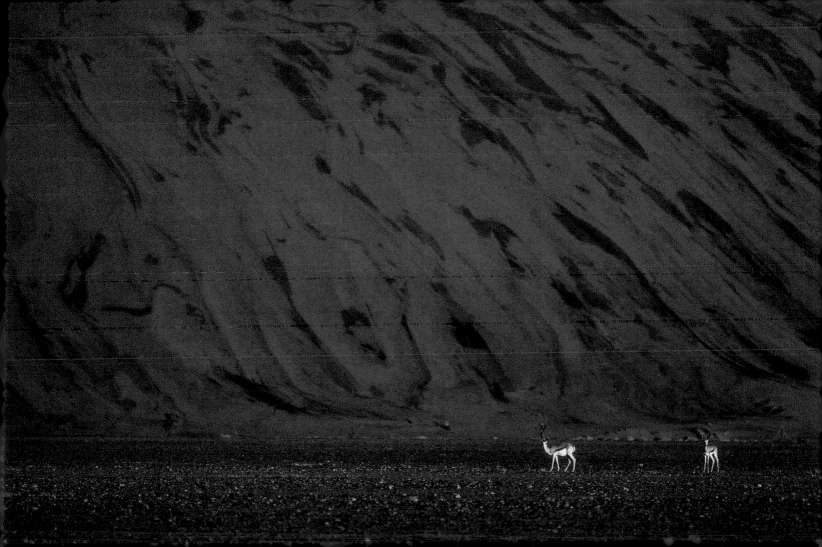

Prevent erosion.

Soil erosion is one form of soil degradation caused by water and wind, and aggravated by human development practices. The texture of the soil, the angle of the slope it is on, and the quality of the vegetative cover all play a part in erosion. Erosion degrades the health of the soil; impacts water quality through runoff, and damages riverbanks and pond edges. Some indicators of problems with erosion include bare spots on the lawn or property, muddy water in a stream or drainage ditch, exposed tree roots, silt build-up, and the widening and deepening of stream channels.

Minimize erosion by mulching, and installing gutters and downspouts that discharge onto the lawn (protect the soil at the outlet using splash blocks or drainage tile).

Klyuchevskaya Volcano, Kamchatka, Russia

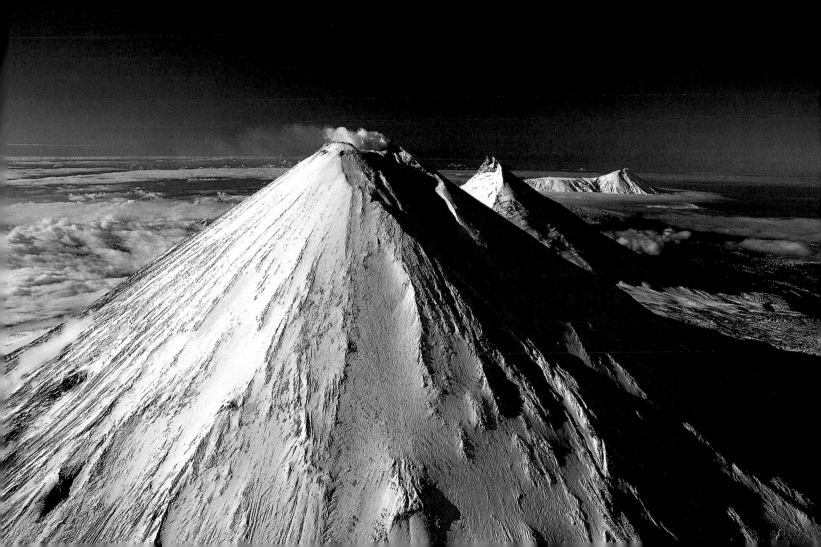

Reduce the amount of water your toilet uses.

In the United Kingdom, each of us uses around 150 litres of water at home each day. The toilet is the biggest water waster in the bathroom; a standard toilet made before 1994 can use up to 9 litres per flush.

By placing a bottle filled with sand or water in your toilet cistern you will reduce the volume of water used with each flush. Don't use a brick as pieces of decaying brick can get into the toilet's system and cause leaks. Better still; replace your toilet with a low-flow toilet, which can decrease water use to 3 litres for every flush.

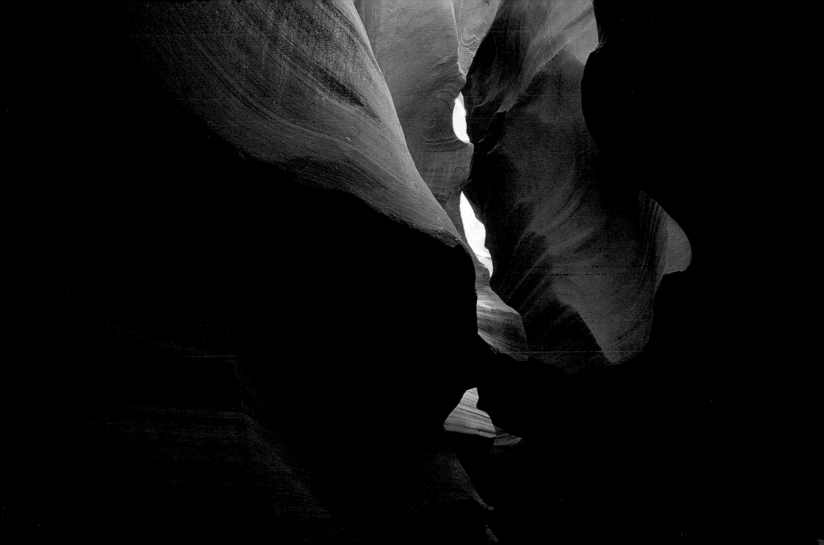

Recycle your mobile phone.

Mobile phones are laced with toxic components like lead and mercury. On average, mobile phones in the United Kingdom are discarded and replaced with newer models after only 12 months—we buy 18 million new phones every year but recycle only 5% of our old ones. In developing nations, reconditioned mobile phones can help people in areas that lack reliable landlines to stay in touch with relatives living and working abroad, look for jobs, and stay up to date on industry and political news that affects them.

Your mobile phone can have a second life. Many charities collect old phones, refurbish them, and send them to people in need. You can resell a newer phone on eBay. And if your phone really can't have another life, contact the manufacturer of your phone—they all now operate take-back programmes that will recycle it properly, disposing of the toxic materials it contains.

The Bahamas

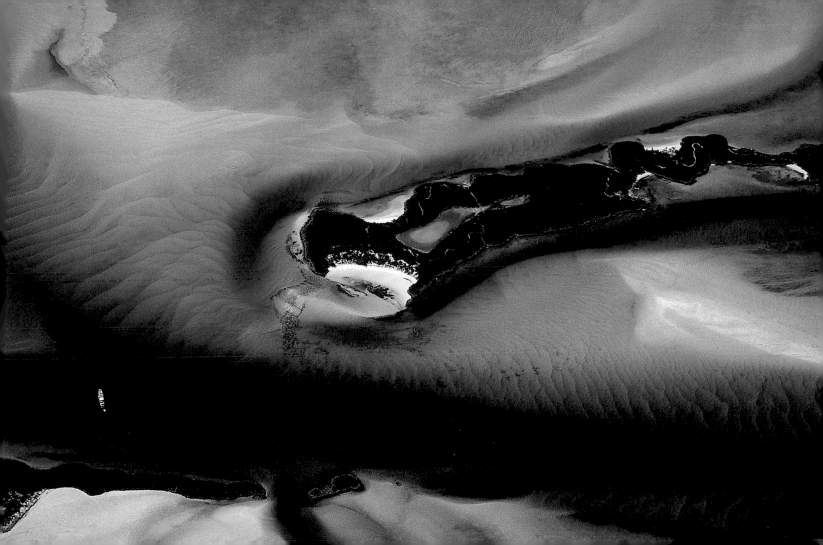

Buy organic food.

World consumption of chemical pesticides and fertilizers is growing: It leapt from 30 million tonnes a year in 1960 to 140 million tonnes in 2000. These chemicals not only consume large amounts of energy in their production, but degrade the soil and groundwater, kill beneficial insects as well as the so-called pests, and can leave traces in the crop itself, which will enter your body when you eat. Organic farming spares the environment from this degradation and your body from these toxins.

You can change this by buying organic. Some good choices to start with are apples, red and green peppers, carrots, celery, and spinach; these products retain very high levels of pesticide residue. You can then broaden the range of products for which you buy organic at your own pace. Visit your local market and ask stallholders about their growing methods. Many small farms follow the principles of organic agriculture but cannot officially advertise as being organic because they have not obtained certification — a difficult and expensive process.

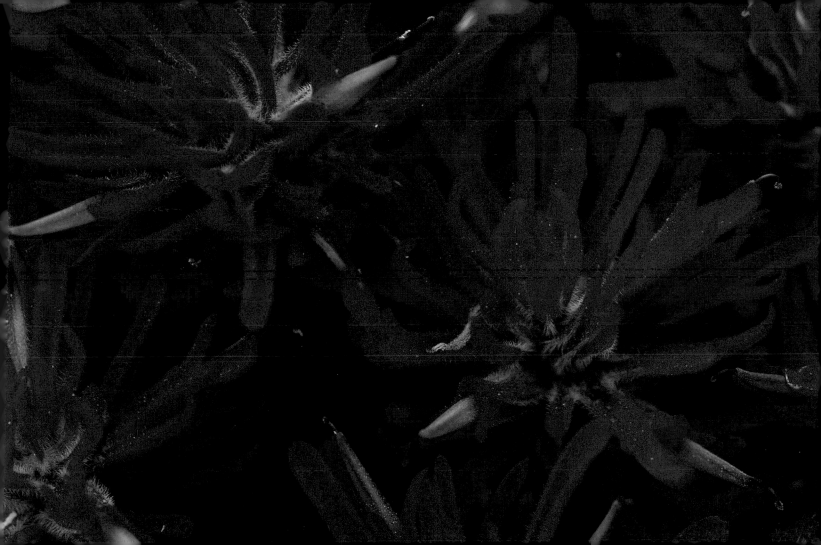

Calculate your ecological footprint.

Want to know your real impact on the planet? An ecological footprint is the amount of land each of us would need to sustain our individual consumption of resources from fossil fuels to food. Currently, the global ecological footprint is 23% bigger than what the earth could technically regenerate in a year. Based on current population there are roughly 1.8 hectares worth of resources per person. The average American uses 9.6 hectares (second only to the United Arab Emirates), while the average UK citizen uses 5.6 hectares, the average Chinese person uses 1.7 hectares, and the average Bangladeshi uses only 0.5 hectares.

Calculating your personal footprint will give an idea of where you stand compared to the national averages — and the more sobering picture of how many planets would be needed to sustain life if everyone shared your footprint.

Orangutan, Malaysia

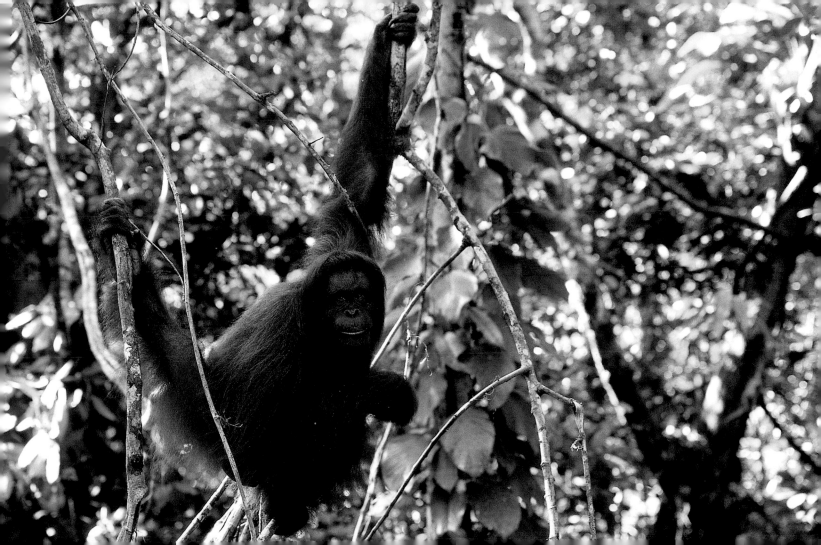

Do not feed wild animals.

Whether they are birds or mammals, on land or at sea, feeding wild animals changes their diet and can alter their behaviour. They may grow accustomed to the presence of humans and risk becoming dependent on receiving food instead of seeking it out themselves. In addition, touching them may endanger their health by exposing them to illnesses to which they are not immune — as well as putting your own health at risk.

Be content to watch wild animals from a distance without trying to attract them with food. Make sure you put your own food and waste out of the reach of wild animals, so they are not tempted to help themselves while you are not looking.

Marine iguanas, Galápagos Islands

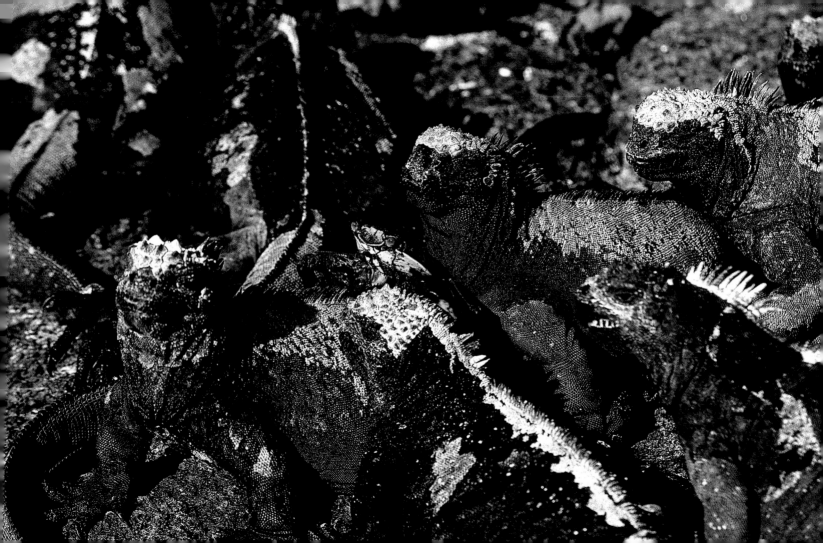

Invest in socially responsible companies.

Socially Responsible Investing (SRI) not only looks at the bottom line, but also at the environmental and social impact of where your money goes. SRI seeks out companies that demonstrate that they have obligations toward the environment and society, and not just to the consumer; companies that develop collaborative relationships with employees and investors; and businesses that are honest and transparent in their reporting processes. Such investments support projects that encourage social integration and job creation, as well as initiatives in areas such as ecology, renewable energy, fair trade, and organic farming and food. Many of these are sectors of high growth, so investing responsibly can reap good financial returns too.

Make ethical investments — there are now many funds and packages out there. Show businesses that investors and customers care about more than just the bottom line — that improving the conditions of the planet and our societies is just as important as making money.

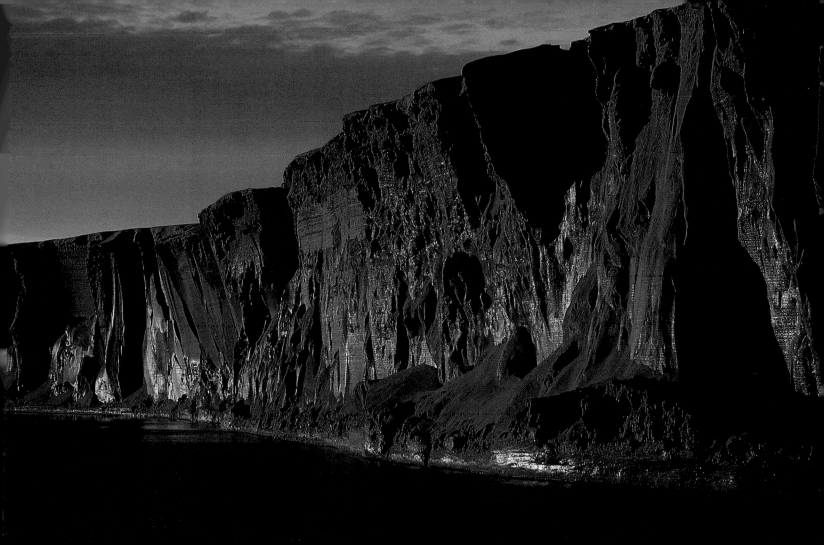

Use your fridge properly.

Fridges and freezers require large amounts of energy to chill foods, but with a little care you can reduce their impact on the environment without losing any of their benefits. Perhaps the greatest impact on energy use of a fridge is the temperature of the room it is in. A 5°C decrease in the ambient room temperature can decrease energy use by 40%. Do not place your fridge or freezer near a heat source, such as a cooker, heater or radiator, or a south-facing window.

Don't put hot dishes in the fridge, or overfill it — and defrost your freezer regularly as a build-up of ice means that more energy is used to keep it cold. Make sure doors close tightly — if the seal loosens, the cool air will escape wasting energy. If you hear the compressor go on a lot you may have a leak, so get your fridge serviced.

Hoarfrost, Sweden

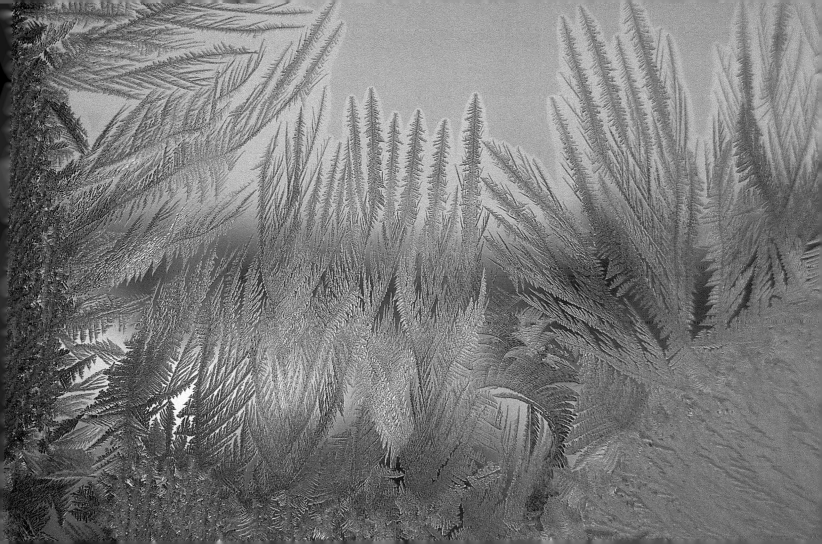

Coffee, milk, and sugar: Say 'no' to individual portions.

Coffee in miniportions uses 10 times as much packaging as when it is purchased in bulk. This extra packaging adds 20% to 40% to the cost of a product and produces a large amount of unnecessary waste.

At your workplace, suggest that individual servings of coffee, tea, sugar, and milk be replaced by large packages for everyone's use. You will reduce the amount of packaging and the cost. The price of individually packaged foodstuffs is often much greater than bulk packets, so your company will save money too.

Atacama Desert, Chile

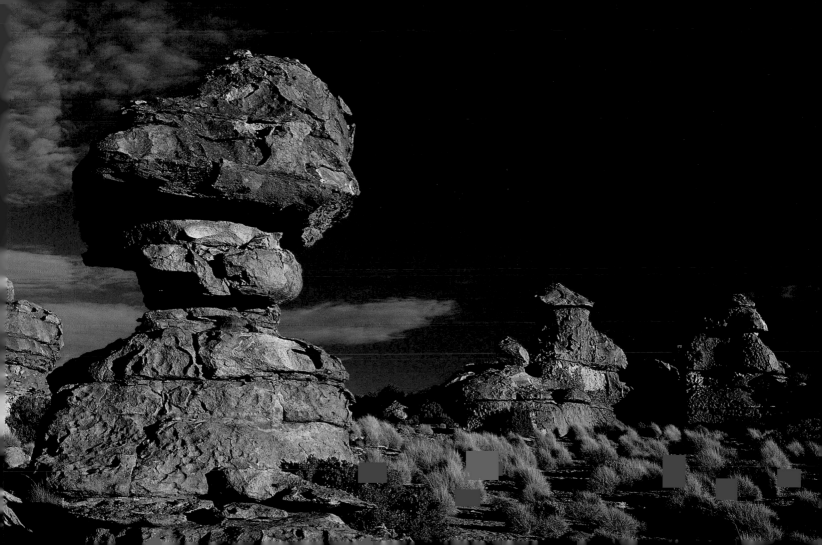

Use the sleep timer.

Scientists say that in the coming years the habitats, natural resources, and species that make up life on earth will no longer be able to adapt beyond the increases in global temperatures. The tipping point is set to 2°C, which will result in dramatic rise of sea levels. To remain within the limits, worldwide greenhouse-gas emissions would have to be cut by around 60% now.

TVs and stereos often have sleep timers, which allow the appliance to shut off after a given amount of time. If you normally fall asleep watching TV or listening to music, use the timer to avoid wasting the energy of the appliance running all night.

Swans, Japan

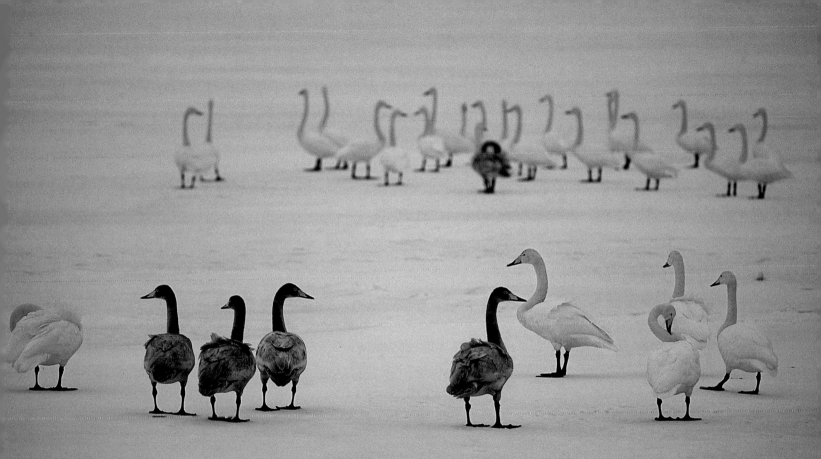

Switch off lights you don't need.

In the space of a century, world energy demand—used for electricity, heating, and transport, for example—has increased twentyfold. If current trends continue unabated the world's energy consumption will double by 2030. Most of this energy comes from oil, gas, and coal, which produce greenhouse gases. Greenhouse gases are naturally present in the atmosphere and maintain temperatures on earth that are favourable to life but as we now know, too much greenhouse effect leads to warming of the global climate.

Make a point of switching off lights that do not need to be on, especially when you leave a room, and try to use daylight wherever possible. The less that electricity is used, the less energy is needed, and the less greenhouse gas is pumped into the atmosphere.

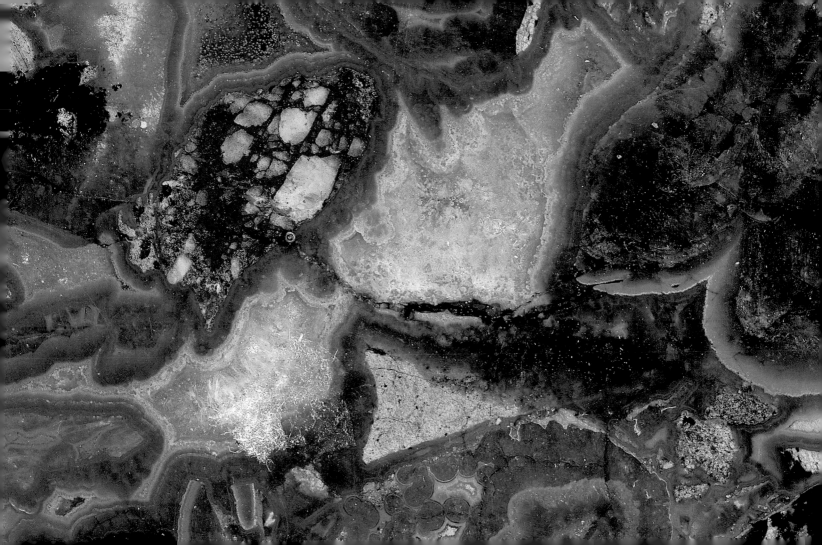

Refuse to buy objects made from ivory.

Massacred for the ivory that is its defence against attack, the African elephant has almost disappeared from the planet. In Kenya and Tanzania about 70,000 African elephants were killed each year between 1975 and 1980. Between 1980 and 2000, their numbers fell from 1.4 million to 400,000.

Although the international ivory trade was banned in 1990, ivory jewellery and statuettes can still be bought in African and Asian markets. Traders may offer to sell ivory objects illegally. Don't give in to the temptation to buy them: This encourages trafficking and, since this trade is illegal, you will not be allowed to take them home.

Piton de la Fournaise Volcano, Réunion

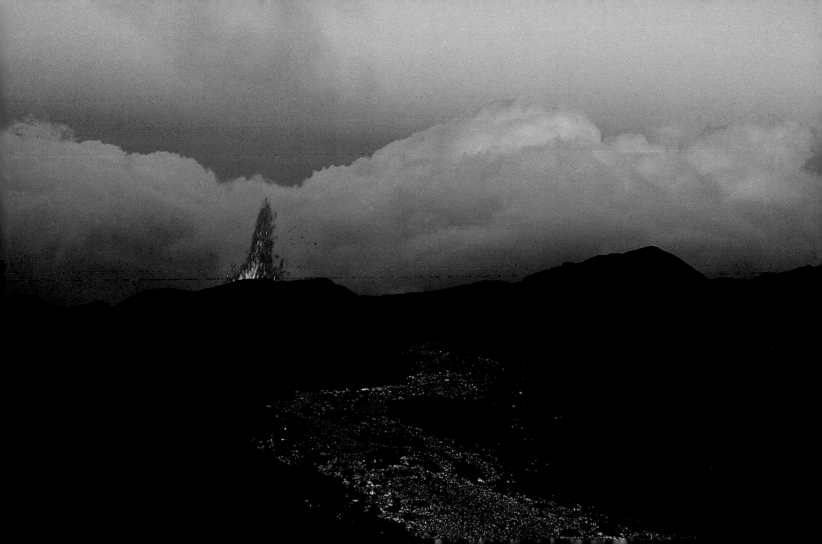

Rediscover your grandmother's remedies.

Chemicals have invaded our lives. In the 1980s there were 500 times as many chemical products as during the 1940s. Today, an average family uses over 100 litres of various chemical cleaners each year. These products, which generally contain substances harmful to your health and the environment, find their way into water, air, and soil and can stay there for many years.

Rediscover your grandparents' natural remedies: washing-up liquid for removing oil stains, white wine vinegar for removing mould or mildew, baking soda for scouring, cedar chips for keeping moths away, lemon juice for polishing copper or disinfecting surfaces, and many more.

Gorilla, Rwanda

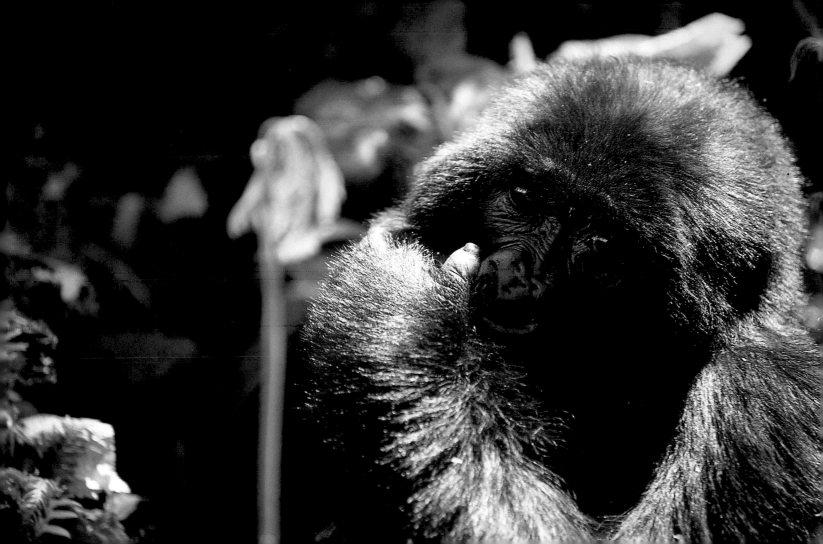

Drive more slowly.

It has taken nature 250 million years to produce the oil that we will probably use up in the next century. The United Kingdom consumes more than 60 million barrels of oil for transport every year, and this continues to rise, making a huge contribution to climate change.

Fuel efficiency declines quickly when travelling above 97 kilometres per hour. Going from 89 to 121 kilometres per hour can increase your fuel consumption by 20% or more. Even decreasing your speed by 8 kilometres per hour will boost your fuel efficiency by a couple of gallons.

River, Iceland

Write to manufacturers urging them to keep genetically modified (GM) crops out of animal feeds.

In 2005, 222 million acres of transgenic crops were grown worldwide, although we have little idea about how these affect local ecologies and wild species. Present labelling regulations do not require disclosure of products from animals that have been fed GM crops (such as meat, fish, eggs, or dairy products). Eighty percent of GM crops find their way into our food by this indirect route.

You can write to farmers and distributors and urge them to keep GM crops out of animal feeds, and lobby the government for better labelling. This way, you will keep them off your plate, and protect the environment.

Sea lion, Galápagos Islands

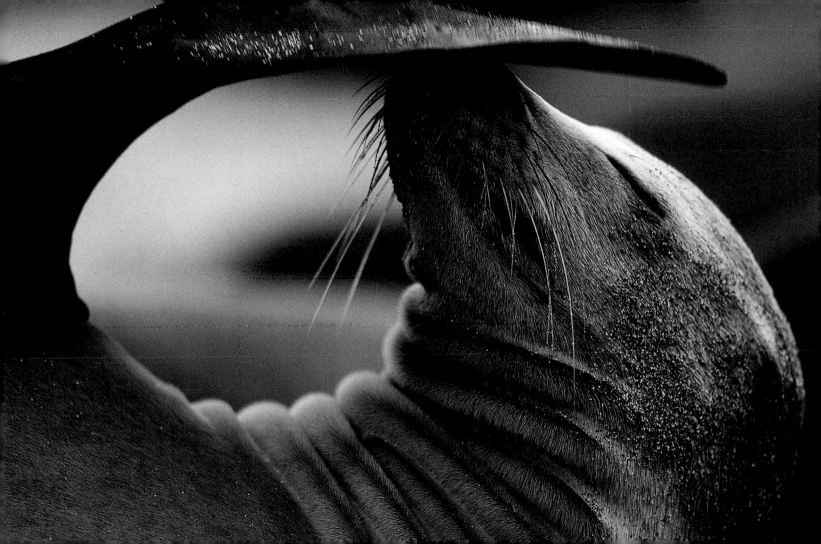

Do not throw out your children's old toys.

Unchecked consumption of the world's natural resources and increasing production waste are mostly because of the actions of the United States, Europe, and Japan, home to 20% of the world's population. A European produces around 5 times as much waste as someone in a developing country. During his or her lifetime, a child born in an industrialized country will consume more resources and generate more pollution than 40 children in a developing country.

When your child outgrows a toy, it is pointless to keep it as a relic; encourage your child to donate old toys to charities, or to children's hospitals or foundations, and explain the benefits of doing this.

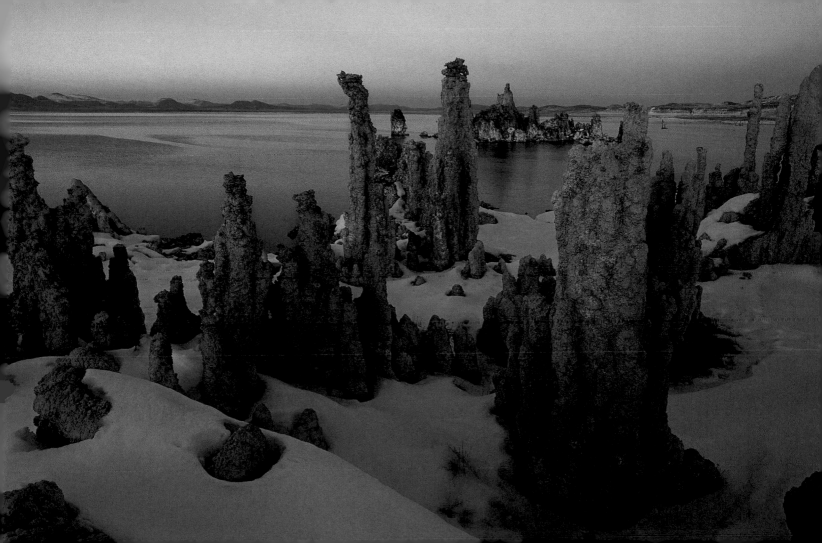

Avoid big-box stores.

In wealthy countries today, consumers travel by car to do their shopping in big-box stores built on the edges of urban areas. They are often seen as cheap and convenient, but this comes at a price to the environment and to the local economy. Supermarket chains exert a high degree of control on the supply chain of food and other goods, which they use to force down farm prices or to import products from countries where labour is cheap and environmental legislation almost nonexistent. They favour intensive agriculture rather than local, mixed farms and every new supermarket causes hundreds of jobs to be lost from local businesses.

Shop closer to home. Not only does supermarket food travel miles to the store and promote unsustainable farming, it also uses excess packaging, contributes to the urbanisation of green spaces, and adds to pollution through the use of cars. Do your shopping locally and by foot, if you can.

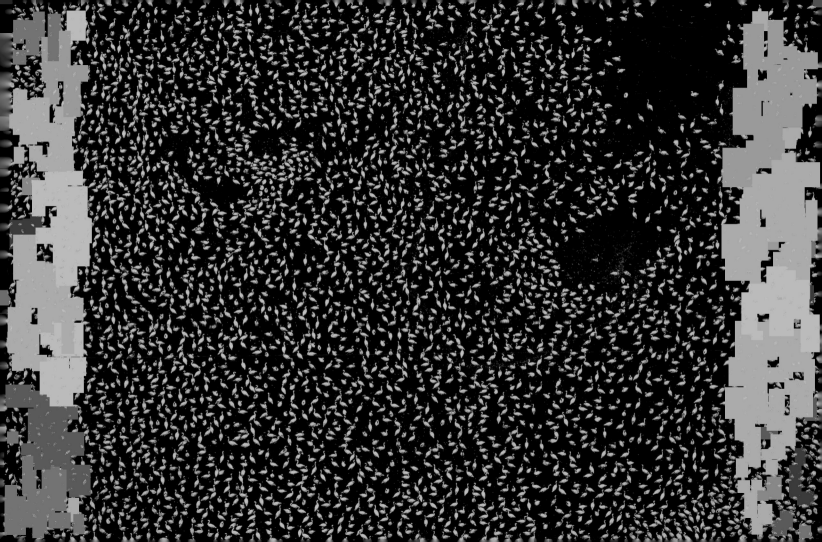

Green your workout.

A chain of gyms in Hong Kong is experimenting with treadmills that capture the energy generated by joggers, sending it to a battery that helps to power the gym. But until such practises are widespread, the average fitness centre excels at wasting energy. First, there's the electricity needed to power all of the machines, lights, and the personal TVs. Then there's the air-conditioning needed to keep a room full of sweating people at a reasonable temperature; not to mention the large amounts of laundry, the sale of bottled water and other drinks, and the equipment that is bought and replaced before the end of its lifespan.

Instead of joining a gym, go outside for a walk, jog, or cycle ride. In the United Kingdom the British Trust of Conservation Volunteers has created a Green Gym program where participants burn calories while doing environmental conservation activities like tree planting or creating and maintaining community gardens.

Lake Magadi, Kenya

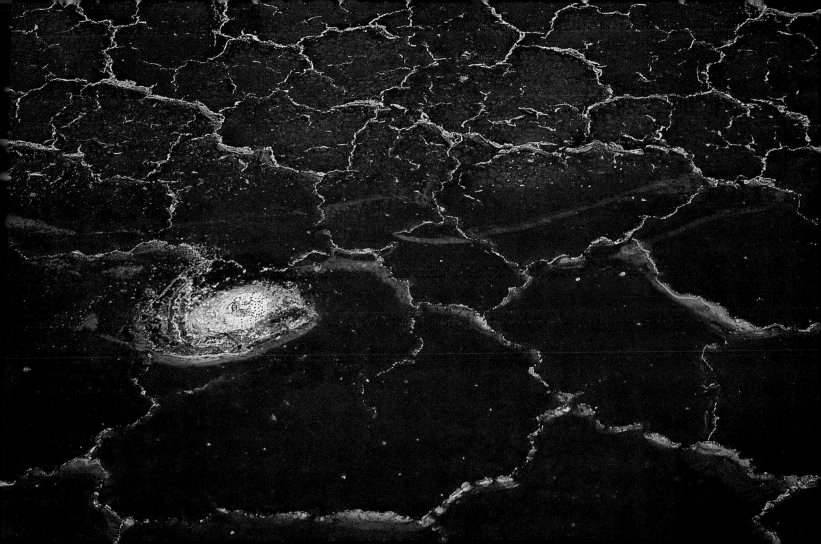

Support animal-friendly or animal-free circuses.

Wild animals used in circuses or travelling shows rarely live in humane conditions; they are often deprived of any kind of regular veterinary care, and are usually chained in one position for long periods of the day with no opportunity to move. Legislation meant to protect these animals is ineffective and rarely enforced. In addition, the transitory nature of circuses means that violators are rarely, if ever, pursued and prosecuted.

Do not visit circuses or travelling shows that keep wild animals in captivity unless you are sure that they are treated humanely, and lobby for better enforcement of animal protection rules.

Clown fish, Australia

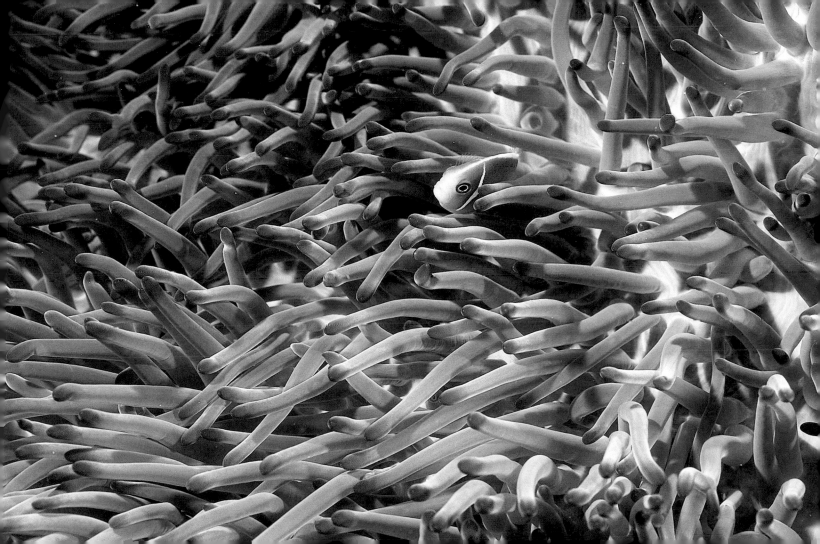

Use public transport.

Air pollution is at the top of the list of problems caused by motor vehicles, followed by car accidents, noise, erosion of habitats by roads, and damage to plants and animals. Cars take up a lot of space in cities, where 4 out of 5 trips are made by car. This congestion costs us dearly: It is estimated that the United Kingdom loses £20 billion in wasted time every year.

Use public transport wherever possible — a bus can take 40 single-passenger cars off the road — and start car sharing. You could also encourage your company to allow employees to work from home; if every worker stayed at home for a day a week, the UK's emissions would reduce by 1%.

After the eruption of Mount
Pinatubo, Philippines

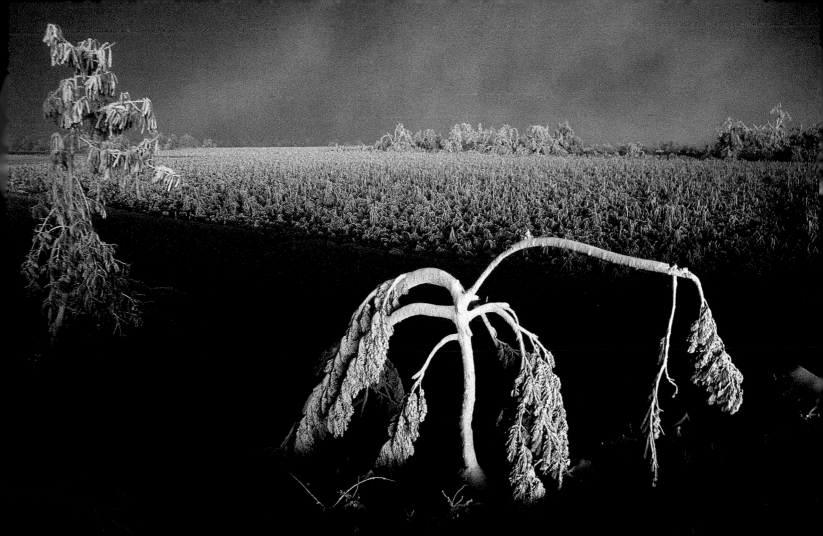

Have your boiler serviced regularly.

Domestic hot water should never be above 60°C. Above that temperature the high heat can lead to limescale and corrosion of pipes and apparatus. Limescale increases heating costs by insulating the water from the heating source, and therefore more energy is needed to heat the water. Moreover, a badly maintained boiler can also lead to air pollution within the home.

To check whether your boiler is poisoning the air in your home or using too much energy, have it serviced once a year. If your boiler is more than 15 years old, consider replacing it with a newer model, which is likely to be at least 30% more efficient.

Waves, United States

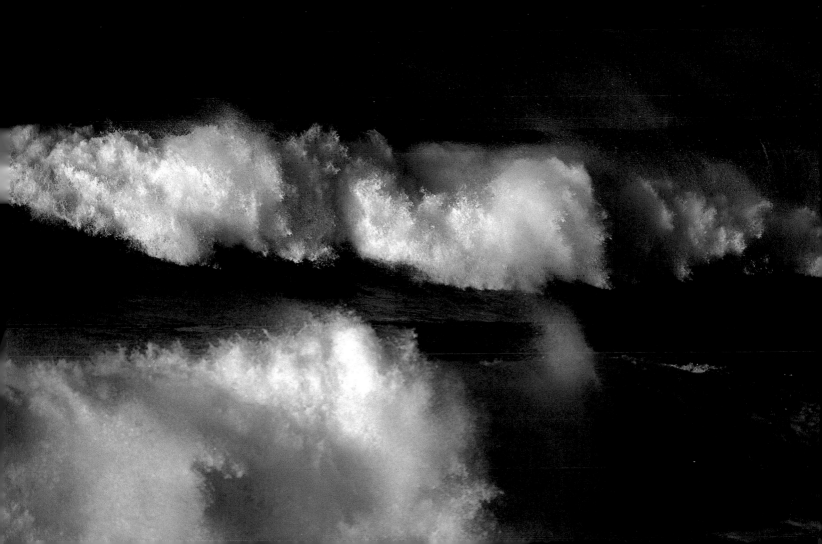

Don't eat at fast-food chains.

One billion people around the world live in poverty. More than 800 million of them go to bed hungry every night. In 2000, the United Nations made a commitment to halving the number of malnourished people in the world by 2015 by making it one of the 8 Millennium Development Goals; by the end of 2007 they were only one-third of the way toward realizing this goal. Meanwhile, no part of the world is spared the wave of fast-food chain restaurant openings, a veritable standard-bearer of globalization.

When you next need a quick bite, think about where you go and try a local café rather than a fast-food chain. Make your children aware of the other results of mass-produced food: polluting industrial agriculture, poor nutritional quality, mountains of nonrecyclable packaging, and standardization of tastes.

River, Iceland

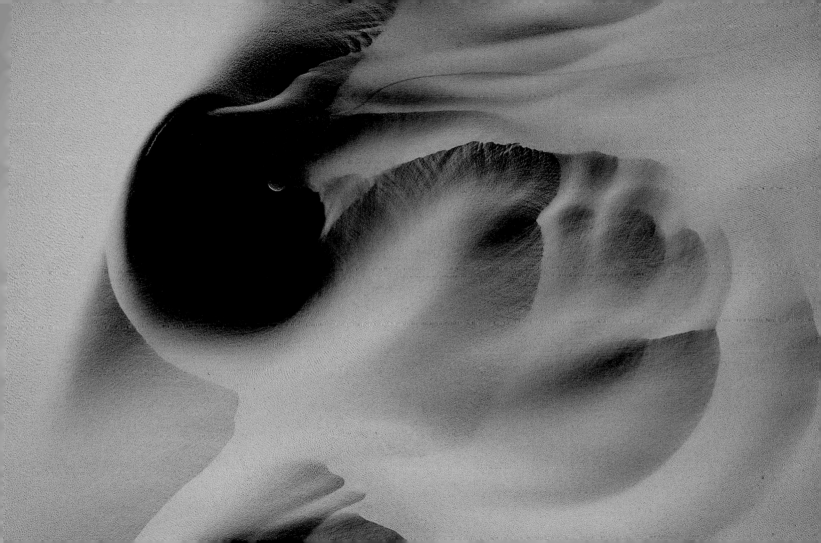

Turn off your cooker early.

Climate change will have severe repercussions on plant and animal life. By changing natural habitats, it will create havoc, especially with species distribution. Many species whose habitats will change will not be able to migrate quickly enough, will have nowhere to go, or will not have time to evolve and adapt to new conditions. Climate change is likely to threaten a quarter of the world's species directly and certain studies have even suggested that by 2050 almost 1 in 5 species will have disappeared from the planet, even in the unlikely event that global warming is minimal.

There are many small ways you can save energy and reduce greenhouse-gas emissions. In the kitchen, switch off the cooker a few minutes before cooking is complete. You will make use of residual heat, which will continue the job while saving energy.

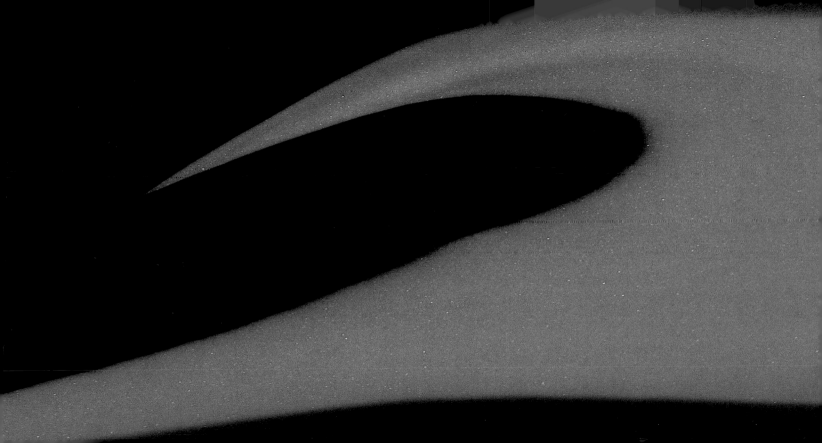

Compost nonrecyclable cardboard and paper.

You can reduce the volume of your waste by 80% simply by recycling and composting all waste that is suitable. Reducing the waste that goes to landfills helps keep the countryside clean and reduces our use of raw materials, as well as the energy used to extract and process them into products.

Grass cuttings, food waste, and other compostable items account for about a quarter of our annual waste. You can add some types of nonrecyclable paper and cardboard (such as tissues, wipes, egg cartons, and ash from your fireplace) to your compost as well. Their fibres will aerate the compost and help the organisms that cause decomposition.

Dwarf birches, Iceland

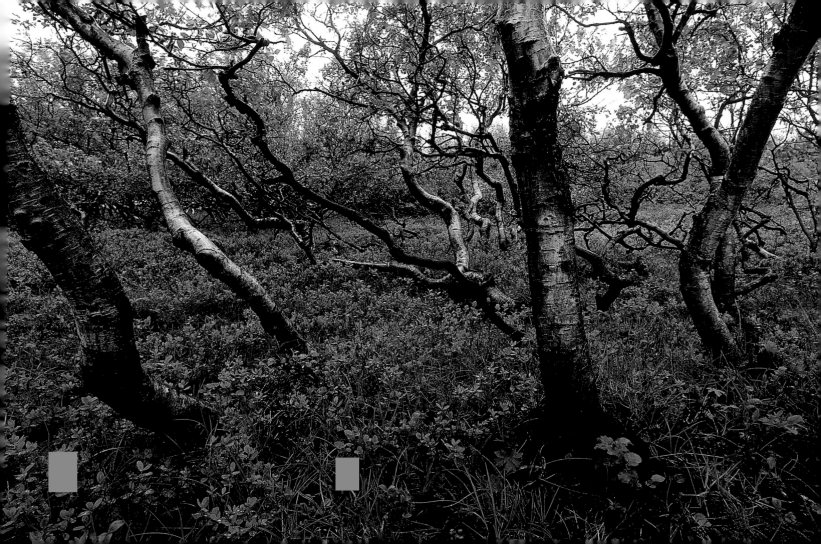

Pack waste-free lunches.

Making packed lunches is a good way to eat more healthily and economically, but a packed lunch can generate a tremendous amount of waste if it is wrapped in disposable bags, plastic wrap, or tinfoil and contains a lot of individually packaged goods like juice containers. The average child that brings his or her lunch to school generates roughly 30 kg of waste every year.

Everything in a waste-free lunch is consumed, recycled, or reused. Start with a reusable lunch box and make sure drink containers, sandwich and snack containers, and utensils are also reusable. Use cloth napkins. Pack fruit rather than snacks that come in plastic packets. If you have to use plastic bags, buy recycled ones and reuse them as much as possible. Sending your child to school and yourself to work with a waste-free lunch will save you money, provide more nutritionally balanced meals, and reduce landfill waste.

Clouds, United States

Choose your bank wisely.

Financial institutions use your money to make investments; and many major banks grant huge loans to enterprises such as fossil fuel plants and unsustainable forestry. You often have very little control over which businesses receive your bank's money, but some banks have ethical policies or accounts, or offer special credit cards that send a portion of the fees you pay to finance charities. Some community investment banks are some of the greenest banks around and many offer credit cards to nonmembers who funnel up to 50% of funds directly into environmental stewardship in a particular region of the country or into small business loans for low-income and underserved customers.

Research your bank's investment and lending policies, and its commitment to reducing its own carbon footprint — and if it's not good enough, switch to an ethical or cooperative bank.

Replace mothballs with natural deterrents.

The mothballs people place in wardrobes give off naphthalene and paradichloroben-zene fumes. The former is a carcinogenic substance; prolonged, repeated exposure to high concentrations can damage the nervous system and affect the lungs. Exposure to high levels of naphthalene can cause headaches, fatigue, and nausea. Most toxic substances we use are intended to eliminate something, so we should not be surprised that they are detrimental to our health.

In your drawers and wardrobes, choose bags of lavender or cedar chips, which smell so much nicer than mothballs. Protect delicate woollen clothes by keeping them in sealed boxes.

Wayana Indians, French Guiana

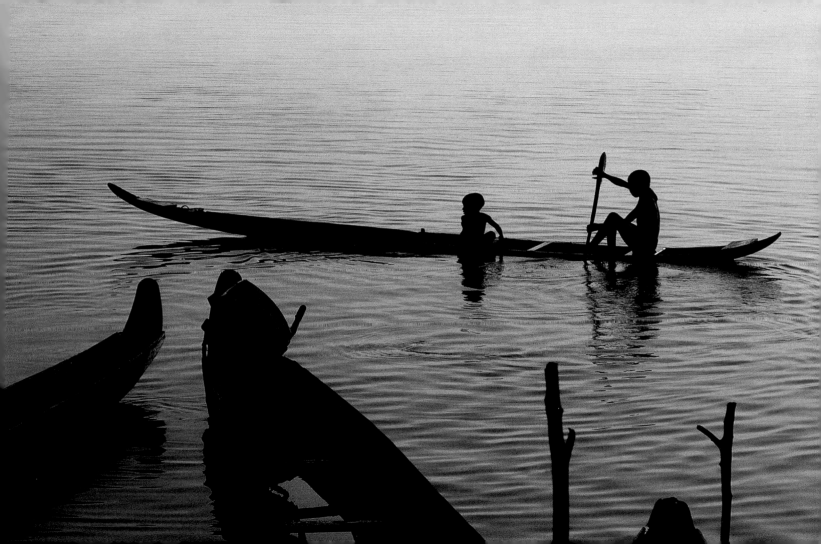

Be a citizen scientist.

For more than a century, amateur bird-watchers have helped conservationists keep an eye on early winter bird populations. Each year the Royal Society for the Protection of Birds in the United Kingdom has organized the Garden Birdwatch, an all-day census undertaken by a huge network of nature lovers. This is the biggest bird census in the world and a project that no one group of scientists would have the time or funding to accomplish on their own.

Lend your eyes and a little of your time to help with the next survey. You could learn how to recognise common and rare birds, including sparrows, cormorants, finches, herons, and owls. Other major projects monitor watersheds or weather patterns, or you could speak to the warden at your local park or nature reserve to see if they could use your help on your next walk.

Autumn, Acadia National Park, United States

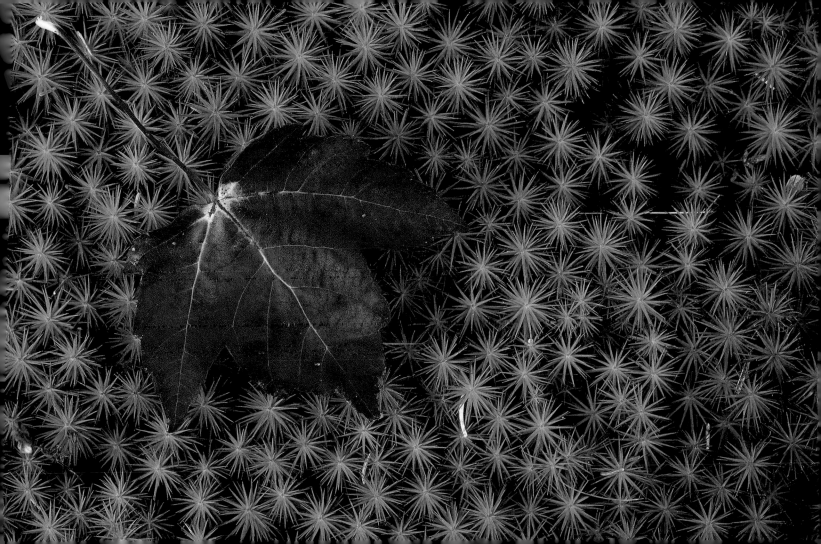

Turn off the tap while you brush your teeth.

Earth has been nicknamed the 'blue planet' because of its abundance of water, but this is misleading. If all the water on earth could be contained in a big bucket, the frozen freshwater at the poles and in glaciers would fill a small cup, and all the freshwater available to people — lakes, rivers, and groundwater — would fit into a teaspoon. Our natural freshwater reserves are not expandable, and they must be shared among an ever-growing global population.

Turning off the tap during the time it takes to brush our teeth saves almost 19 litres of water. That is more than an average citizen of Kenya uses in an entire day.

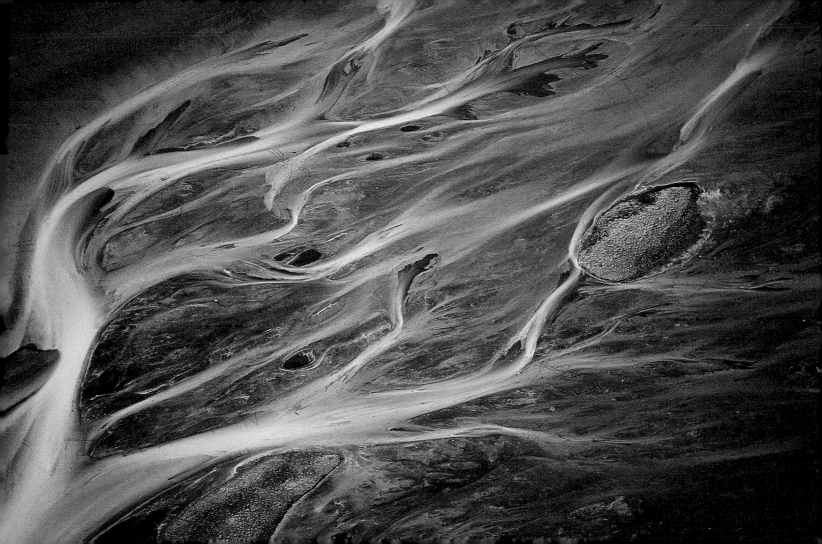

Recycle magazines and newspapers.

For every tonne of paper recycled, a huge amount of energy and resources are saved—over 3,000 litres of water, and enough electricity to power a 3-bedroom house for a year. In addition, recycling paper produces 5% of the air pollution caused by making it from scratch.

Paper is one of the easiest things to sort and recycle, so make sure you don't throw away any used paper and cardboard. It can be used to make new paper and cardboard, as well as packaging, tissues, paper napkins and tablecloths, and toilet paper. As for your magazines, before putting them in the recycling, offer them to the waiting room of your local doctor, dentist, or hairdresser, where they will be read again and again.

Baobabs, Madagascar

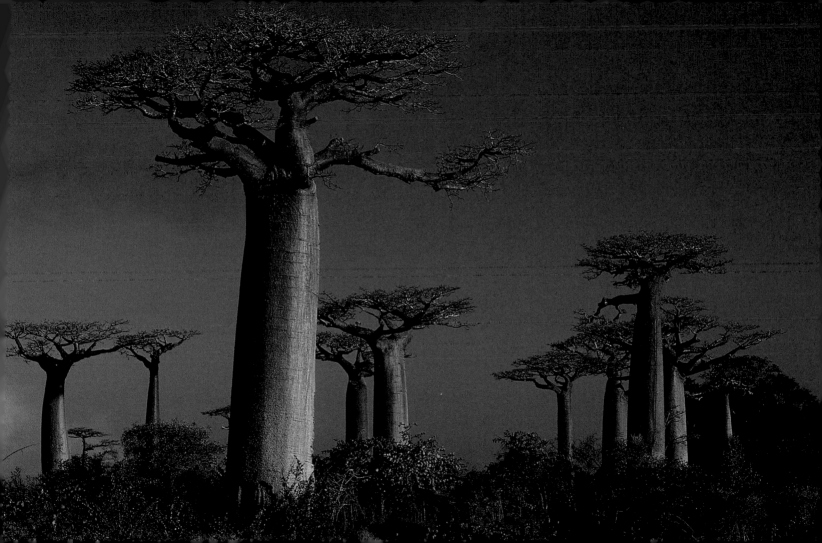

Do not litter the mountains.

Mount Everest, the highest point on the planet, has been a well-travelled destination for decades. As many as 300 climbers a day may gather at base camp during the peak season, and the area has suffered considerable pollution as a result. Recently, several cleanup campaigns have removed piles of trash from the roof of the world; the first operation at base camp eliminated 30 tonnes of waste. Nor has Mont Blanc in France been spared by the 3,000 climbers who trample its summit every year. Between 1999 and 2002, cleanup operations removed almost 10 tonnes of waste from the summit alone. The fragile environments of the high summits are sensitive to the slightest disturbances and easily damaged by mass tourism.

Do not contribute to the degradation of high places; leave nothing behind and pick up what others irresponsibly throw away.

Tabular iceberg, Antarctica

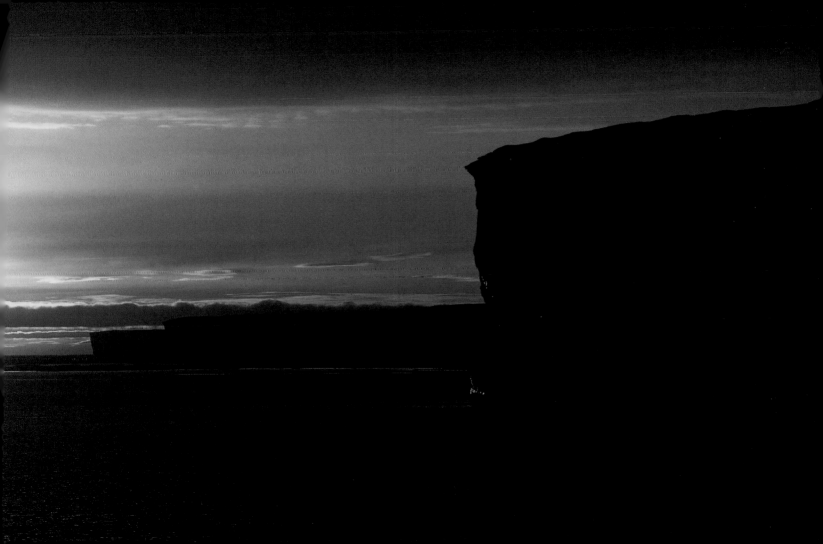

Turn the tap off while you wash dishes by hand.

When a tap is turned on, over 6 litres of pure drinking water flows out every minute. We are easily fooled by the generosity of our taps. Each time we use them, a large part of the water goes down the drain without even being dirtied.

When you wash the dishes by hand, fill the sink or a washing-up bowl, rather than washing each plate under a running tap. Hand-washing dishes typically uses about 63 litres per session. Better yet, invest in a water-efficient dishwasher — if you use a machine wisely, it can use as little as 10 litres of water, much less than even careful hand-washing practices.

Dunes, Algeria

Don't prerinse dishes.

Your dishwasher will use the same amount of water and energy whether or not you prerinse your dishes. In most cases, simply scraping off food scraps should be enough for your dishwasher to do its job, especially if it is an updated model. Prerinsing can waste up to 20 gallons of water.

If certain types of dishes or foods prove problematic for your dishwasher, set aside a small amount of dishes to wash by hand — fill up the sink basin rather than let the tap run while you wash. Otherwise, let the dishwasher do all the work.

Air bubbles trapped in ice,
Canada

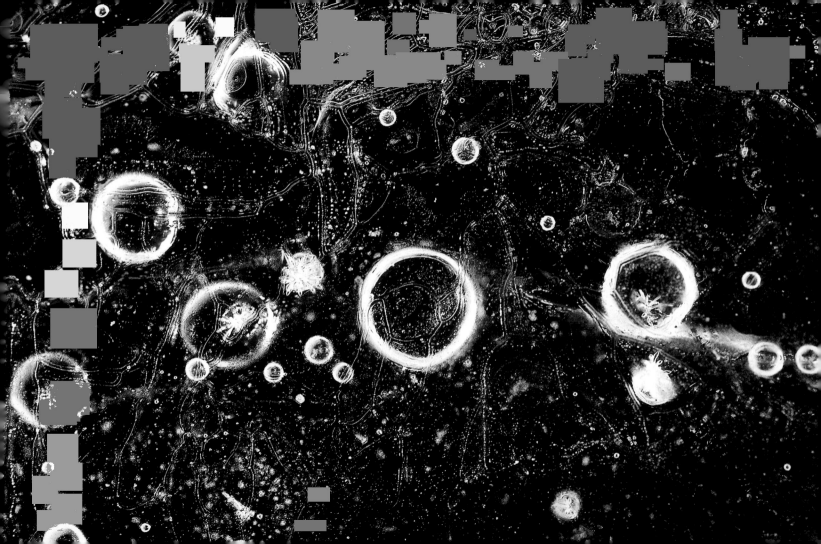

Collect rainwater.

Nature gives us water for free. Like solar and wind energy, collecting rainwater is a means of protecting the environment in a sustainable way. The rain that falls on the roofs of our houses could cover as much as 80% of our current annual domestic-water consumption. In addition, collecting rainwater prevents it from flowing along the street, picking up pollutants, and depositing them into storm drains and eventually into our waterways. Rainwater collection systems do double-duty, conserving water and protecting our environment from pollutants.

Have a rainwater collection system fitted to your house to meet your outdoor water needs, like watering the garden and washing the car. At the very least, put a plastic dustbin beneath your rain gutter to collect water.

Sossusvlei dunes, Namibia

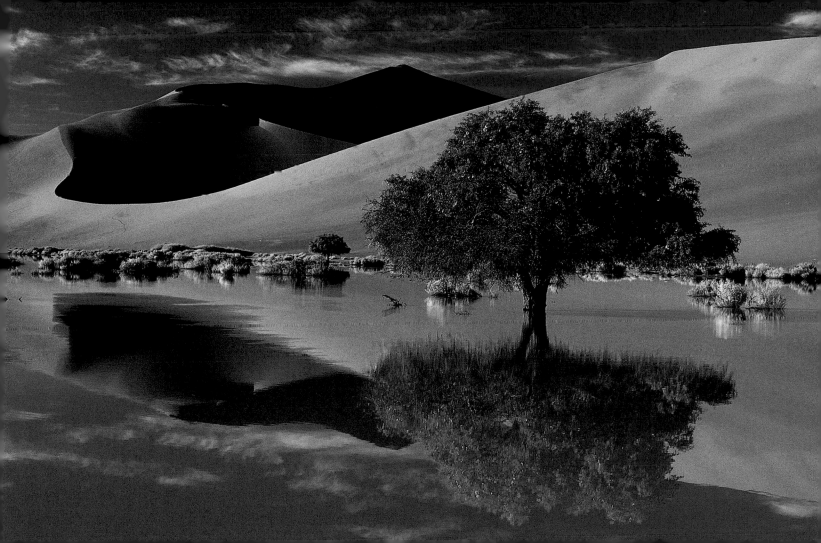

Check that others obey the law.

National environmental agencies, burdened with protecting and restoring your country's environment, may fail to do so, at times out of negligence but sometimes due to lack of funding. Do not let your local authority put environmental concerns last on the list of budgetary priorities—human health and safety are at stake. Pay attention to your local council's policy decisions, and monitor the trend in funding for environmental programmes.

Do not hesitate to approach a lobbying group, or to alert watchdogs or the media about a government body or a company if they do not comply with environmental legislation.

Piton de la Fournaise Volcano, Réunion

Recycle actively and effectively.

Take part in your local recycling programme: Note the collection times and learn how to sort from your local council. Proper sorting is vital to making your recycling efforts meaningful — contamination in a recycling container can mean that it can't be recycled and will be diverted to a landfill. Be sure to consult the guidelines for your local recycling scheme to find out what you can include in your recycling collection. Recycling is important, but it is essential to do it properly.

If you are uncertain about what to do with a particular item of waste, call the council or your nearest recycling facility — don't just throw it in with your recyclables or other rubbish.

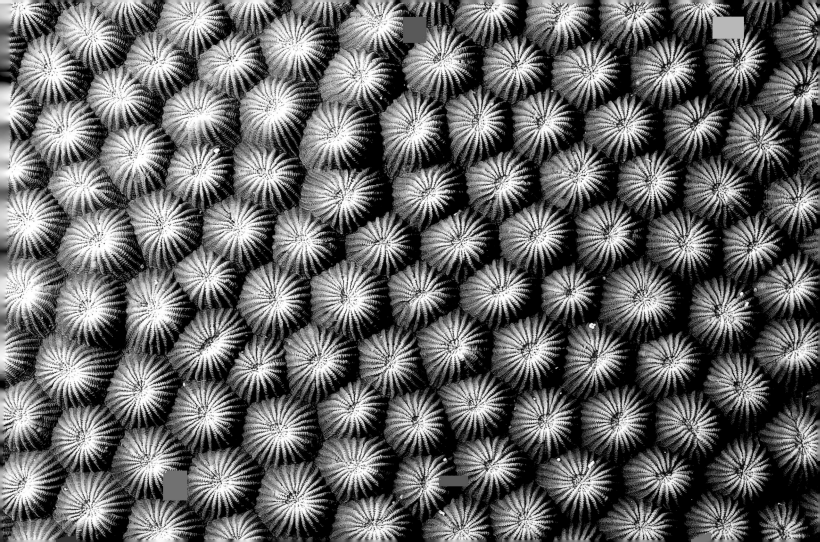

Don't idle your car engine.

Since 1900, emissions of carbon dioxide have risen dramatically as a result of growing consumption of coal, oil, and gas, and its concentration in the atmosphere is the highest it has been in the last 20 million years. An average passenger car in the United Kingdom produces nearly 4.3 tonnes of carbon dioxide per year.

When you start your car engine, you don't need to run it while remaining stationary in order to 'warm it up'. Instead, just drive gently for a few miles: The engine will warm up while avoiding needless pollution, carbon-dioxide emissions, and fuel consumption.

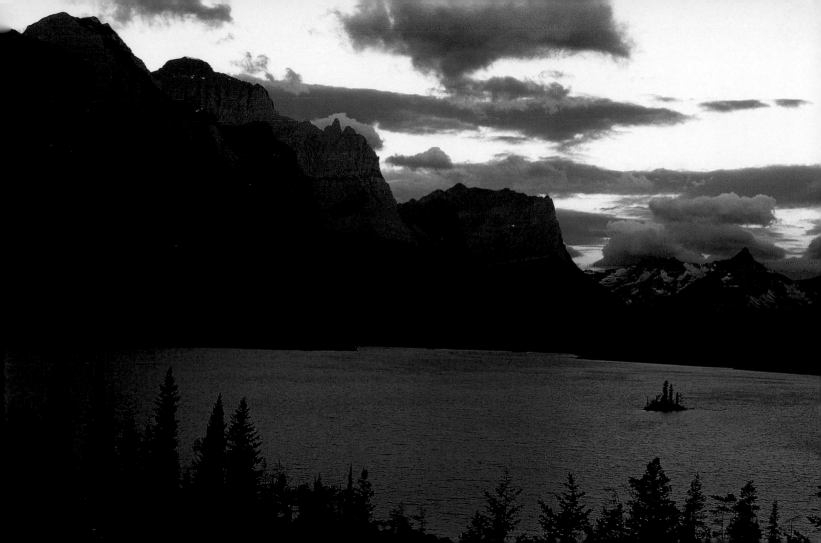

Plant native vegetation in your garden.

If you plant greenery that only thrives in a specific climate, you could expend huge amounts of water, fertilizers, and other growing aids just trying to keep it alive. Indigenous plants are already accustomed to the demands of their environment, and they often require much effort to keep healthy—that means less wasted water, less fertilizer, and less need for pest control. Planting native species also encourages natural biodiversity and lessens the risks associated with introducing non-native plants that could spread and change natural habitats, thereby affecting local wildlife.

As our climate changes to become drier in summer, choose native, drought-resistant species such as beautiful grasses or succulent plants that do not require watering.

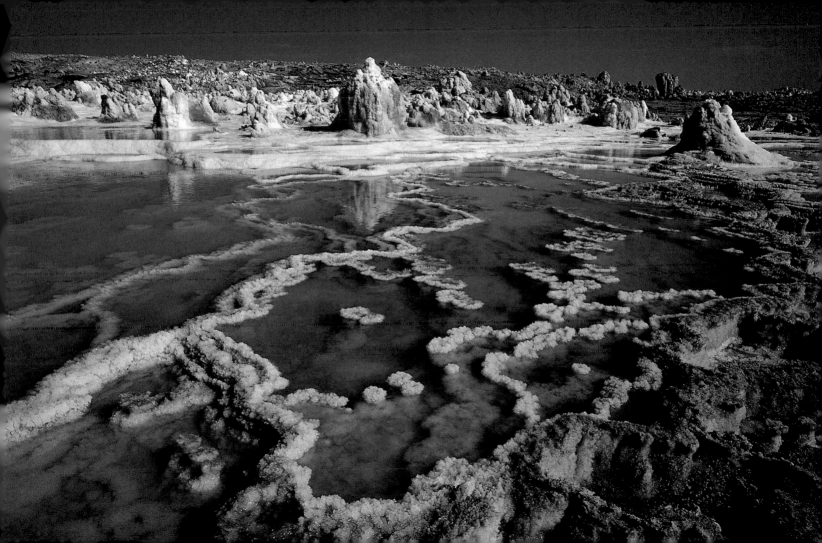

Suggest composting at your children's school.

School canteens create an enormous amount of organic waste that could be turned into compost. Many schools already compost their waste, and do so in ways that allow students to participate in the process—whether through work in science lessons, by growing vegetables in on-site gardens or by simply making the students responsible for sorting their recyclables and organic materials at every meal. This can not only reduce waste but also teaches young people about the importance of reducing waste, and how composting works.

For your children's canteen, or your workplace cafeteria, take the initiative by explaining the economic and ecological advantages of composting. If there isn't space to compost on site, you can arrange for the organic waste to be collected for composting elsewhere.

Islets, Galápagos Islands

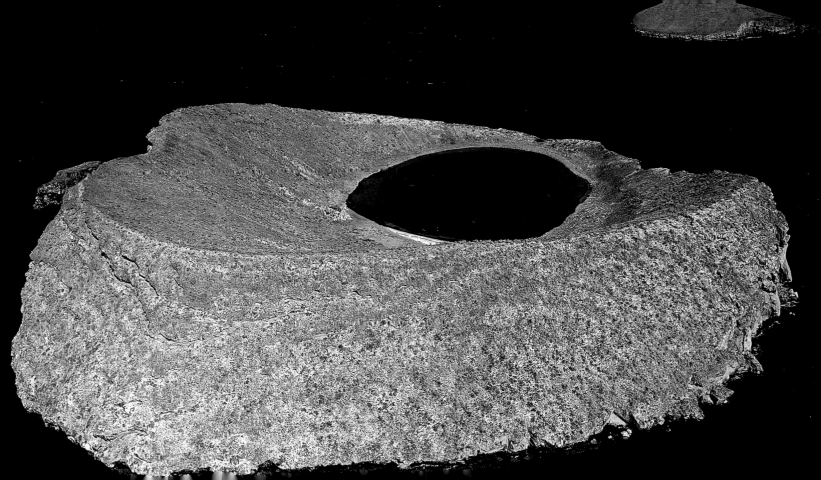

Arrange a better bouquet.

A lovely bunch of flowers bought from the florist or the supermarket may have been grown in a greenhouse thousands of miles away (Kenya is the largest supplier of cut flowers to the European Union). Apart from the environmental issue of transport over long distances, the boom in horticulture in some developing countries has a high social and environmental cost. In Colombia, the flower industry uses enormous amounts of polluting pesticides and exposes poorly paid garden workers to chemicals that may be carcinogenic or toxic. In drier regions, such as Kenya, horticulture requires substantial amounts of water and, as a result, overuses local water resources.

If you want a traditional bouquet, seek out organic and fair-trade flowers. Organic flowers are grown without toxic pesticides; fair-trade flowers are harvested on farms that provide better health and safety standards and higher wages for their workers. Look for the Fair Trade or VeriFlora labels, which ensure that your flowers come from farms with high environmental and labour standards. And consider giving a potted plant from a local nursery as a gift rather than a bunch of flowers. It will last far longer.

Cactus flower, Mexico

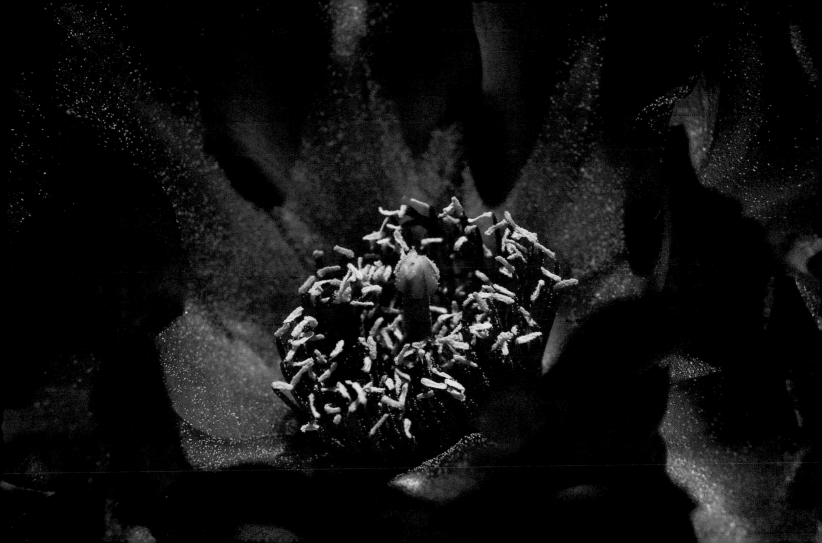

Save energy when you cook.

In March 2002, an iceberg 85 kilometres long and 64 kilometres wide broke off the Antarctic shelf. That same year, the inhabitants of the Tuvalu archipelago, in Micronesia, were forced to evacuate their islands as sea levels rose. In order to slow the warming of the seas and rise of the sea level, we must reduce world emissions of greenhouse gases quickly and drastically. This is all the more urgent because the greenhouse gases already in the atmosphere will continue to have an effect for about 10 years. Global warming will therefore happen no matter what we do.

Small things really make a difference. Be sure always to put a lid on your cooking pots; in this way you can reduce the energy used for cooking by between 20% and 30%. And you will save time, too.

Coral Island, Australia

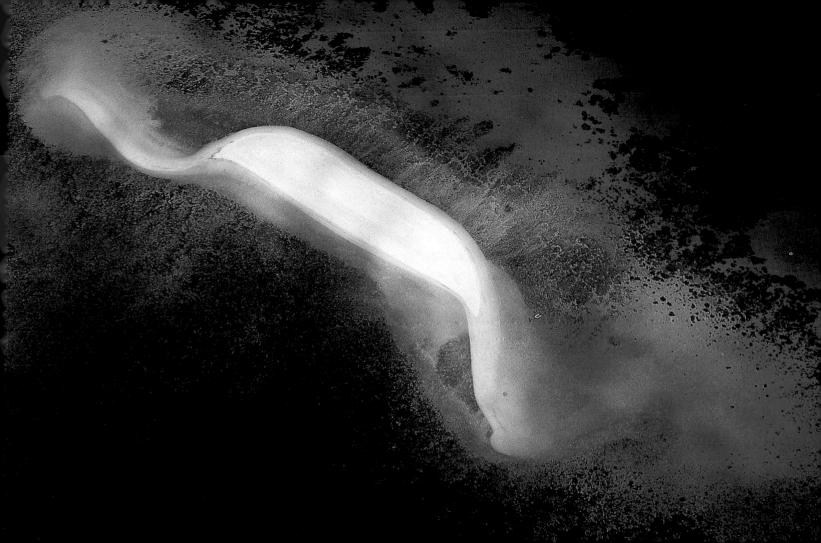

Rent a green car.

Most of the major car rental agencies now have some hybrids in their fleets; specialised local agencies have more alternatives like electric cars. Nationwide car-sharing programs like Streetcar are now found in most cities and large towns—a low yearly membership fee allows you to reserve cars (many of which are compact and fuel efficient) for a few hours or by the day from any of the companies pick-up points—generally, conveniently located in residential areas. By becoming a member, you help these car-sharing ventures to grow further.

The next time you rent a car, rent green. The bigger the demand for hybrids and alternative-fuel vehicles, the greater the investment in these programs by big agencies.

Dune, Mauritania

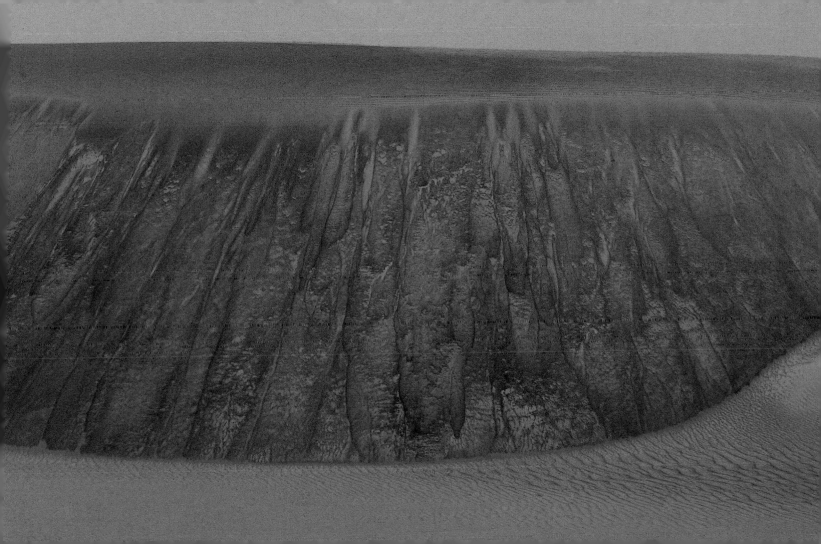

Insulate your home.

Even if you do not drive a car, you can take action to reduce climate change. Through its consumption of energy (for hot water, heating, electricity, and lighting), an average dwelling produces 6 tonnes of carbon dioxide per year—more than a car does. In Europe about a quarter of all emissions of carbon dioxide, the main greenhouse gas responsible for climate change, comes from homes.

To reduce the need for heating, you can prevent heat from escaping: Insulate the roof, floors, and walls with fibreglass wool, rock wool, mineral wool, cork, cellulose (from recycled newspapers), or hemp. This will save 20% on your heating bills, and will pay for itself within 5 years at most.

Mountain goat, Waterton-Glacier International Peace Park, United States

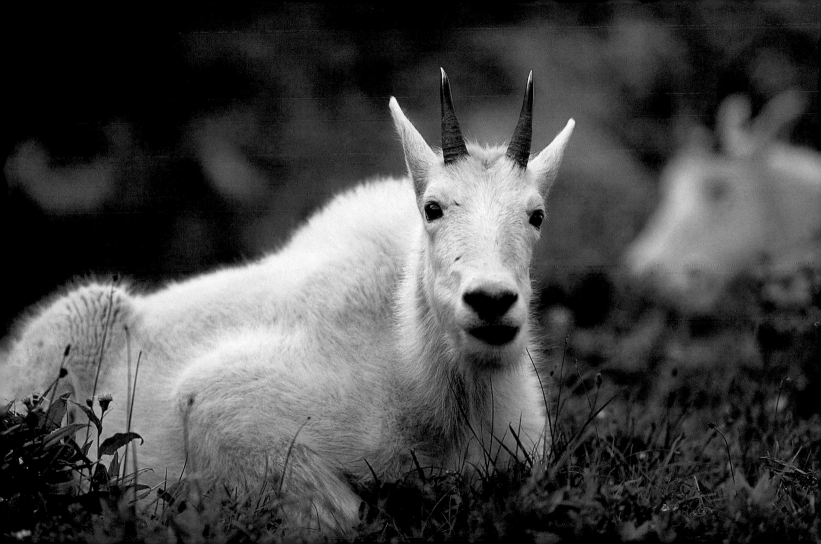

Do not use aerosol air fresheners.

The CFCs (cholofluorocarbons) in aerosols are now illegal in the European Union, but artificial air fresheners are still an energy-intensive and toxic way to produce a 'nice' smell. Each year the United Kingdom uses around 600 million aerosol cans, yet aerosol propellants contain flammable and nerve-damaging ingredients as well as tiny particles that can lodge in your lungs. Fragrances of all kinds can provoke allergic and asthmatic reactions.

Replace artificial air fresheners with potpourris, essential oil diffusers, candles, incense, fragrant plants (for example, citronella or honeysuckle), citrus fruit peels, or oranges studded with cloves. And remember that aerosol cans can now be safely recycled, so include them with your metals for collection.

Acacia tree, Mali

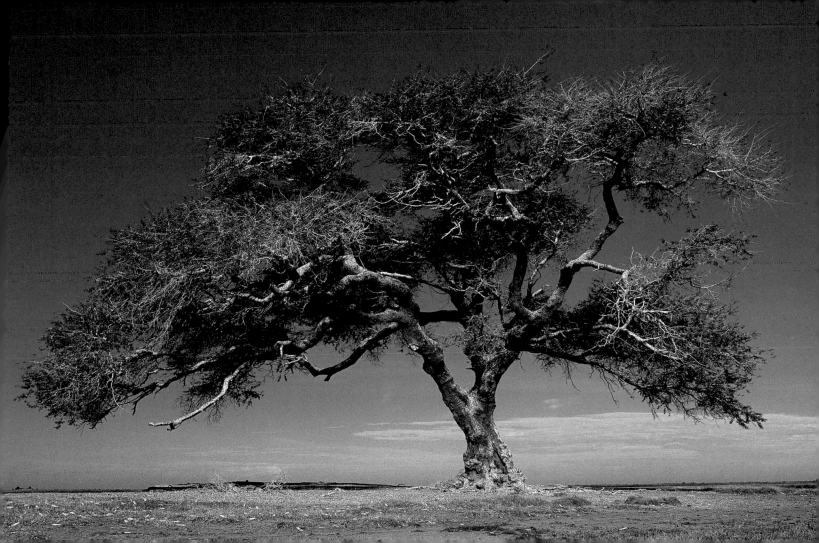

Become a liftsharer.

Liftsharing websites are an easy way to find 'buddies' to share your car, immediately making your transportation at least twice as energy efficient. Or if you don't have a car or don't want to use yours, you can find someone who travels to the same location as you every day and share a ride to work. It is easy and safe, and will not only halve your use of petrol but also halve the costs of driving to work.

Sharing your car with one other person immediately takes a car off the road, and thus reduces your carbon emissions by half. Sign up today with your local liftsharing network — you'll be amazed how easy it is to make new friends.

Arches National Park,
United States

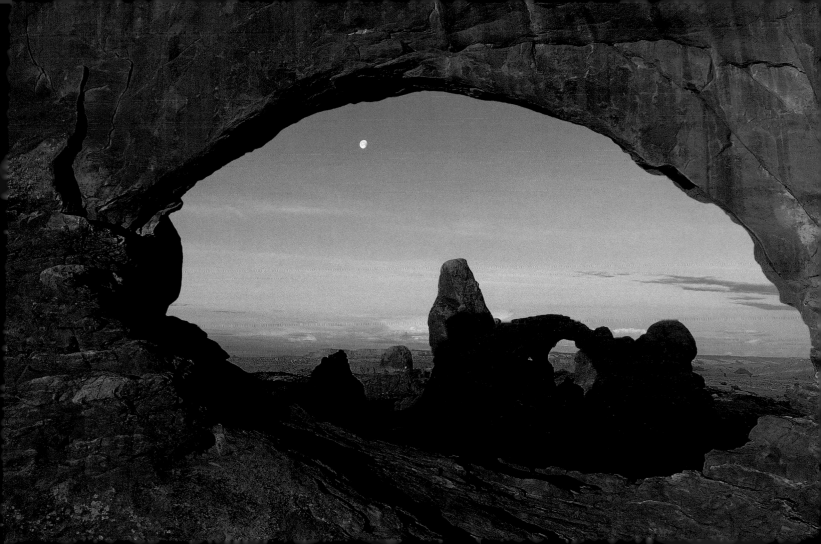

Make your next car a hybrid.

Hybrid cars combine an electric motor and an internal combustion engine. They run on electricity in town and use petrol at motorway speed at which point, ingeniously, the batteries are recharged by the movement of the car. Thanks to this optimized use of energy, hybrid cars offer excellent performance and are much cleaner in town; they produce 75% less pollution than standard vehicles.

Hybrids are still more costly than comparable cars, but prices continue to drop as more models are produced and the demand for fuel-efficient cars grows. If you have to buy a car, make sure it is the most efficient model you can find.

Caymans, Venezuela

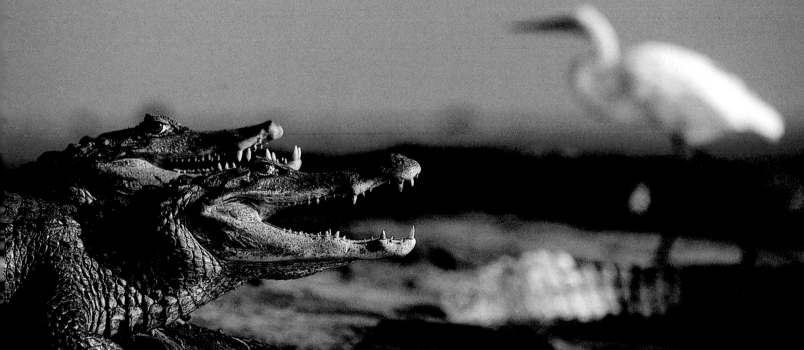

Use a low-flow showerhead.

To attempt to meet our escalating need for energy, humans have built dams and diverted rivers: 60% of the planet's rivers have been tamed in this way, and more than 45,000 large dams produce 20% of the world's water. Building these dams, however, has displaced between 40 and 80 million people—few of whom were consulted beforehand—and has caused extensive deforestation and species loss. Showers account for 12% of household water use, adding up to more than 6,600 litres per year.

You can reduce water consumption by replacing your showerhead with one that aerates and increases the flow of the water to produce a finer spray. A low-flow showerhead can use around 8 litres per minute, depending on the model (much less than a conventional showerhead); it costs around £10 for a standard model up to £100 for a designer model. Many have 'pause buttons' as well, so you can stop the water flow while you soap up.

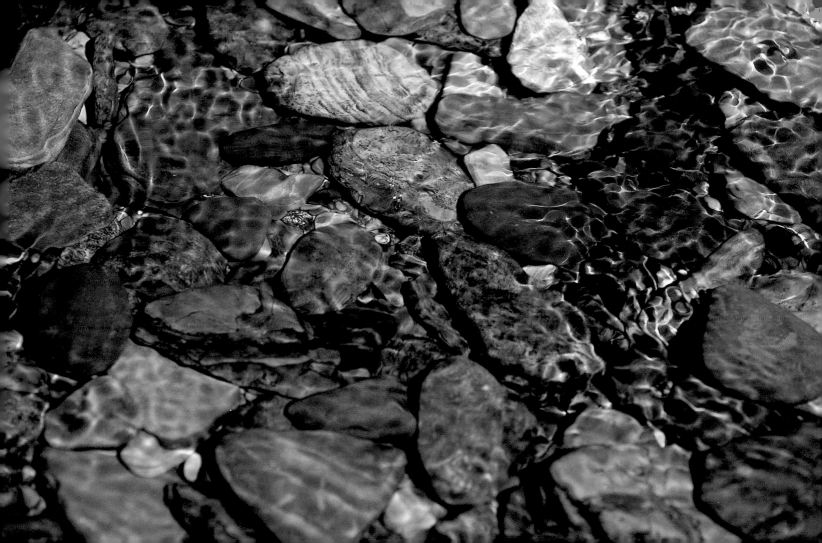

Donate your leftover medicines so that they can be distributed for reuse.

In developing countries, every day 30,000 people die for lack of medicines or the money to buy them, while we throw our unused medicines in the dustbin. But there are humanitarian organisations that collect these unused medications and redistribute them to the poorest people around the world. One organisation, Aid for AIDS annually redistributes nearly £2.5 million of medicine to people in developing countries who are HIV-positive or living with AIDS.

Find a charity near you that accepts unused medicine donations. This is also a safer choice for your household, because it will reduce the amount of medicine that could fall into a young child's hands. Forty percent of poisonings involving children are a result of ingesting medicines.

Bacteria, Kamchatka, Russia

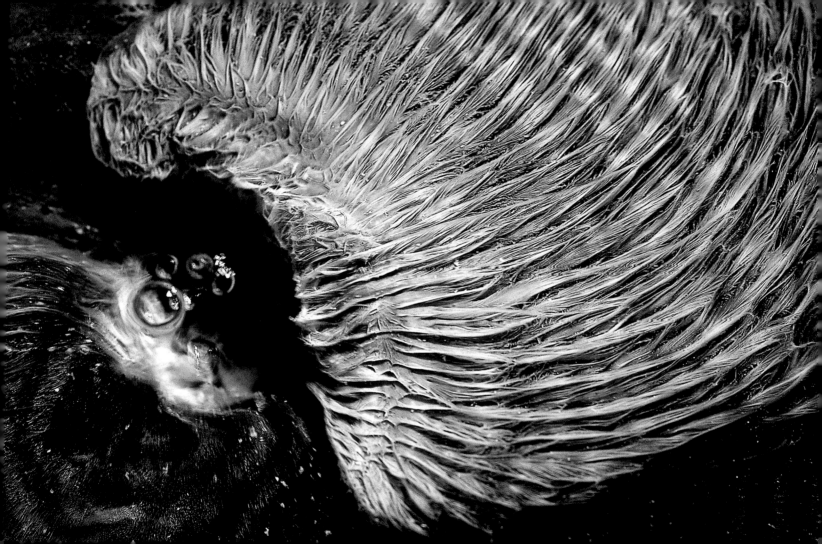

Have your heating checked and maintained regularly.

Air pollution is always more obvious in the middle of a traffic jam than when you are back at home. However, even indoors, you are not immune from harmful emissions, especially carbon monoxide. This gas is produced by incomplete combustion of coal, wood, gas, or fuel oil, which may be caused by a blocked flue, the use of old or badly maintained stoves, boilers, or oil heaters, or clogged ventilation ducts that prevent air circulation. Carbon-monoxide poisoning creates many incidents per year in the United Kingdom and in Europe some leading to fatalities. And poorly functioning boilers use more fuel, meaning more pollution and higher bills.

Keep your air clean: Have your home and water-heating equipment checked and maintained by professionals — and don't forget the ventilation ducts.

White Desert, Egypt

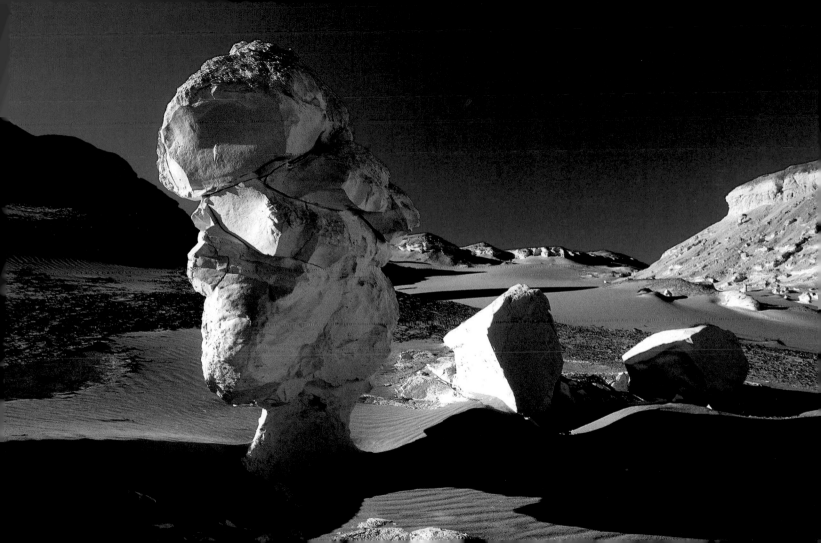

Make compost with organic waste.

In nature, compostable waste, like the waste found on the forest floor, decomposes into soil through the action of microorganisms, and returns energy and nutrients to the forest floor. Our rubbish contains a large amount of organic waste, which, instead of being returned to the natural cycle, is cut off from the soil and added to our landfills.

Leaves, branches, and grass from the garden, eggshells, fruit and vegetable peelings, coffee grounds, tea bags, and bread from our tables can all join the compost heap. If mixed well, turned regularly, and kept sufficiently moist, in a few weeks this will yield compost, a natural fertilizer that is good for the soil. Whether you make a compost heap or use a bin, there is certainly a composting option suitable for the amount of space you have available.

Birch, Lassen Volcanic National Park, United States

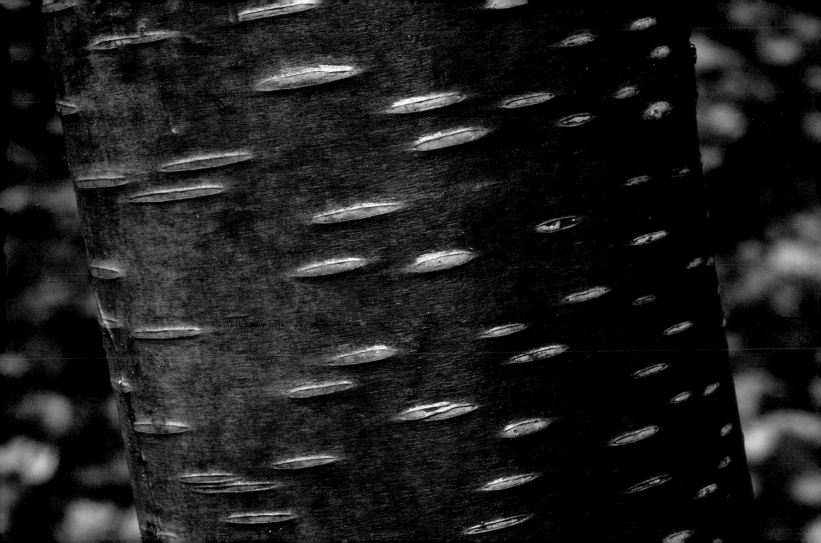

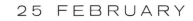

25 FEBRUARY

Reuse water.

One-third of the world's population is living in areas with moderate to severe water shortages. More than 2.7 billion people will face severe water shortages by 2025, according to the United Nations, if we keep increasing our use at the same rate. The United Kingdom actually has less water resources per person than Spain or Portugal, due to the density of its population.

Look for ways to use leftover water. Water that has been used to wash vegetables can be left in the sink to clean dishes. You can water indoor and outdoor plants with water that's been used to cook pasta or vegetables. When you have a shower, trample lightly soiled clothes or towels underfoot while you wash, or wash them in the bath after you get out.

Anaconda, Venezuela

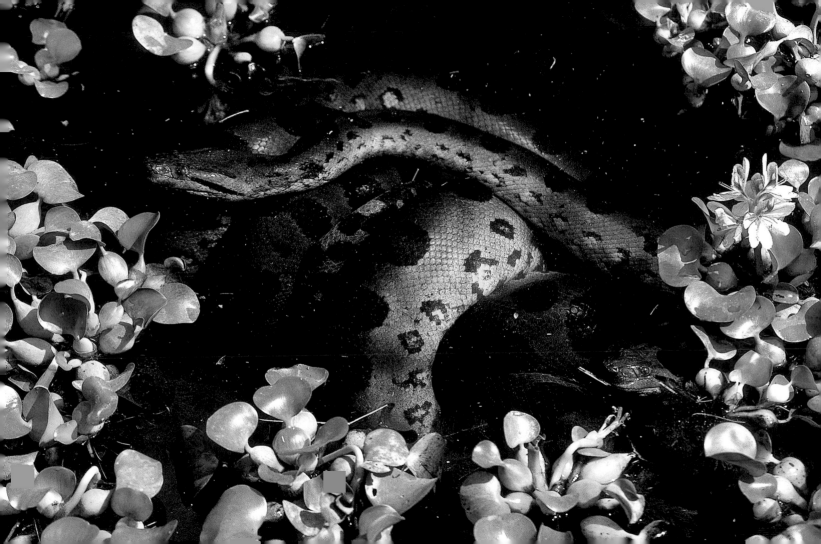

Do not drop litter when travelling.

UK domestic waste now goes to different destinations, depending on where you live and the type of waste. London exports 70% of its municipal waste to other places for treatment or disposal and the majority of solid waste still goes to landfills. Across the country the average rate of recycling is 31%. However, this is not the case everywhere. Worldwide, only 20% of household waste is treated in one of these ways. In some poor countries, rubbish bins are rare or altogether absent.

Do not drop your litter just anywhere — especially if you are on an excursion — even if the environment already appears to be dirty or strewn with dumped waste. Take your litter back to where you are staying and dispose of it properly.

Seashell, France

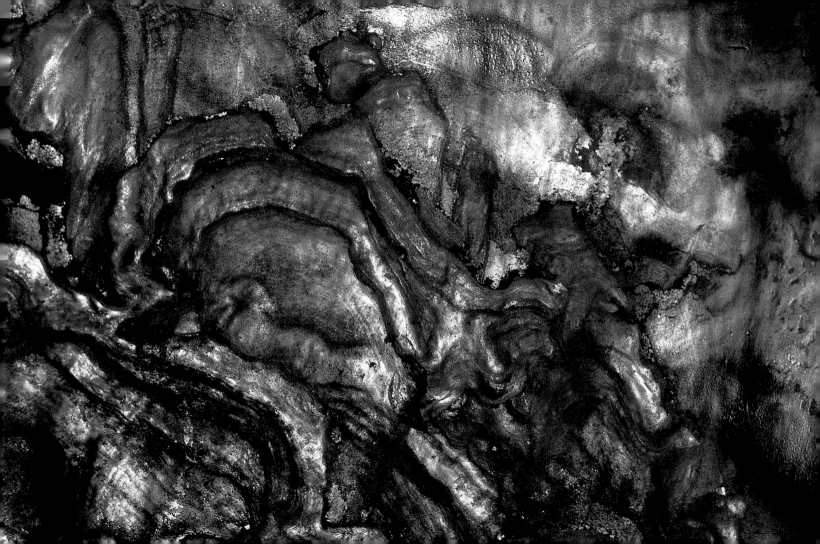

Switch to paperless bills.

Paper and cardboard account for about one-fifth of household waste. This is equivalent to over 4 kg of paper waste per week.

Sign up for online banking and pay as many of your bills as possible electronically. Be sure you decline the option to receive paper statements when you sign up for these programmes. Don't print receipts when you withdraw cash at the machines as they are yet another source of litter and almost always unnecessary — all withdrawals and debit transactions show up on your online banking statement within 24 hours if not immediately.

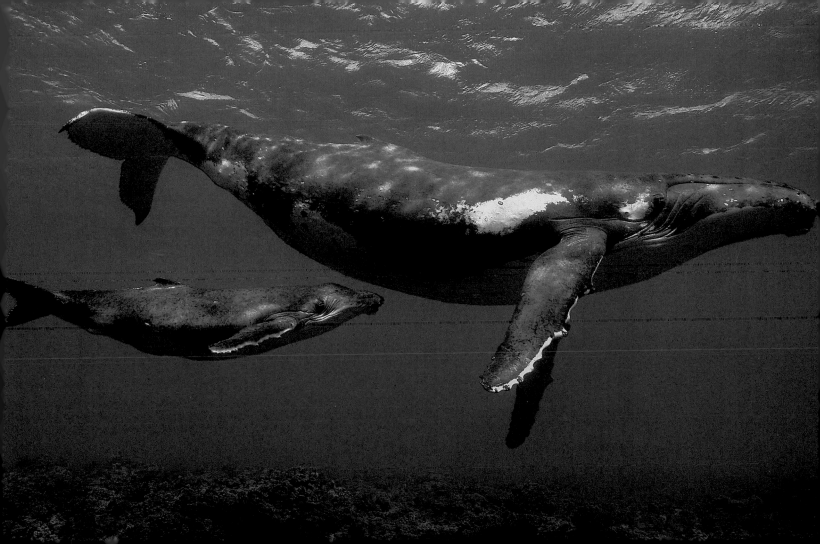

Do not defrost in the microwave.

Renewable energy — from the sun, wind, the heat under the earth's crust, waterfalls, tides, the growing of vegetables, or the recycling of waste — is infinite. Harnessing it produces little or no waste or polluting emissions. In countries like Germany, government officials have recognized the benefits of investing quickly and heavily in these technologies and already 12% of their national energy supply comes from renewable energy production, with future targets to triple this as well as cut down electricity use by 11%.

Rather than adding to your electricity bill by using the microwave to defrost your food, remember to take food out of the freezer earlier and let it defrost at room temperature.

Erg (sand desert), Mauritania

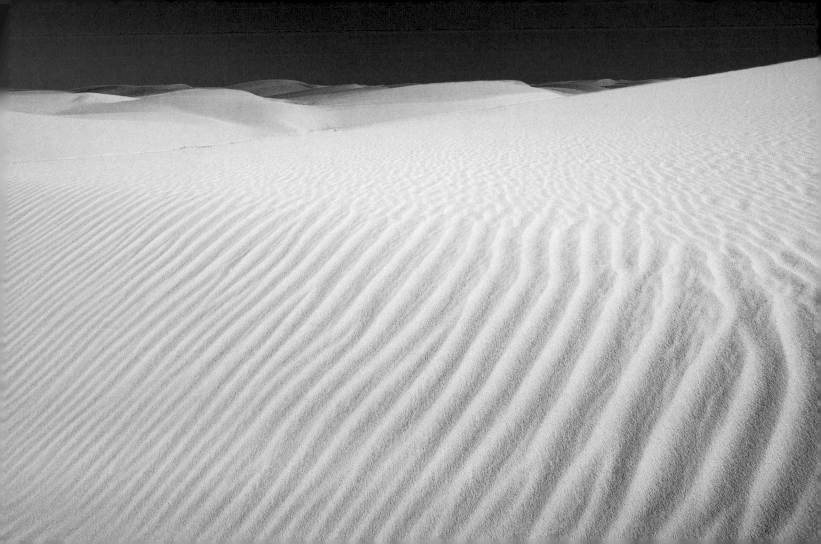

Boil only as much water as you need.

Whether you use an electric kettle or a saucepan, heating water uses energy. There is no point in doubling the energy you use, for no purpose: Boil only what is necessary. A study found that if all British people did this on just one day, the energy saved could power all the country's streetlights through the following night.

When you boil water for tea or a hot drink, try to boil only what you need, or pour the surplus into a thermos flask to keep the water very hot until you need it.

Thunderstorm clouds,
United States

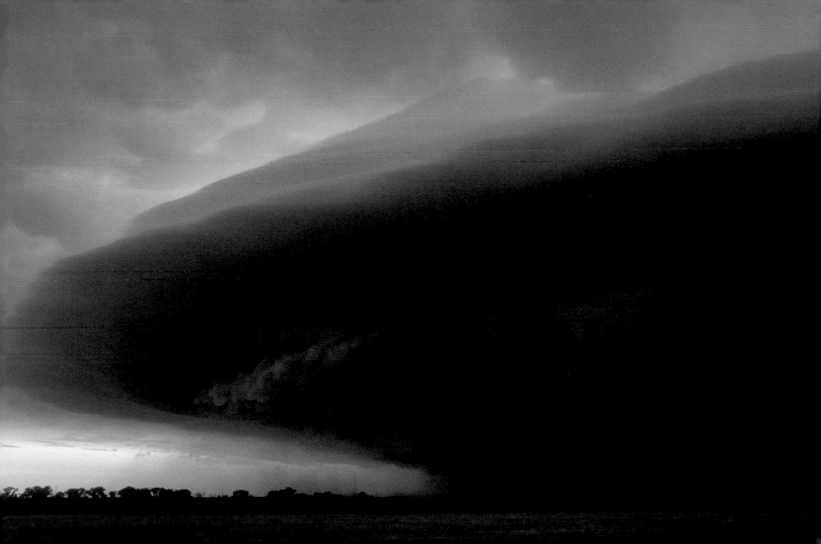

Research the impacts of aquaculture before eating farmed fish.

At present, fish farming accounts for 43% of the world's fish production. This is unlikely to change as the world's demand for fish grows along with its population, and many wild species continue to be in peril because of over-fishing. Aquaculture is often criticized for its negative environmental impacts: To produce 1 pound of farmed salmon, 3 pounds of wild-caught fish are needed to provide meal and oil. And, like all intensive farming, fish farming uses chemicals and antibiotics, which affect humans.

There is such a thing as sustainable aquaculture: Tilapia, catfish, and many varieties of shellfish can often be farmed safely. Organisations like Seafood Watch and the Marine Stewardship Council have developed strict criteria for sustainable fish farming and offer advice to the public about how to choose the best fish. Look out for their logos on the fish you buy.

Cherry blossoms, Japan

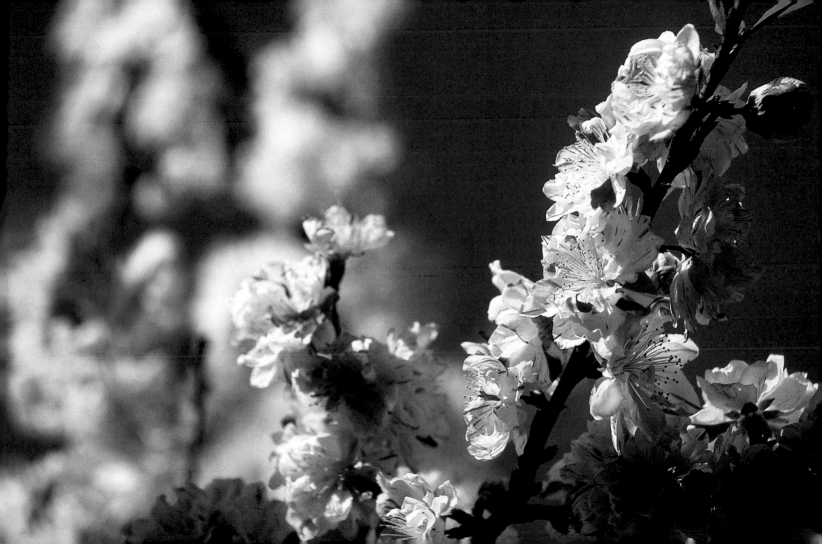

Introduce environmental education to schools.

Many local environmental charities or natural reserves offer free or low-cost education presentations or field trips for school-aged children — often it is simply a matter of asking. They usually focus on environmental problems facing your area, or tours of the natural features it has to offer. They often tailor their programmes to the national curriculum, ensuring that children can easily make the link to their classroom education.

If you would like environmental education to have a higher priority in your children's school, spend some time investigating the organisations that offer educational resources. It is a good way to increase awareness among students, teachers, and other parents.

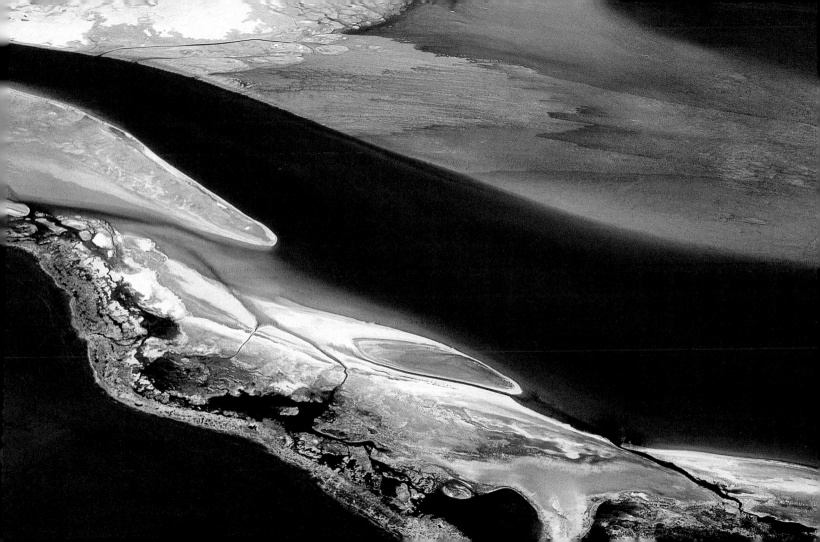

Consider a career move.

Today universities offer many courses in environmental fields—from policy to education to business administration. If your job is at odds with your concerns, consider moving in a different direction. You might not have to reinvent the wheel: You can offer your current skills to businesses who are trying to be greener—they all need consultants, marketing professionals, lawyers, accountants, assistants, and so on.

Think about working in an environmental field, whether it be business, consultancy, conservation, or recycling. Green business is one of the fastest growing sectors of the economy, and demand for green products, renewable energy, and new technology is only going to grow as resources become more scarce.

Volcanic lake, Kamchatka, Russia

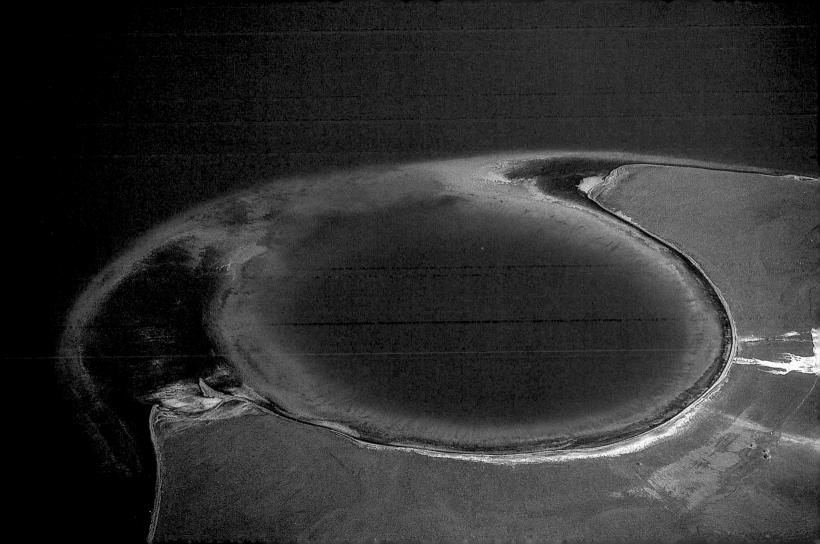

Discover Slow Food.

The Slow Food movement began as a response to the industrialization of the food system, and the subsequent loss of food varieties and flavours. The movement began in 1986 in Italy and has moved around the globe. In 1900 there were about 200 varieties of artichokes in Italy: Today only a dozen survive. The mission of the Slow Food movement is to: educate consumers on land stewardship and ecologically sound food production; encourage cooking as a method of strengthening relationships between people; further the consumption of local, organic, and seasonal food; and create a collaborative, ecologically oriented community.

Opt for diversity and discover Slow Food. This international movement opposes the standardization of tastes imposed by fast-food. It has more than 80,000 members in 50 countries.

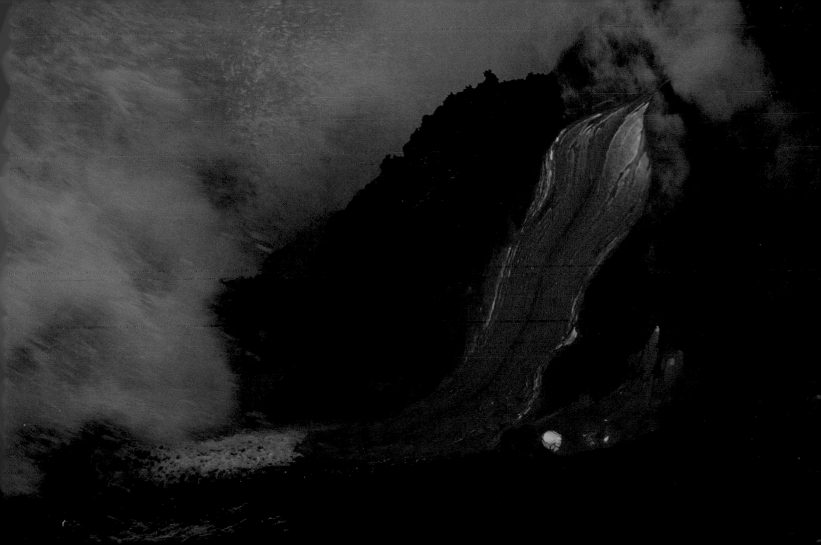

Get rid of your car.

The toxic fumes emitted by industry and vehicles contain nitrogen dioxide and sulphur dioxide. In the air, these compounds are converted into nitric acid and sulphuric acid, and fall back to earth in rain. Acid rain eats away at the stone of historic buildings, destroys forests, acidifies lakes and rivers, and attacks crops. Atmospheric pollution has done more damage to the Acropolis in Athens in 25 years than natural erosion has done in 25 centuries.

If you live in a large city and use your car only occasionally, consider using public transport and/or joining a car-sharing or lift-sharing program. It often works out to be more economical if you take into account the cost of buying a car, depreciation, insurance, petrol, and parking.

Glacier corridor, United States

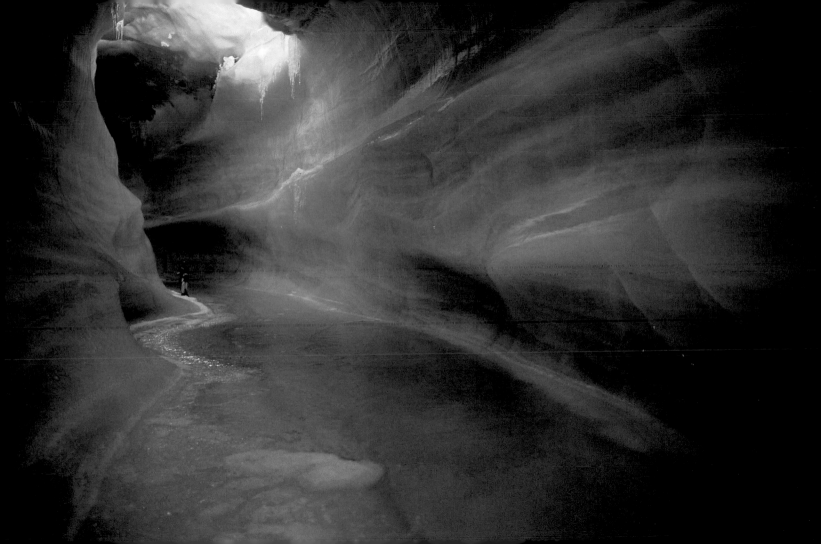

Reuse waste paper.

Europe, North America, and Japan combined are home to just 20% of the world's population but swallow up 63% of its paper and cardboard. Increasing consumption of these products is relentless: The wealthiest countries use 3 times as much paper today than they used in the 1960s. By 2010, the volume of paper used worldwide could increase by as much as 50%.

To avoid contributing to this overconsumption, cut back on your paper use, and keep reusable paper products, such as manila envelopes and file folders. Cut scrap paper into quarters and use it to write phone messages rather than buying a new pad. And recycle all eligible paper and cardboard products.

Mehedjibat *erg* (sand desert), Algeria

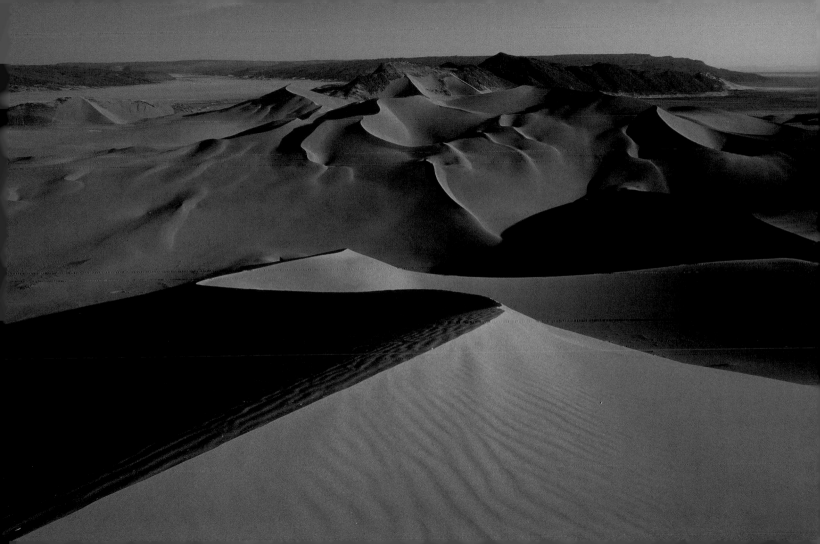

Properly dispose of old car batteries.

Car batteries are rechargeable electric cells containing lead and acid. These substances are extremely toxic to nature: A battery left in the countryside pollutes nearly 6 square metres around it for several years. The lead used in cars, in general, is the largest remaining source of lead pollution, and the majority of current lead use is for car batteries.

To recycle your old battery, call your local authority or car dealership to find out where to bring it, or take it to your local recycling centre.

Sea of clouds, Indonesia

Say 'no' to digital displays.

At present, a quarter of the world's population controls three-quarters of the energy produced on the planet, while a third of the world's population does not even have electricity. For example, the United States uses 22 times as much energy per inhabitant as India does, whilst the average European uses 12 times as much. Part of the energy consumption in wealthy countries is due to superfluous gadgets.

_____

If you are choosing between two different models of fridge, cooker, or microwave, choose the one with a mechanical display rather than one with a digital display; the digital display is always on and wastes energy.

Rain forest, Costa Rica

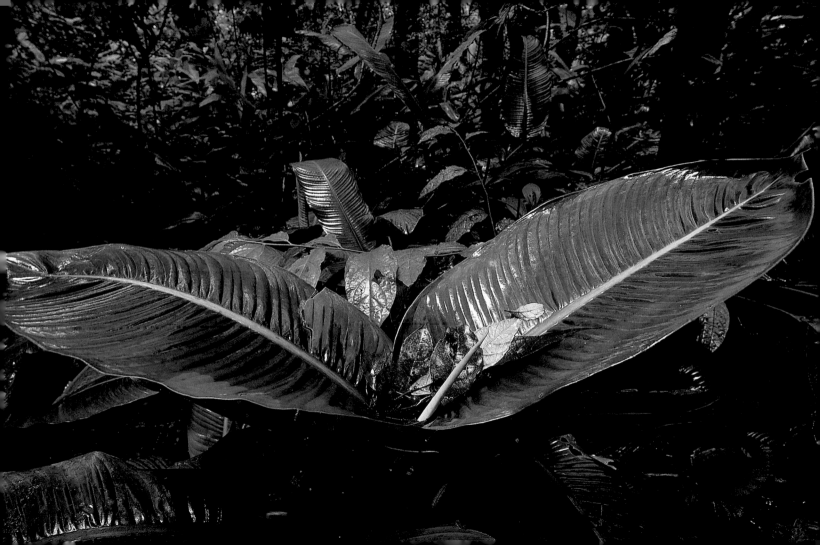

Ventilate your home regularly.

Indoor air pollution affects all enclosed spaces. This can be caused by a ventilation system that does not remove stale air properly, by a faulty gas stove or heater, or by the improper use of products that require a high degree of air circulation to dissipate pollutants, such as paints, varnishes, and household cleaners. Some pollutants, such as mites and molds, are of natural origin.

On average, we spend 80% of our lives in buildings. The quality of the air indoors can therefore have a major effect on our health. To circulate the air and remove pollutants, ventilate your indoor space regularly and generously, even in winter.

Tsingy, Madagascar

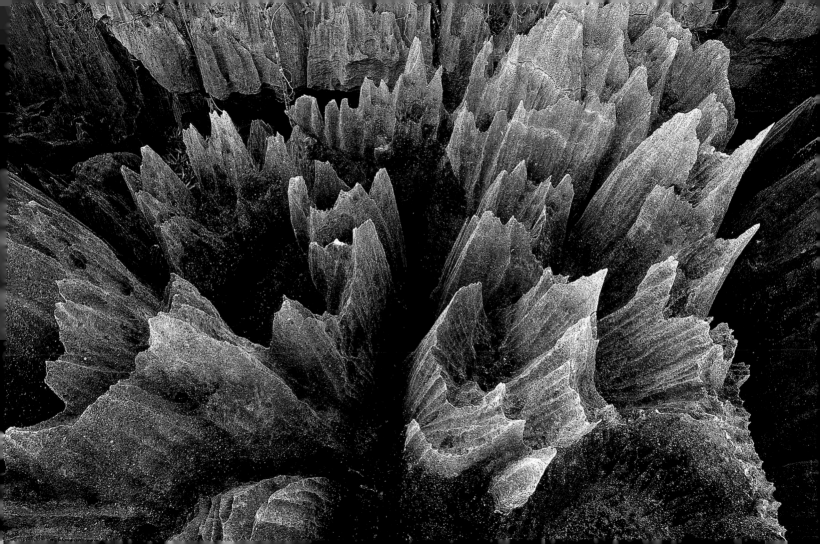

Take a different approach when buying clothes.

We rarely question the social and environmental impact of the clothing we buy. Who made it and what is it made of? How far did it travel before being sold? Polyester, nylon, and fake fur are not biodegradable, and their manufacture from nonrenewable petrochemical products requires large amounts of water and energy. Growing cotton uses large quantities of pesticides. Wool, linen, and hemp, on the other hand, are more environmentally friendly, as is organic, locally made cotton. Green designers now have a slew of renewable and biodegradable fabrics to choose from, including cloth made from bamboo, and many of them make high-end duds from recycled materials, too.

Choose clothing and shoes that are made from organic crops, and manufactured near where you live, or fairly traded. Consider buying second-hand clothes from thrift stores and consignment shops, and buy well-made clothes that won't go out of style in one season.

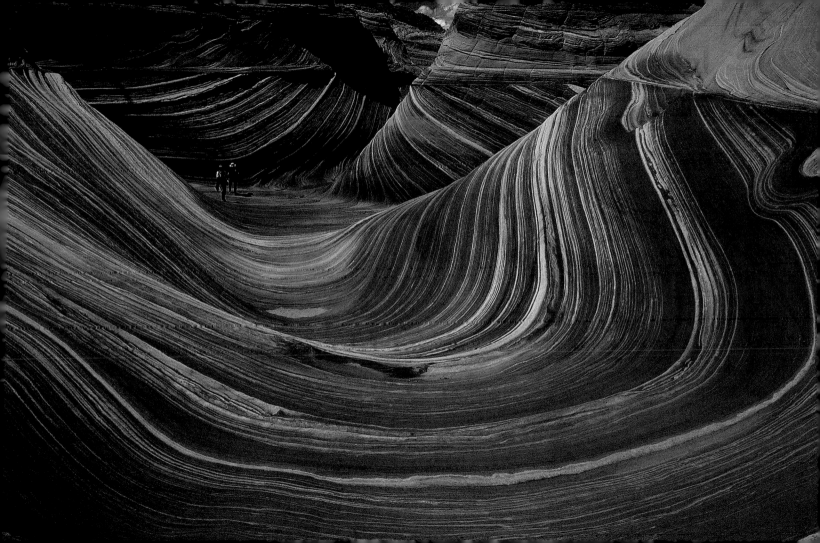

Make your holiday carbon-neutral.

Many people now buy carbon credits to offset the emissions generated by their air travel. But your impact doesn't end when you step off the plane, so try to calculate the emissions for your entire trip. Travel Green estimates that the average 1-night hotel stay generates 15 kilograms of carbon dioxide. In response to this some hotels have started to offer emissions-offset programs to guests, usually a few pounds per night. Car and boat travel should also be part of the equation when estimating how much carbon your trip produces.

Remember that carbon-neutral is not synonymous with sustainable, so be sure to stay in eco-friendly accommodations, use public transport, be conscientious of water and energy use (particularly in nations where these resources are scarce), dispose of waste properly, and tread lightly in general.

Grand Teton National Park,
United States

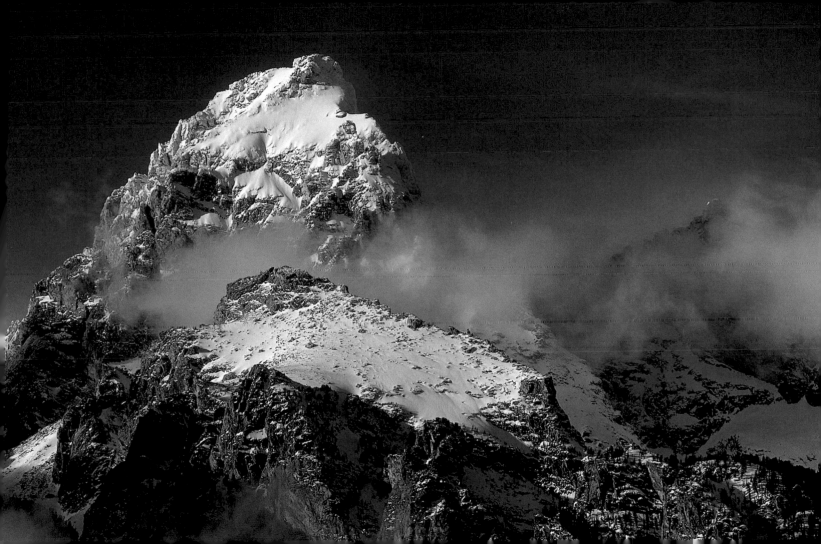

Don't keep exotic animals as pets.

Over the last decade it has become fashionable to keep exotic animals as pets. These animals, snatched by the thousands from their natural habitats and carried to the other end of the world, end up in captivity, where they usually survive for a short time, being suited neither to their new climate nor to life out of the wild. The black market for exotics has devastated the populations of some unfortunate species. The highly sought-after horned parrot of New Caledonia, for example, has been the victim of ferocious poaching: Only 1,700 remain in the wild. Similarly, there are more tigers in captivity than living in the wild, and only a small percentage are those in zoos; the rest live in circuses, roadside menageries, big-cat rescues, and in backyards, as pets.

Think carefully before imprisoning a languid iguana or a brilliantly coloured parrot in your home.

Marine iguana, Argentina

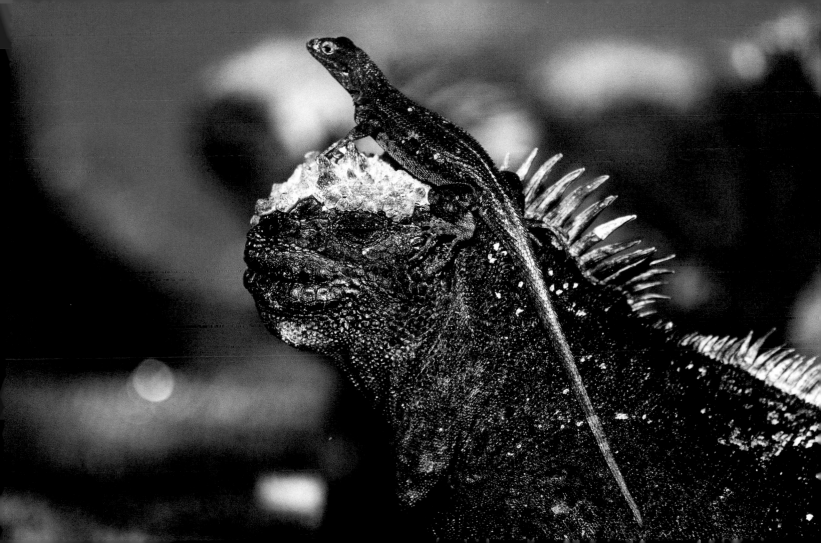

Invest in products and souvenirs that encourage sustainable living.

During the last century, whales, tigers, rhinoceros, and elephants reached the edge of extinction. Every day, several dozen species vanish from existence. Half the plant and animal species on earth may disappear before the end of the twenty-first century. Overexploitation is one of the leading causes, because poaching—whether for meat, eggs, feathers, or skins—is very lucrative and is a strong temptation to people living in poor countries.

In developing countries, poaching often brings greater profits than respectable jobs in a sustainable industry. The best way to discourage poaching is to invest in products that have been developed sustainably, for a fair wage, in equitable conditions. It may take some extra work, but do some research on the country you are visiting and seek out sustainable cottage industries that employ native people. Then buy their wares.

Caterpillar, Death Valley National Park, United States

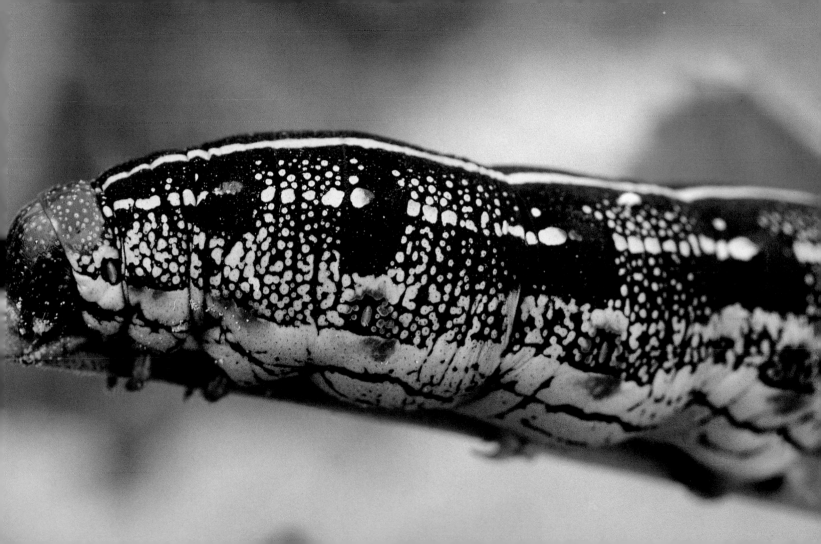

Choose products with less packaging.

When we buy something, we tend to look at its quality and its price. Little attention is paid to the packaging, even though it accounts for part of the cost of the
product—sometimes a considerable part. Why does a tube of toothpaste have to come
in a cardboard box? Why do printer cartridges come in both cardboard and plastic
packaging?

**When you have a choice between equivalent products, choose the one with less
packaging—even better if that packaging was made from recycled materials and
is fully recyclable itself. If a favourite brand of yours uses excess packaging for its
products, ring or e-mail a complaint.**

White Desert, Egypt

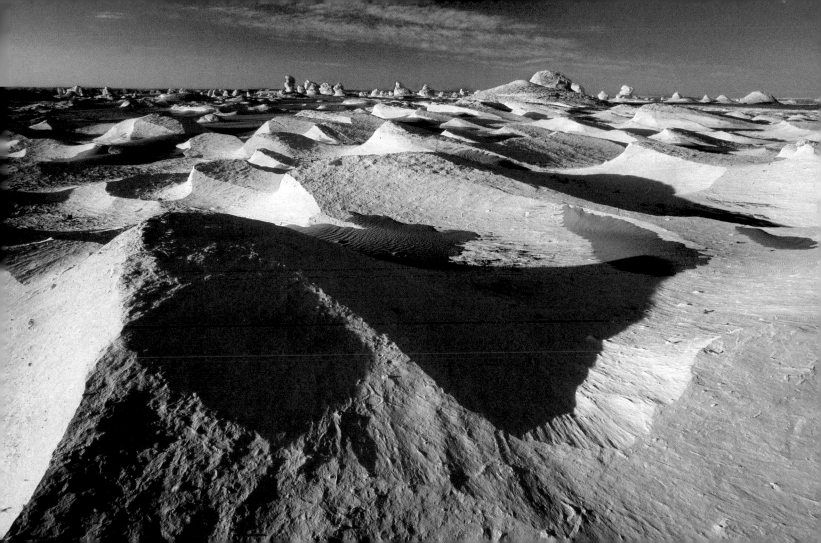

Find out how your local authority manages waste.

In addition to ecological benefits, recycling also creates jobs. More than 1.5 million people worldwide are employed in the recycling industry. Recycling creates 36 jobs per 10,000 tonnes of recycled material compared to 6 jobs for the same amount of material brought to traditional disposal facilities.

Ask your local authority how it manages your area's waste. Is it dumped or burned, and where? If your local authority has not put in place a comprehensive recycling program, ask why. Encourage other voters to ask similar questions.

Iceberg, Greenland

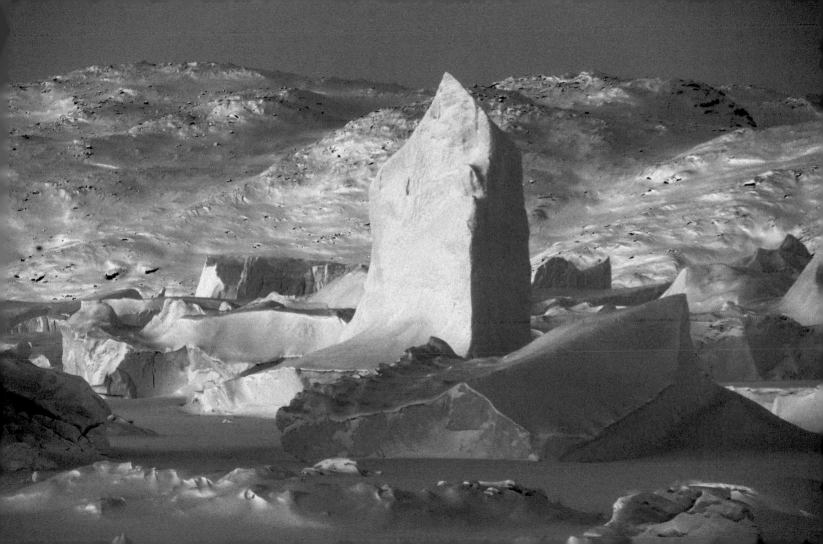

Drink better beer.

On average, a UK citizen drinks nearly 100 litres of beer a year — and around 80% of this is bought from just 4 multinational producers who care little about their environmental impact. Many of them have bought up previously independent brands and now produce these 'traditional' beers in huge factories. But there are still many small independent breweries around the country, sourcing their raw materials locally and taking sustainability seriously. Some of these have taken major steps to reduce their environmental impact. They buy power from wind farms or generate their own energy, invest in technology to make brewing less energy intensive, send grain waste to local farms or use it for composting. Responsible brewers can use up to 50% less water than industrial brewers, who need 5 to 6 gallons of water to create 1 gallon of beer. Some breweries have gone organic, only using pesticide-free barley and hops, and most independent brewers also use less artificial additives as the flavour in their beer is the product of hard work, not a chemical formula.

So, next time you are in a pub or bar, ask for a local beer to try — it will probably taste better, and you will be supporting the local economy too.

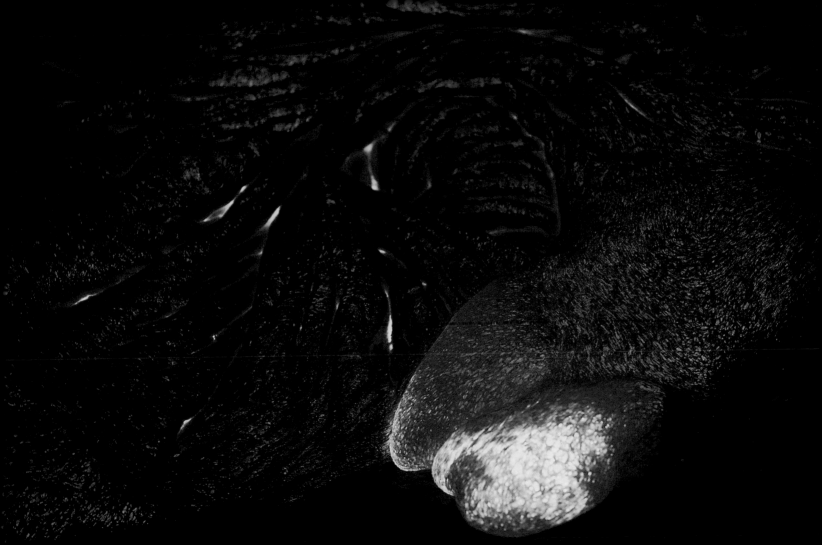

Use aerators on your taps.

Every day the average UK citizen uses around 150 litres of water at home — compared to an average of around 30 litres in Africa. Water is an increasingly precious commodity; with summer droughts now a regular occurrence in Europe and likely to become more common as climate change continues.

You can reduce your domestic consumption by having taps fitted with aerators — which are very cheap to purchase, starting at around £4. The flow from the tap will feel stronger, but it actually contains less water and more air. Tap aerators can reduce the water usage from your taps by up to 75%, so look out for them in your local hardware shop or online.

Niagara Falls, United States

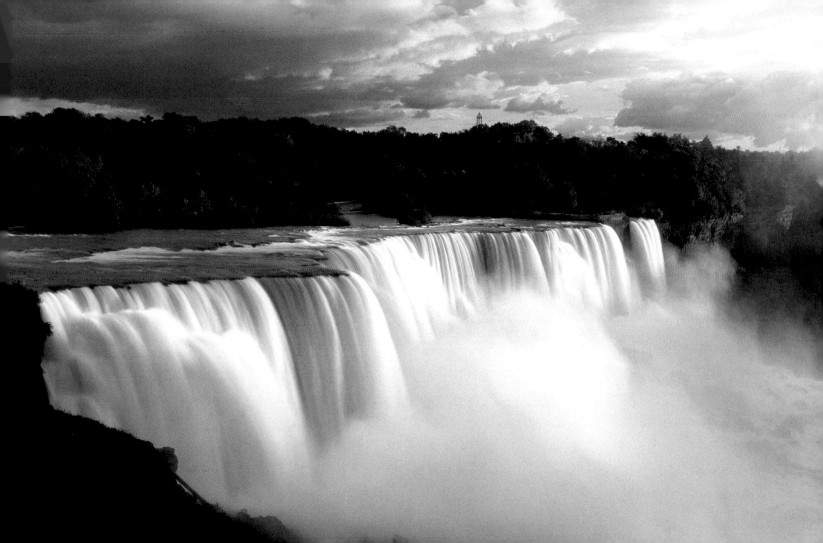

Know the pros and cons of MP3s.

Downloading music means you get the music without the CDs and those bulky plastic jewel cases (most of which are made from polystyrene and not easily recycled). Although downloading music produces a fraction of the emissions involved in putting an actual CD in an actual store, the e-waste generated by computers and MP3 players, which have incredibly short shelf lives, has its own disadvantages.

You can help make your MP3 player a more ecologically sound investment by buying the greenest equipment you can find (that includes your computer), burning as few CDs from MP3s as possible (on rewritable discs), making sure you don't leave your MP3 player charging all night, and extending the life of the player. There are now repair shops that fix players that are past warranty or seem beyond hope; these same organisations also buy broken players and resell them. And as you're making the transition to digital, recycle old CDs by giving them away or taking them to a second-hand record store.

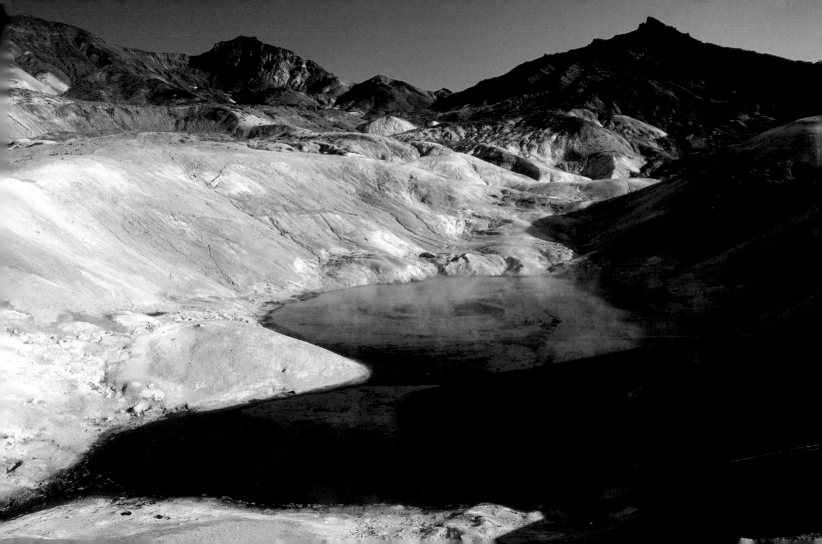

Change your car over to LPG.

Liquefied Petroleum Gas (LPG), often known as autogas, is a mixture of propane and butane. When used as a vehicle fuel it is often referred to as autogas. The simple chemical makeup of the gases ensures that they are clean burning. LPG is produced as a by-product in both the extraction and refining stages of oil production. In the past it has been considered waste and flared off. It is particularly abundant in the North Sea's 'wet' crude oil. LPG costs around a third of the price of petrol, and produces around a third of the emissions — so you win both ways. In the United Kingdom there are now around 1,500 petrol stations that also sell LPG, so you don't need to worry about supply.

You can change your car over so it can run on both conventional petrol and LPG. It is not expensive and can save you money in the long term, as well as helping to slow down climate change.

Atacama Desert, Chile

Celebrate the arrival of spring by doing something for the earth.

Every year, nearly 15 million acres of land become desert, worldwide. Overgrazing, excessive deforestation, rain and wind erosion, and salt contamination all cause soil degradation. Already, desertification has affected a global area equivalent to the combined territory of United States and Mexico, and every day the earth's productive capacity is reduced. The planet will need to feed roughly 8 billion people by 2025. We must seek to halt the practices that cause desertification and invest in methods to stop it.

The spring equinox falls on March 20 or 21 every year. On that date, day and night last equal lengths of time. It is an ideal opportunity to offer the planet a few hours of respite. This spring equinox, make a gesture for the earth — the choice of what to do is vast.

Mount St. Helens National
Volcanic Monument,
United States

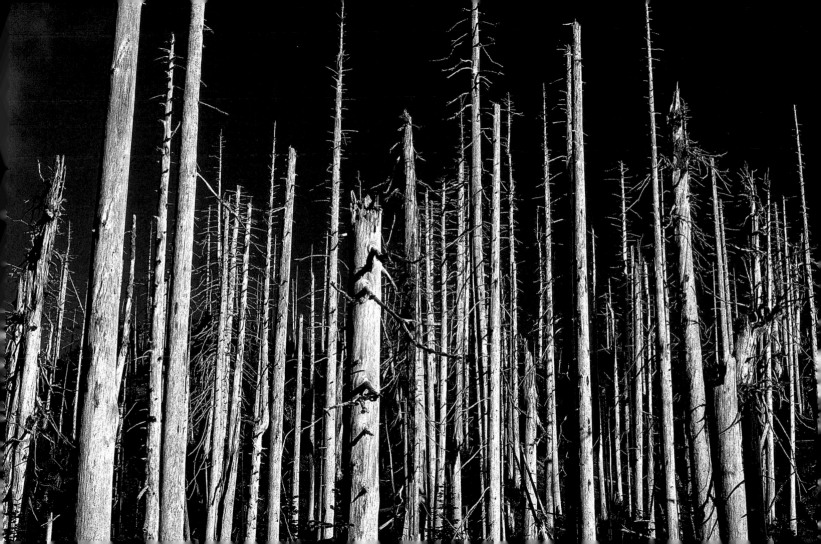

Do not let children play with water.

It seems to us so natural that our taps deliver clean water that we assume it is a lifetime guarantee to everyone. This is not the case. Every morning, millions of people walk several miles to collect the water that is essential to meet their modest needs. The average African woman walks more than 5.6 kilometres per day to obtain water for her family — or the equivalent of a marathon every week. March 22 is World Water Day every year, and aims to make people in the world aware of the importance of preserving this vital resource.

Teach your children to treat water with respect. The tap in the bathtub and the garden hose are not toys — do not let your children play with the running water.

Autumn, United States

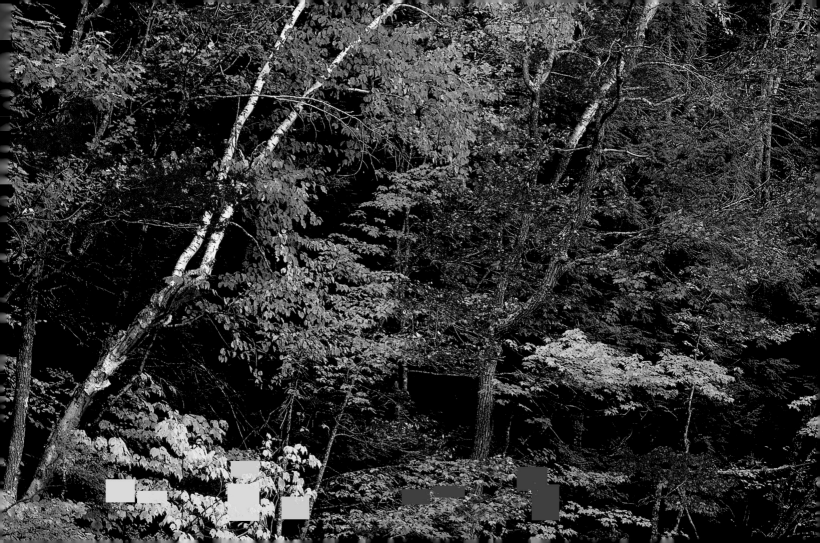

Run your dishwasher only when it is full.

A large volume of the water taken from nature to meet humanity's growing needs is drawn from rivers. Rivers such as the Colorado in the United States and Mexico, the Jordan in the Middle East, the Indus in Pakistan, the Yellow River in China, and the Nile in Egypt vanish into the earth at certain times of the year in certain places because their flow is not enough to reach the sea. Rivers and streams in Europe and the United States suffer the same fate because of groundwater depletion. This happens during the dry months of the summer when the base flows of rivers are low and water is being pumped to irrigate lawns and gardens, as well as for use in homes.

Using a dishwasher is more efficient than washing up by hand — washing under a running tap uses around 60 litres each time, while an efficient dishwasher can use as little as 10 litres per cycle. To further save water, use the dishwasher sparingly — only run it when it is completely full.

Guelta (water hole), Niger

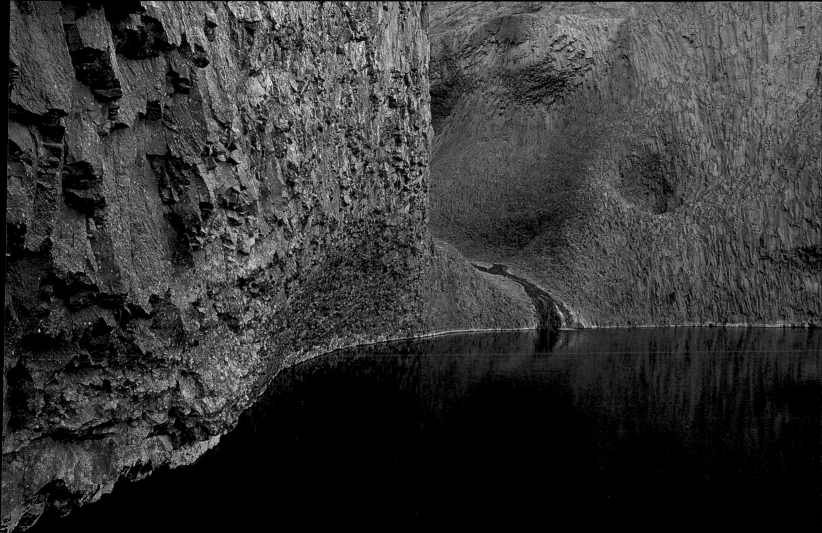

Try trading skills instead of buying services.

People all around you have a wealth of specific talents and knowledge that perhaps you do not share. Your own abilities may take another form. These may range from the sophisticated—computer programming, financial investment, or portrait photography—to the basic, like lifting boxes or feeding a cat while the owner is away.

Instead of looking in the phone book for a service for hire, reach out to your neighbours and friends and offer to swap skills. Perhaps someone living near you will offer the help you need in moving house, in exchange for your help with child care. It is another way of encouraging a more humane society.

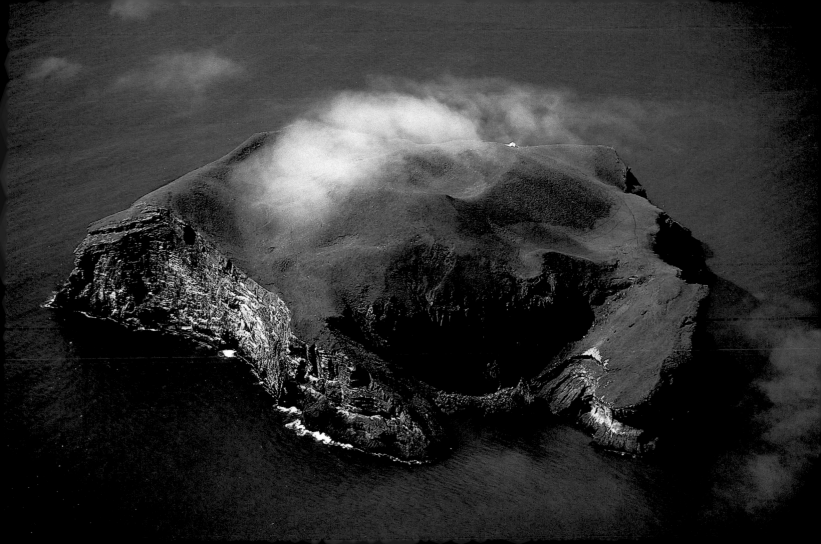

Water your garden in the evening.

All the water we use runs into rivers, where it flows to the sea to evaporate and fall back to the earth once more as rain. This endless process is called the water cycle. The water that quenches our thirst today may have been drunk by dinosaurs millions of years ago, for the amount of water on our planet is always the same. We need to look after it as our population continues to grow and our use of water increases.

Wait until evening to water your garden; during the cooler hours of the night, plants lose less through evaporation, and use half as much water. Also keep the weather forecast in mind: There is no sense watering your garden if rain is due. And don't water your lawn in the dry summer months — your shrivelled grass will become green as soon as the rains return.

Dunes, Chad

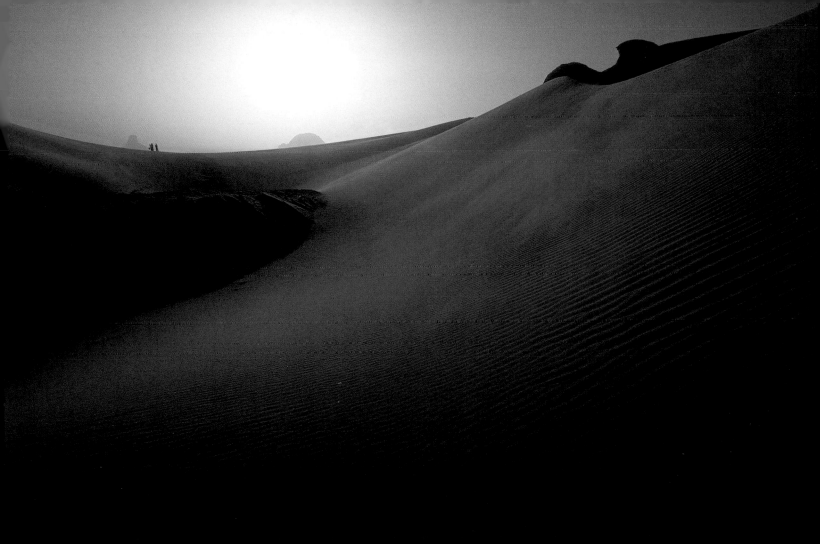

Choose a dishwasher with a 'booster' heater and lower your water heater temperature.

More than a third of the electricity used by an average household goes to supply power for washing machines, dishwashers, and clothes dryers.

To reduce this consumption of energy, choose a dishwasher with a 'booster' heater. This will add a small amount to the cost of a new washer, but means you can lower the temperature of your boiler so it should pay for itself in water-heating energy savings after about a year. Some dishwashers have boosters that will automatically raise the temperature, while others require a manual change before beginning a wash cycle.

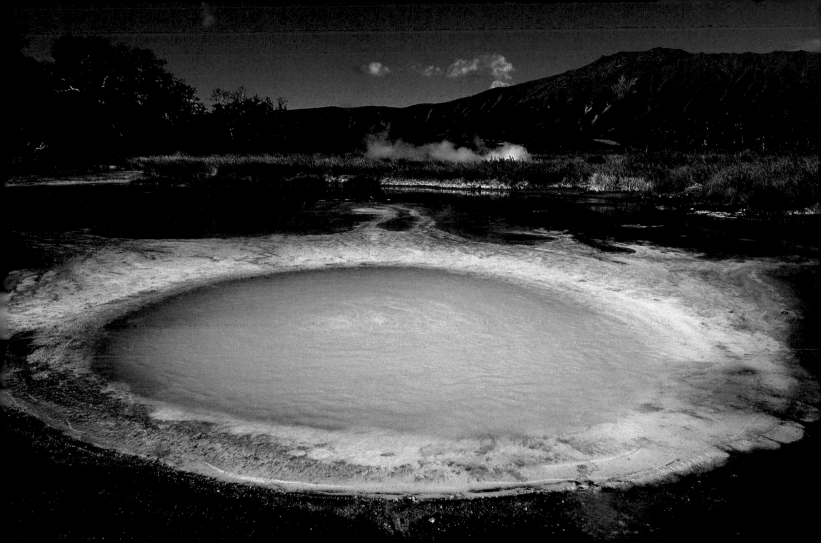

Consider a toy library.

Too many children never experience childhood. A total of 218 million children between the ages of 5 and 17 are forced to work and almost 126 million work under dangerous conditions. More than 300,000 young boys worldwide are enlisted as child soldiers. Many are not even 10 years old.

To teach your children values that are not oriented exclusively toward consumption or buying things, consider organizing a toy library with their friends in the afternoons. The variety of shared toys will certainly please them, and the toys will be used by more than one child.

Arches, Chad

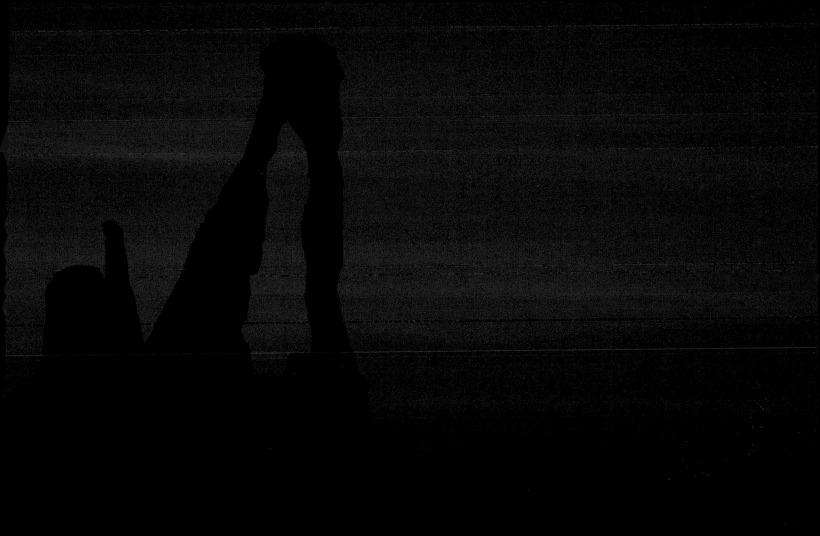

Leftover and stripped paint should go to the dump.

Painting the house is a polluting business. Cans of leftover paint, soiled cloth and packaging, solvents, and glue become mixed up with other household waste. They have a damaging effect on the decomposition of the gases produced by incineration and on the effluent from dumps. If the liquids are poured down a drain, their toxicity interferes with the processes of water-treatment stations. Half of all this waste is not treated and thus ends up in rivers and the sea. Three quarters of marine pollution comes from fresh water.

There are several ways to minimize the polluting effects of painting your house: Use eco-friendly paints, take careful measurements, and buy only the amount of paint that you need; once you are done with the project, take leftover paint to a paint exchange program, or donate it to a local charity. Finally, if you must dispose of the paint in the trash, be sure to let it dry completely (adding sawdust or cat litter as needed) before putting it in the garbage.

Glacier, Greenland

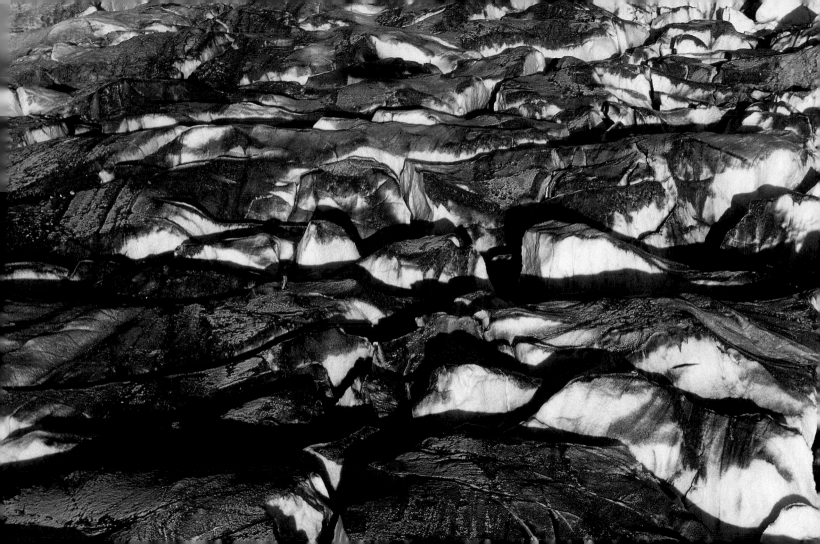

Participate in a Lights Out program.

Cities around the globe have staged Lights Out events, in which residents and businesses are encouraged to turn off all nonessential lights for 1 hour. In 2007 London saved 750 megawatts of electricity when nearly 2 million lightbulbs went dark—enough to power 3,000 TVs for a year. Earth Hour, Sydney's local event, went global in 2008.

Find out about upcoming Earth Hour and Lights Out events and encourage friends and local businesses to participate. On a smaller scale you can stage personal lights out events anytime—shut everything off, including computers and TVs during peak usage hours, light up a few nontoxic candles or solar-powered lanterns, and relax with family and friends.

Leatherback turtle,
French Guiana

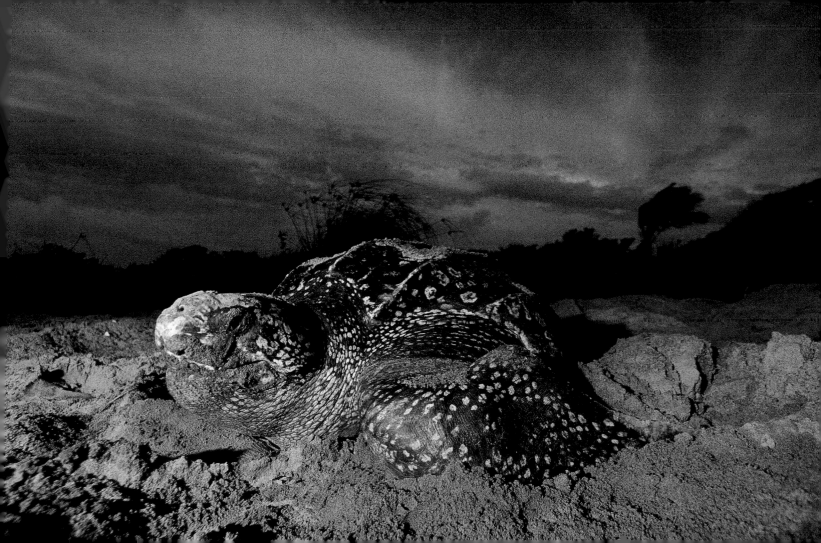

Take a shower rather than a bath.

More than a third of humanity lacks adequate sanitation. It is estimated that half the world's hospital beds are filled with patients suffering from preventable, water-borne diseases. The World Health Organization estimates that more than 2.5 billion people do not have access to basic sanitation, and more than a billion people use unsafe sources of drinking water. This lack of access to clean water kills 4,000 children every day.

Don't take for granted what the rest of the world sorely needs. A bath uses up to 100 litres of water, while a 5-minute shower takes around 30 litres — and even less if you fit an aerator or low-flow showerhead.

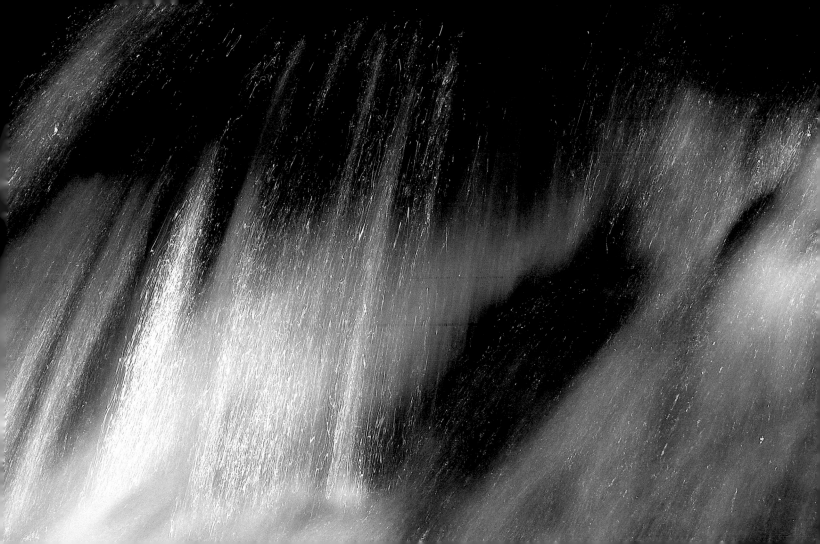

Use technology rather than travelling.

To reduce the risk to climate change, the concentration of carbon dioxide in the atmosphere would need to be reduced by one-third to one-half of what it is now. That means that the Kyoto Protocol, which was considered too demanding by the United States — the world's chief producer of greenhouse-gas emissions — falls far short of what is needed to stabilise our global climate.

Reduce transportation costs and save time by using the Internet or telephone when possible. Many tasks can be carried out by video conferencing, telephone conferencing, and e-mail rather than by meeting face-to-face.

Red ibis, Brazil

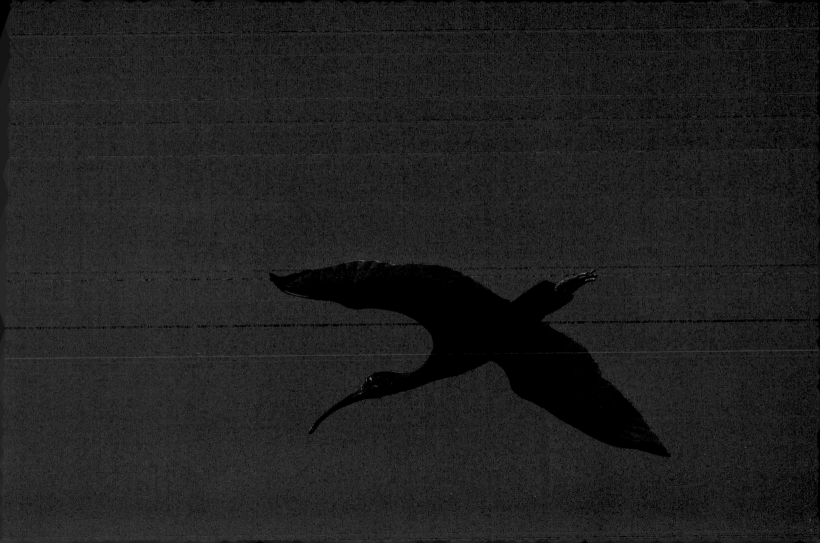

Fair trade isn't just for coffee and tea.

Fair trade accounts for a small fraction of world trade—only 0.5% of coffee sold in the world is fair-trade certified. Yet it directly benefits more than 7 million people in about 70 countries and enables them to meet their needs for food, health, housing, and education. However, broadening the fair-trade market to embrace new cooperatives in developing countries relies on demand, which in turn depends upon the awareness of consumers in Europe, the United States, and Japan.

Don't stop with fair-trade coffee and tea. Broaden your purchasing to include other widely available fair-trade products, such as bananas (in the United Kingdom 1 in 4 bananas sold are now fair trade), chocolate, honey, orange juice, pineapples, rice, sugar, and even flowers.

Yellowstone River Canyon, United States

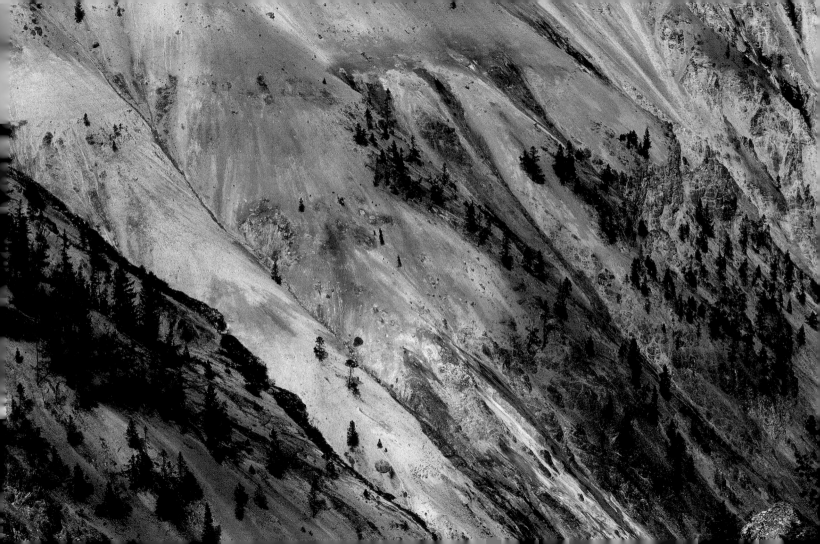

Report fly-tipping.

Illegal dumping or fly-tipping is a major problem. Apart from being a blight on the landscape, bulky waste can also contain dangerous substances that can pollute the soil, water, and air. It should be a concern to everyone, since illegal dumping often is seen as a 'gateway' act; if it is tolerated, it sends the message that other illegal activities may also be tolerated. Dumping household, industrial, and commercial waste is an illegal act considered an offence that leads to prosecution.

If you notice illegal dumping happening in your neighbourhood, make a note of the location, the surrounding environment, and the type of waste, and report it to your council or local authority. They have the power to have it properly removed, even from private land.

Icebergs, Greenland

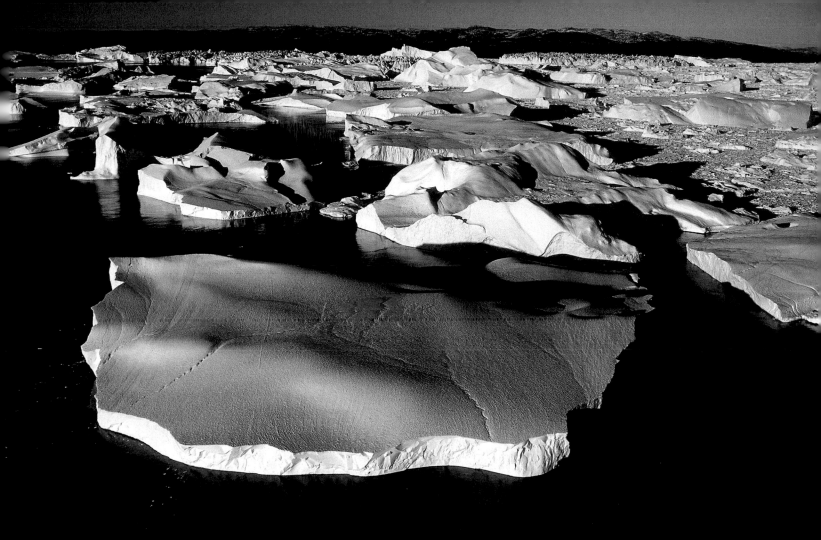

Do the small things, but don't lose sight of the big picture.

Making small adjustments to our daily habits is important. For example, if every household replaced one regular bulb with a compact fluorescent, it would prevent the equivalent of the emissions generated by 800,000 cars. However, we cannot alleviate the strain on our planet simply by buying better dish soap or using rechargeable batteries. As we implement the small improvements, we must keep in mind the need for greater change. Reducing the amount of petrol we use by driving hybrids is good, but creating public transport systems that eliminate the need for cars is much better. Some of the big-picture actions we should keep in mind are ridding ourselves of oil dependence; reducing the amount of land we require for food and limiting the environmental impacts of big agriculture; reimagining our communities and living standards to curb unsustainable suburban sprawl; and electing officials, from the local level to the presidency, who have clear environmental priorities and policies.

Don't compartmentalize your efforts: Understand where each gesture fits into the larger context of sustainability and always look for ways to make a leap toward greater change.

Giant clam, Australia

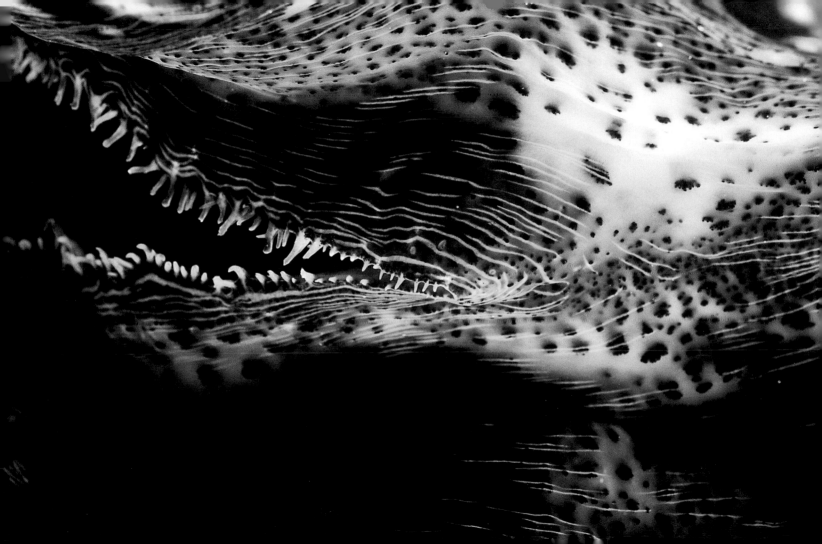

Try an electric bicycle.

Preserving the quality of the air around us is indispensable to life. Air pollution kills three times as many people as road accidents. It causes respiratory diseases (chronic bronchitis, asthma, sinusitis) and is responsible for 3 million worldwide every year.

Try an electric bicycle. It is an attractive alternative to the car for short journeys. The electric motor ingeniously spares your legs by reducing the effort needed to pedal, and the removable, easily rechargeable battery has a range of 20 to 40 kilometers, depending on the terrain. Above all, it emits no pollution, is silent, and is considerably faster in city traffic.

Uzon Caldera, Kamchatka, Russia

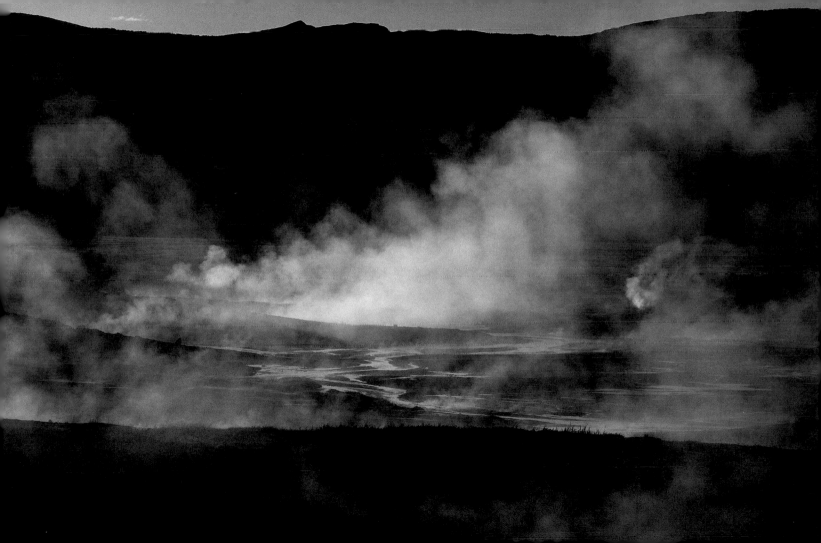

Get your school to go green.

There's more to greening our schools than advocating for healthy lunches. Recycling programs can reduce waste in both the cafeteria and the classroom. School buildings can receive green retrofits that reduce energy use and remove toxic substances. School grounds can go from chemical-drenched lawns to food-producing gardens and outdoor earth-science labs.

Join with fellow parents — and teachers and students — to demand that your school pass a resolution that addresses the whole picture of sustainability, or join the Eco-Schools programme. You will provide a framework that will ensure future administrative decisions are approached from a planet-saving mindset.

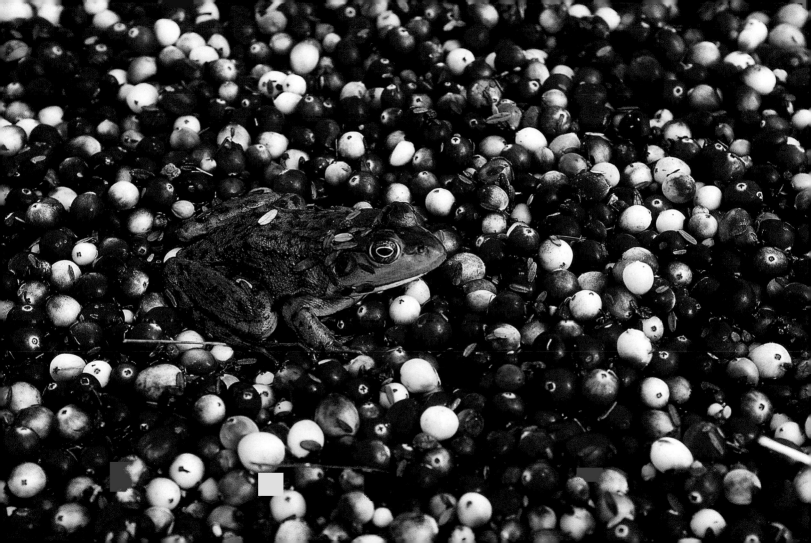

Ask your school to put the 'field' back into the field trip.

Most children view field trips as one of the small perks of enduring another school year. Even trips to educational institutions like museums and historic sites generate the kind of excitement that textbooks often fail to do. Field trips are great motivators and in turn great opportunities to introduce children to the natural areas close to them, and get them thinking about possible solutions to environmental issues.

Suggest that your school dedicate one or more of its annual field trips to environmental education. Visits to recycling centres, hands-on work at urban and city farms, or walks with park wardens are just a few examples of trips that can inspire children to take action to protect the environment.

Emperor penguins, Antarctica

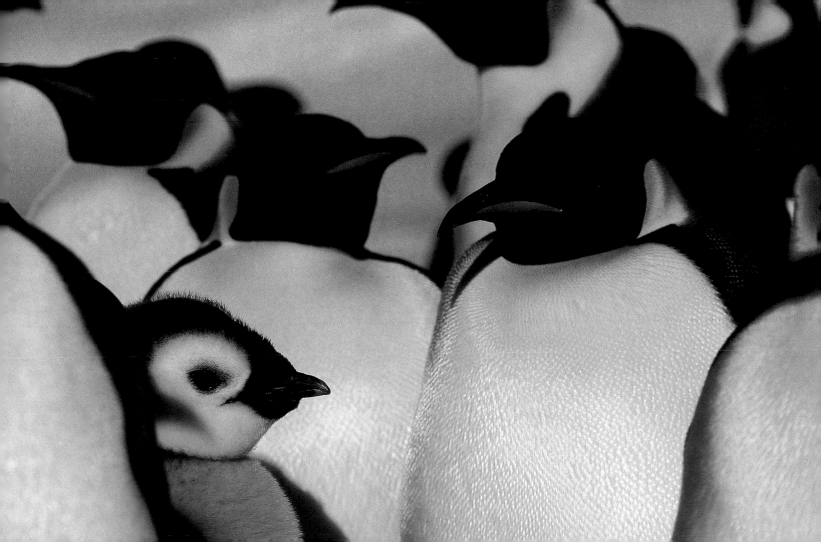

Take a minute to think about the next generations.

By the middle of the century, the earth will be home to 9 billion people: an additional 3 billion mouths to feed, all needing housing, water, and light. In 2050, if each inhabitant of developing countries uses as much energy as someone living in Japan did back in 1973, world energy consumption will be 4 times what it is today.

Other generations will live on the earth after us. How will we keep up with the demands on our shrinking resources? What are we going to leave for them?

Bacteria, Kamchatka, Russia

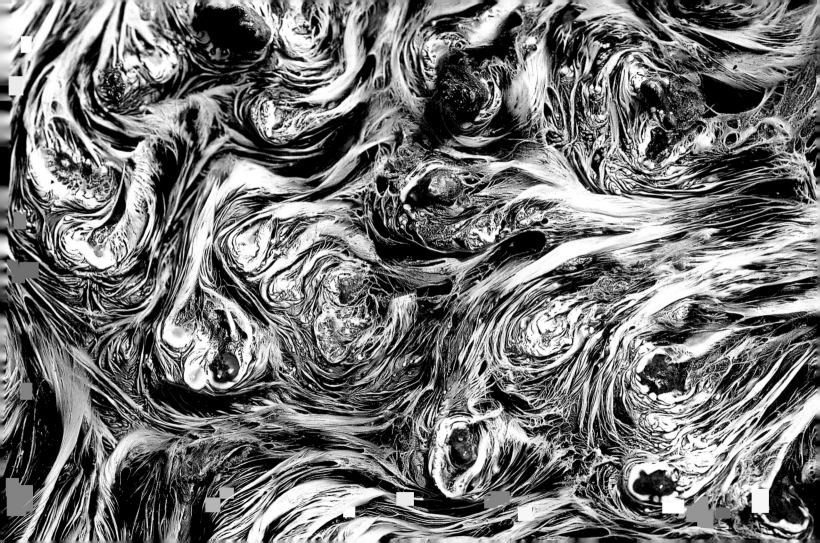

Go bicycling as a family.

Half of all adults and 1 in 5 children in the European region are overweight. A third of these are already obese and numbers are accelerating. Part of the reason for these extra pounds lies in the power of TV and in lack of physical exercise. Make time to take your children out on a bike ride, an activity that is as beneficial for their health as it is environmentally friendly.

Take more trips closer to home. Instead of planning a long family car trip, explore your local flora and fauna by bike. If you live in an urban environment, be sure to teach your children safe riding habits when sharing the streets with cars; if you live in a rural area, encourage your children to use their bikes as much as possible, rather than relying on the family car.

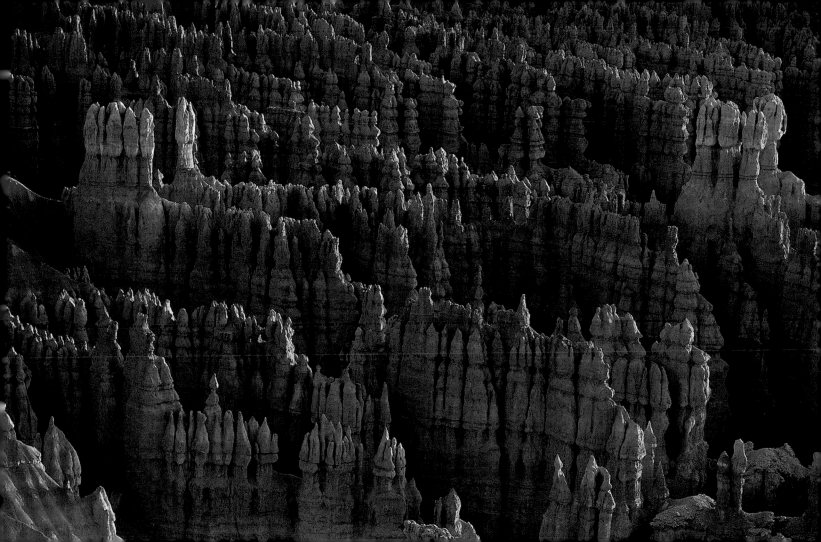

Use rewritable CDs or flash drives to back up files.

CDs are recyclable but only a few companies offer this service, and tonnes of discarded discs end up in landfills every year. The manufacture of a CD uses around 1 kilogram of carbon dioxide, in addition to the oil-based plastics that it and its case are made of.

Forgo the spindles of cheap one-use CDs that fill the shelves of office supply stores and spend a little more on a small pack of rewritable ones. Store data on rewritable discs or on a USB flash drive.

Scorpion fish, Thailand

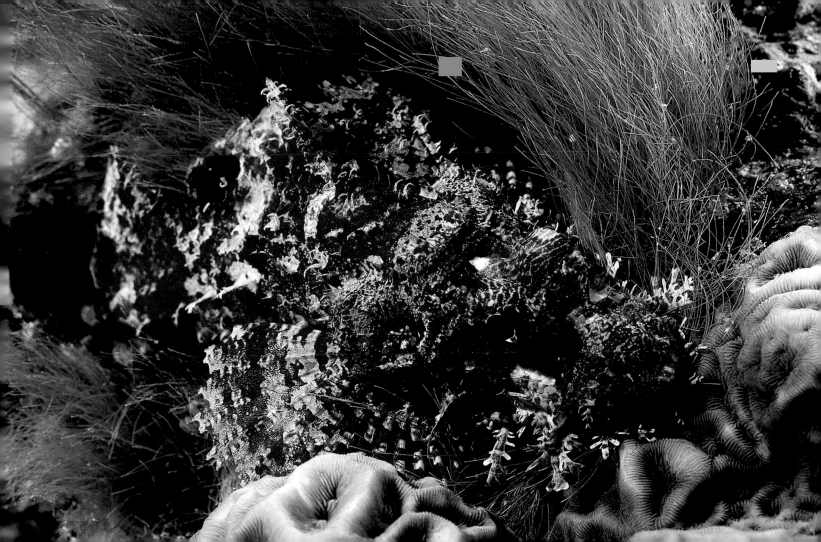

Buy organic food for your baby.

Studies have shown that human exposure to pesticides can cause neurological disturbances, increase the frequency of certain cancers, damage the immune system, and reduce male fertility. Pesticides also degrade soil and contaminate drinking water, leading to significant cleanup costs. These chemicals also kill nontargeted insects and affect organisms throughout the food chain. A conventional farmer can use any of 450 different authorized pesticides; an organic farmer can use just 7 natural pesticides, and that usage is strictly controlled.

If 'going organic' for the whole family seems daunting, at least give priority to feeding organic food to babies and young children. Pesticides can increase susceptibility to certain cancers by breaking down the immune system's resistance to cancer cells. Infants and children are among those at greatest risk.

Grand Staircase-Escalante
National Monument,
United States

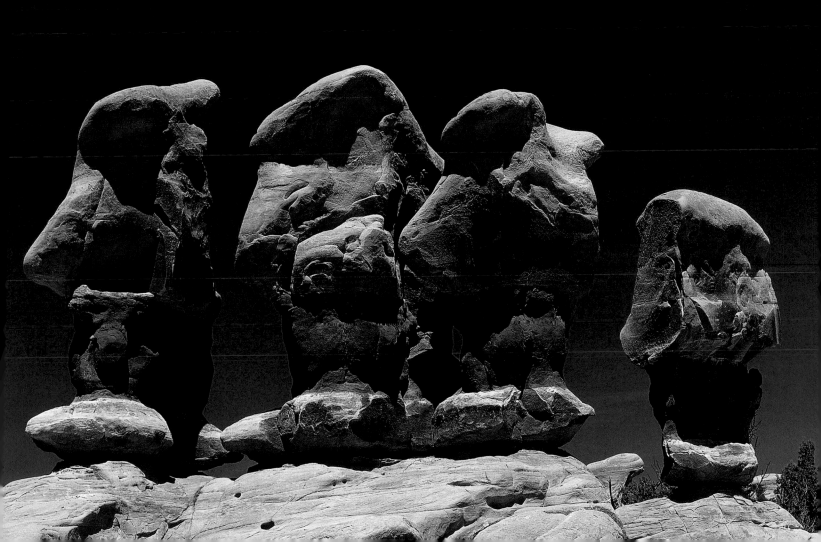

Check the air filters on your car.

One of the most common causes of a drop in fuel efficiency is dirty or clogged air filters. Dirty filters reduce the amount of air entering the engine, causing incomplete combustion of fuel. This can reduce your fuel economy by around 10%—the equivalent of over 10 pence being added to the price of your petrol.

An easy way to check whether your air filter needs changing is to take it out and shine a torch on it. If light is allowed through, it is probably fine; if it stops the light, buy a new one.

Salar de Uyuni, Bolivia

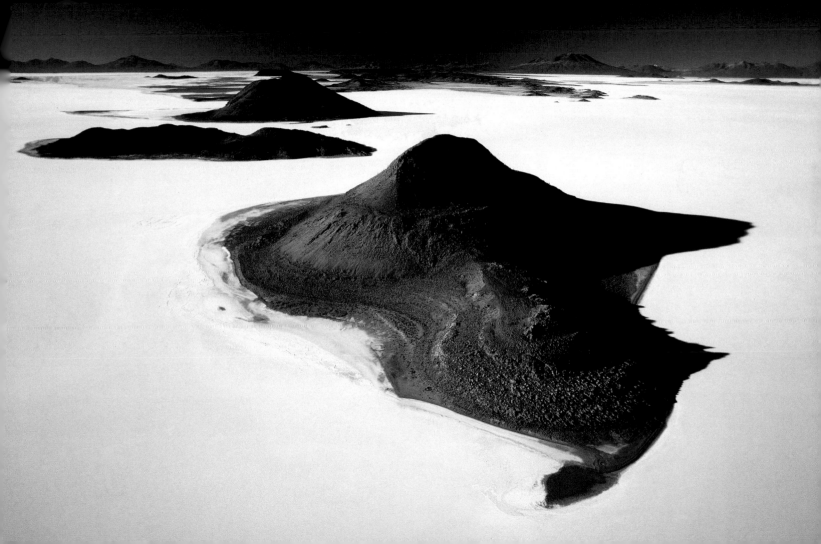

Use natural treatments for plant diseases.

In both agriculture and gardening, the intensive use of chemicals and defoliants impoverishes the soil, which, in the long term, becomes sterile. Repeated, systematic treatment with these agents encourages the development of resistance in the targeted pests. Since the 1950s, the number of insect and mite species immune to insecticides has increased from a dozen to about 450.

The best way to deal with plant diseases is to prevent them in the first place. Choose the right plants for your site, use disease-resistant varieties, keep a clean garden, create well-balanced soil, don't overwater, and mulch to prevent weeds from spreading.

Seeds, Shenandoah National Park, Virginia

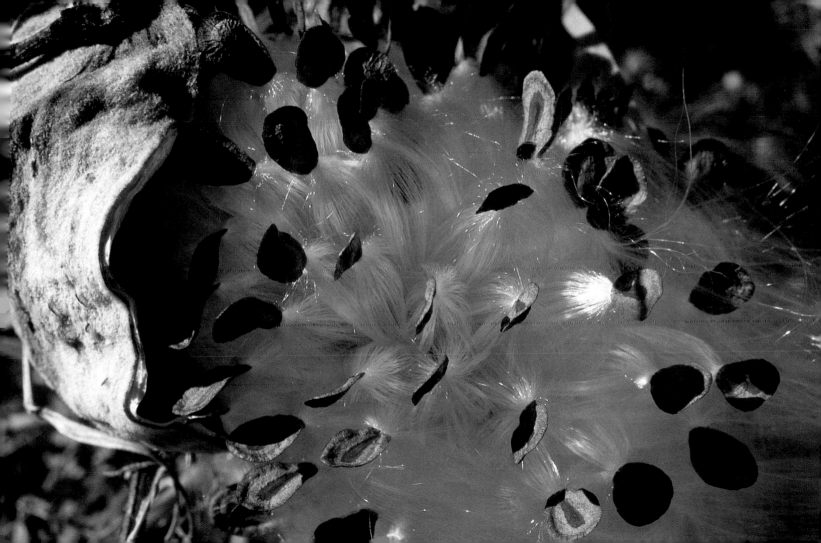

Sport fishermen: Respect the sea.

Worldwide, the depletion of the oceans' fish stocks is due to over-fishing on an international scale. The fish that are caught are ever smaller; they have not reached maturity or been able to reproduce, and thus are not able to perpetuate their species and replenish stocks. Do not make this mistake when you go fishing for pleasure.

Observe the size limit for fish, crustaceans, and shellfish. You can find out which species are covered by restrictions by asking your tourist office, the port authority, or the marine and fisheries department. Make sure you tell your fellow fishermen, if necessary. And do not catch more than you need.

Namib Desert, Namibia

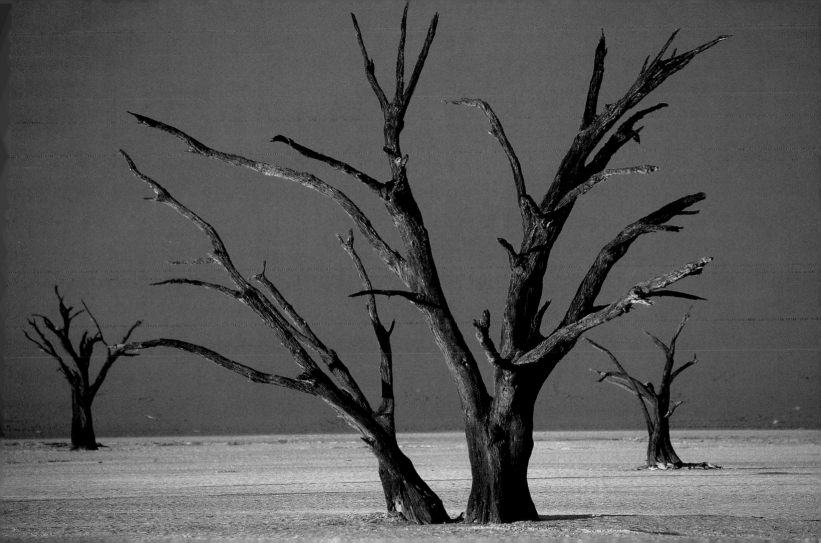

Offset the greenhouse-gas emissions your air travel produces.

Although planes are technically public transport, air travel is not greener than car travel — in fact, it's far more destructive. A 747 jet aircraft consumes 19 litres of fuel per 1.6 kilometres flown. Air travel accounts for 70% of the United Kingdom's transport-related emissions each year. Around the world, air emissions are expected to triple by 2050. There are many Internet sites that enable you to calculate the greenhouse-gas emissions your next air journey will produce. One transatlantic flight produces almost half as much carbon dioxide as a person produces, on average, in meeting all their other needs (lighting, heating, and car travel) over a year.

Many organisations and airlines offer carbon credits, the money from which funds clean energy or reforestation programs; even travel-booking sites have started to offer these credits as add-ons when you purchase airline tickets. If you can't avoid flying, make sure you offset the impact of your trip.

Elephant, Kenya

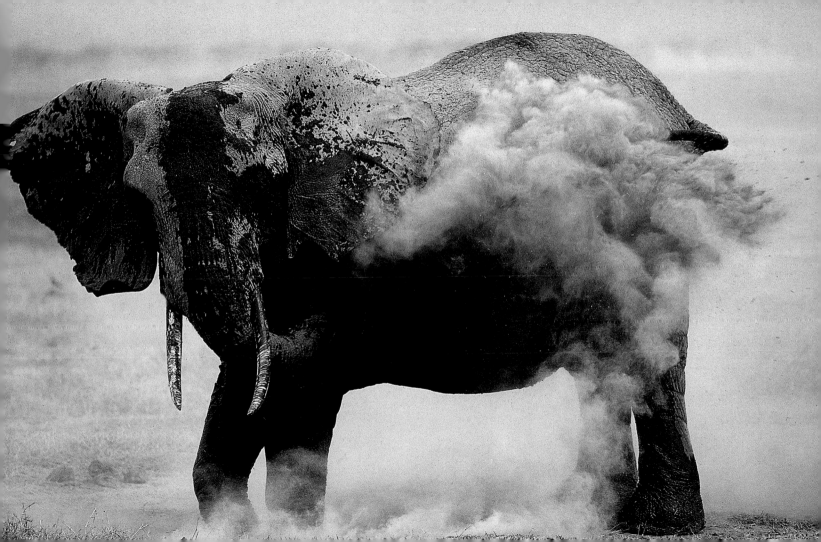

Don't waste food.

Thirty percent of the food we buy in the United Kingdom gets thrown away because we don't eat it before it goes off—and all of it has used energy in the process of farming, processing, packaging, and transporting it to the shops. We have forgotten the ways our grandparents used to make the most of food by freezing, cooking leftovers, and being careful with our store cupboards.

When shopping, check the 'best before' dates and choose the packets that will last the longest. In your fridge, make sure that the items that will go off fastest are nearest the top or the front. If you notice vegetables beginning to turn, make soup—you can cook up a big batch, then freeze it in portion sizes to be reheated when you need it. And when you buy in bulk or on special offer, freeze what you won't eat quickly—it will be cheaper, and you won't risk it going off.

Drifting ice floe, Antarctica

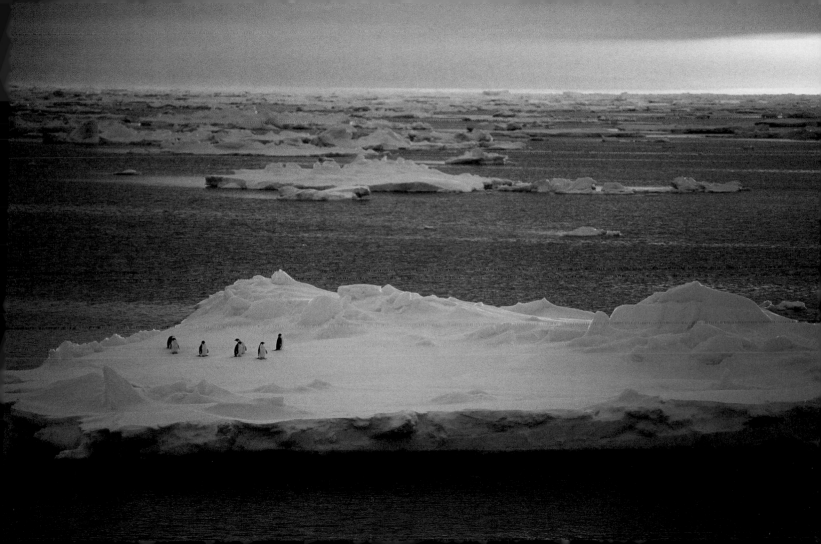

Be unobtrusive while out walking.

The farmland bird index for Europe has declined by 34% since 1966. One in 8 of the world's birds face extinction. Birds are vulnerable to habitat damage from intensive agriculture and forestry, the growing impact of development on the land, unrestricted water use, and pollution of all kinds.

When you are out walking, treat wildlife with respect. Do not disturb animals, especially young animals and chicks. Watch them discreetly, at a distance, without disturbing their quiet and tranquillity.

Orangutan, Malaysia

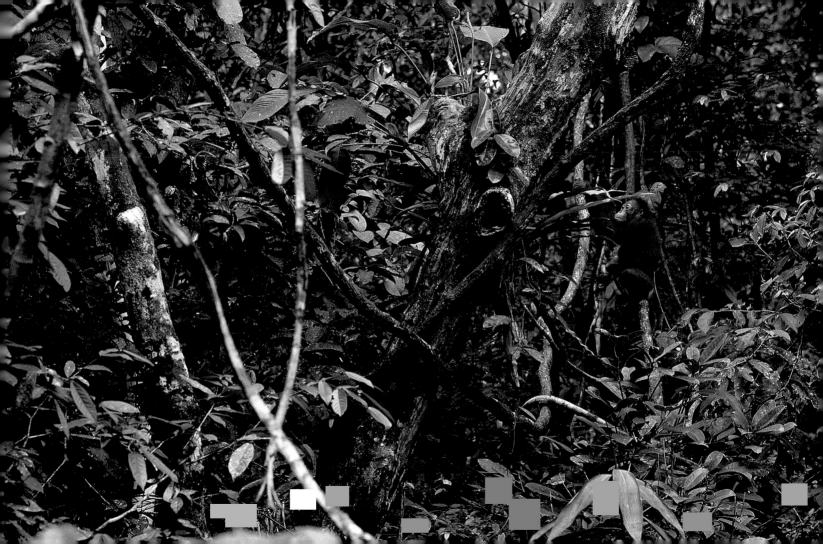

Trace leaks.

On average about half the water in cities and in distribution grids worldwide is lost to leakage. A faucet that leaks 1 drop per second can waste up to 12,000 litres of water per year. A leaking toilet can lose 570 to 750 litres a day.

Trace the leaks in your home's plumbing. Test your toilet by adding a few drops of food colouring or dark-coloured drink mix to the tank's water. Wait 30 minutes and then check the bowl to see if any of the coloured water has leaked out of the tank. Use your water meter to help you find other phantom leaks: Take readings before and after a 2-hour period in which no one uses any water — if there is any discrepancy you might want to call a plumber to check for leaks.

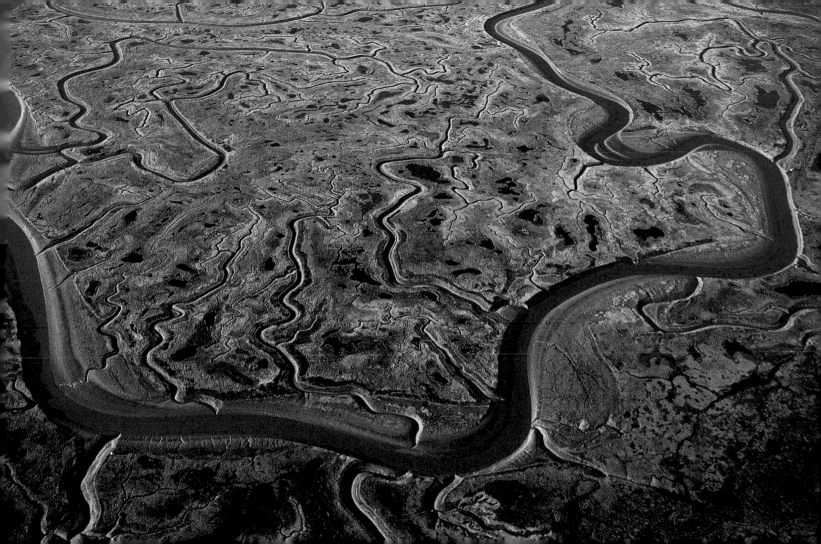

Count your carbon calories.

Every food product you purchase has 2 caloric values: the amount of energy you receive from it (the value printed on the side of the package), and the amount of energy required to produce it. In today's food industry the second caloric value comes from a variety of sources: namely, the human energy involved in production, and the fossil fuels that drive the machinery used in the farming process and power the production of chemicals. Some of the statistics are hard to swallow: The modern production and distribution system spends 10 to 15 calories for every calorie it produces; the United States expends 3 times the energy per person for food that developing countries use per person for all energy activities.

Tesco, the United Kingdom's biggest supermarket chain, has started to add 'carbon labels' on selected products to help shoppers understand the carbon footprint of each purchase. Until everything we buy is labelled, we can be conscious consumers by studying carbon scorecards compiled by organisations like Climate Counts which rate major global companies based on their efforts to reduce their carbon calories.

Salt lakes, Chad

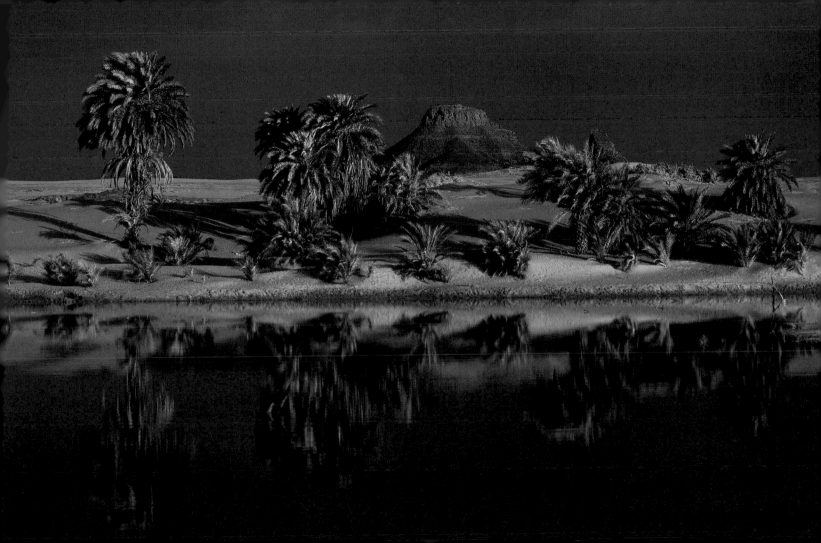

Create a green roof.

Green roofs aren't just a few potted plants—they have soil layers and drainage systems. They help filter air pollution, extend a building's life by protecting it from ultraviolet rays, reduce storm water runoff (which can instead be collected and recycled within the building), and keep interiors cooler in summer. They can also help mitigate the urban heat island effect, where cities absorb large amounts of heat through the large amounts of concrete and asphalt they contain.

Though most examples of green roofs are currently found on larger buildings, it's possible to add a simple green roof to many homes. If you have a flat roof, you can easily find a system that you can install—or think about making a brown roof that can be as simple as layering gravel and some soil on your roof, and is also good for wildlife and cooling. If you live in a flat, ask the managing agent or landlord for a green roof retrofit next time the roof is repaired.

Erta Ale Volcano, Ethiopia

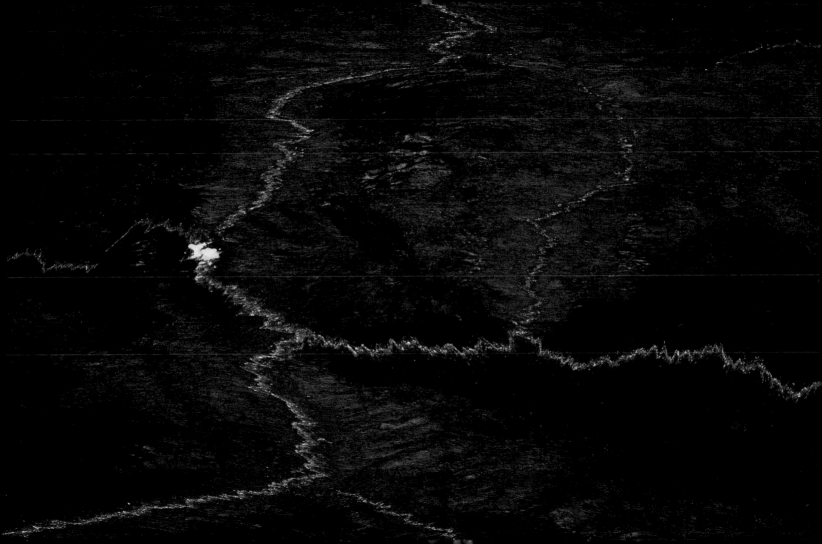

Weed by hand.

Each year gardeners pour millions of litres of chemicals onto their lawns. Excessive use of herbicides and other pesticides threatens biodiversity and freshwater resources, two essential elements of life on earth.

Avoid using chemical weed killers. To remove weeds from your garden, hoe regularly, and pull weeds out before they can seed. Vinegar or lemon juice can also be used to kill some weeds.

Lobelia, Uganda

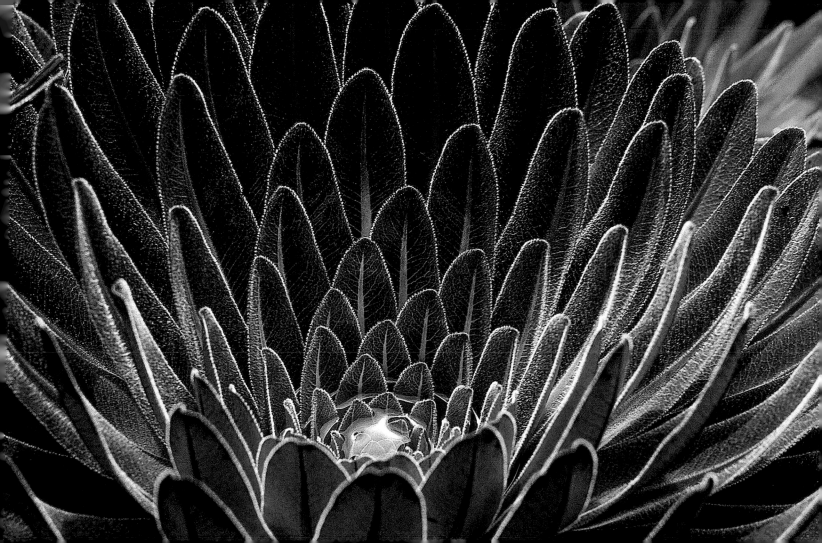

Protect rivers: Don't pollute storm drains.

No fewer than 114 great rivers, or half the planet's biggest watercourses, are severely polluted. The Ganges, sacred though it is for Indians, receives 1.7 billion litres of wastewater every day, which transform it into a vast open sewer. Worldwide, about 2 million tonnes of waste are poured into lakes and rivers every day. As a result, at least a fifth of the planet's 10,000 species of freshwater fish are either extinct or are in danger of extinction.

Protect rivers from all pollution. Don't dump toxic substances into storm drains, which can discharge into water bodies without any filtration or treatment. Also, don't drop litter in the street or countryside. Sooner or later, it will be washed into a river, lake, or harbour.

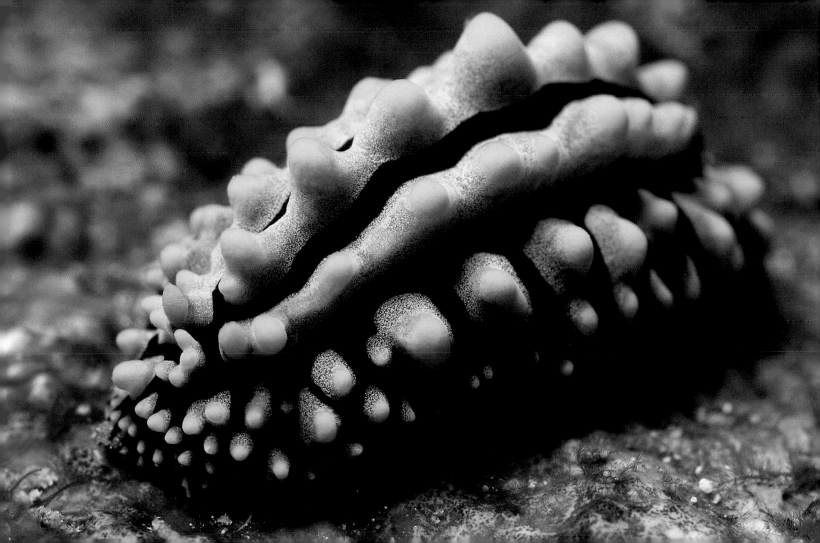

Do something for the planet on Earth Day — and every day.

In 1998, 25 million environmental refugees fled from desertification, deforestation, industrial accidents, and natural disasters. This was more than the 23 million who became refugees because of war. As a result of climate change, environmental refugees will become ever more numerous, driven from their homes by droughts, floods, extremes of weather, or rising sea levels. The United Nations estimates that by 2010 the world will have 50 million environmental refugees; by 2050 we may have as many as 150 million refugees as coastal flooding, erosion, and desertification worsen.

Every year on April 22 more than 180 countries celebrate Earth Day. Join the party: Take part in events organised that day. Then, through your own behaviour, make every day an earth day.

Salar de Uyuni, Bolivia

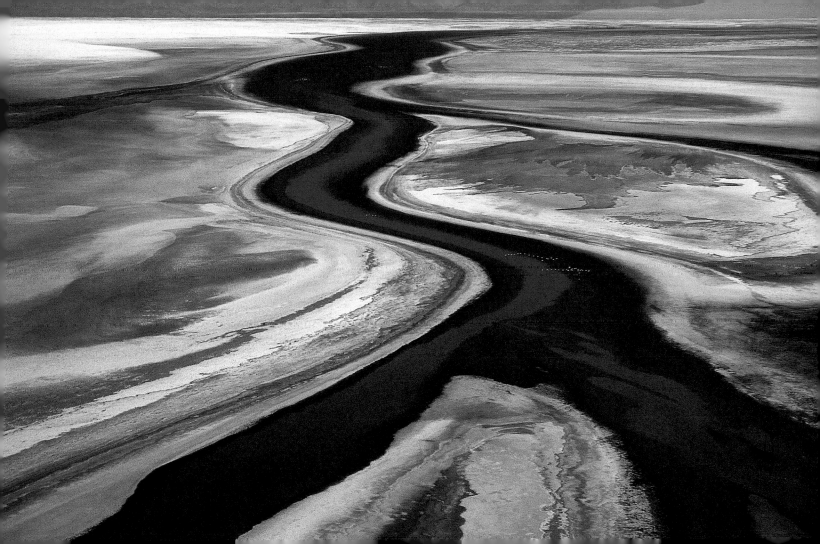

Apply Slow Food principles to the rest of your life.

The credo of the Slow Food movement can be extended to many different arenas, from clothing design to architecture. The Slow movement asks us to slow down, engage with, and reflect upon all of the things we bring into our life, whether goods or experiences. 'Slow design' artisans produce handmade goods of high quality in which materials are sourced locally (and are often recycled) and nothing is mass-produced. A 'slow home' is designed by an architect (instead of a developer) who takes time to tailor the property not only to the needs of the owner but also to that of its environment. 'Slow travel' may mean you spend all of your time in one place and really get to know it instead of moving restlessly from city to city or sight to sight.

A slow life focuses on quality, social and environmental responsibility, creativity, and personal engagement — an antidote to conspicuous and hasty consumption of inferior, mass-produced goods and experiences.

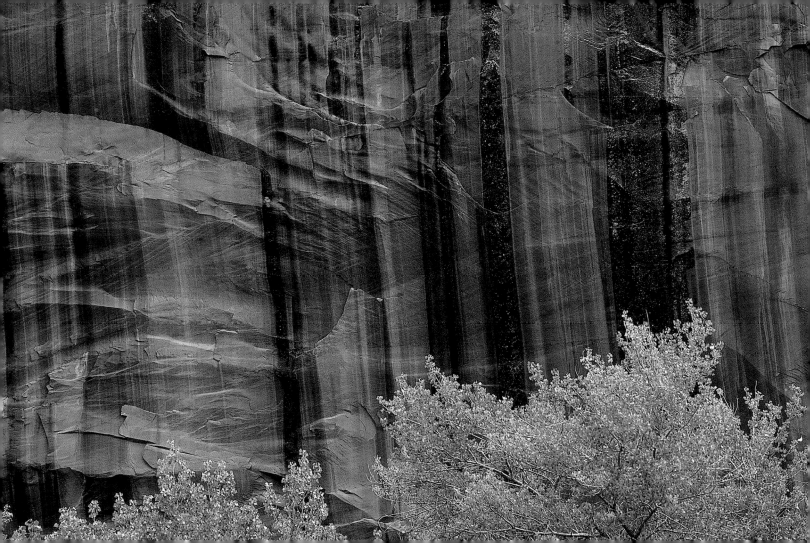

Choose compost and natural fertilizers rather than chemical fertilizers.

Overuse of chemical fertilizers containing nitrogen contributes to pollution of water by nitrates. Highly soluble, these chemicals are easily washed away by rain and carried into rivers and aquifers. Nitrates contribute to the eutrophication of rivers by causing them to become overrich in nutrients, so that algae grow rapidly and deplete the oxygen supply, which suffocates all water life. Large amounts of nitrates in groundwater interfere with drinking-water supplies.

In your garden, use natural fertilizers (stone meal, bone meal, or wood ash) and compost made from organic waste to improve soil structure and fertility naturally, effectively, and sustainably.

Palm tree, Malaysia

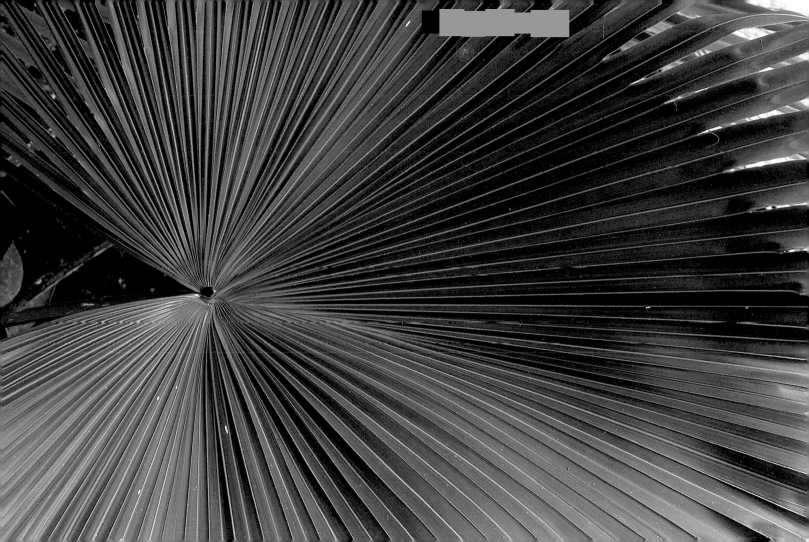

Give your home a 'spring green'.

A spring clean is a great way to clear out clutter, shake off winter doldrums, and refresh our living spaces. Before you throw something out make sure it cannot be reused; DIY magazines and Web sites offer lots of fun and creative ways to repurpose common household items. Sort through all throwaways to make sure you're recycling or donating as many items as possible. Take the time to perform simple, resource-saving repairs like fixing leaks. And as you take stock of your home, make a list of the things you want to improve upon: toxic or inefficient products that still need to be replaced and energy-conservation measures that you have yet to adopt.

Make your spring clean greener — prioritise recycling, reuse, and repair. And make sure you buy eco-friendly cleaning products to do it with.

Guelta (water hole), Chad

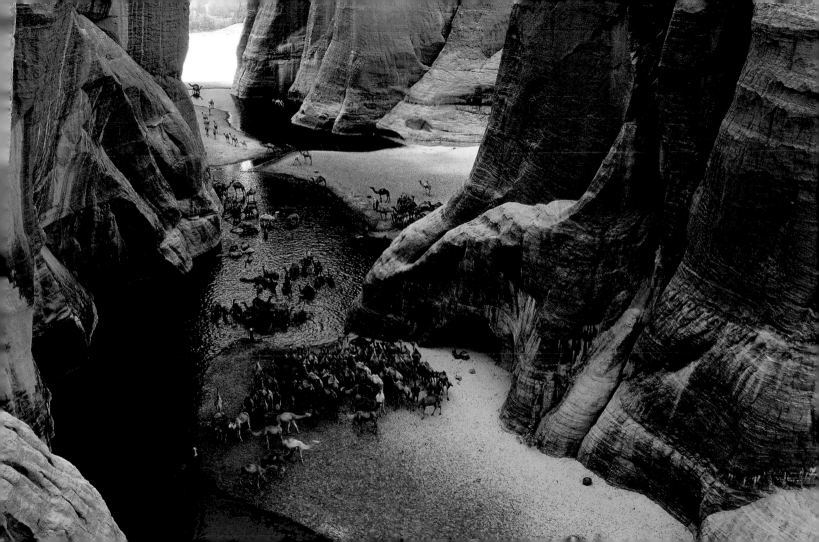

Do not pour cooking oil down the drain.

A city of 100,000 people produces over 300,000 litres of wastewater every day. Before returning to nature, this dirty water must first be cleaned in a treatment plant.

Avoid pouring food oils in the sink: vinaigrette, oil from tuna cans, and oil used for frying as they form a film on water that interferes with the functioning of water treatment plants by suffocating the bacteria that remove pollution. It is better to put used cooking fat aside in a closed plastic container that, once full, can be discarded with other nonrecyclable waste.

Iceberg, Greenland

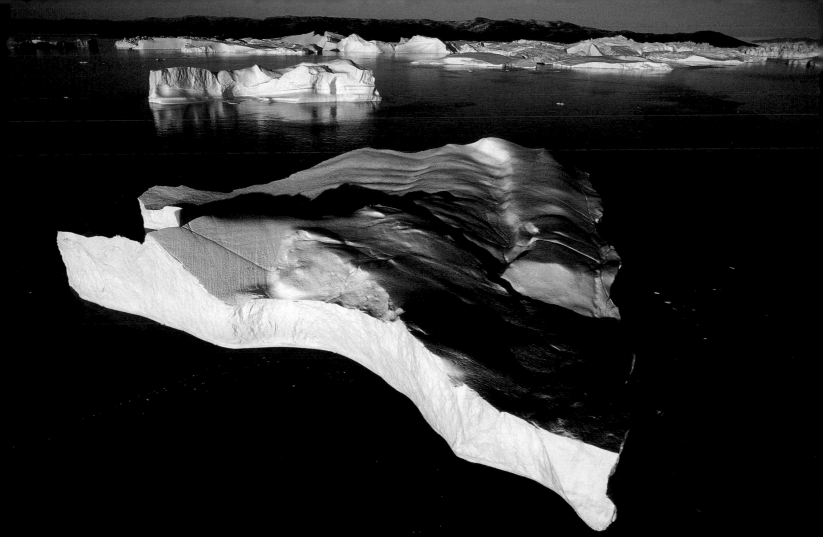

Buy toilet paper made from recycled paper.

Every year 25 million trees go into the production of toilet paper, paper towels, napkins, facial tissues, and handkerchiefs for EU consumers. Europeans use about 22 billion rolls of toilet paper per year.

If every home used recycled rolls, it would save millions of trees. But don't grab any package emblazoned with '100% recycled'. Always look for the percentage of post-consumer content (these vary, but several brands use up to 80%). The presence of post-consumer waste asserts that a certain amount of raw materials came from recycled paper. In addition, look for FSC (Forest Stewardship Council) certification, which means any virgin materials used were harvested sustainably, and avoid products with fragrances, dyes, inks, and chlorine bleach.

Saguaro National Park,
United States

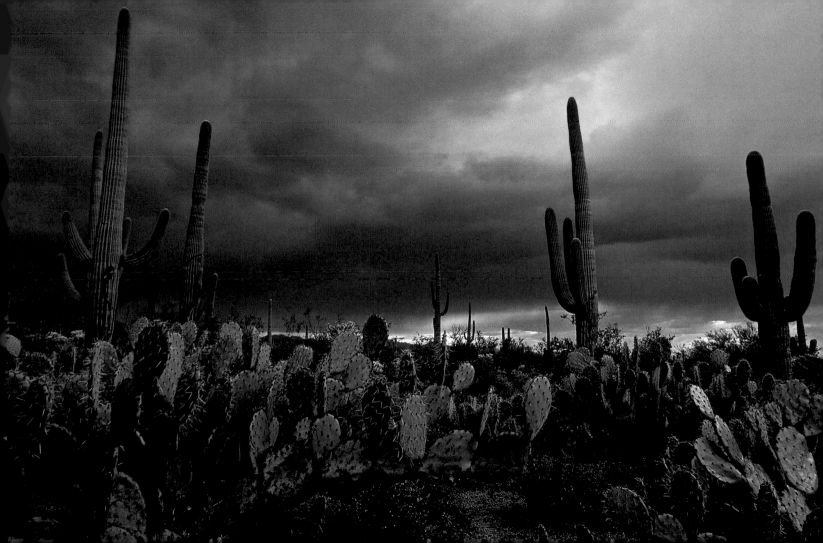

Use solar thermal collector panels to produce hot water for your home.

Solar energy is available everywhere. It is free and easily harnessed by fitting solar thermal collector panels to your roof. These panels use sunlight to heat hot water and can be easily fitted to your existing hot water system. They can produce all the domestic hot water you need, without producing noise, pollution, or dangerous waste in the process.

Solar thermal collectors are efficient and one of the cheapest forms of renewable energy equipment. They can be installed on virtually any roof, and government-funded grants and tax breaks are often available for such installations. Find a local installer today.

Antarctic peninsula

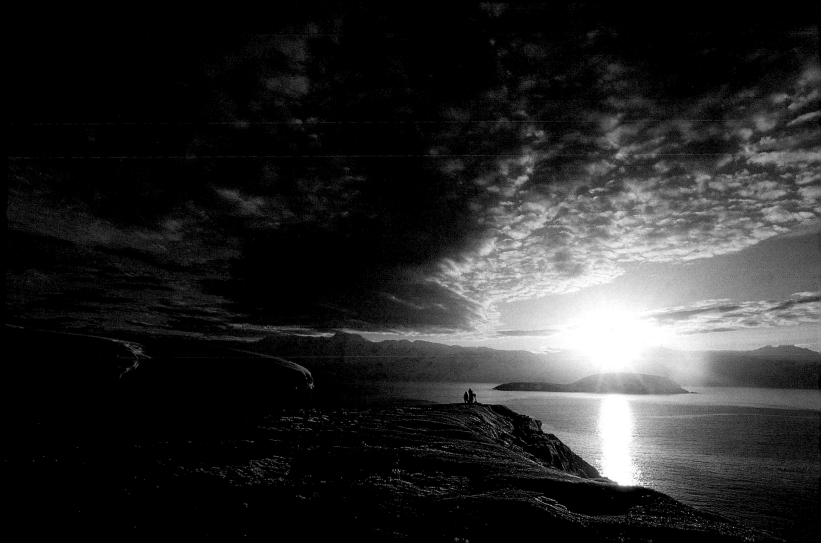

Shop at the local market.

Three quarters of the edible varieties of produce that were cultivated at the beginning of the twentieth century have disappeared. Today's fruits and vegetables, which have survived the race to increase productivity, are mostly hybrid varieties chosen for their ability to withstand the various demands of mechanized farming and produce distribution. Picked prematurely and ripened artificially, once they are on the shelf, their appearance is almost perfect—and generally hides their lack of flavour and nutritional value. The produce in a supermarket is generally sourced from large, intensive factory farms that squeeze smaller farmers out of business.

Buy your fruit and vegetables in the market, from local producers. You will be supporting the local economy, and your purchases will be environmentally friendly, because they involve less transport and packaging, and therefore less waste and pollution. They will taste better, too.

Lake Turkana, Kenya

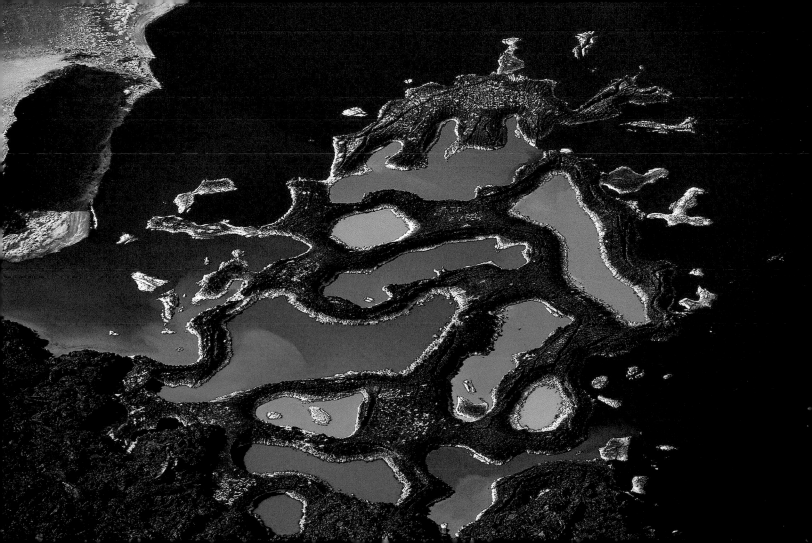

Demand organic products in your cafeterias and canteens.

Every year throughout the world about 3 million people are poisoned by, and 200,000 die from, pesticides. In fact, today these products are between 10 and 100 times more toxic than they were in the 1970s. A common way for pesticides to affect human health is for the chemicals to seep into groundwater supplies, which provide the bulk of our drinking water. Since it takes several centuries for these supplies to be replaced, this contamination poses a grave threat. Therefore, practicing less-polluting agricultural methods also safeguards the future of our drinking water supplies.

Organic food has a place in educational institutions and places of business: Help your child's school and the cafeteria at your workplace to buy more organic and locally grown products.

Piton de la Fournaise Volcano,
Réunion

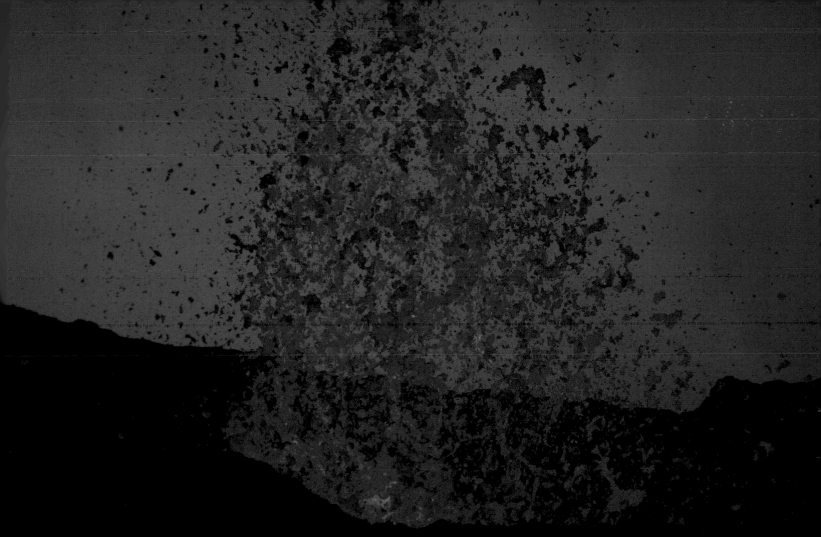

Choose 'draft' quality when printing, and recycle your toner cartridges.

Printer cartridges contain pollutants such as aluminium, iron oxide, and plastic but the cartridges are perfect for reuse and recycling. Whether damaged or empty, they can be dismantled and reassembled; defective parts may be recycled and refilled cartridges are of comparable quality to new ones. Toner powder, which is highly toxic, contains chemical pigments made from cyanide. If this finds its way to the dump, it will contaminate soil and water. During the recycling process, this powder is instead incinerated at 1,482°C.

The best way to reduce the pollution produced by ink cartridges is to use less ink. Make 'draft' quality as your default setting and only print when necessary. Recycle your used cartridges, or use one of the many companies that collect, refill, and return them to you to use again.

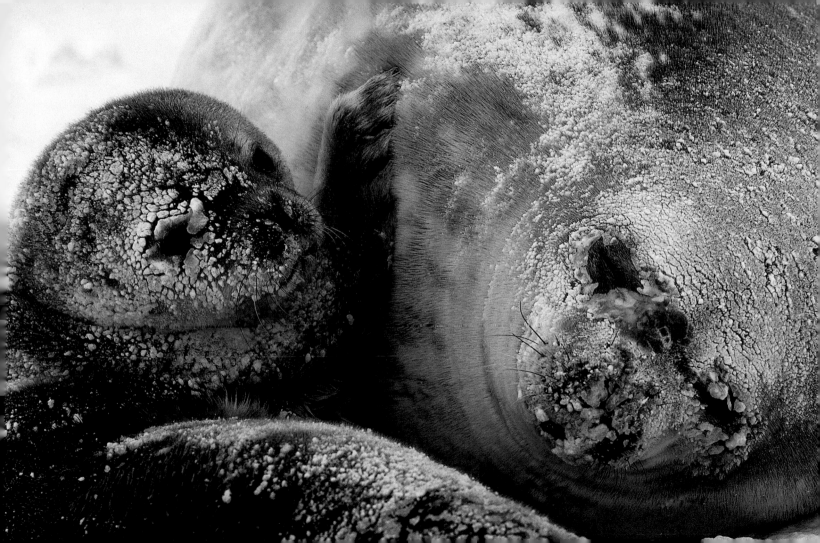

Order an organic vegetable box.

The average UK potato may travel as far as 1,287 kilometres from field to kitchen in a journey that leaves a trail of serious environmental and societal consequences. The food shipping industry relies heavily on cheap energy sources, and air pollution from food transport contributes to our smog-choked atmosphere. Farmers see only a fraction of the price of their produce in the shops, while the rest is paid to various middlemen in the food production process. Unable to compete with large-scale farms, small farmers are forced to close up shop.

Locally delivered organic vegetable boxes mean that your food miles will be dramatically reduced, and you will be supporting independent farmers to get a fair price for their goods. You will learn more about the seasonality of food and may discover new vegetables, as well as develop a relationship with your local food producers — and getting a box delivered will save you from driving to the shops.

Erg (sand desert), Algeria

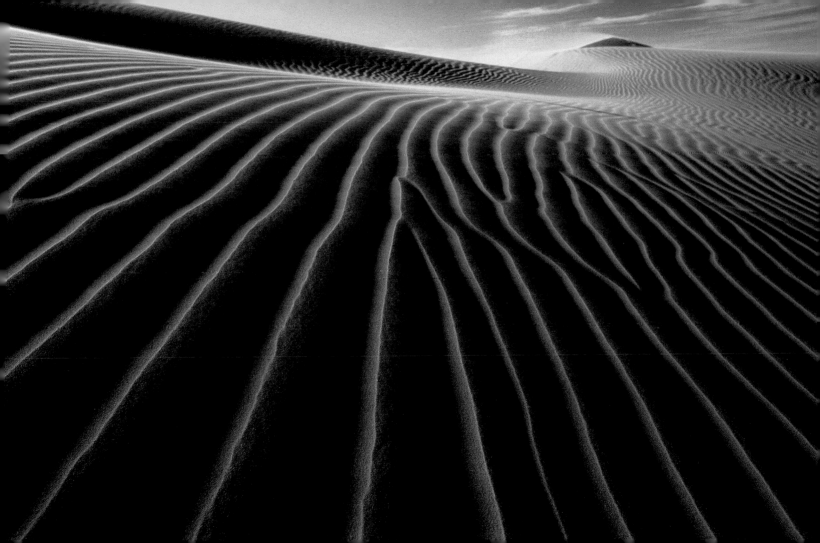

Mulch your garden to protect it from evaporation and weed growth.

When weeds appear in the garden, there is a strong temptation to eliminate them using environmentally damaging chemicals. But you can prevent them from growing in the first place by using natural mulch cover that also helps to keep moisture in the soil. Protected from weeds as well as from drying out excessively, the garden will be healthier.

You can mulch the soil around the base of plants, trees, and bushes using hay, dried grass cuttings, leaves, wood shavings, chippings, and so forth. Mulching also protects soil from the action of sun and wind, and helps to keep it moist.

Acid lake, Vanuatu

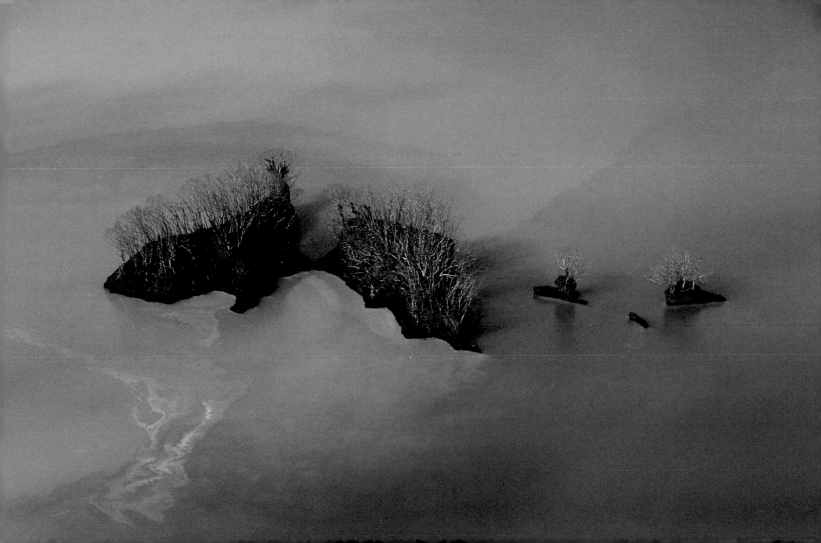

Invest in a new boiler.

Water heating accounts for around 80% of a home's energy use. The new generation of combination boilers can be up to 90% efficient, compared to older gas boilers that operate at around 50% efficiency. Given that heating takes such a large amount of energy, investing in a newer boiler can save money and cut your carbon-dioxide emissions significantly.

Consider upgrading your boiler — many energy companies give discounts if you buy through them. In the United Kingdom, look for a SEDBUK — a rating which indicates the most efficient type — and make sure you get it serviced regularly to keep it operating at the maximum efficiency.

Ice floe, Antarctica

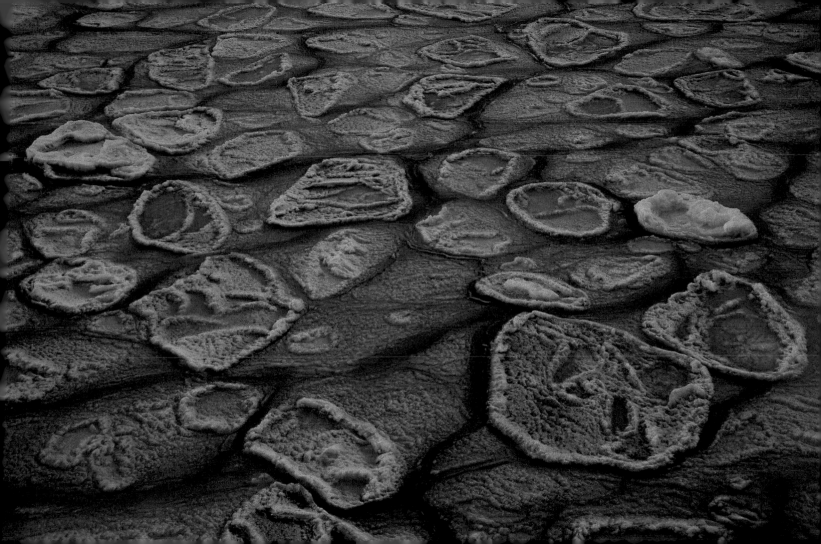

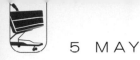

Use concentrated dishwasher liquid.

Packaging has gone beyond the function of protecting a product and informing the consumer, and has become a marketing tool. Overpackaged goods vie with each other to seduce potential buyers at first glance, so that a product that was not on the shopping list ends up in the shopping basket.

When buying dishwasher liquid, ignore boxes of individually packed tablets and instead choose less polluting and more easily carried alternatives, such as refillable packages, especially concentrated liquids. Dishwasher detergent in tablet form is also higher in phosphorus, which disrupts ecosystems when released into our waterways.

White Sands National Monument, United States

Protect endangered habitats.

Approximately 15,589 plant and animal species face extinction. In Europe, 1 in 6 species of mammals is in danger of disappearing, and 1 in 3 species of freshwater fish. As many as 50% of Europe's plant species are also threatened by global warming and the destruction of habitat by intensive agriculture and urbanisation.

Threatened and endangered species can be found throughout the United Kingdom and Europe in all kinds of ecosystems. Learn the species that are listed in your area and commit to assisting in the preservation of their habitat.

Osprey Reef, Australia

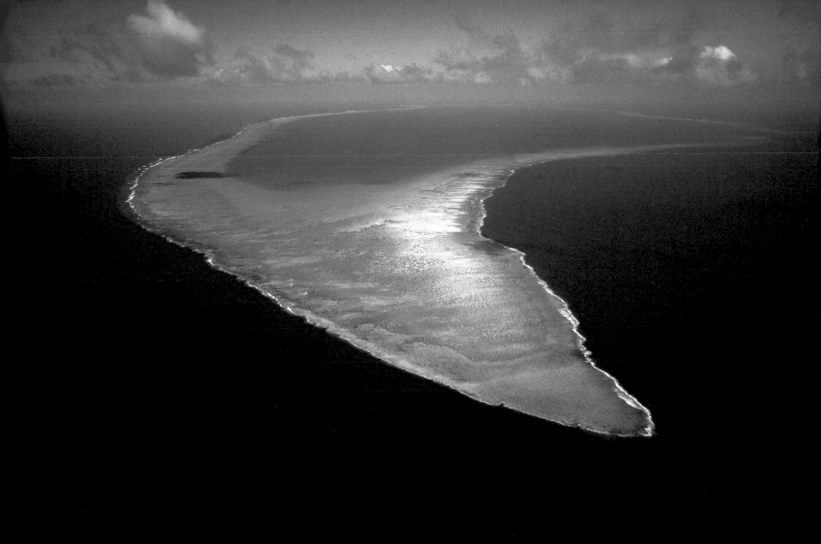

Install a dual-flush toilet.

All our buildings are supplied with drinking water, yet only 1% of the water treated to those standards is actually drunk. A dual-flush toilet can reduce the use of potable water for nonpotable actions. A dual-flush toilet has two buttons—use a full flush for solids or a reduced amount of water to flush liquids.

Look into replacing your old toilets with dual-flush versions. Dual-flush fixtures can allow you to reduce your household water consumption by half.

Monument Valley National
Monument, United States

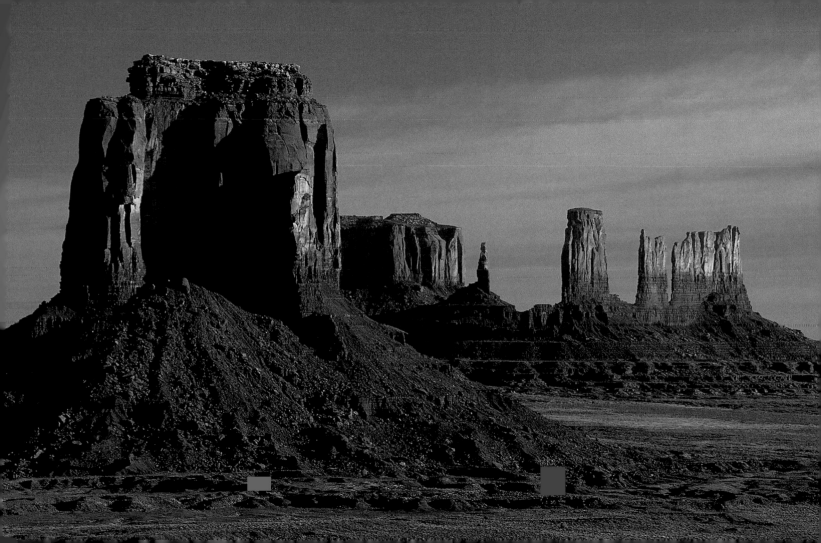

Choose cruelty-free cosmetics.

It is often difficult to distinguish between companies that do and do not test on animals. Many companies do not label their products clearly and others make confusing statements — for example, a label claiming 'this product has not been tested on animals' may mean that the final product may not have been animal tested, but the individual ingredients could have been. So even if the manufacturer claims to be cruelty-free, the ingredient supplier could have tested on animals.

If you want to buy genuinely cruelty-free cosmetics, look for products approved under the Humane Cosmetics Standard (HCS). The HCS is the world's only international criteria for cosmetic and toiletry products that are genuinely not tested on animals. By offering a single, internationally recognised set of cruelty-free criteria, the HCS helps ethical consumers avoid animal-tested cosmetics and toiletries. Check the labels on the cosmetics you buy.

Lake Natron, Tanzania

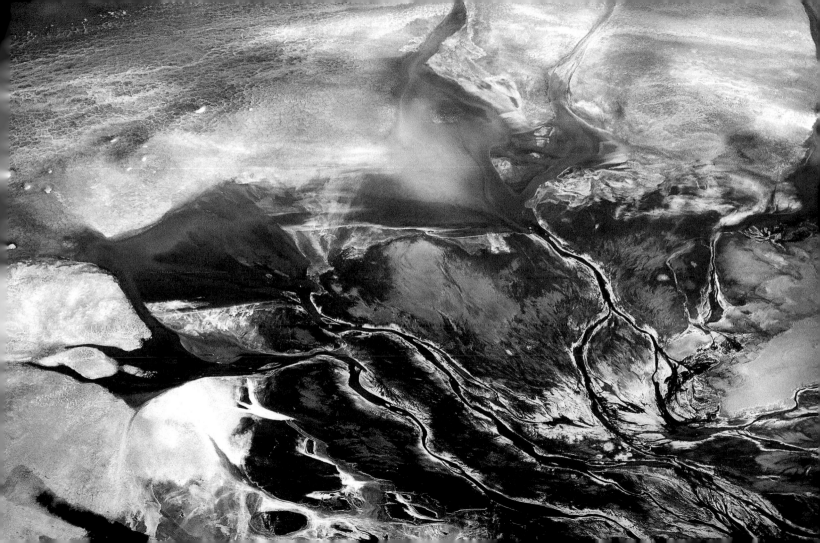

Buy products that are durable and can be repaired.

Manufactured products often require a degree of raw materials and energy from the environment out of proportion to their final weight. If wealthy countries maintain their present rates of consumption, each individual will consume an average of 100 tonnes of the earth's nonrenewable resources and more than half a million litres of fresh water each year (30 to 50 times the amount that is available for each person in the poorest countries). Buying durable, well-made goods that can be repaired will help reduce the impact of this consumption.

The next time you buy something, ask the seller about the length of its guarantee, how easily it can be repaired, and whether spare parts are available.

Descent into a glacial crater, Greenland

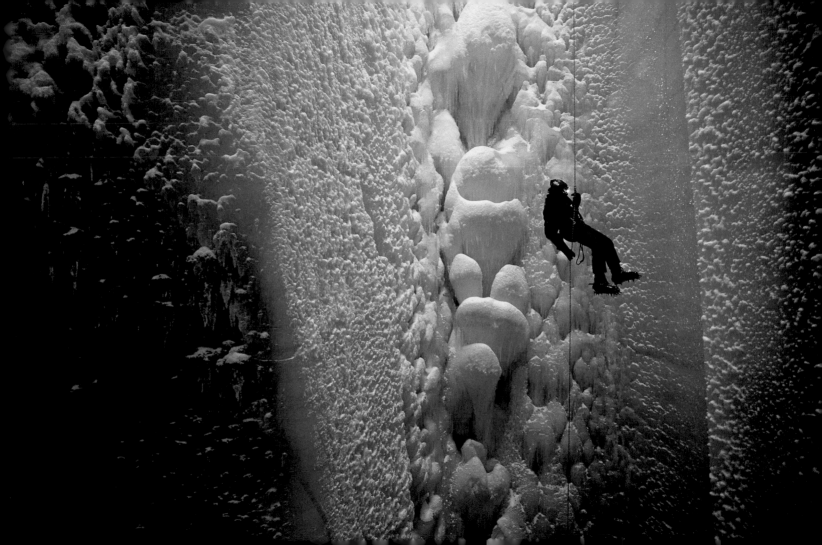

Get on your bike.

Preserving the quality of the air around us is indispensable to life. Air pollution kills 3 times as many people as road accidents. It causes respiratory diseases (chronic bronchitis, asthma, sinusitis) and is responsible for 310,000 premature deaths in Europe each year.

Get on your bicycle, rather than using your car, and not only will you help make the air cleaner, but you will be fitter and healthier too. And with congestion so bad in our cities, your journey will probably take less time as well.

Sandbars, The Bahamas

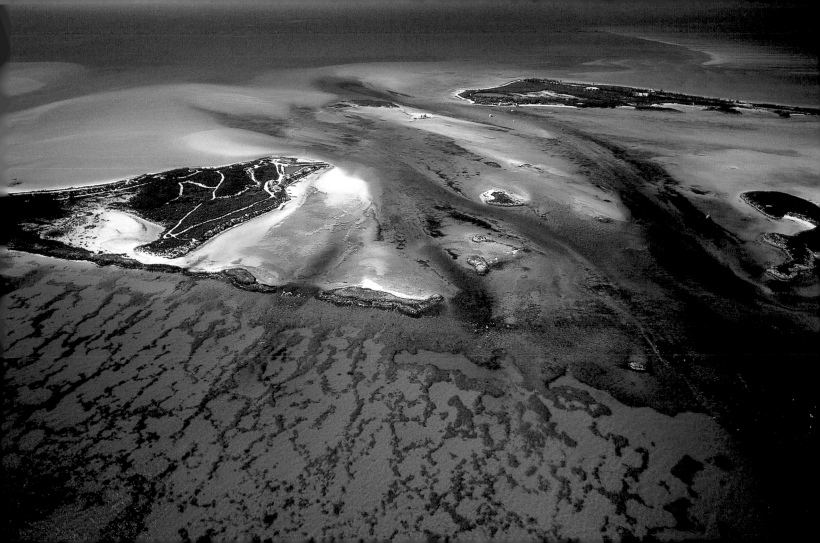

Keep ash and eggshells to use in the fight against slugs.

Eliminating unwanted visitors to the garden does not necessarily require chemicals. Tricks and traps sometimes work much better, are easier on your wallet, and cause absolutely no damage to the natural environment.

Use cunning to wage war on slugs and snails. Drive them away by spreading ash or crushed eggshells around the plants you wish to protect or, alternatively, plant herbs. Slugs dread pungent aromatic plants. You can also lay planks alongside your flowerbeds. All you need to do is turn them over regularly to collect and destroy the slugs that seek shelter from the sun beneath them.

Atchafalaya River, Louisiana

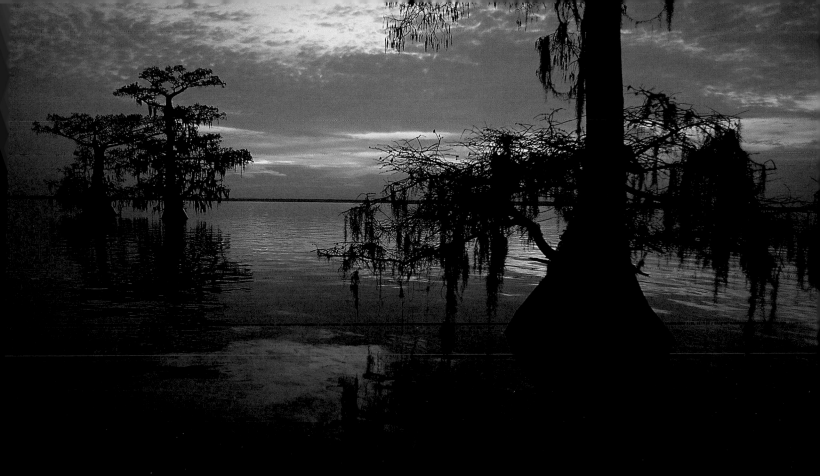

Visit local nature reserves and parks.

Our green spaces constitute an extraordinary natural and cultural heritage. National parks and forests; nature reserves and bird sanctuaries; local parks and community gardens offer insight into natural and cultural histories. The landscapes of national parks might inspire awe and wonder, while small local green spaces tell us much about our communities, history, and ecology.

Find a green space in your area. Learn about the species that inhabit it and any developments that might threaten it.

Massif Central, France

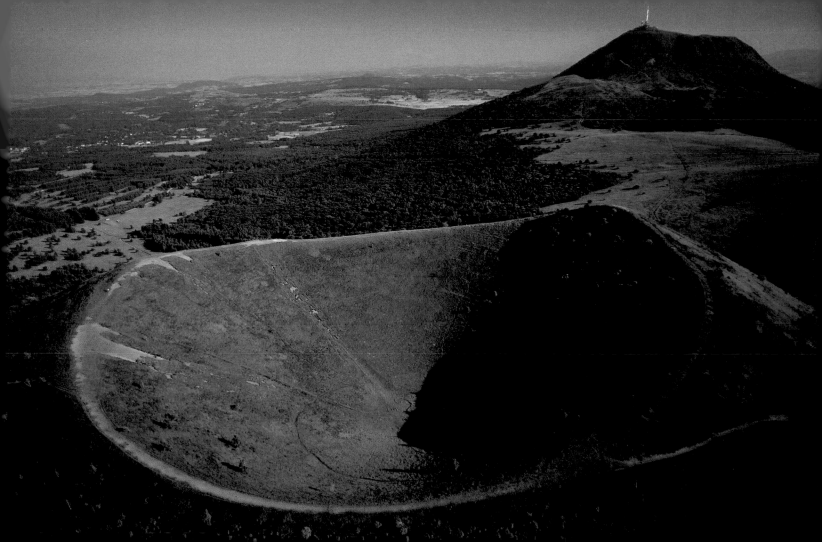

Give your clothes a second life.

Fashions change and clothes gradually accumulate in wardrobes. On average, the manufacture of 1,000 items of new clothing produces over 200 kg of waste as cloth, paper, and packaging. If old clothes are in good condition, they can be put back into circulation on the second-hand market, sold cheaply, distributed to charities, or if you know how to sew, altered into new garments. The second-hand market offers an economic, environmentally friendly alternative to new clothes.

Sift through your clothes, and donate those that you no longer wear to charity, or put them into clothing banks. Clothes that are too damaged to be worn again can be used as cleaning rags, or recycled to make paper. And you can also buy your clothes at second-hand or vintage shops, which is an increasing trend — keeping up with fashion, while also consuming less.

Dallol Volcano, Ethiopia

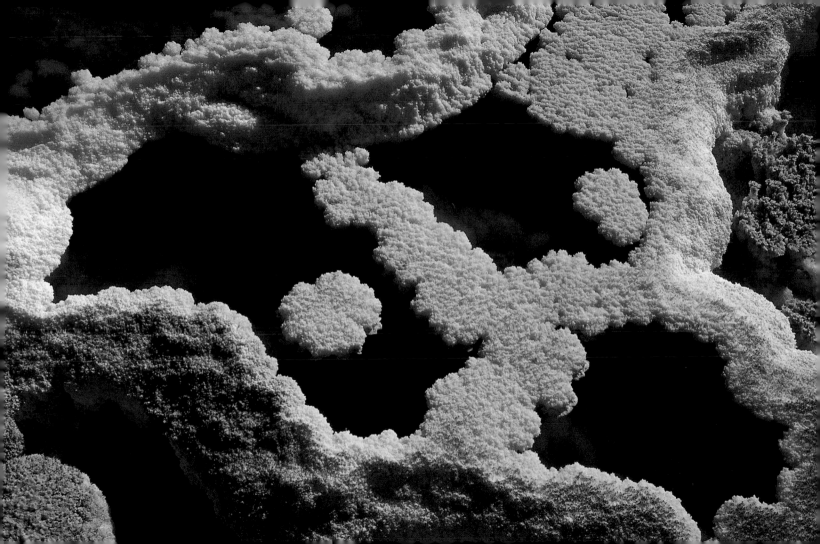

Freshen the air naturally.

Plug-in or aerosol air fresheners not only create nonrecyclable waste, they pollute the indoor air we spend more than 50% of our time in with phthalates and chemicals like benzene and formaldehyde. Plug-in room deodorizers also constantly drain energy.

To freshen the air without polluting your home, try burning beeswax candles (make sure that any scent added is not from chemicals), hanging bundles of dried herbs or lavender, filling a bowl with pinecones, or drying rose petals in baskets.

Lake Magadi, Kenya

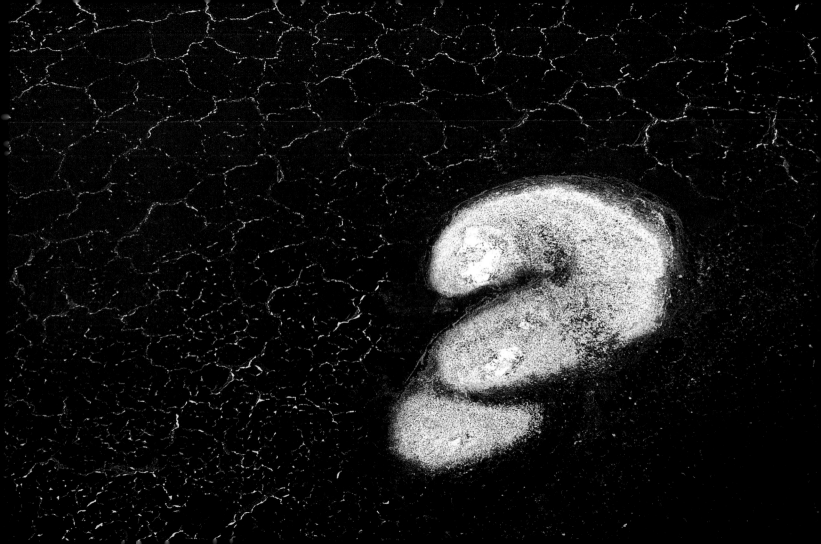

Do not print out your e-mail.

Paper and cardboard, which are both recyclable, make up 80% of office waste. Despite the concept of the paperless office, workplaces continue on an upward trend in paper use. To reduce this wasteful consumption, do not automatically print out the e-mails you receive.

Organize your computer to file your e-mail electronically, and only print out e-mail when it is essential. The average office worker uses 10,000 sheets of paper a year — don't be part of the statistic!

Stream, Greenland

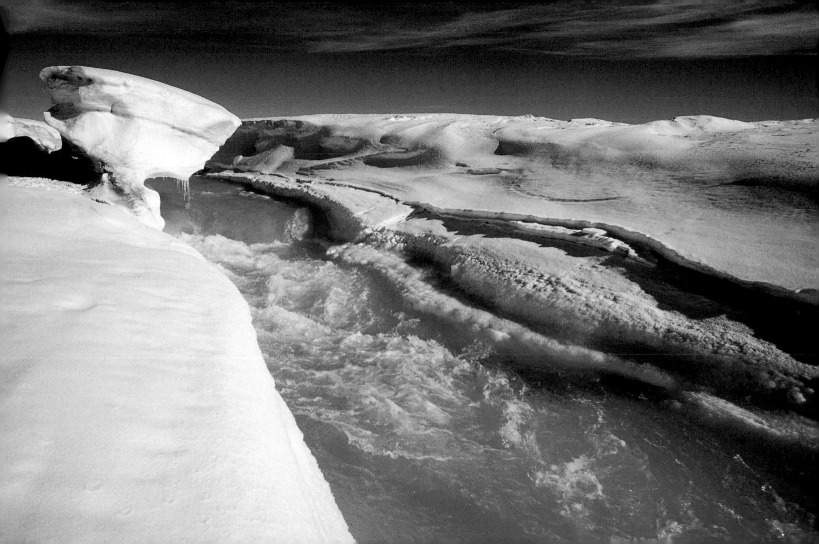

When you go for a walk, respect the environment.

Nature constantly provides us with a multitude of free goods and services: clean air to breathe, a favourable climate, food (including a considerable reserve of biodiversity), fresh water (that is naturally purified), medical treatments (many of which remain undiscovered), energy resources, natural plant pollination by wild species (notably of a third of the plants we use for food), and more. Our dependence on the natural world should encourage greater respect in us, since the future of our species depends on it.

Walking or hiking is a very environmentally friendly way of seeing the countryside. However, when on a walk, always keep to the footpaths. Stay out of sensitive areas such as meadows and wetlands unless there are designated paths. And if you are visiting very sensitive areas, minimize the risk of spreading invasive species or disease by making sure you're not transporting insects, pollen, or seeds.

Dallol Volcano, Ethopia

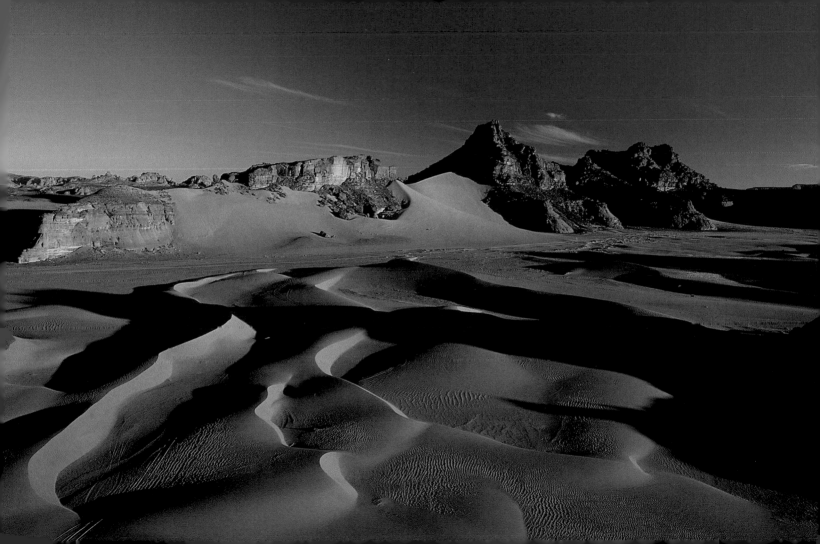

Check into alternatives before sending old or unwanted carpet to the landfill.

In Western Europe, over 1.6 million tonnes of carpet is thrown away each year and most of it was replaced for reasons other than wear. Replacing a carpet is not only economically expensive, but also environmentally costly. Much modern carpet is made of plastics and is not biodegradable, so finding ways to prolong the lifespan of carpet is an important part of reducing the toxic waste we create.

If you're just tired of the colour, find a service that will redye your carpet rather than replacing it. These companies can also restore an old carpet to its original quality. Several companies now also offer carpet recycling services, or your local authority may collect carpet to be recycled. If you have a garden, carpet can be used as a mulch to suppress weeds.

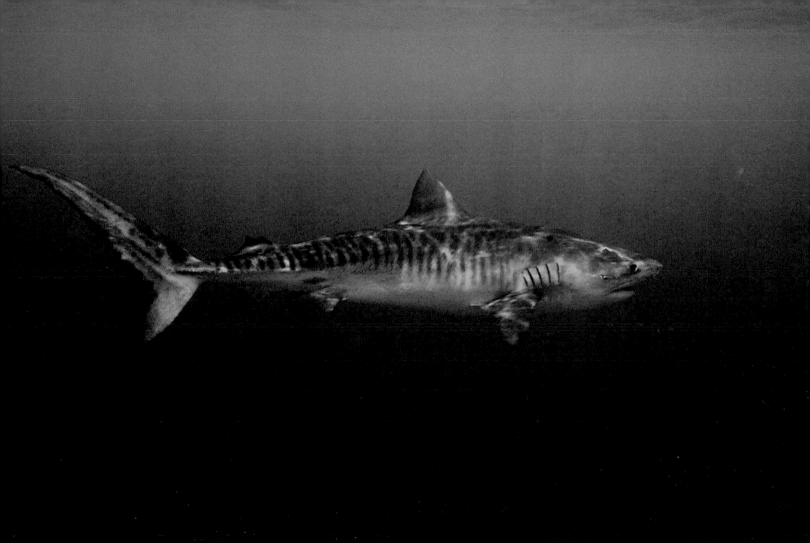

Find alternatives to cling film.

Most cling film or plastic wrap cannot be recycled, and some contain PVC or phthalates—not something you want covering your food. Aluminium foil is a friendlier option because it can be recycled and 100%-recycled versions are readily available; however, foil can react with some foods and leach aluminium. Better 'plastic' wraps are available, too. Look for corn- or starch-based bioplastics that are biodegradable and recyclable.

In the kitchen, cut down on the need for cling film or foil by covering dishes with other dishes or pot lids, or by using reusable plastic containers or old takeaway boxes. In packed lunches, pack foods in reusable containers.

Paesine, metamorphic limestone, Italy

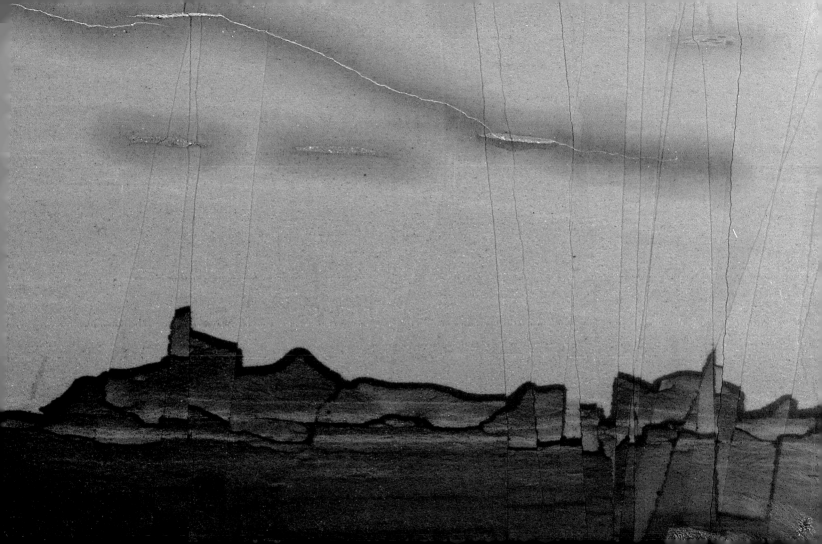

Sign petitions.

The size of a budget allocated to a certain activity gives an indication of its economic importance or humanitarian value. Worldwide defence spending is over £500 billion, whereas international development aid does not even amount to £30 billion. Yet public pressure is hugely effective in changing the way our governments spend their money — and it is easier than ever to sign up, thanks to a host of online tools.

What sort of world do we want? Support public campaigns — sign petitions. By keeping quiet, we become the architects of global catastrophe.

Wayana Indians, French Guiana

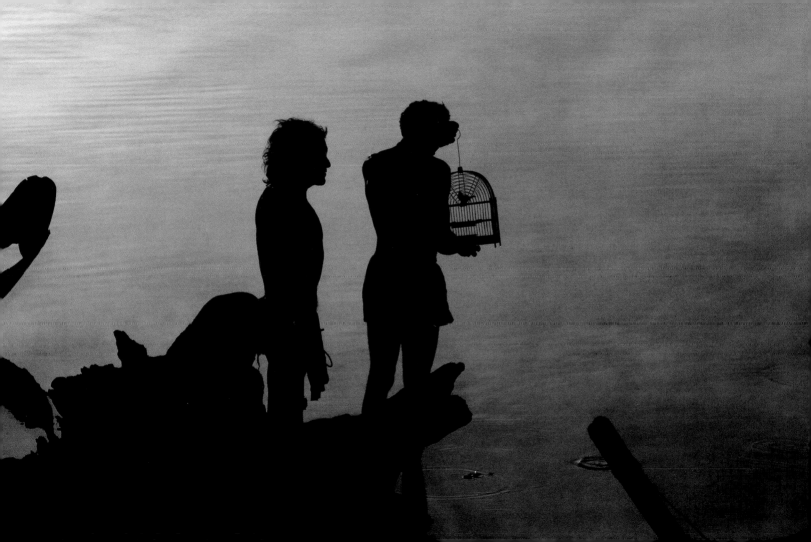

Clean the coils on your fridge.

Fridges are notorious energy guzzlers — and they're always on. They use about 5 times the energy used by TVs and more than twice as much energy as dishwashers or washing machines.

Check the electricity consumption of your fridge and freezer: Dust or pet hair on the coils at the back can cause your compressor to have to work harder, and may increase energy use by 30%. Clean the coils every 3 months. Keep the inside clean, too. The more jam-packed the fridge, the harder is it for the cold air to circulate.

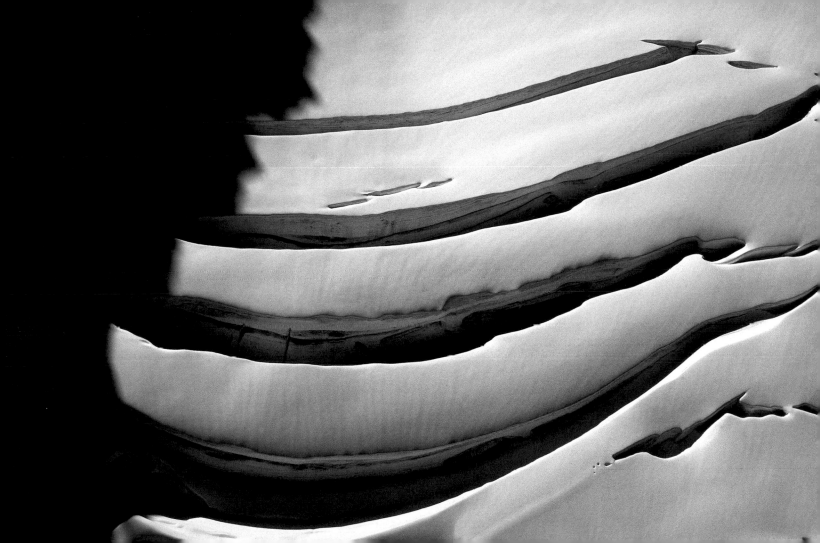

Use cycle couriers.

With the materials and resources that it takes to produce a single midsize car, 100 bicycles could be produced. Cars contribute not only to global warming, but also to local air pollution, causing asthma and many other respiratory problems. In town, the bicycle, which produces neither greenhouse gases nor pollution, is an ideal form of transport—quick, flexible, and cheap.

For your business, use cycle couriers if you can. You will be contributing to improving urban air quality, supporting a sustainable means of transport, and reducing your company's carbon footprint.

Pink flamingoes, Kenya

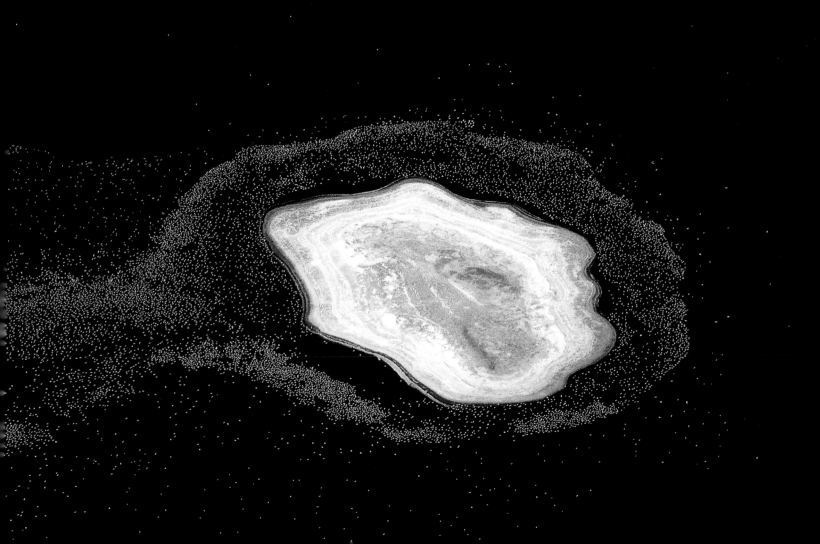

Reduce the amount of electricity used for lighting.

Electricity for lighting accounts for an average of 15% of your annual electricity bill, and is the second biggest item after refrigeration. By taking a few simple measures, you can save up to 70% of the money you spend on electricity for lighting. You will also preserve the planet's energy resources and its atmosphere.

Choose natural light wherever possible, switch off unnecessary lights, and replace your conventional bulbs with energy-saving ones. Do not use halogen lights as spotlights, and install lighting with motion-sensors on your stairs and in hallways.

Piton de La Fournaise Volcano,
Réunion

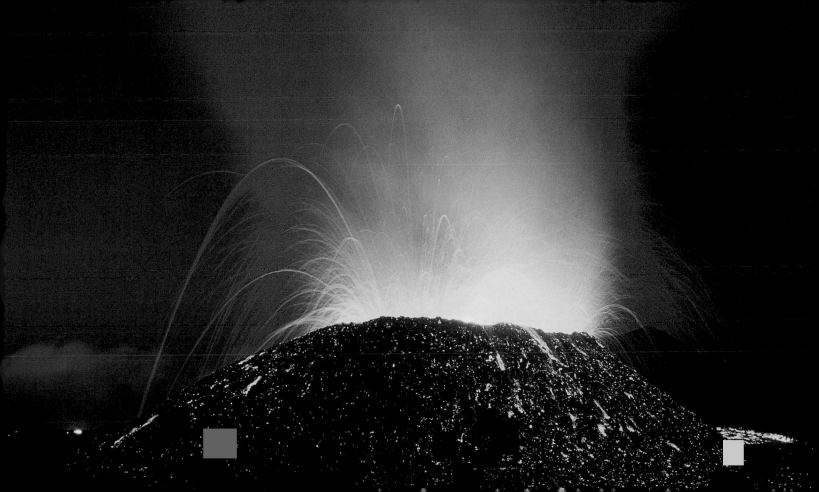

Strive for a Zero Waste household.

Eighty percent of what we produce is thrown away within 6 months of its production. The Zero Waste concept goes beyond just recycling, to take in reducing the amount of waste that is created in the first place, and new strategies to reuse waste products. Zero Waste programmes, which seek to reduce and conserve resources, have been successful in moving many communities toward a zero-waste reality — Vienna in Austria has been particularly successful and now has some of the lowest levels of waste of any developed nation.

In a Zero Waste home nothing ends up at the landfill — all waste and unwanted items are reused, recycled, or composted. Try to get your own home as close to zero as possible, and lobby your town or city to adopt a Zero Waste policy.

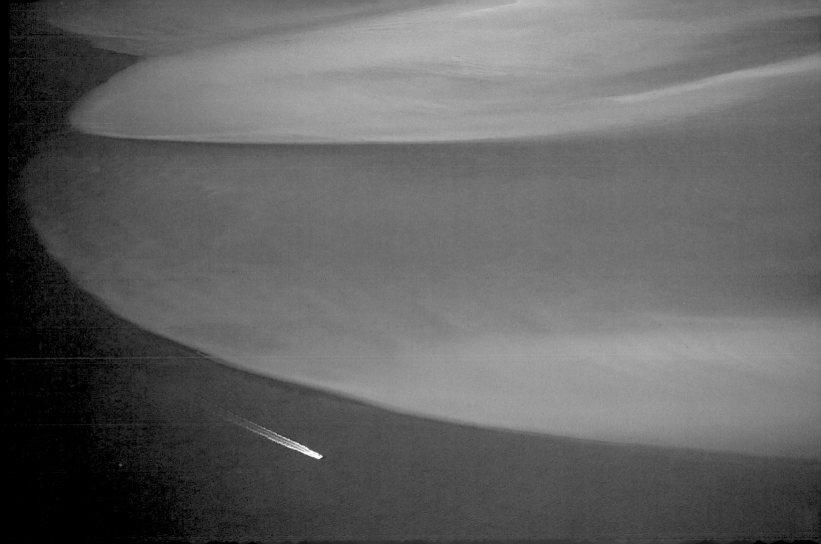

Putting the hoe to the soil makes watering more effective.

Among gardening jobs, hoeing is one of the most significant. It is essential for the health of the soil and for removing weeds, and hoeing aerates the soil and allows it to retain moisture. It is crucial after a heavy rain because the surface of the soil, smooth and packed tight by raindrops, will cause water to run off the next time it is watered. Loose, well-worked soil allows water to reach the roots of plants and drains water better, rendering watering more efficient.

Hoe your garden! Smart water use is essential when trying to make your garden as environmentally friendly as possible.

Desert, Algeria

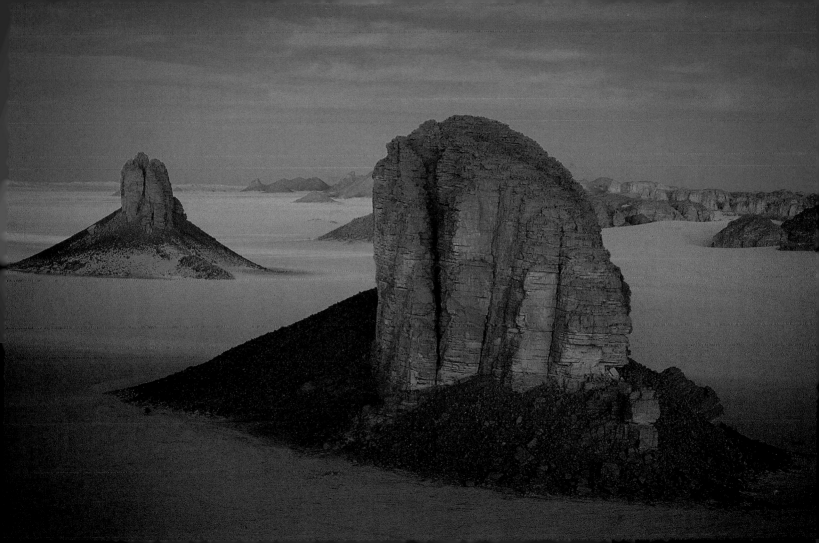

Think green when building or renovating.

Tomorrow's dwellings will have to be of high environmental quality. The Code for Sustainable Homes, which is being introduced in the United Kingdom, enables the reduction of energy consumption and emissions of carbon dioxide by means of highly efficient insulation, the use of renewable energy, and better integration of dwellings with their natural environment. Using recycled rainwater reduces the consumption of fresh water and keeps polluted storm water from entering waterways. Moreover, the Code for Sustainable Homes guidelines helps create a healthy, comfortable indoor environment. An environmentally friendly building is not more expensive, and in fact, pays for itself in less than 10 years, thanks mainly to its savings in energy and water.

If you are planning to build or renovate your home, find out about the Code for Sustainable Homes standards and look to The Association for Environment Conscious Building (AECB) as well as zero-energy buildings. You will enjoy the satisfaction of respecting nature and turning to it for your day-to-day comfort at the same time.

River, Iceland

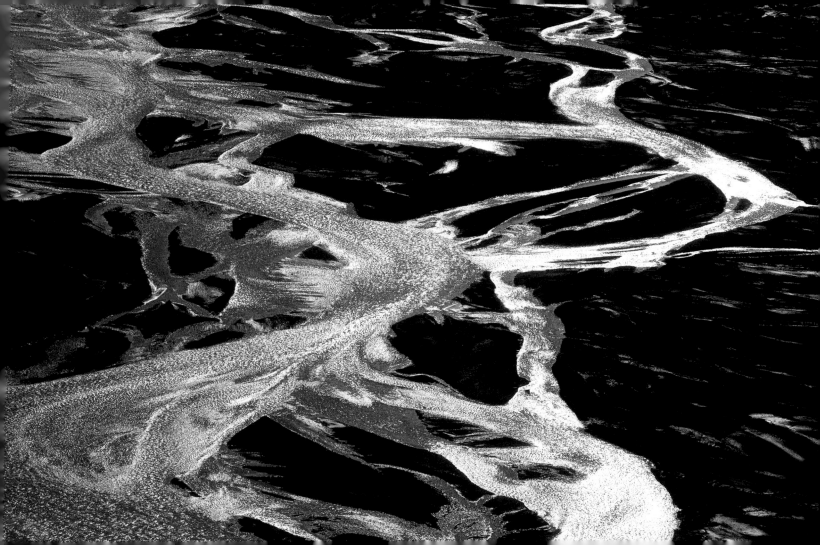

Respect tropical reefs.

A refuge for prey, lair for predators, shelter, nursery, food source, and spawning ground: Coral carries out a multitude of functions. Despite its appearance it is not an inert mineral but alive and growing extremely slowly. It takes coral a year to grow 10 centimetres, and it may have taken it more than a century to grow a metre-long block. In a fraction of a second, a clumsy kick or blow with a flipper can destroy a coral formation that has been growing for centuries.

If you are on holiday by a tropical lagoon, do not walk on the reef. When diving, be careful of your flippers. And never break off a branch of coral to take home as a souvenir.

Coral, Australia

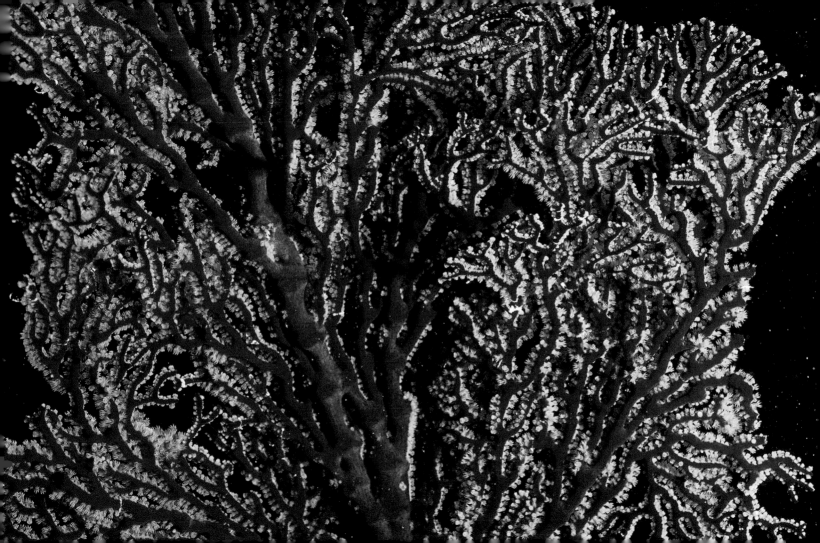

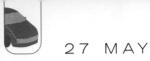

Wash your car with recycled water — or no water.

When you wash your car in your driveway, runoff (including any cleaners you're using and contaminants like motor oil and petrol) goes directly into storm drains without being filtered or treated. In addition, washing your car yourself generally uses more water than the average car wash (between 300 and 530 litres versus 140 litres).

Eco-friendly car washes properly treat and recycle runoff and use biodegradable soaps. Some even use 'waterless' methods — car-cleaning sprays that are free of phosphates and use nontoxic, plant-derived solvents, requiring only about 0.17 to 0. 24 litres of water to activate. These sprays are also available to consumers who enjoy the ritual of the summer driveway wash.

Ténéré *erg* (sand desert), Niger

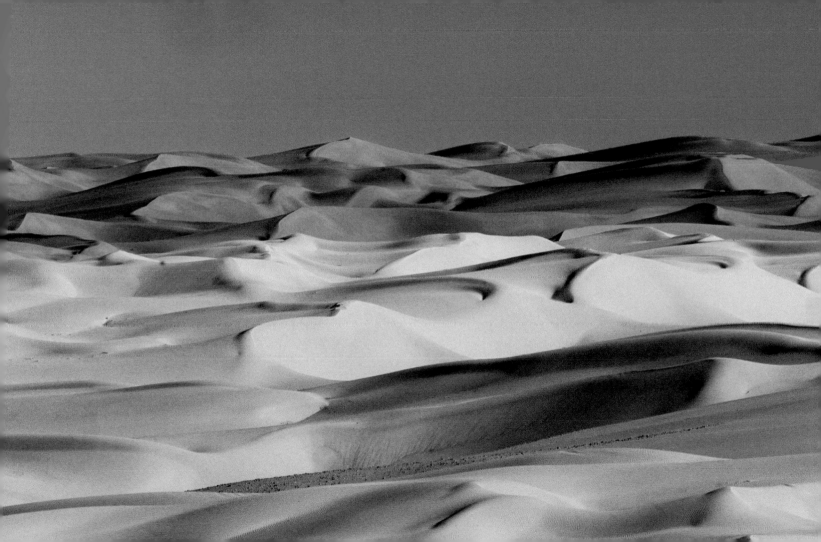

Recycle your tin cans.

Tins (generally now made of steel) are 100% recyclable. One tonne of recycled steel saves 1.1 tonnes of iron ore, 600 kg of coal, 50 kg of limestone, and the thousands of litres of water needed to produce steel. Steel recycling saves 75% of the energy it would take to create the substance from raw materials.

Make sure you recycle your tins and metal scraps: They will be transformed into new cans, or into sheet metal for various uses.

Frozen lake, Greenland

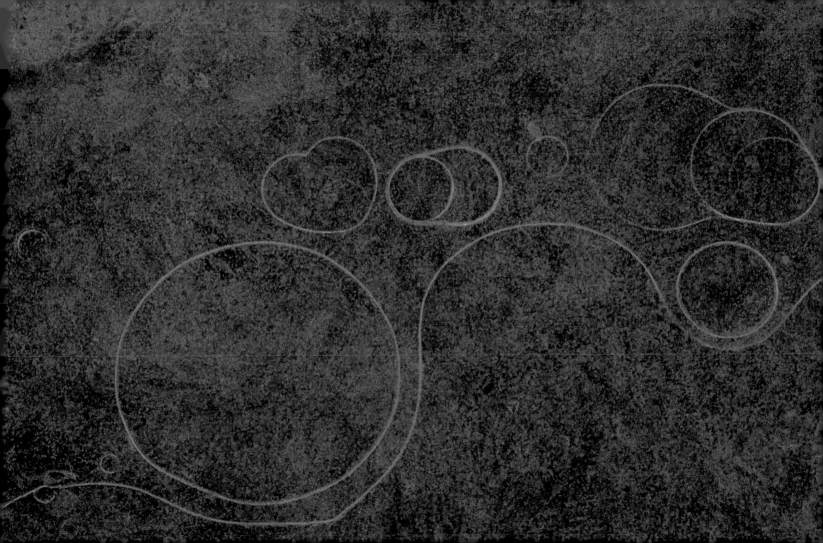

Grow your own vegetables.

Spraying pesticides on crops increases productivity in the short term. The long-term use of chemicals, however, produces resistance in pests while wiping out their natural predators. The farmer must increase the dose, thus exacerbating pollution of the soil, air, and water. As a result the world market in agricultural pesticides has almost tripled over the last 20 years.

Rediscover the flavour of something you have grown yourself. A vegetable garden or a few vegetables grown in window boxes will provide produce that is free of both pesticides and superfluous packaging. Cucumbers, potatoes, and courgettes have high levels of pesticide residue when grown conventionally, but can be grown easily in containers or in your garden.

Volcanic cone, Iceland

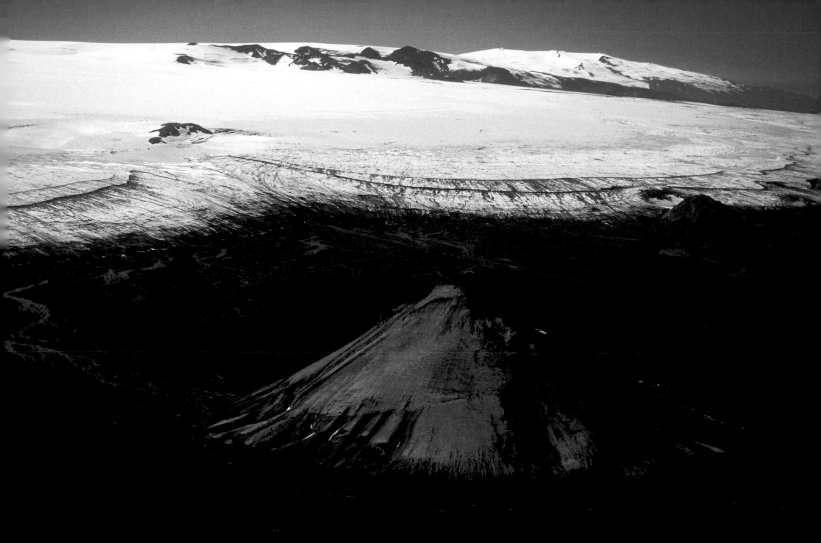

Sort your waste to reduce the amount that needs treatment.

More than 40% of our waste is incinerated. Incineration reduces its volume by 90%, thus saving space in landfill sites. It also produces energy that can be converted into electricity or heating. However, the burning also produces fumes that contain dioxin (which is carcinogenic), acid gases, and other toxic particles. Antipollution regulations demand that they be treated with filters which, once saturated with toxins, also become waste that requires disposal.

By sorting waste (glass, paper, batteries, engine oil, aluminium, and so forth) that can be recycled or composted, UK households recycled around a quarter of their waste in 2006, although around 80% of our waste could have been kept out of landfills. We've got scope to do a lot better.

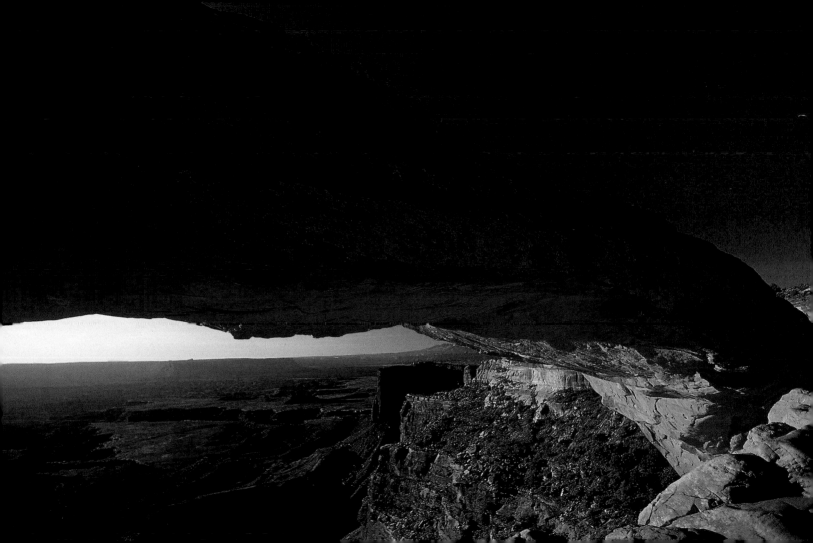

Wash laundry only when it is dirty.

The quality of freshwater is constantly deteriorating because of heavy contamination by polluted storm water running off streets; organic matter; fertilizers; and chemical waste from agriculture, industry, and households. The large quantity of the waste and poisonous products poured daily into rivers constitutes a danger that is all the more severe because water use — and the elimination of wastewater — is increasing daily. In some areas, tap water is regularly cut off, temporarily, because of pollution.

It may seem like common sense, but the best way to conserve water in the laundry is to do less of it. Only wash your clothes when they are really dirty; one wear does not automatically make the clothes dirty.

Heron, United States

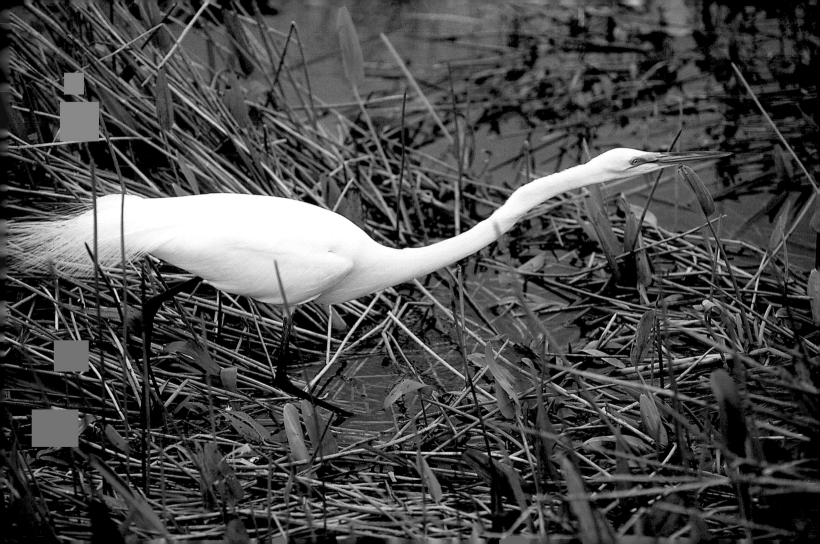

Act to preserve the environment without waiting for someone else to do it first.

It is easy to think that one small, damaging action does not endanger the earth's future. In practice, however, such actions are never isolated events. It is the repetition and accumulation of all these small acts that take on dramatic proportions. In the same way, a small, isolated gesture to preserve the environment may not improve matters on its own but all the simple gestures, repeated every day by millions of people, will have a significant effect when added together. If the majority adopts them as a new way of life, they will contribute to preserving the planet and its riches for future generations.

Do not wait for your neighbour to act. Make the first move. He or she is probably waiting for you to take the first step.

Mud springs, Chile

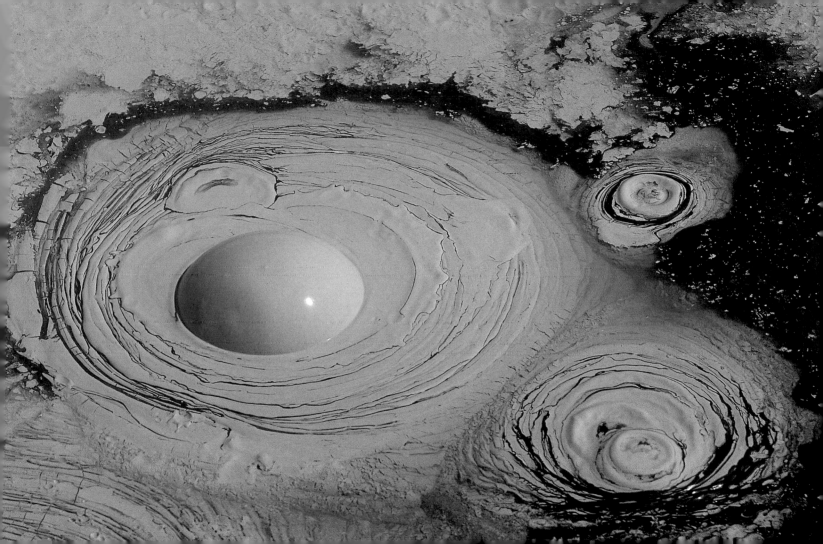

Use power strips to eliminate 'phantom' power leaks.

Many electronics and appliances (particularly anything with a standby mode or a clock) continue to drain power even after they are turned off—in fact, 40% of energy used by household electronics is drained when the devices are supposedly off. The only way to ensure that a phantom current isn't leaching energy from your home is to unplug all of these machines.

To truly flip the switch on all of your various chargers and electronics, plug them into a multisocket surge protector and turn the surge protector off. Some 'smart' surge protectors have sensors that will automatically shut off the entire power strip once they detect that all devices have been powered down.

Ounianga Kébir Lake, Chad

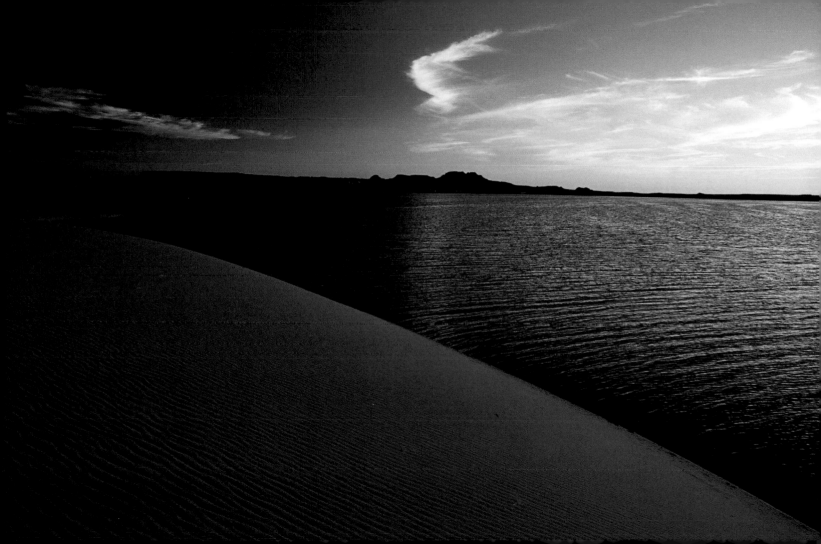

Start an eco-club.

Many tenets of sustainable living involve pooling resources and forming political advocacy committees, so why not start a club to help organise your neighbours and friends around environmental action? From discussing which natural cleaners work best to recruiting volunteers to build a community garden, an eco-club will help disseminate important information and encourage everyone to keep making good choices.

A local eco-club can bring together new arrivals and people who have been working in environmental causes for decades. What's more, they remind us that a shift toward sustainable living isn't just responsible it's fun and energizing. Start a local club in your town.

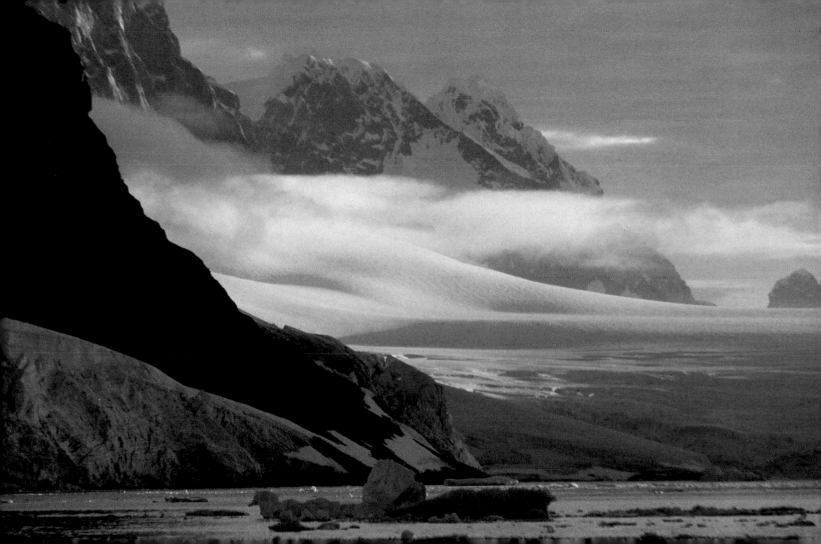

If you go fishing, respect your surroundings.

Contrary to appearances, the ships that sail the world's oceans are responsible for only a small part of the pollution of the seas. Oil spills account for only 2.5% of pollution, and cleaning ships' tanks at sea accounts for 25%. Most pollution (about 70%) comes from the land by means of what is emptied into rivers and estuaries. In 1996, the authorities on Corsica found a stranded whale with more than 9 square metres of plastic sheeting in its stomach.

When you fish from the shore leave pebbles, rocks, and empty shells where you found them, for they may shelter unobtrusive animal life. Make your children aware of the need to respect sea and shore habitats, which teem with life but are vulnerable.

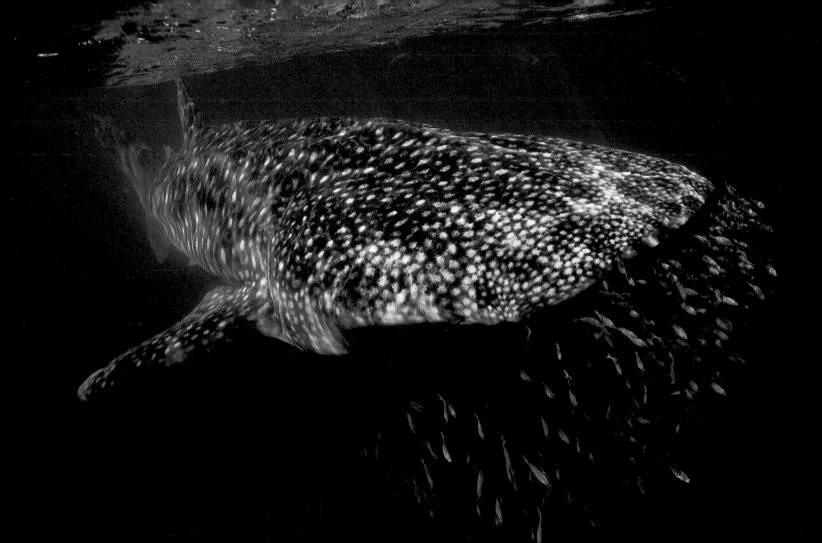

Recycle glass.

Glass can be recycled indefinitely. In the United Kingdom, we produce around 2.5 million tonnes of glass waste every year, and all of this could be recycled into new glass containers, as well as made into road surfacing and other materials. The aim for 2008 is to recycle around 70% of this and at present it looks like we are unlikely to meet this target.

Keep your glass in the production stream — and make sure you recycle properly. Remove corks, and plastic and metal lids and rings from bottles. Windowpanes, light bulbs, mirrors, Pyrex items, porcelain, and earthenware are not recyclable and will contaminate your recycling collection.

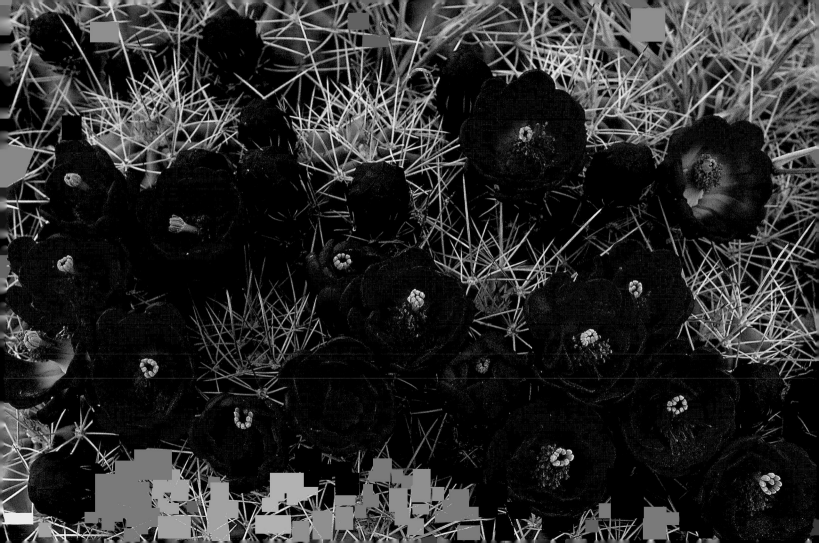

When renovating, think reclaimed, recycled, and renewable.

Flooring, cabinetry, shelving, countertops, tile work—you can find sustainable options for all components of a renovation or redecoration. Reclaimed wood is a wonderful alternative to new lumber; old-growth wood salvaged from demolition sites is often harder and of higher quality and has real character. Bamboo and cork are both renewable materials that can be made into flooring (bamboo can be used in cabinetry as well). Though linoleum doesn't sound very glamorous, it's surprisingly green, made up of cork and wood dust, rosins, and linseed oil. For new wood, buying FSC-certified products ensures that you are not supporting clear-cutting operations. Recycled-glass tiles are beautiful and recycled glass can also be made into countertops that resemble ceramic or marble. Composite countertops from recycled paper waste and water-based resins are indistinguishable from standard plastic laminate counters, but are more heat-resistant and nontoxic.

Ask builders about incorporating eco-friendly materials when you renovate your house. Don't worry if your area lacks retailers that stock these products as many materials such as tiles and flooring can be ordered online.

Sandstone, United States

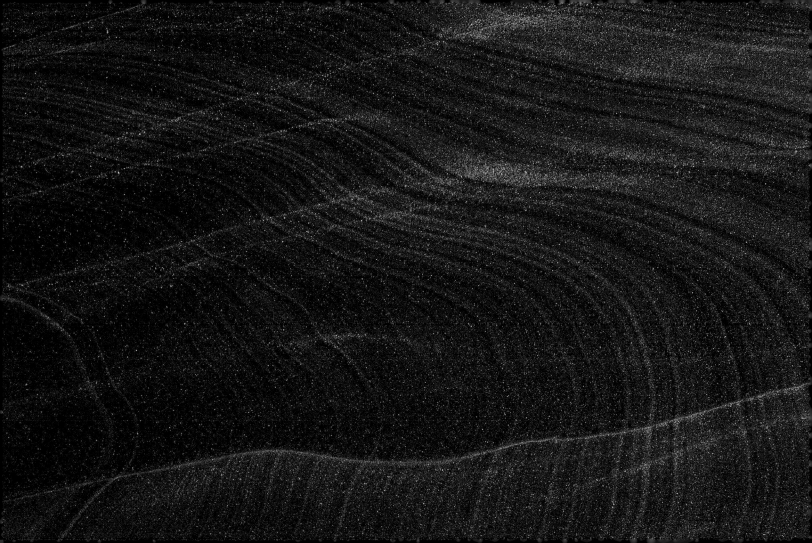

Unplug mobile chargers and AC adapters.

World energy consumption rose by 2.4% between 2005 and 2006. In 2030, world energy demand is expected to grow by 57% to 17.7 billion TOE (tonnes of oil equivalent) as opposed to 11.4 billion TOE used in 2005; electricity use will account for 22% of the total increase. Faced with such forecasts, can we really believe that the damage being done to our natural environment—first and foremost global warming—has any chance of diminishing?

We often leave mobile phone chargers and adapters plugged into the wall after they've finished charging our devices. However, they continue to drain energy from the socket until they are unplugged. If only 10% of the world's mobile phone users routinely unplugged their chargers, it would save enough energy each year to power tens of thousands of homes.

Mount Pinatubo, Philippines

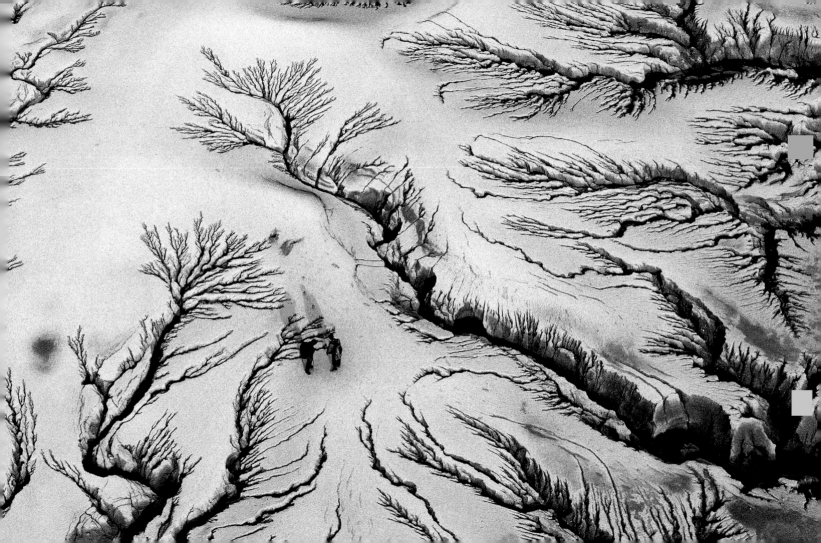

Urge your local council to upgrade its buildings to certified environmental standards.

Most countries now have a system of rating buildings according to their environmental performance — LEED in the United States and BREEAM in the United Kingdom are 2 examples. While many local authorities now demand that new buildings meet a minimum standard, in Europe most council-owned properties are older and waste significant amounts of energy.

Lobby your local authority to upgrade its buildings and thus to lead by example. Ask them to set a minimum standard of environmental performance for their existing buildings as well as new ones — they can install new boilers, double glazing, insulation, and more efficient heating systems to reach ambitious targets.

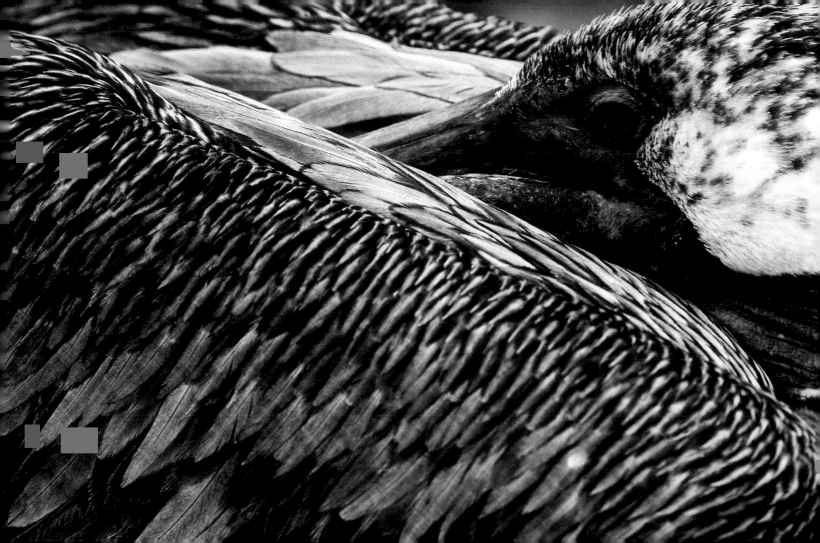

Practise sustainable tourism.

Tourism has become the world's biggest industry, and exotic destinations jostle for space in brochures and glossy magazines. The developing countries, however, often gain nothing; only 30% of the money spent by tourists remains in the host country. Still, there are new ways of going on holiday that promote equitable tourism.

Support local businesses as much as possible; seek out hotels that pay their workers fair wages, give back to the community by supporting humanitarian projects, and use local sources for everything from public transport to restaurant food; and use tour operators that respect fragile habitats and can show visitors what local conditions are really like. When you travel, you can also have a positive effect.

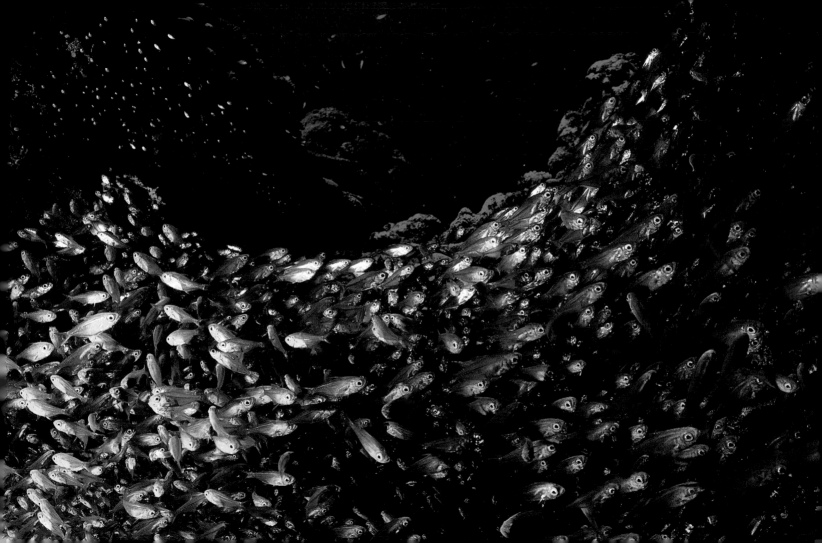

Recycle your old running shoes.

Around 338 million pairs of shoes are bought each year in the United Kingdom, yet less than 18% of this number is recycled when they go out of fashion. Serious joggers need to replace their running shoes often to avoid injuries, and every year millions of pairs of sneakers get thrown away.

If your shoes are still in good shape, you can donate them to charities or through sports shops and they'll be given to someone in need. If your shoes are too dog-eared to be reused, they can be recycled to live again as playground surfaces, running tracks, and basketball courts. Some big athletic shoe companies run recycling programs and also accept brands other than their own. Nike has recycled more than 20 million pairs of shoes since starting the program.

Lake, Chad

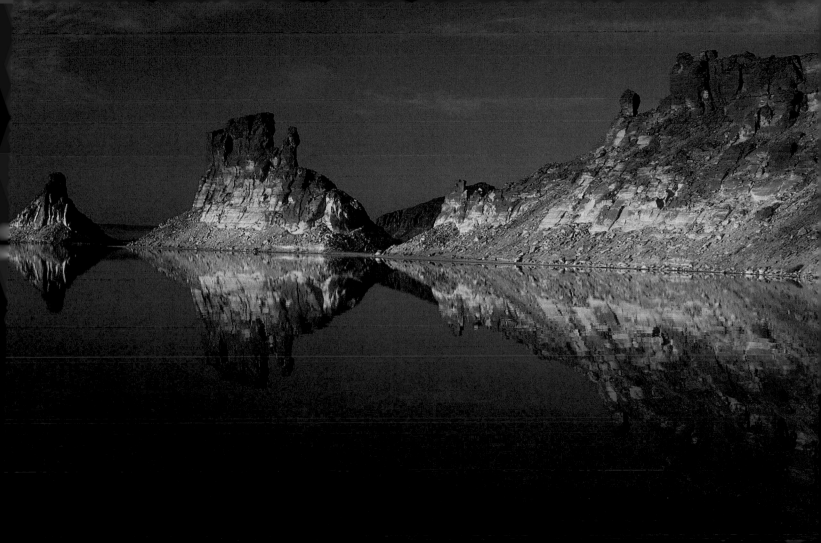

Install your boiler close to where hot water is used.

Thanks to the sun, wind, rivers, and geothermal energy, human beings are able to tap into renewable energy sources that neither pollute nor produce waste that can threaten the future of the planet for generations to come. If we used the best available technology in our buildings and in transport, industry, food, and services, global energy use could be cut in half. Until these sources are widely used, however, we should not forget that the smartest energy use is not using energy.

It is best to locate your boiler close to the hot water's exit points — such as the kitchen and bathroom — to reduce the waste of heat through pipes.

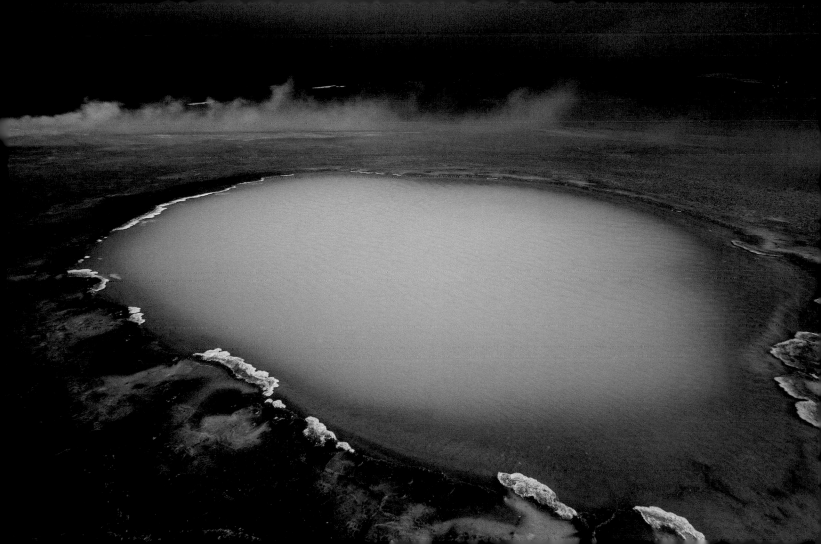

Buy or grow unusual varieties of fruit and vegetables.

In its headlong rush for profitability, the agriculture industry favours the most productive and pest-resistant types of produce at the expense of many domestic varieties of fruits and vegetables regarded as less efficient. There exist more than 7,500 known varieties of apples in the world. Today only about 8 to 10 are available in UK supermarkets and since the beginning of the twentieth century, 80% of tomato varieties, and 92% of lettuce varieties have been lost, or survive only in special conservation facilities.

Standardization is gaining ground, and biological diversity is in free fall. Consider varying your choices of fruits and vegetables; try different types, and rediscover the flavour of heirloom varieties. Local farms often revive these and sometimes develop their own delicious types of produce based on them. There are several nonprofit organisations which help gardeners collect and exchange rare heirloom seeds to grow.

Orangutan, Malaysia

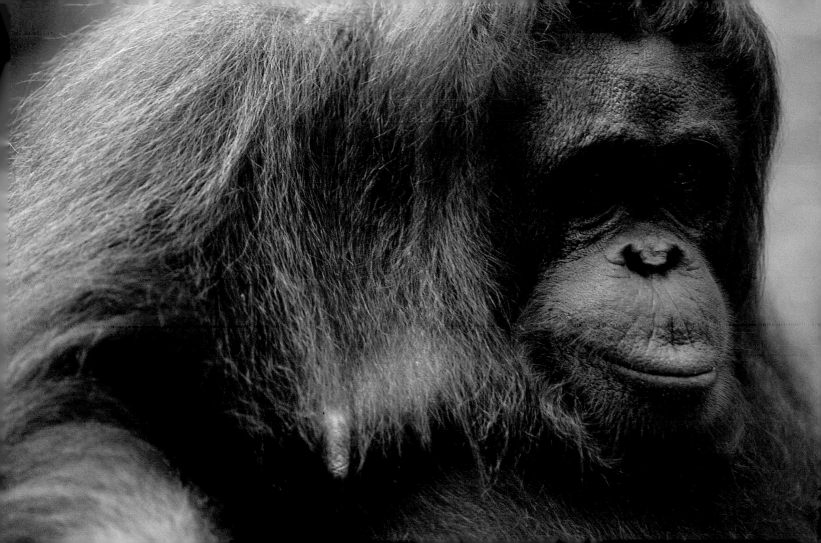

Identify your least-efficient appliances.

Replacing all of your old or inefficient appliances and electronics can be costly—it's usually a multistep process. But an inefficient fridge can use two and a half times the energy of a modern A-rated fridge, which can add up to £50 a year—making it well worth the cost of replacing it.

You can use websites, or devices like the Kill-a-Watt and the Wattson, to help you assess the efficiency of your appliances, from sound systems to fridges. They calculate how many kilowatts per hour an item uses and what that translates to in terms of cost each month. Once you know which gadgets are the worst performers, you can prioritise—you'll know which ones need to be replaced first and you'll better manage your energy consumption.

Ice floe, Greenland

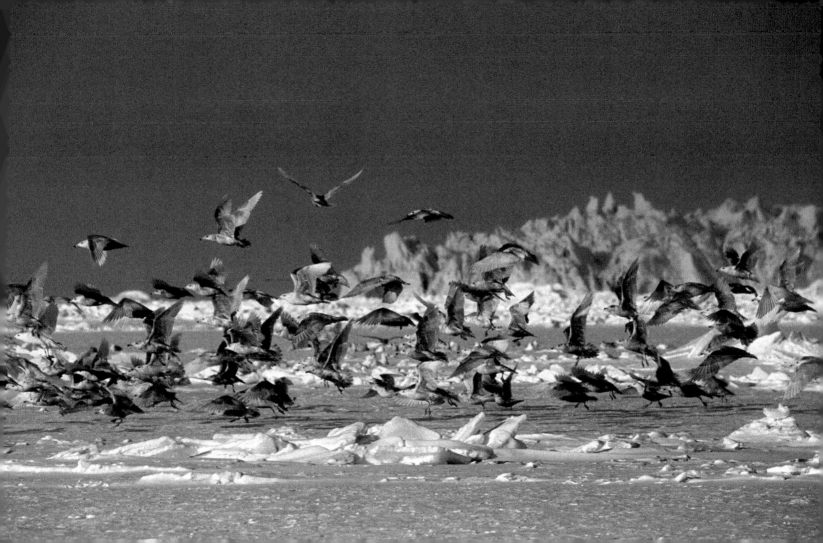

Think twice before booking a cruise.

The average cruise ship generates up to 760,000 litres of sewage and 3.7 million litres of wastewater every week. Over the past 5 years several major operators have been heavily fined for illegal dumping of waste at sea. In addition, cruise ship anchors cause coral-reef damage; a ship anchoring for one day can rip up as much as half an hectare of reef.

   Not only do cruise ships produce a tremendous amount of waste, they promote a hit-and-run type of tourism where great numbers of people descend on a port for a very short period of time, many only go on tours or to shops and restaurants affiliated with the cruise line. Often small communities bear the burden of the pollution caused by the ships without truly reaping the benefits.

If you want to book a cruise, forgo the 'floating cities' for small ships that offer a more personalised experience and focuses on the destinations, not the onboard amenities.

Fishermen, Mali

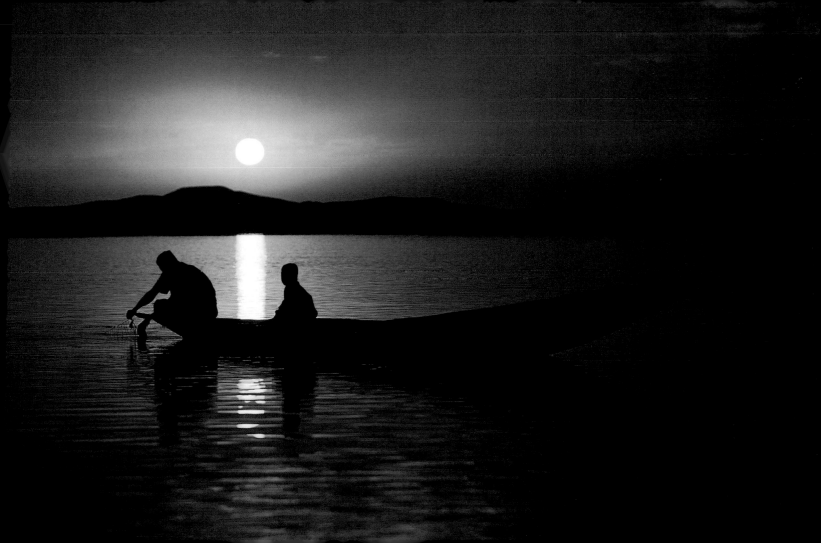

Choose cooking oil in glass bottles.

Glass is the recyclable material par excellence: It can be reused or recycled indefinitely, without loss of weight or quality. Unlike paper, the primary benefit of recycling glass comes not from protecting the original source of the material, but rather in conserving the energy it would take to create the new material. Recycled glass melts at a much lower temperature than the raw materials needed to make glass, thus using less energy.

Cooking oil is available in nonrecyclable plastic bottles, and in infinitely recyclable glass ones. Make the right choice.

Ténéré Desert, Niger

Drink tap water.

The world market for bottled water, estimated at $100 billion per year, is flourishing. In Western Europe alone, consumption of bottled water rose to about 273 million litres in 2006 from just 30 million litres in 2000. However, the most natural of all drinks is much less natural once it is packaged. To contain the world's bottled water, 2.45 million metric tonnes of plastic are required. Manufacturing the bottles, packing, and transporting the water (25% is drunk outside its country of origin) uses natural resources and energy and generates mountains of waste, since most plastic bottles are not recycled. Plus up to 40% of bottled water is actually tap water, not spring water as it claims to be.

Do not forget that our tap water is treated to be perfectly drinkable, and its quality is rigorously checked. Moreover, it can be as much as 10,000 times cheaper than bottled water.

Lake Chad, Chad

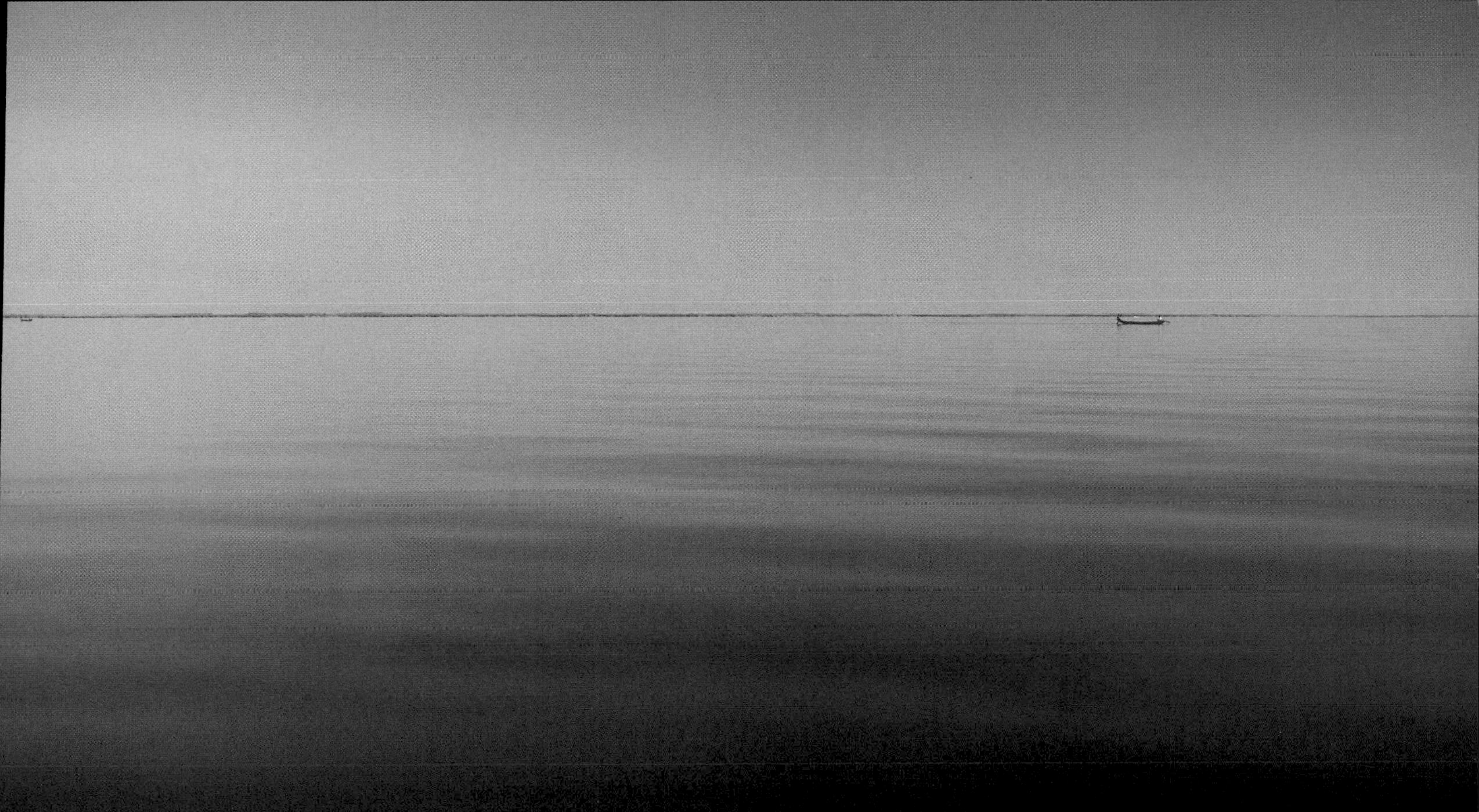

Divers, respect the sea.

A tiny rise in sea temperature is enough, in some cases, to disturb the growth of coral and cause bleaching, and there have been many instances of this in recent years as a result of global warming. In general, corals recover afterward, but if the stress to which they have been subjected is too intense or too prolonged it can kill between 10% and 30% of the colony. When this happens, all the fauna living on the reef suffer, and fish stocks are also affected.

When you are diving in tropical seas, be as discreet as possible. Use your flippers carefully to avoid damaging anything around you; do not touch anything and do not feed the animals to avoid interfering with their behaviour. When you are not diving, remember all the ways to save energy, and thus limit climate change.

Nudibranch, Australia

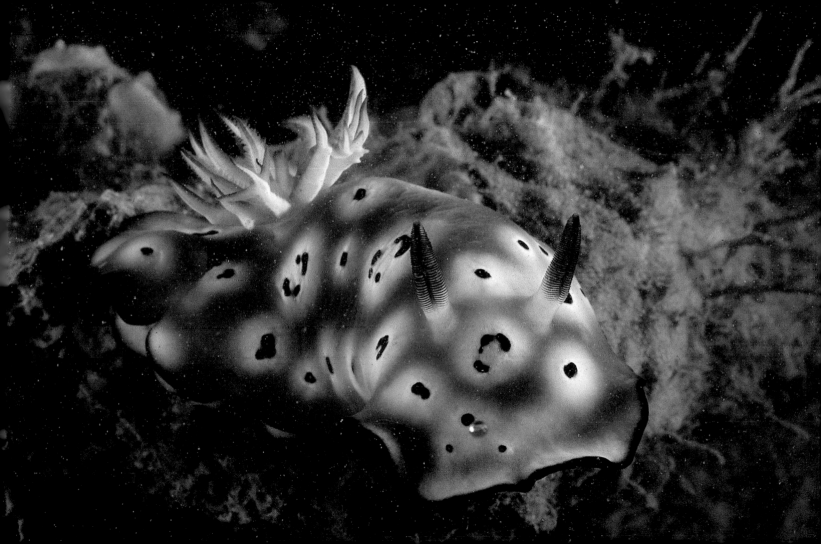

Buy retreaded tyres.

Every year, about 290 million tyres are scrapped. Of this number, 45% are used for fuel (to provide energy), and 29% are recycled to make material for industrial use. That said, 275 million tyres still sit in stockpiles that breed rat and mosquito populations and cause air and water pollution.

Retreading uses half as much energy as making a new tyre. To encourage this economical and environmentally friendly practice, choose retreaded tyres.

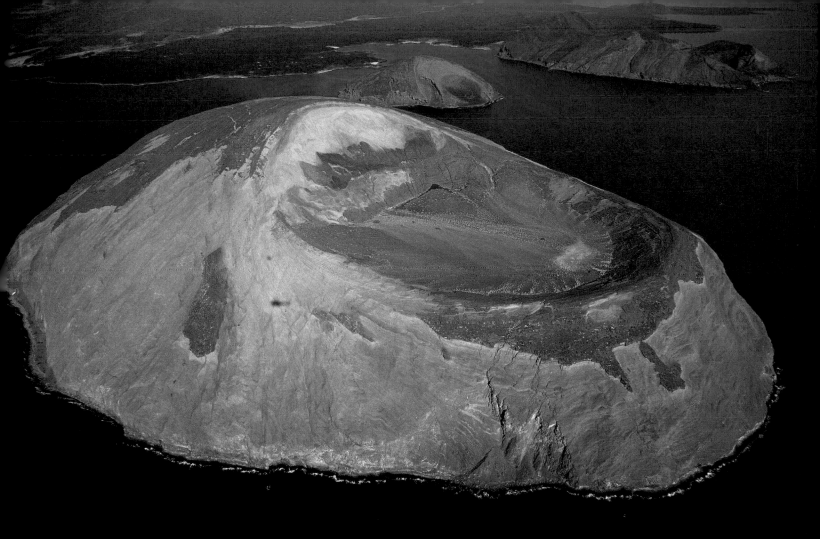

Support the Blue Flag when on holiday.

Every year, billions of litres of wastewater from cities are poured into the Mediterranean. Three-quarters of this water has not been treated. To help limit marine pollution, the Blue Flag, a European eco-label, annually rewards and honours local authorities and vacation resorts for their efforts toward achieving a quality environment—for their water quality; for educating and informing the public; for environmental management and safety; and so forth. The Blue Flag's high profile acts as an incentive to local elected officials who do their best to gain and keep this distinction.

Look for the Blue Flag when you choose a beach for your holiday. In 2007, it was awarded to almost 3,200 beaches and marinas in 38 countries in Europe and elsewhere.

Andaman Island, India

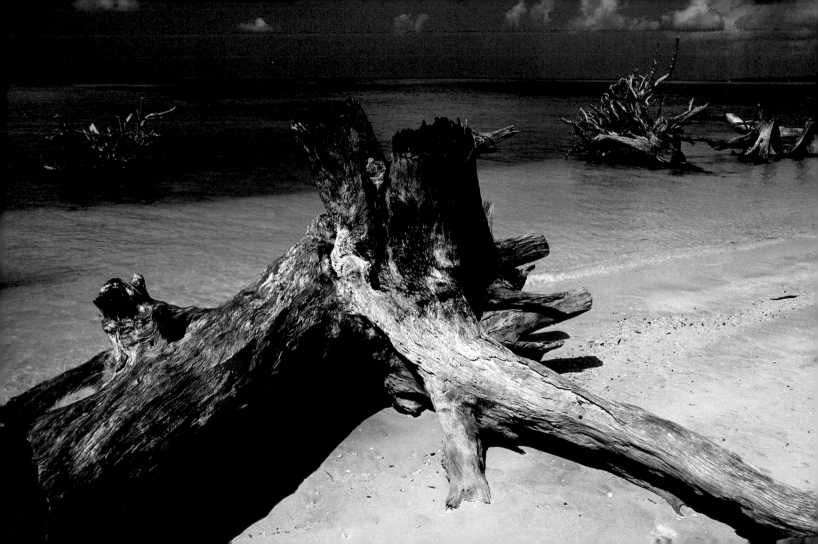

Stay at hotels that have comprehensive environmental policies.

A lot of hotels recycle, and many are starting to address water consumption by making daily towel and sheet laundering optional. But those efforts alone do not make a hotel green. If a hotel is of new construction did it choose its site wisely and/or seek BREEAM or other environmental certification? Does it make use of local food or does it import everything from miles away? Some hotels conserve energy with sensors that shut down power and air-conditioning when no one's in a room, and cut water use with low-flow fixtures and dual-flush toilets. Others go as far as installing solar arrays and grey water recycling systems. Hotels can reduce food waste by composting and donating edible leftovers to charitable organisations. They can protect groundwater and the health of their customers and workers by only using eco-friendly cleaning products. Furthermore, a green hotel limits the amount of printed material it issues and uses recycled papers and nontoxic inks for brochures. And a hotel cannot be considered green unless it treats its workers well and pays them living wages.

Support hotels that are truly making the effort to reduce their impact. The Green Tourism Business Scheme is one organisation that can help identify such properties. If your favourite hotel is behind the curve, let them know that their customers demand greater change.

Laguna, Bolivia

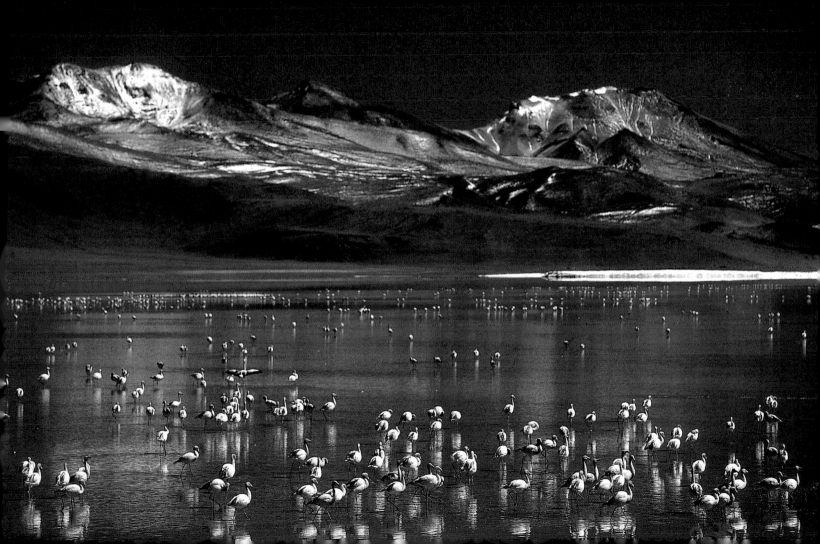

Try not to use your tumble dryer.

Roughly 40% of British households use a tumble dryer frequently, and if each of these 10 million households didn't use their dryer once, it would save over 18,000 tonnes of carbon dioxide. Of all household electrical appliances, the clothes dryer consumes the most energy. It uses 2, or even 3, times as much power as a washing machine.

The cheapest and most environmentally sound way of drying the wash will always be to hang it up. If you have to use the dryer, don't overload it, clean the lint trap regularly, and use the permanent press option to finish the drying cycle using residual heat. Invest in a dryer with a moisture sensor — it will shut off as soon as your clothes are dry.

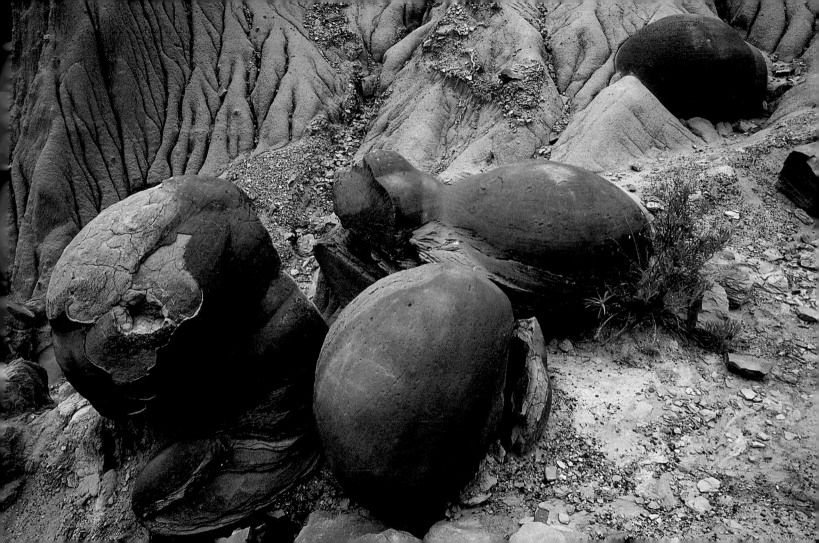

Make sure your appliances are efficient.

Every time you use an appliance or turn on your lights, resources are used to generate the electricity needed to run the appliance. Ninety-five and four-tenths percent of the electricity produced in the United Kingdom comes from traditional, nonrenewable resources, which are the number one cause of industrial air pollution in this country. The remaining 4.6% is generated from renewable resources, such as solar, geothermal, small hydro, biomass, and wind.

To minimise your energy use, make sure that all your appliances are as efficient as possible. The European Union now requires all white goods, lightbulbs, and many other appliances to display their energy rating on the label — aim for an 'A' rating whenever you buy something new.

Altiplano, Bolivia

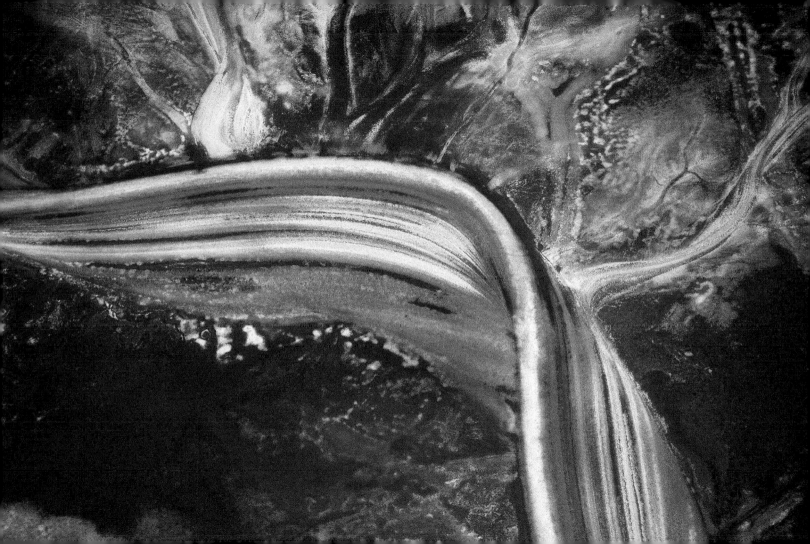

Ask for the MSC (Marine Stewardship Council) label.

Worldwide, fish stocks are in free-fall. Populations have dropped by a third in less than 30 years. Now there are labels that encourage good practice, by identifying products that come from sustainably managed fisheries; that is, areas where efforts are made to preserve the natural marine environment and the richness of species, while guarantee-ing a decent wage for fishermen. In this way consumers can encourage ecologically responsible fishing practises.

Look for seafood products bearing the label of the Marine Stewardship Council, an independent, global, nonprofit certifier of sustainably produced seafood.

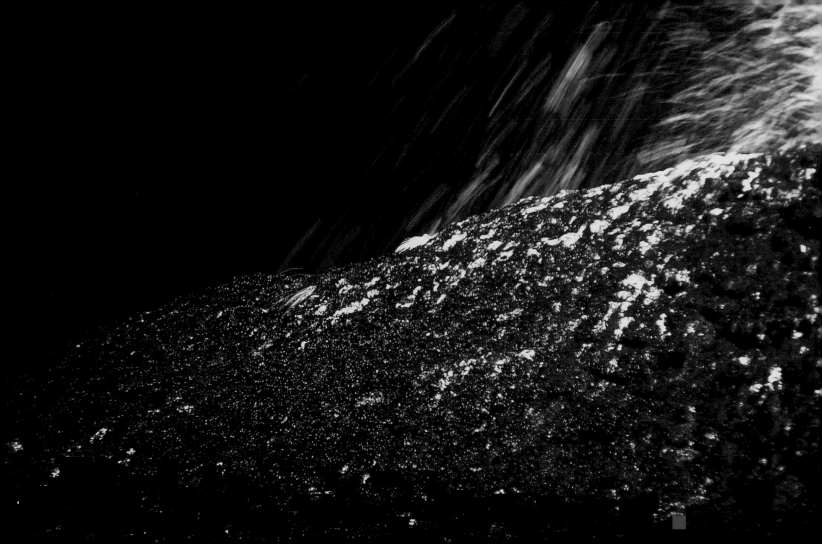

Moderate your air-conditioning use.

The world's energy consumption is increasing relentlessly as standards of living rise. Air-conditioning, a modern comfort, has a particularly voracious appetite for energy. If it is used to excess (that is, to produce cold rather than a comfortable temperature) it uses large quantities of electricity pointlessly.

By being content with a degree or two less, you can save up to 10% of daily energy consumption. Use it in moderation in your car as well. Fans generally use much less energy and can help circulate the cool air, so that your air-conditioner doesn't have to work quite as hard. Lastly, make sure the unit you buy is the correct size — believe it or not, if an air-conditioner is too large for the space it cools, it will do its job less efficiently (it won't remove the humidity from the air as well as a properly sized unit), wasting even more energy.

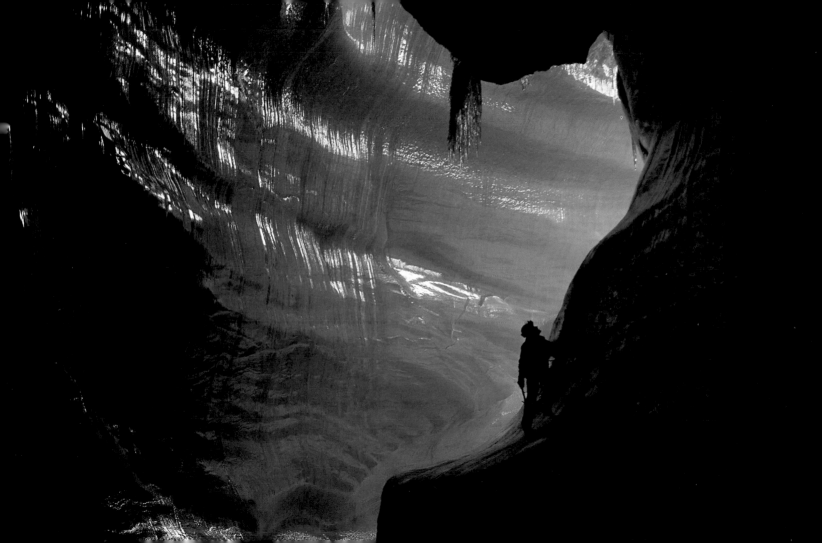

Choose a trailer rather than a roof rack.

A roof rack on a car contributes to pollution and climate change. When loaded, it increases wind resistance by up to 15%, which is reflected in fuel consumption. Even when empty, it increases consumption by 10% at the same speed.

If you need to carry a large amount of luggage when you go on holiday, use a trailer — or ship bags and bicycles to your holiday destination by train, which will produce less pollution. If you must use a roof rack, remove it when you don't need it.

Blizzard on the ice cap, Greenland

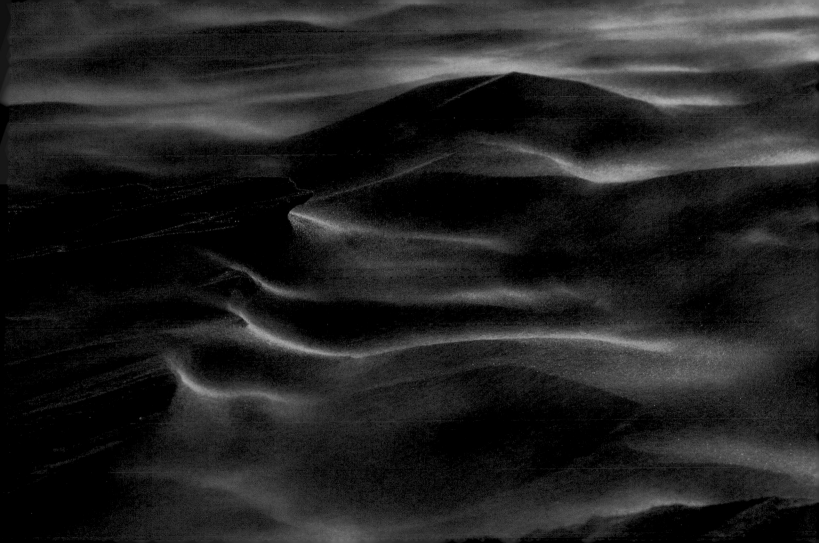

Decide what you want before you open the fridge door.

Replacing a 10-year-old fridge bought in 1990 with a new A-rated model would save enough energy to light the average household for over 3 months, and save more than 136 kg of pollution each year. In a well-equipped household, the fridge alone accounts for a third of electricity consumption (20% for the freezer and 12% for the refrigerator).

In order to avoid increasing your already high consumption needlessly, close the refrigerator door as soon as you have taken out what you need. Every time you open it, up to 30% of the cooled air can escape. And remember, that the tidier the contents, the less time the door needs to be kept open.

Icebergs, Greenland

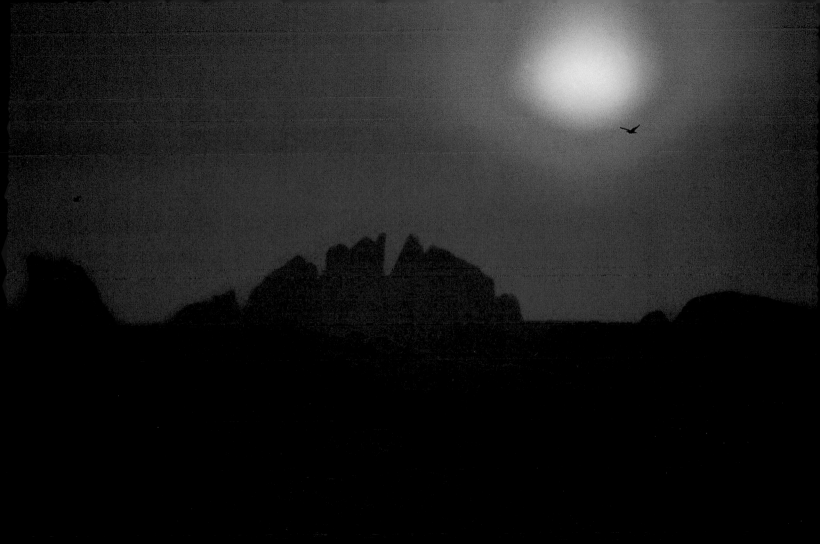

Make those around you aware of the problems.

Not everyone has the same level of awareness of environmental problems, although there is general agreement that the planet should be preserved. It is up to you to convey the urgency of the problem and to share the solutions that you have learnt.

Spread your knowledge and help those around you (family, friends, neighbours, and colleagues) become aware of the need for a good quality environment, and to conserve resources. Encourage them to take simple actions with this in mind.

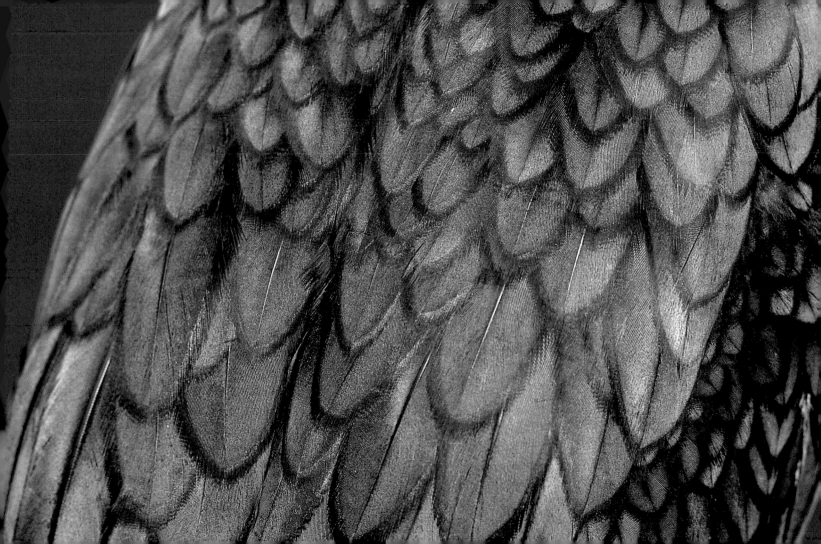

Reduce your meat consumption, and you'll feed the world.

In the United States and Europe, two-thirds of the grain produced each year is destined for livestock feed. More than half of the grains produced worldwide are not fed to humans. If it were, it could feed 2 billion people. Intensive farming is too costly in natural resources such as water, soil, and energy sources and will not be able to sustain the 8 billion people predicted to be living on earth in 2030.

Begin to reduce your meat consumption slowly. Choose 2 days a week to eat vegetarian and increase the number of days at your own pace. The variety of foods for vegetarians and the availability of local farm-fresh organic produce make the vegetarian lifestyle more appealing than ever, and you will be helping to relieve a small part of the pressures of our global appetite.

Cayman, Venezuela

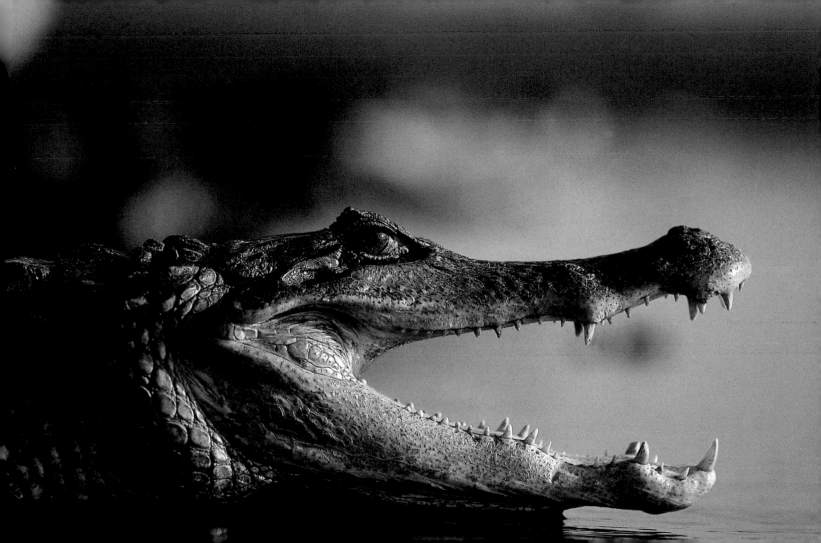

Do not waste water where it is scarce.

About 65% of the water human beings use is pumped from underground aquifers. However, more is drawn off than is naturally replaced because impervious surfaces such as pavements and buildings prevent rainwater from entering the ground. As a result, aquifers are gradually being drained dry. Some aquifers close to the sea — in Spain, for example — have started to fill up with saltwater. In India, the water table has dropped between 0.9 and 2.7 metres over three-fourths of the country's area. In some Mexican towns there is barely enough water to provide 19 litres per day per resident.

In developing countries the average tourist uses as much water in 24 hours as a local villager does to produce rice for 100 days. Avoid wasting this precious liquid: Take short showers, don't ask your hotel to wash your sheets and towels every day, and don't leave the tap running when you do things like brush your teeth.

Namib Desert, Namibia

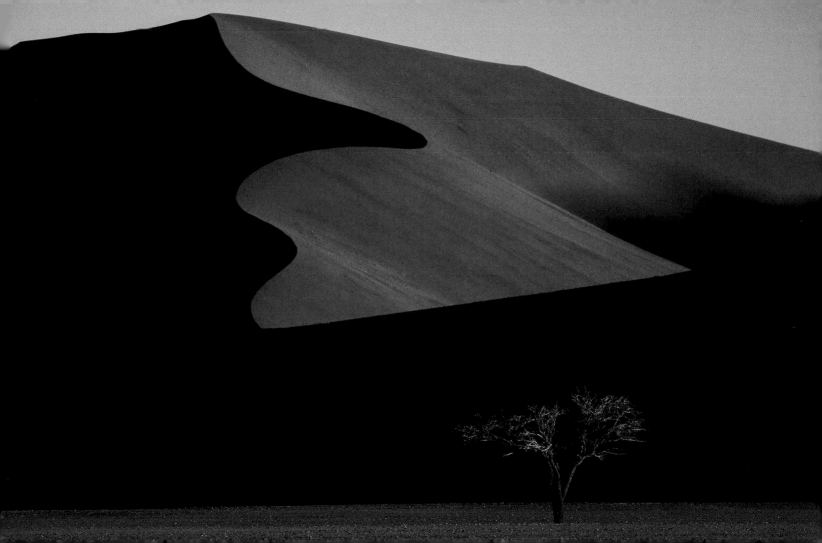

When you go on holiday, give your home a rest, too.

Holidays are generally a high-impact activity, especially when it involves air travel. Make sure your home isn't using up resources while you are thousands of miles away.

Before you leave turn off as many appliances as possible. Clean out the refrigerator and turn the temperature down. Turn off boilers, or in winter set them to the lowest temperature that you can. Turn off air-conditioning or heating systems (or, if you need minimal heating to stop condensation and mould, turn the heat down as low as possible). If you can, turn off the water — a leak or burst pipe is a terrible thing to come home to and a terrible waste of water. Unplug all AC adapters and electronics, especially those that continue to draw power through digital clocks and 'standby' modes.

Icebergs, Greenland

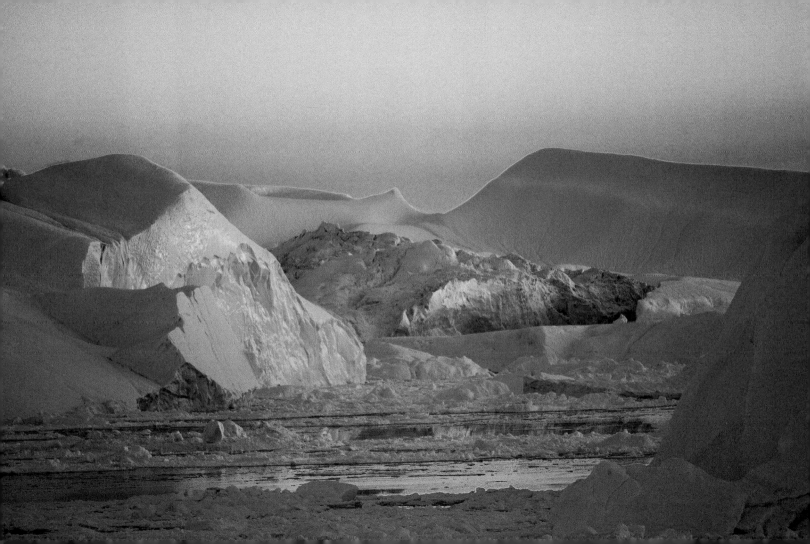

Use heat for weeding.

Everyone knows that using too much fertiliser, insecticide, weed killer, and fungicide on crops damages the environment—in particular, water resources. However, most of us do just that in our own gardens and produce the same type of pollution.

You can dispense with chemical weed killer, for example, by using heat: Pour boiling water on the weeds. The weeds darken almost immediately and turn brown within a few hours, much like the effect of a contact herbicide, but there is no toxic residue and the area is immediately safe for children.

Acacia, Niger

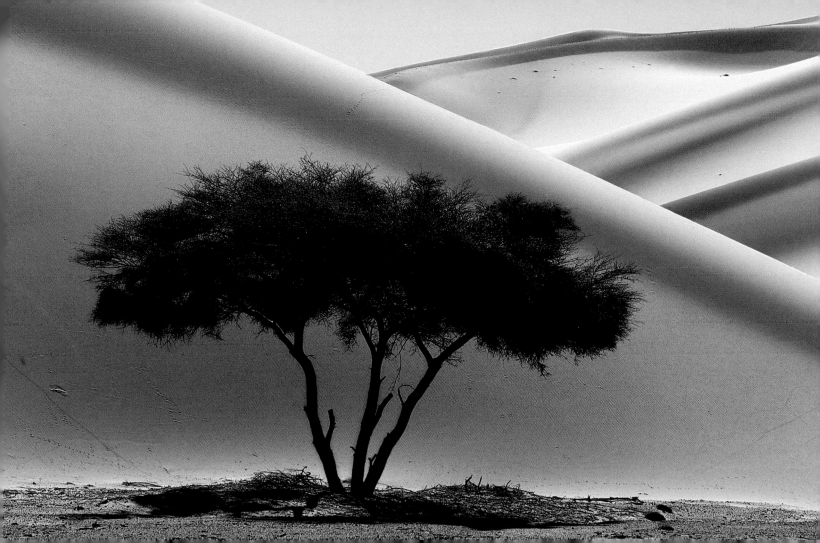

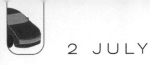

Take the train rather than the car.

Most people start their day in a car, fighting traffic and boredom. A passenger on a train, whether travelling for business or pleasure, has the option to work, sleep, read, or chat with fellow passengers. Many companies offer refunds for season tickets, while car use for commuting doesn't count against tax, so it may be cheaper to take the train, and it will almost certainly save you time.

Discover the comfort of train travel. Your journey will be safer and less tiring, and you will considerably reduce your contribution to global warming.

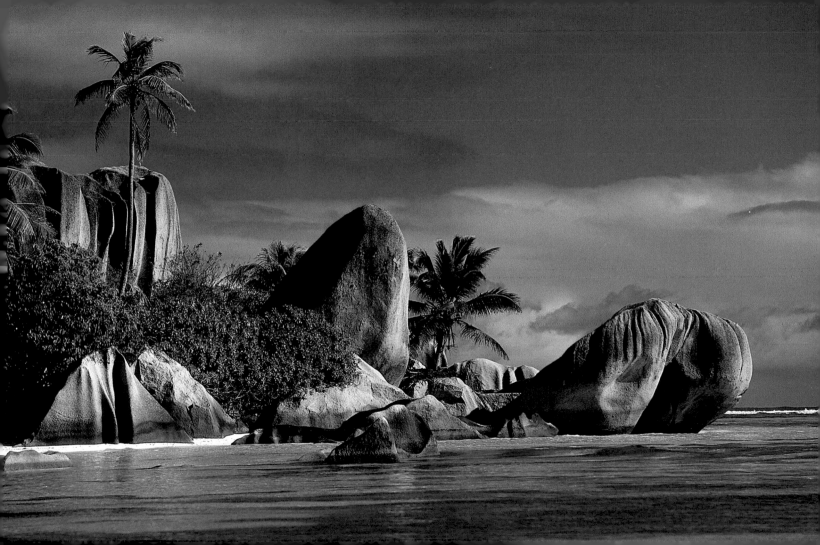

Quit smoking.

Everyone knows that tobacco is harmful to our health. More than 3,000 substances have been identified in tobacco smoke, including nicotine, which causes addiction; tars, which cause cancer; and carbon monoxide. Moreover, smokers pollute their immediate surroundings. However, the damage does not stop there: Every year about 600 million trees go up in smoke to provide space to cure tobacco leaves; tobacco farming accounts for 5% of deforestation in Africa. Cigarette butts are a huge source of litter and can take a decade to break down.

Smoking is simply not part of a sustainable lifestyle. While you cut back, avoid smoking in enclosed spaces, and keep to smokers' areas in public places. Look for organic tobacco and hand roll to avoid nonbiodegradable filters.

Fog, United States

Celebrate Independence Day.

Make the 4th of July your day to become independent from the cost of wasted energy and products — and celebrate in style. Have a barbecue with sustainably produced charcoal made from reclaimed scrap wood, not gas. Don't use lighter fluids. Buy local food to put on it, from organic producers. Use real glasses and cups — if you don't have enough for a party, hire them from a local off-licence — and fill them with locally produced juice or beer. Make decorations from old magazines and newspapers — get your children to lend a hand. And at the end of it all, compost and recycle as much waste as possible.

Celebrate your independence from oil and electricity — and make it a better celebration for the environment.

Blue octopus, Australia

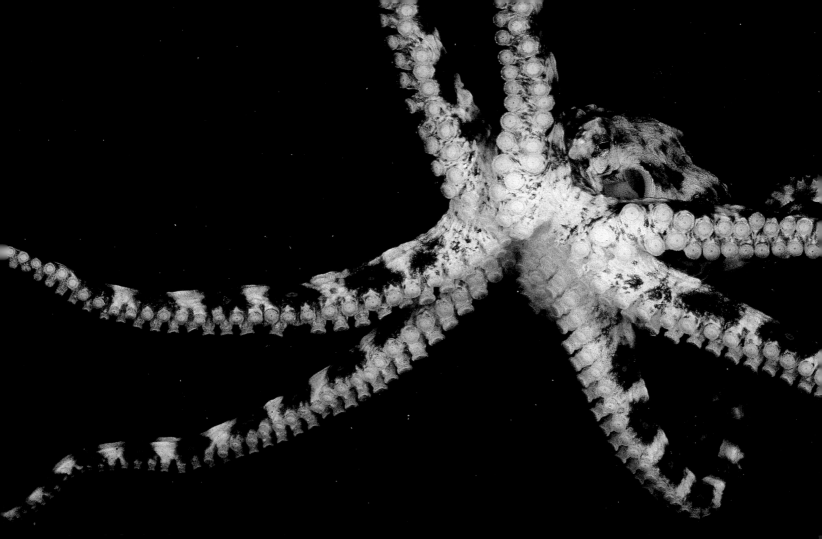

Take bulky waste to reuse centres.

How do you deal with old appliances, furniture, old plaster, sheets of metal, and everything else that does not fit in your dustbin? Traditionally, this type of waste went straight to the landfill, but a growing number of reuse centres can take everything from old furniture to plumbing and lighting fixtures to lumber and flooring.

Before you send an old wardrobe or bed to the dump, find out about your local reuse centre online. Anything that's not salvageable should be properly disposed of. If you cannot take it to the dump yourself, your local authority will have information on door-to-door collection services.

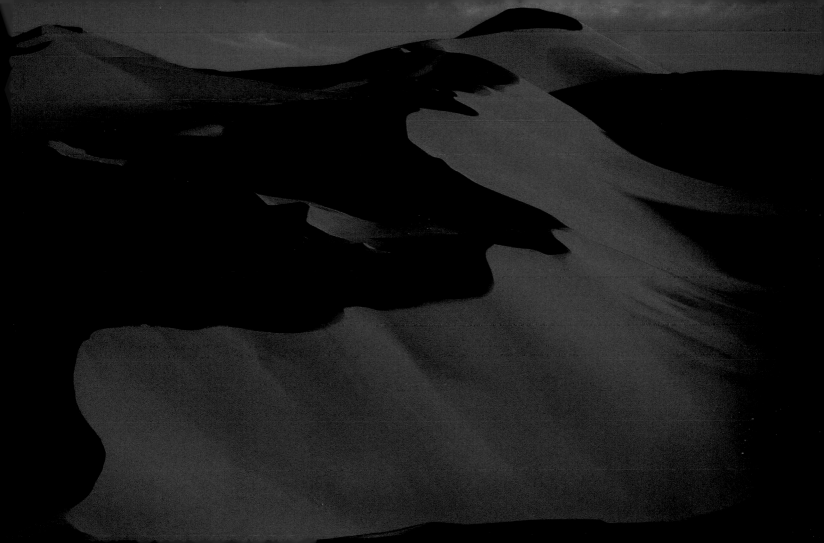

Check where your purchases are made.

Everyone knows that private cars pollute. But we often forget that most of the items we use in our daily lives travel long distances, too. The environmental impact of transporting food and consumer goods is considerable: The farther a product travels, the more greenhouse gases are emitted.

To minimise this waste of resources and pollution, check the label to see where the fruits and vegetables or household goods and toys you buy come from. If it's possible to get a similar item of the same quality from a local source, do so.

Tungurahua volcano, Ecuador

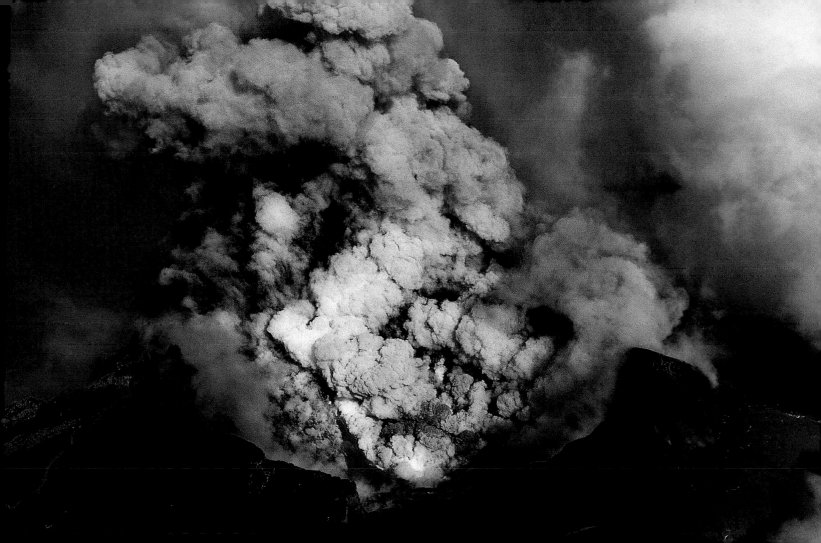

Telecommute or videoconference.

In Britain the number of teleworkers has risen sharply in the past years and now account for 8 percent of all workers amounting to 2.2 million. Teleworking reduces traffic and pollution considerably.

If you can do your job remotely, ask your employer to consider trying a telecommuting scheme — the summer is a great time to make this request as the pace slows at many businesses while people go on holiday and take advantage of shortened summer hours.

Videoconferencing, though not exactly carbon neutral — it does require a lot of electronics and energy — is far more eco-friendly than travelling to business meetings.

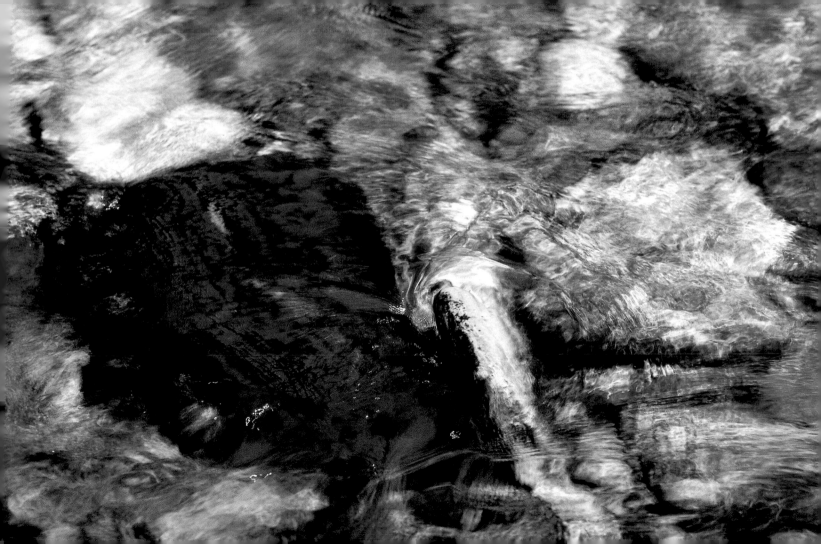

If you don't like tap water, use a filter.

Bottled water is the fastest growing drinks market in the world, worth £20 billion and counting. Yet in the developed world, we are delivered clean, safe water for a tiny cost to the environment and us. A bottle of water takes more water to make than it will hold, and many bottled water brands use the same sources as tap water, just treating it to taste a little better.

You can make tap water taste better yourself for a fraction of the cost by using a filter, or adding a little lemon juice to a jug of water. Or, simpler still, you can get rid of the taste of chlorine by leaving a jug of water in your fridge for a few hours: Chlorine is volatile and will evaporate. Keep a few water bottles to refill every day and take them out with you — and remember that almost every café or restaurant will give you tap water for free if you ask.

Dallol Volcano, Ethiopia

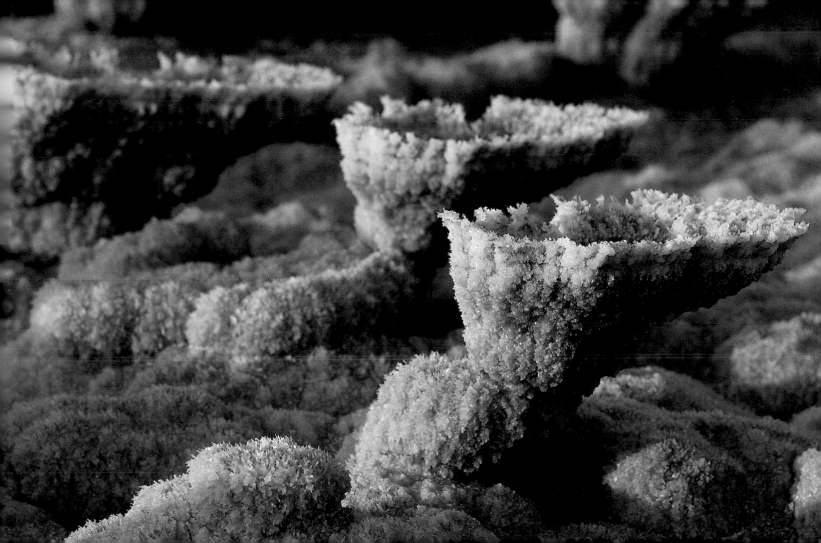

Use eco-friendly sunblock.

There is a difference between sunscreen (which uses chemicals to absorb and reflect the sun's harmful rays) and sunblock (zinc- or titanium-based formulations that physically block UVA and UVB rays). Protecting your skin from the sun is important to your health, but many of the chemicals in brand-name sunscreens are incredibly harmful to coral and marine life. Each year swimmers add roughly 4 to 6 million kilos of sunscreen and tanning products to our oceans. Recent studies show that parabens, cinnamate, benzophenone, and camphor derivatives—all common ingredients in commercial sunscreen—can cause dormant viruses in coral reef algae to bloom, which can eventually kill the coral.

Protect yourself and our oceans by using biodegradable sunblocks that don't contain harmful chemicals. Better alternatives are on the horizon, but for now products that have titanium dioxide and zinc oxide as active ingredients, and all-natural (even better, organic) inactive ingredients are the safest.

Sandstone, Chad

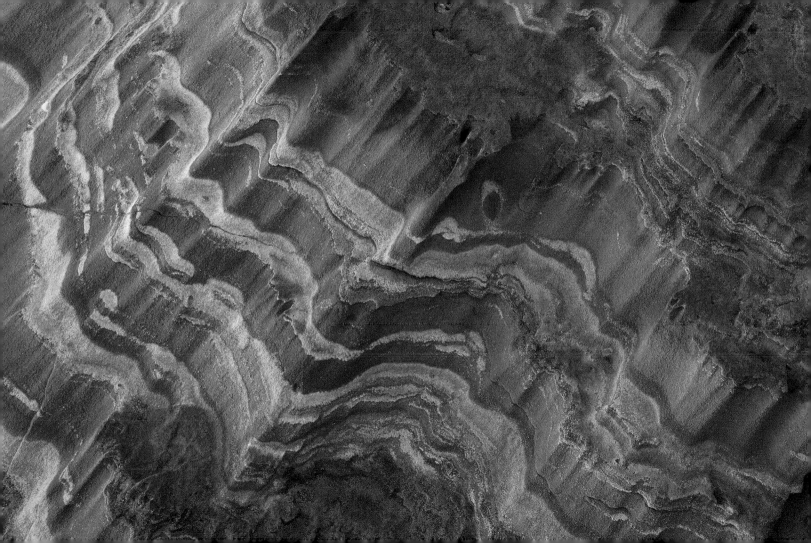

Avoid buying souvenirs made from protected species.

Overexploitation of living things—as a result of hunting, fishing, or excessive harvesting—is one of the main reasons for species extinction. Illegal trade in threatened animal and plant species is the third largest form of trafficking in the world after arms and drugs; this trade affects 13% of the bird and mammal species threatened with extinction. For example, sea turtles, having inhabited the planet's oceans for several tens of millions of years, are now in danger of extinction as a result of human activity.

By buying objects or souvenirs that come from protected species, you are encouraging this traffic and speeding up the extinction of species. When you are on holiday, don't buy souvenirs or gifts that may be made from protected species of animal, plant, or tree.

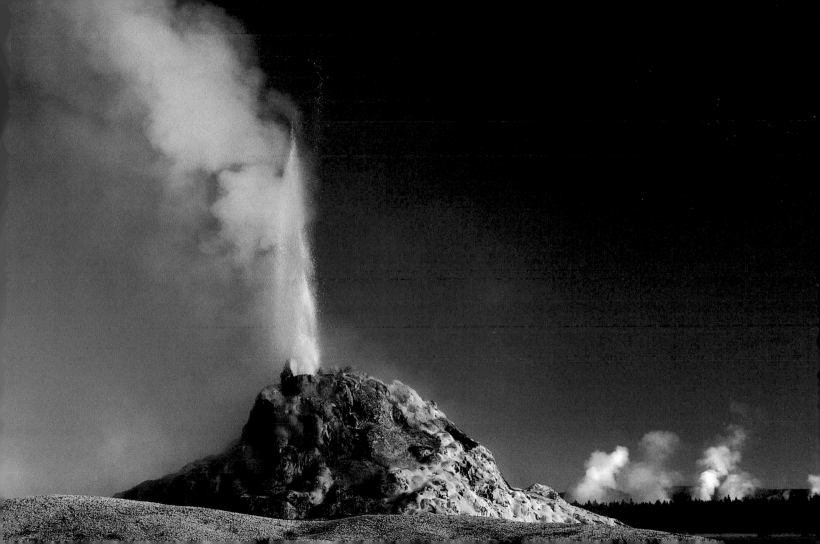

Take your old batteries back to the shop.

Inside a battery, the chemical reaction that takes place produces energy, which is converted into electricity. Most cylinder and button batteries contain toxic metals such as cadmium, mercury, lead, and nickel, which are extremely harmful to the environment. Even though some newer batteries may be disposed of in your household waste, it is strongly recommended that you recycle your alkaline batteries.

Many large shops, and many local authorities, accept batteries for recycling. They may not advertise this fact, so it is always worth asking. Try to limit the number of products you use that require batteries, and buy a battery charger and rechargeable batteries.

Yosemite National Park,
United States

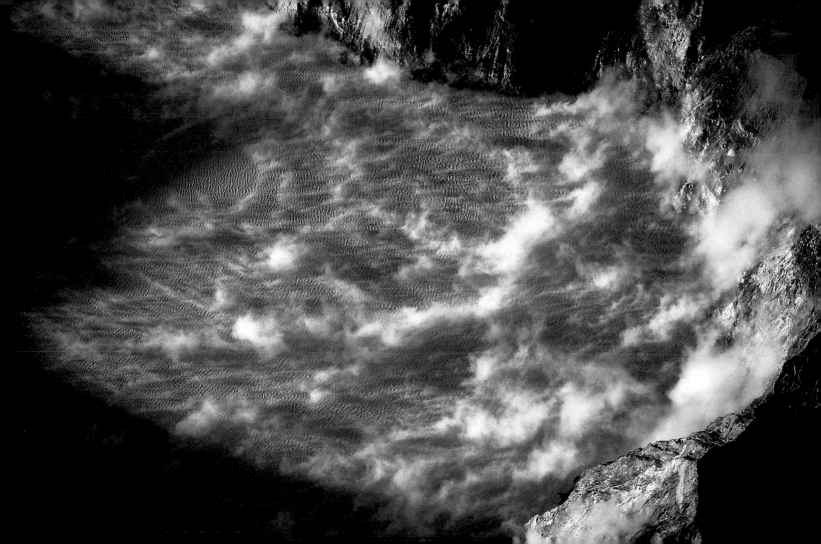

Turn off the air-conditioning in your car.

Do you really need to air-condition your car? Air-conditioning significantly increases the amount of fuel you use, yet simply turning up the ventilation fan is almost always enough to keep your car at a comfortable temperature. Using air-conditioning can make your car up to 20% less efficient, which will affect your wallet as well as the environment.

In your car, turn off your air-conditioning; turn up your fan. But don't open your windows to keep it cool because the extra drag created means that your car has to work extra hard to compensate.

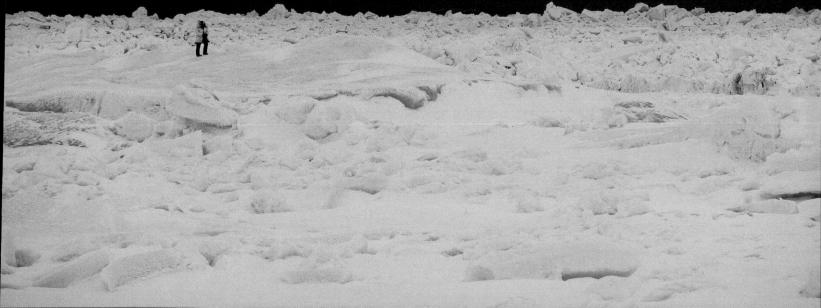

Don't light fires in the countryside or forest.

Emissions of carbon dioxide are one of the chief sources of the air pollution that is causing the proven upheaval in the climate. Nearly 5 tonnes of carbon is released when a hectare of coniferous forest burns. Fires on grassland can spread very quickly, killing wildlife and destroying valuable ecosystems and habitats.

Preserve the planet's natural habitats: Don't light fires in the countryside, ever.

Patagonia, Argentina

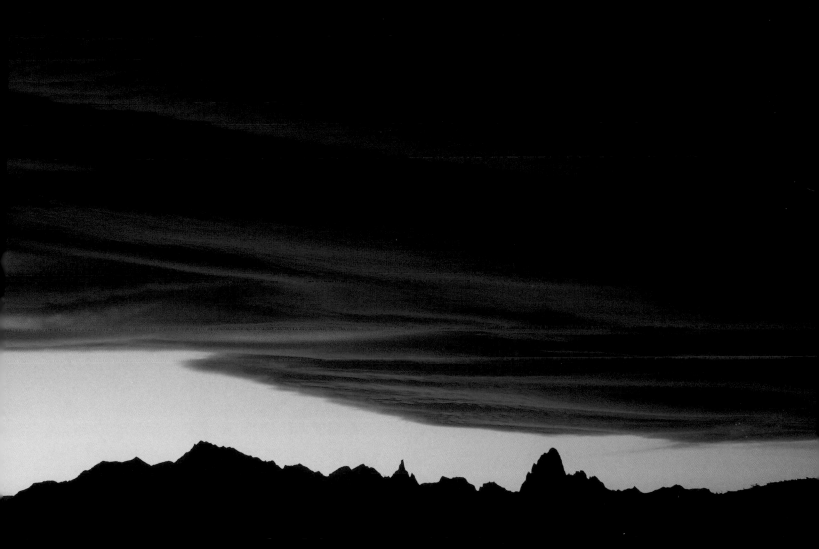

Beware of invasive species. Do not introduce non-native plants or animals.

Nature relies on delicate balances. An alien species, whether deliberately or accidentally introduced into a habitat, may find conditions so favourable that it becomes invasive. Miconia, an ornamental bush introduced to Tahiti in 1937, now covers two-thirds of the island. Caulerpa, a tropical seaweed, monotonously blankets vast areas of the Mediterranean. Closer to home, Japanese knotweed is a major issue in the United Kingdom, smothering rare native plants in many areas of the southwest, and it also can cause structural damage to buildings; and signal crayfish have also become a major problem, out-competing native freshwater species as well as carrying diseases.

To avoid unbalancing the precarious ecological balance of your native region, do not release any exotic animal or plant into the environment, and never smuggle plants or animals in your luggage.

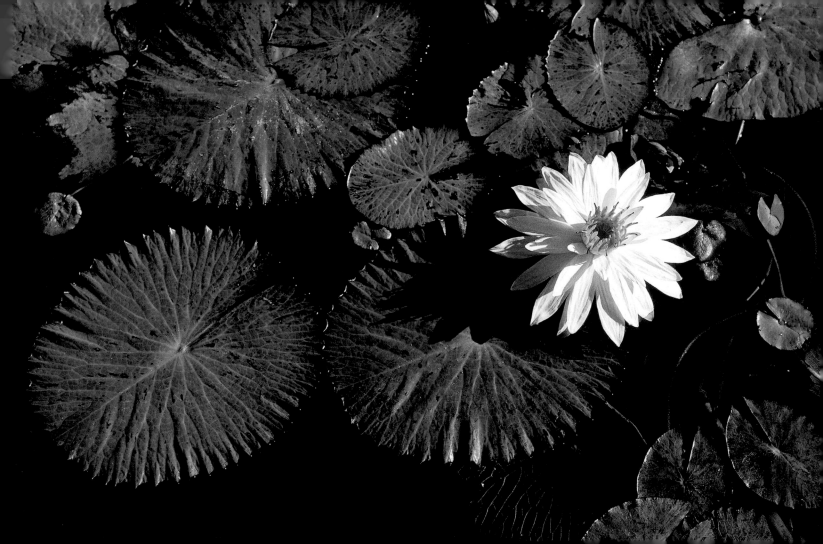

Think twice before visiting endangered habitats.

In the past few years a new type of travel has become popular — some call it 'disaster tourism'. Inspired by news reports of disappearing habitats, some travellers are forsaking typical vacation spots to head to Greenland to get a last look at endangered polar bears or to Tanzania to see Mt. Kilimanjaro before its famous snows are gone forever. Although getting to know an endangered place can be seen as a step toward figuring out how to protect it, make sure your desire to see a spot before it vanishes doesn't compound the problem.

Before booking a trip to an eroding reef or glacier, consider the following. Will increased tourism have any benefits? The Galápagos Islands, for example, are being destroyed by unregulated tourism; if more people rush to see them before they change, it will hasten their demise. Does any portion of the money you spend on your trip go toward helping those communities affected by climate change? Finally, ask the toughest question of all: Are you travelling to the destination to make a difference or to secure bragging rights?

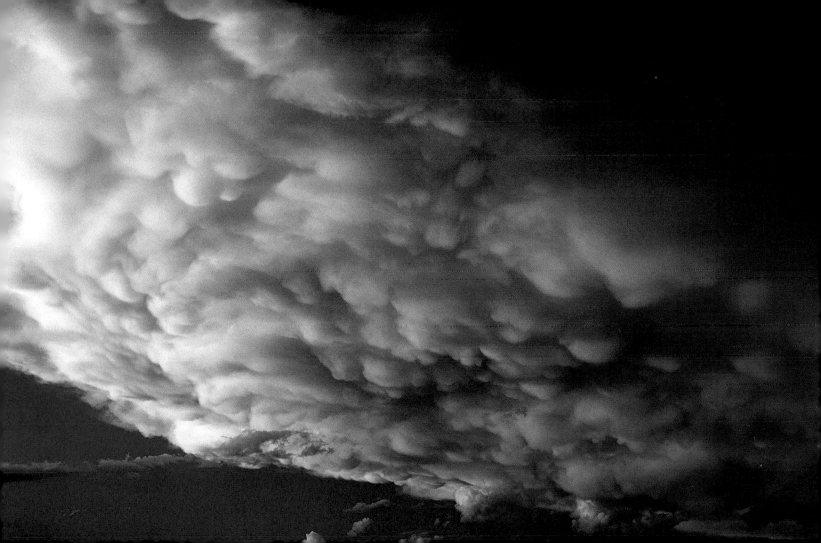

Take your litter with you.

Some waste is biodegradable, decomposing easily in the environment. Other waste does so much less quickly. A tissue dropped outside takes 3 months to decompose, a piece of paper takes 4 months, and chewing gum takes 5 years. An aluminium can decomposes over 10 years, a plastic bottle takes at least 100 years, and a glass bottle requires several centuries.

No matter how quickly you think it will decompose, do not leave rubbish behind. Always take it with you and find a litterbin, or better yet, a recycling bin.

Inactive volcanic cone, Bolivia

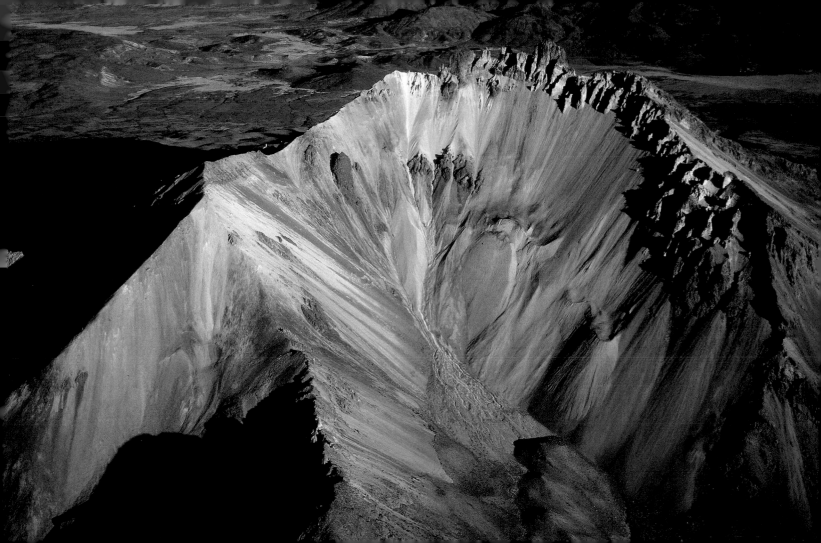

Don't eat farmed prawns.

Mangrove forests, which grow on swampy shores, are a vital habitat for marine life as well as significant to local economies. They offer a refuge and spawning ground for fish and crustaceans; they protect the shore by trapping sediment washed down by rivers; and they slow erosion caused by waves. Mangroves carpet almost a quarter of tropical coasts but this is only half their former extent, for this fragile, unique habitat is continually receding as a result of logging, pollution, and increasingly, the expansion of prawn and shrimp farming, particularly in Asia. Half of the mangroves that remain are considered degraded in some way. The impact of the destruction of mangroves on the coastal ecosystem was recently found to be even more vital when scientists discovered that mangrove forests are crucial nurseries for some coral-reef fish species.

Prawn and shrimp farming has already destroyed an estimated 1 million hectares of coastal wetlands and mangroves. Avoid eating farmed prawns, especially when staying in foreign countries.

Mantis shrimp, Australia

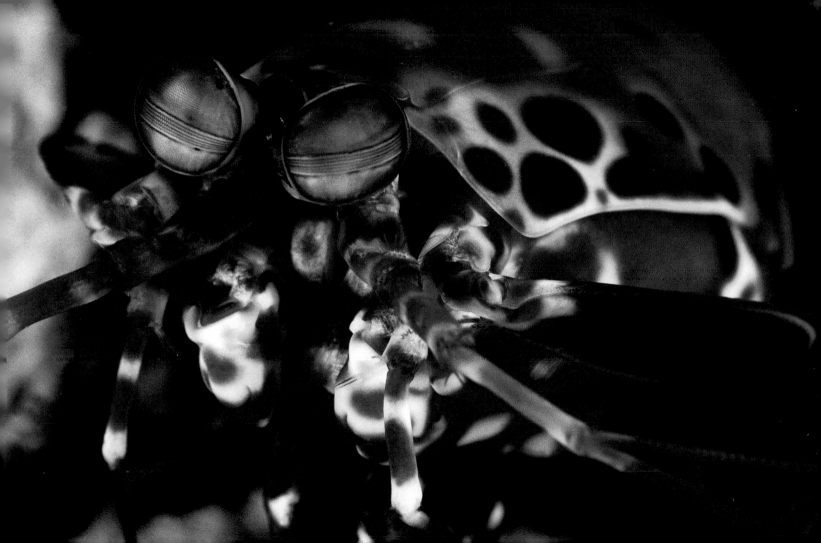

Choose solar-powered heating for your home.

Renewable energy sources produce no greenhouse gases and their reserves are inexhaustible. Why not use the sun to heat your water and your house? Depending on the situation, energy from the sun can supply 40% to 80% of hot water needs, and 20% to 40% of heating needs. A solar hot water heater may allow a 40% to 70% reduction of energy consumption during the summer.

Various grants for renewable energies are available — in the United Kingdom, ask the Energy Saving Trust for advice. And a solar thermal hot water system is the cheapest form of renewable energy technology that you can install, costing from £3200. The sunlight is free, courtesy of Mother Nature.

Ice crystals, Greenland

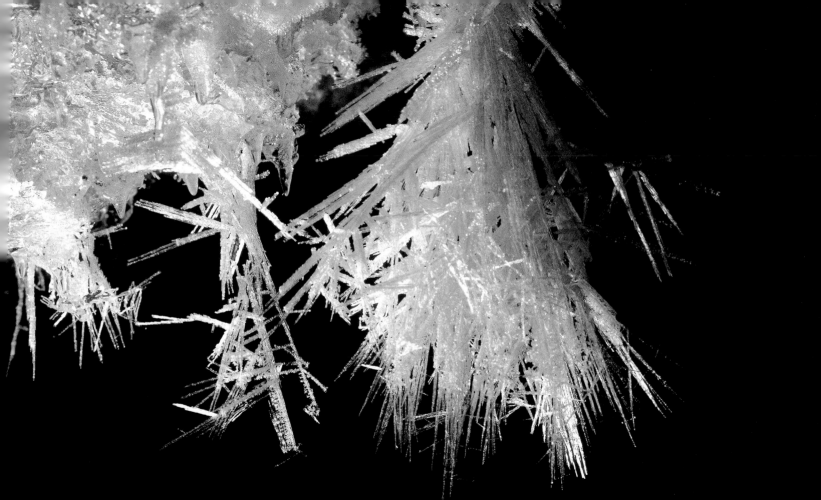

Donate your time to an environmental organisation.

Every country now has a plethora of environmental organisations—local, regional, and national. Some focus on issues of nature and wildlife, some on waste and recycling, others on helping low-income families become more energy efficient. Many people choose to support these organisations by giving a donation or becoming a member in order to support initiatives financially; others give their time to take part in the organisation's activities.

These organisations have a great deal to contribute. They also need you. Investigate the environmental groups in your area, and support their work in some way.

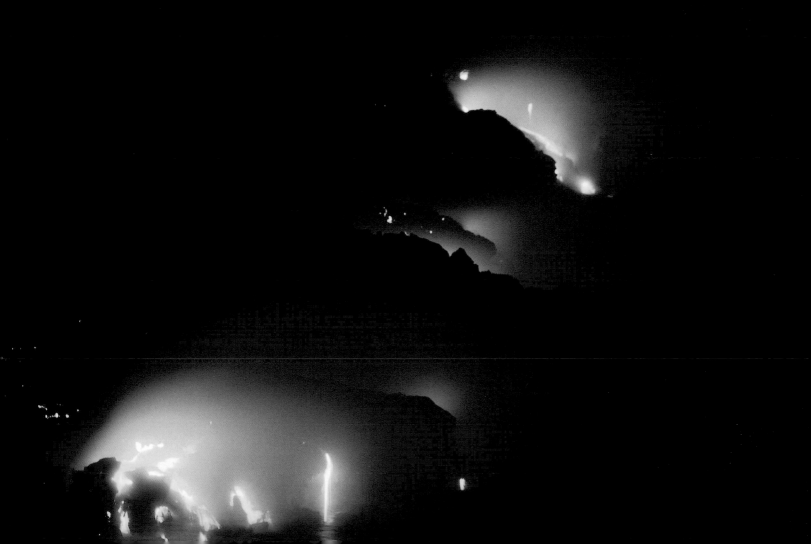

Practise environmentally friendly camping.

Camping would appear to be close to nature and do little environmental damage, but in practise this can vary. Making greener choices about where and when you camp will reduce the amount of impact your camping trip has on the environment.

Always camp in designated campsites; choosing your own site to pitch a tent will impact on habitats and wildlife. If you choose a popular outdoors destination for your trip, choose to go at an off-peak time of year; fewer people in the park will not only add to the enjoyment of your trip but also reduces the amount of impact visitors have on a given day. Take your rubbish with you, and don't dump any wastewater near freshwater sources. Use phosphate-free, biodegradable soaps for bathing and washing dishes.

Olympic National Park,
United States

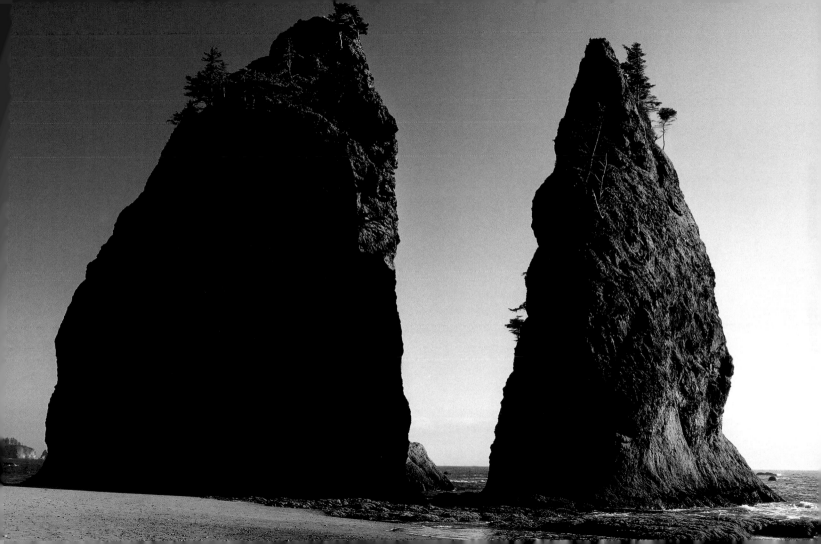

Make your children aware of the natural world that surrounds them.

Before we want to protect something, we must first get to know it. Apathy is often due to ignorance rather than negligence. Those who are young today will soon have the earth's future in their hands. Let us give them the means to do better tomorrow than we have done today.

Suggest nature trips to your children, such as visits to local nature reserves, bird sanctuaries, botanical gardens, walks, and other open-air activities. Give them binoculars, magnifying glasses, notebooks, and pencils. Complement these outings with books, nature guides, and discussions about their newfound knowledge. By broadening their interests you will help to increase their awareness, and learn a lot yourself.

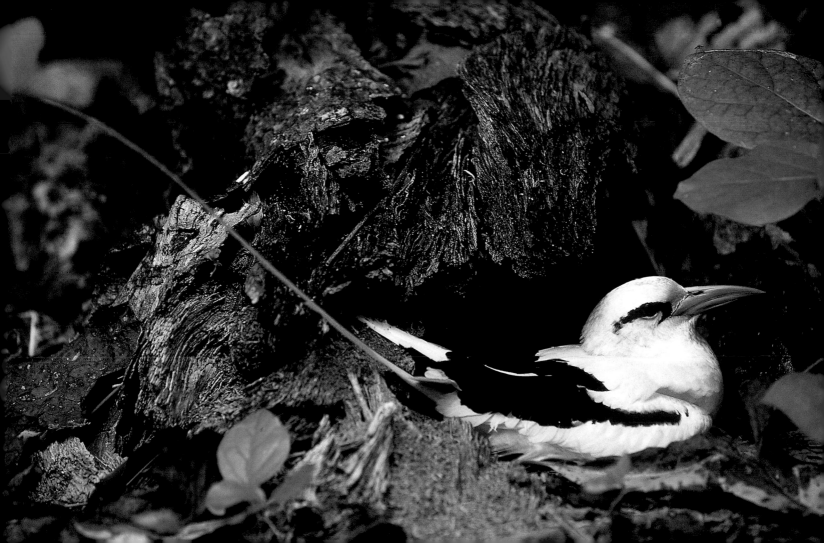

Keep your tyres properly inflated.

Keeping tyres fully inflated reduces wear and lengthens their life, thus saving money—new tyres can be expensive, costing around £300 to replace all four. It also saves precious raw material: It takes 25 litres of crude oil to create a new tyre. Under-inflated tyres can increase fuel consumption by up to 10%. Tests show that a 25% decrease in tyre pressure can cost you 5% to 10% more on petrol and 25% on tyre life.

Make sure you keep your car's tyres at the pressure recommended by the manufacturer. Take 5 minutes every month to check the pressure of your tyres.

Iceberg, Antarctica

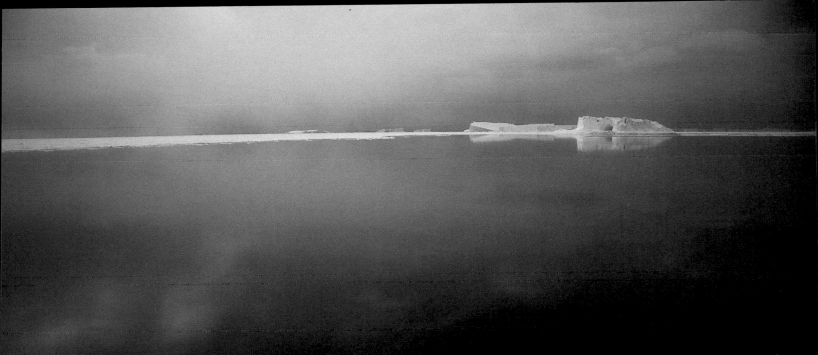

Buy a fridge that does not damage the ozone layer or the climate.

International measures for halting the destruction of the ozone layer stipulate that chlorofluorocarbons (CFCs) in refrigeration equipment must be replaced by hydrochlorofluorocarbons (HCFCs) and hydrofluorocarbons (HFCs), which do not damage the ozone layer. Unfortunately, they do contribute significantly to climate change because they contain chlorine, which makes them far more powerful greenhouse gases than carbon dioxide. The anticipated increase in the use of HFCs by the year 2050 will contribute as much to global warming as all the private cars on the planet put together. Fridges are available that contain neither CFCs nor HCFCs, but use isobutane instead.

When you change your fridge, find out about models that do not damage either the ozone layer or contribute to climate change — and make sure that you dispose of your old one safely.

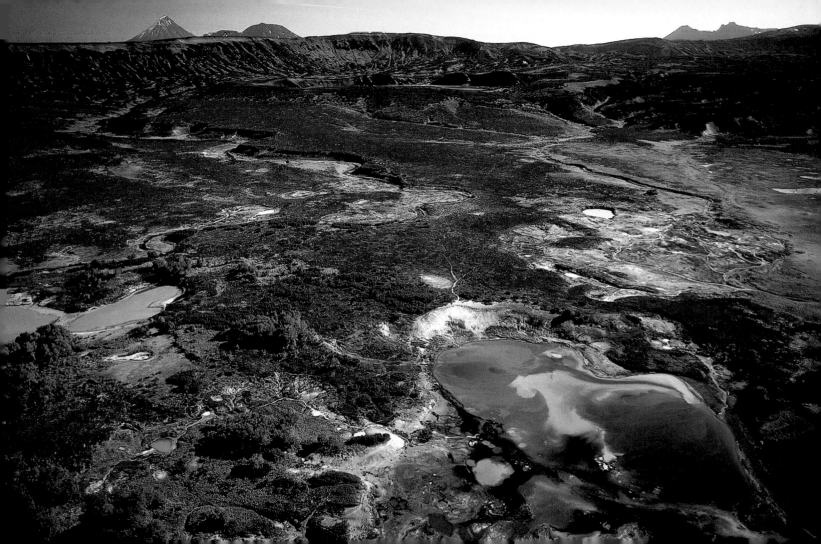

Use the right dose of detergents and other chemicals.

Thanks to the efforts of detergent manufacturers, you now need far less detergent to wash a load of laundry or dishes.

Check the recommended dosage on the packages of the products you use to wash dishes, floors, or laundry, especially for concentrated detergents, and stick to them. Using more soap does not give better results and can cause skin irritation. In addition, it is more costly, wastes more packaging — and therefore natural resources — produces more waste, and contributes to the degradation of already polluted rivers.

Iceberg, Greenland

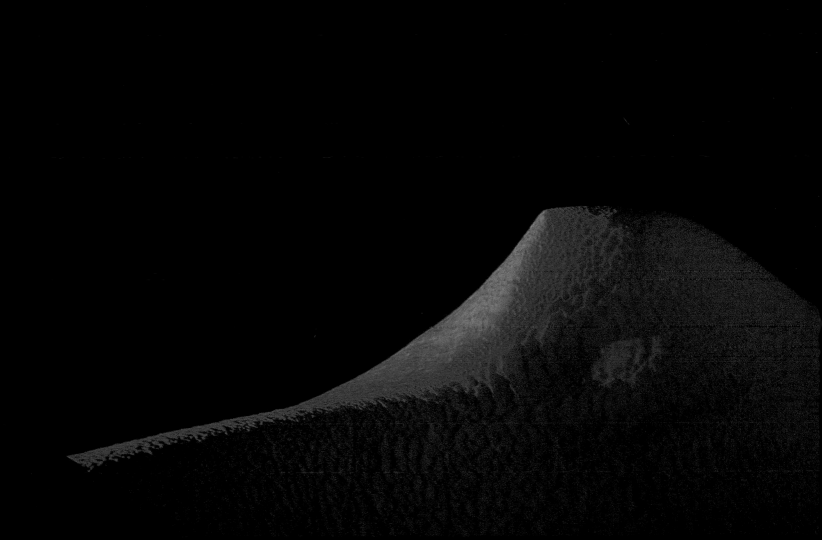

Do not throw away your baby's clothes and accessories.

Joy at the birth of a child is often preceded by a frenzy of shopping for the things that new parents think they need. The list can be long and the bill high, especially since we generally want the best, most attractive, most modern and, above all, the newest products for the latest addition to the family. A large proportion of these accessories and clothes will see use for an extremely short length of time.

To lessen the impact of a new baby on the family finances and to avoid buying things that get used for only a few weeks, borrow what you need from other family members or friends, or from local 'freecycling' networks. Then lend things in turn, sell them, or give them away. If the same plastic bath is passed down among 4 children, that makes 3 fewer baths that need to be manufactured.

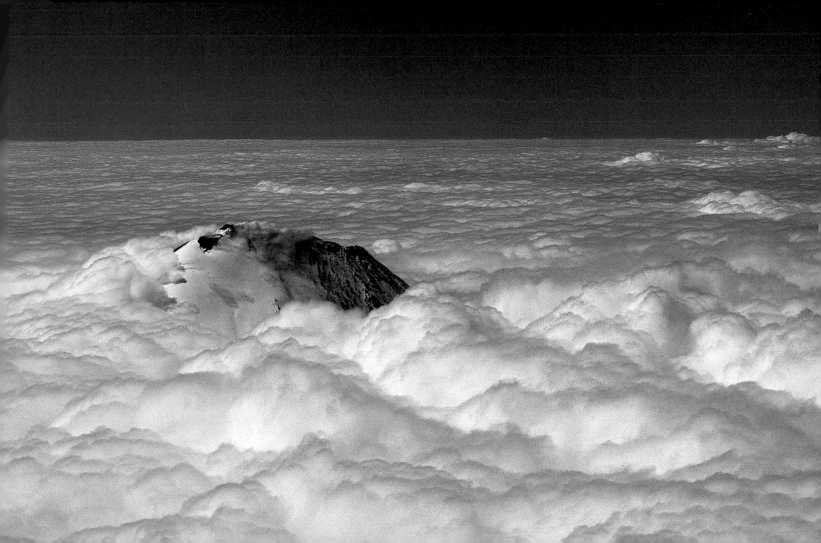

Keep litter out of our oceans.

A motley carpet of some 300 million tonnes of waste covers the floor of the Mediterranean. Some of the waste will remain there, intact, for centuries. A newspaper takes 6 weeks to decompose in the sea, and a cardboard box takes 3 months. A cigarette butt takes 2 years, and a steel can 80 years. An aluminium can will last 100 years, and a plastic bag 300 years. A piece of polystyrene or a plastic bottle will both remain intact for 500 years. Glass lasts even longer.

Vast though it is, the sea cannot absorb all our pollution. It is becoming saturated. Do not leave any waste on the shore, or throw any overboard.

Elephant crossing a sea channel,
Andaman Islands, India

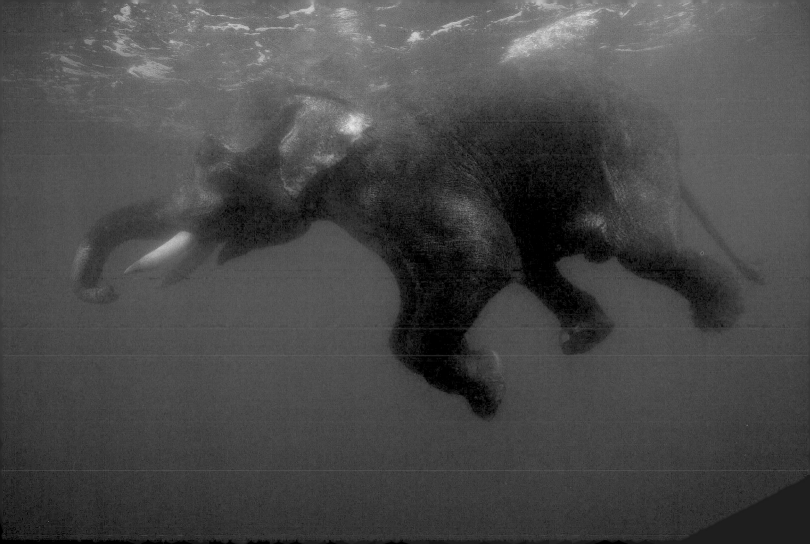

Say 'no' to rare fish species on your plate.

Consumption of fish products has more than doubled in the last 50 years. Today, 52% of the world's commercial sea fish stocks are fished to the limit of their capacity, 17% are over-fished, and 8% are exhausted or slowly recovering. In the waters off Newfoundland, cod stocks are struggling to recover despite a moratorium on fishing. A modern factory ship can catch as much cod in an hour as a typical sixteenth-century boat could haul in an entire season. Only a quarter of the world's fish stocks are moderately fished or under-fished, and species that were once plentiful have become rare.

Watch your consumption of sea bass, swordfish, bluefin tuna, cod, hake, monkfish, sole, and Atlantic salmon — these are just some of the threatened species.

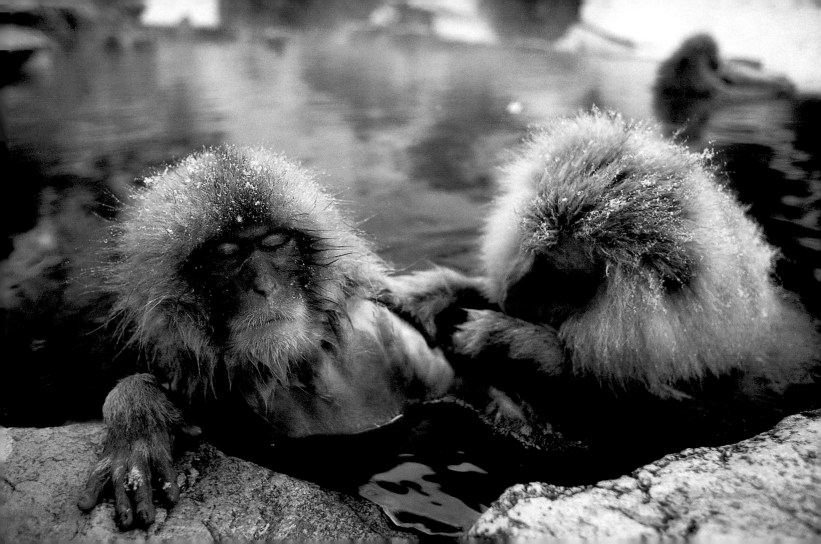

Make a shopping list.

We are easily tempted by things we 'want', but rarely stop to ask ourselves what we 'need'. As a result much of what we buy is surplus to our needs. Shop displays are designed to tempt us to buy what we don't need, without us realising it—and we waste around 30% of the food we buy in the United Kingdom because we don't eat it before it goes bad.

We only have one earth. Do not allow yourself to be trapped into overconsumption; make a shopping list before you go out, and keep to it. You won't forget anything, and you will avoid impulse purchases that you don't need, which can account for up to 70% of what you buy.

Chrysocolla, France

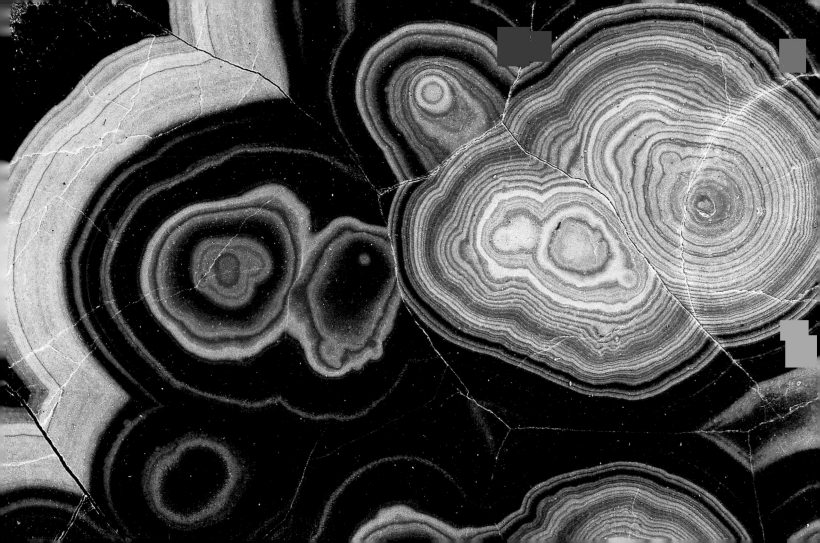

Use your library.

Tropical rain forests are being destroyed at the rate of 22 million hectares a year. Every second a tract of rain forest the size of a football field disappears from this planet in order to provide space for cattle or crops, or to provide wood for paper products and furniture. World wood consumption is expected to rise by 58% over the next 20 years. In some tropical forests, a single tree can be home to up to 100 species. What will be left of this biological wealth?

A typical paperback book uses 3 kilograms of carbon dioxide before it reaches a reader. Even if you can afford it, rather than buying novels and other books new, subscribe to your local library. Libraries are precious civic spaces in which everyone should participate.

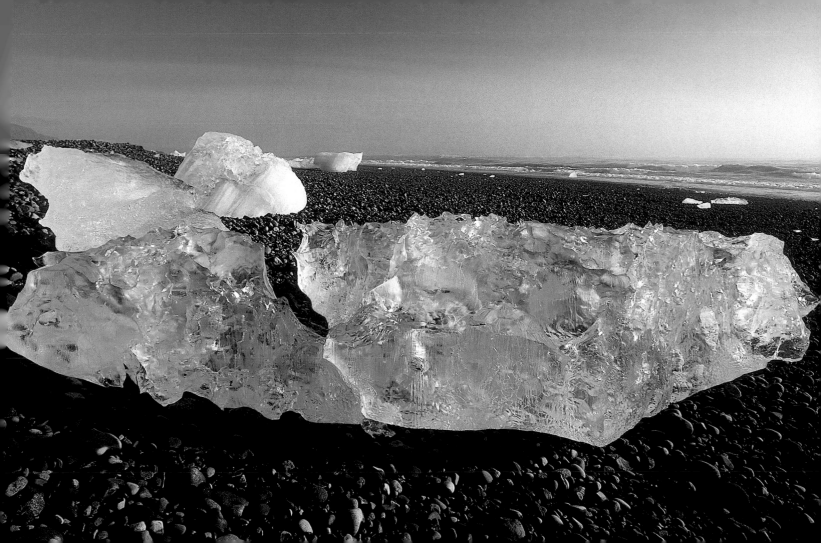

Support environmentally conscious films.

In 2005, Participant Productions, a newly formed film company dedicated to exploring and inspiring social change through filmmaking, released *Syriana.* This drama about the politics of the oil industry went on to earn several major awards. Participant and likeminded companies strive to not only provide socially compelling entertainment, but to do so while doing their part to reduce their impact on the environment. Research has shown that along with its blockbusters, California's film and television industry produces nearly 8.5 million tonnes of carbon dioxide each year. *Syriana* and fellow Participant film *An Inconvenient Truth* were both carbon-neutral productions.

Support filmmakers who are committed to social change and production companies that address the toll moviemaking takes on the environment. If the cinemas in your community don't play such films, arrange DVD screenings at schools or community centres and donate the DVD to your local library.

Baobabs, Madagascar

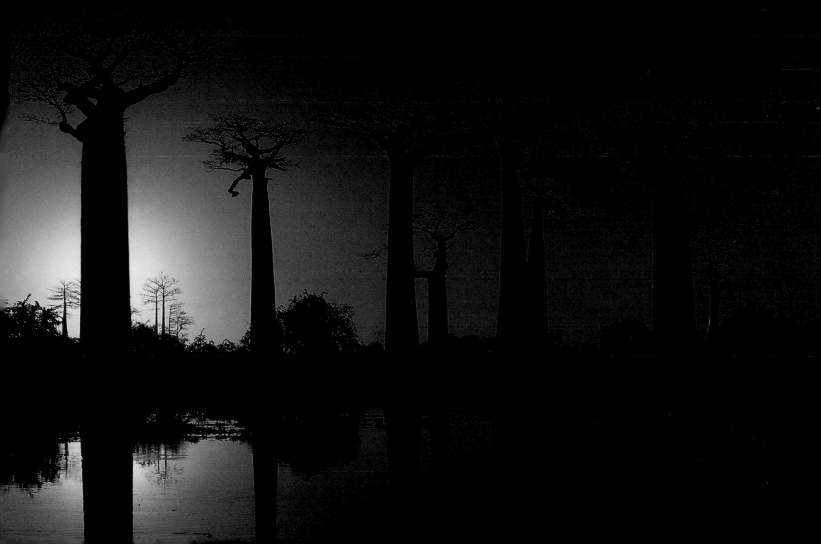

When you eat out, eat in.

In the space of about 30 years the volume of waste generated by household packaging has risen fivefold, and certain materials such as plastic, by as much as 50 times. In the United Kingdom, 3.2 million tonnes of the 26 million tonnes of household waste produced annually comes from packaging. Eleven percent of this waste is plastic of which 40% comes from the 15 million plastic bottles we use every day. Less than 3% of these plastic bottles get recycled. Also, an estimated 25 million tonnes of litter is strewn on the streets every year, almost all from food and drink packaging.

When you stop for lunch during work avoid buying take-away food, which produces large quantities of waste, in particular, nonrecyclable plastic. Take the time to sit down and eat your food at the restaurant.

Green turtle, Australia

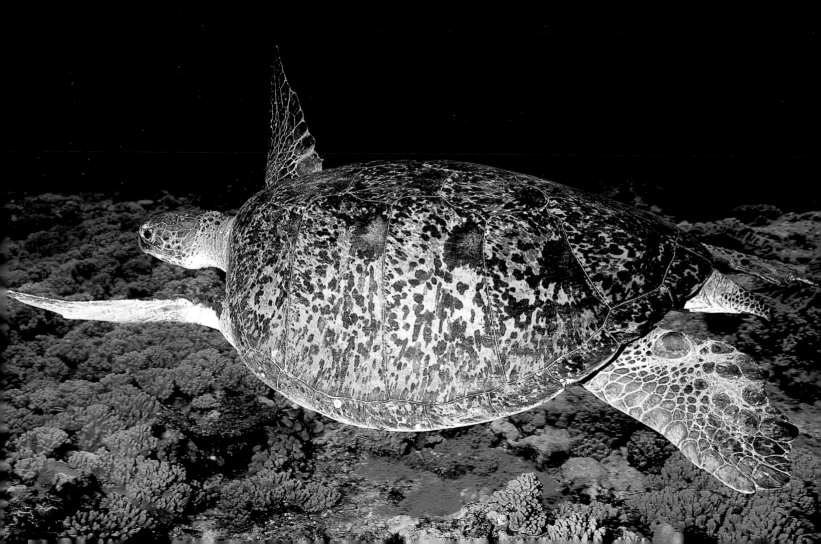

Use nontoxic cleaning products.

The average European household uses and stores a large number of hazardous chemicals in the garage, in cupboards, and under sinks. In the local supermarket we can buy acids, phenols, oil derivatives, corrosive solutions, chlorine, and a whole arsenal of toxic products that are supposedly necessary, according to advertising, to keep our homes clean. Many of these products contain carcinogens, reproductive toxins, and endocrine disrupting chemicals, which can cause long-term or delayed health effects.

Choose environmentally friendly and biodegradable household cleaning products, which do not contain the most dangerous substances or petroleum, which is a nonrenewable resource. Vinegar and baking soda are two simple household substances that make very effective cleaners.

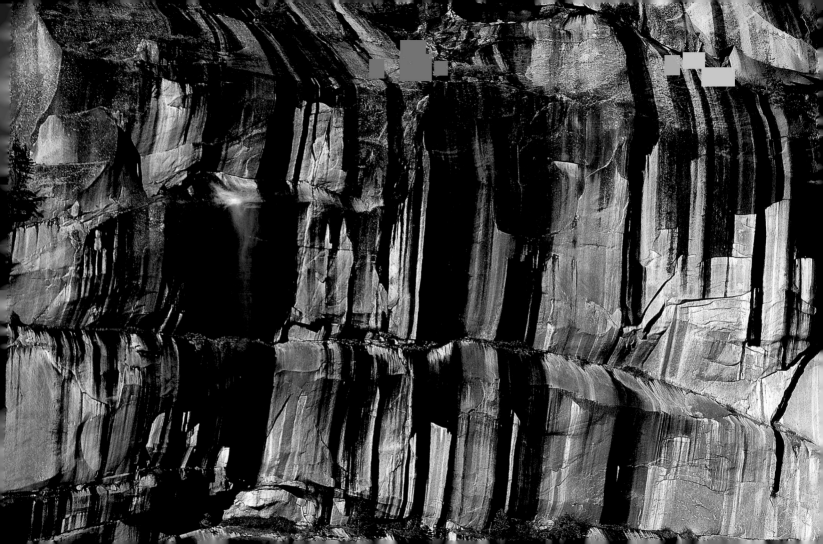

Practice 'voluntourism'.

Whether guarding turtles laying their eggs on Mayotte; helping to protect wolves in Romania, iguanas in Honduras, or griffon vultures in Israel; or assisting scientists in the conservation of endangered primates in Kenya, the possibilities for volunteering for environmental work are endless. Helping in this way enables you to understand a country by living as local people do, while working for the protection of flora and fauna, or habitats and furthering sustainability projects.

Are you looking for a way to spend your next holiday by doing something both original and useful? Consider planning a trip with a charity or NGO that offers short-term volunteer-based holidays; beyond wildlife conservation efforts, you could help build solar power arrays in an African village or teach basic computer skills to a community in Brazil. Or look closer to home and save the carbon emissions from flying — many national charities offer short breaks where you can help with a nature reserve, heritage project, or community initiative.

Ruwenzori Mountains, Uganda

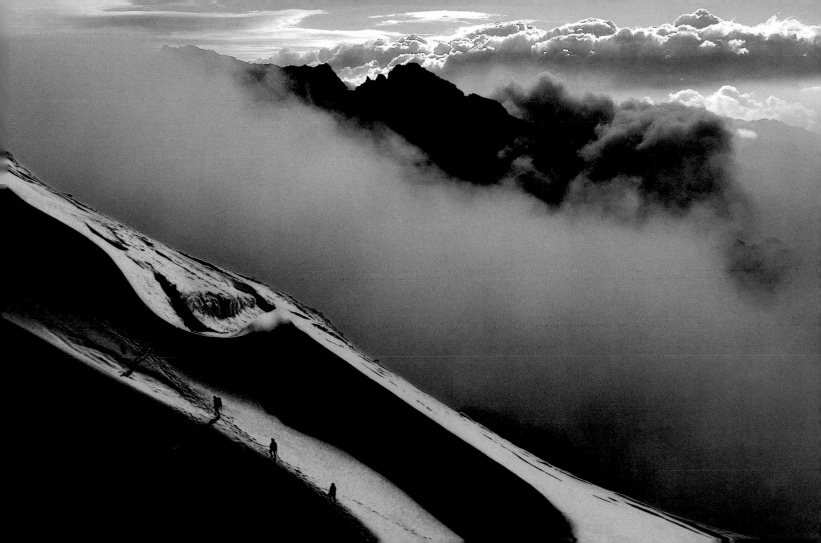

Do not buy foods containing genetically modified organisms.

Humans have mastered technologies that enable them to modify the genes of plants and animals directly, producing genetically modified organisms (GMOs). These transgenic plants—maize, cotton, and soy, for example—are immune to insects and diseases, resistant to drought, and richer in vitamins. Pro-GM groups claim that their products are more efficient and environmentally friendly; anti-GM groups argue that too little is known about the effect of GM foods on the environment, and that multinational biotech groups are the only people who stand to gain. Currently, 5 companies control all of the genetically engineered crops in the world, with Monsanto producing 90% of all genetically modified crops.

Until more is known of the effects of GM foods on society and the environment, try to limit the amount that you buy. Look for 'No GM' or 'GM-Free' labels.

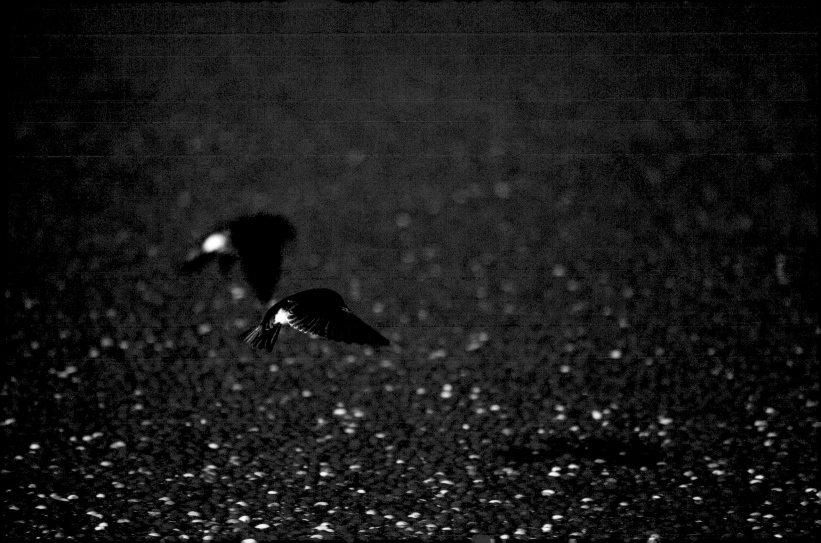

Take the train rather than the plane.

Each year, aviation generates as much carbon dioxide as all the human activity in Africa. Carbon-dioxide emissions are not the only environmental concern. Deicing airplane wings creates 750 million to 2.2 billion litres of wastewater each year.

Avoid travelling by plane for journeys less than 400 kilometres. The European train network is fast, cheap and fun — you can take sleeper trains overnight to go skiing, or for weekend city breaks, for less than the cost of a flight and hotel, and without the hassle of airports.

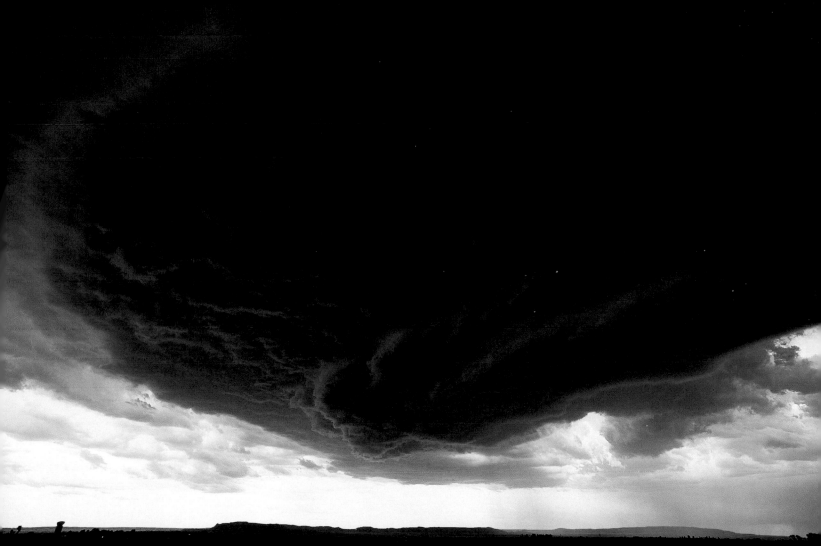

Hire a bike, not a car.

For getting around town, the bicycle has some unique advantages: It is clean, silent, compact, fast, and economical. Many European cities have extensive bike-sharing networks where, for a low fee, subscribers receive a swipe card that gives them access to bicycle stations all over the city; once they've finished their ride they can return the bikes to any designated point. Most recently, Paris started a program that boasts 20,000 bikes. In the first month of the program it was reported that each of the bikes was being used an average of 6 times per day. And many holiday destinations offer cycle hire for tourists.

Next time you think of hiring a car on holiday, think about a bike instead — it's cleaner, greener, and gets you fit, too.

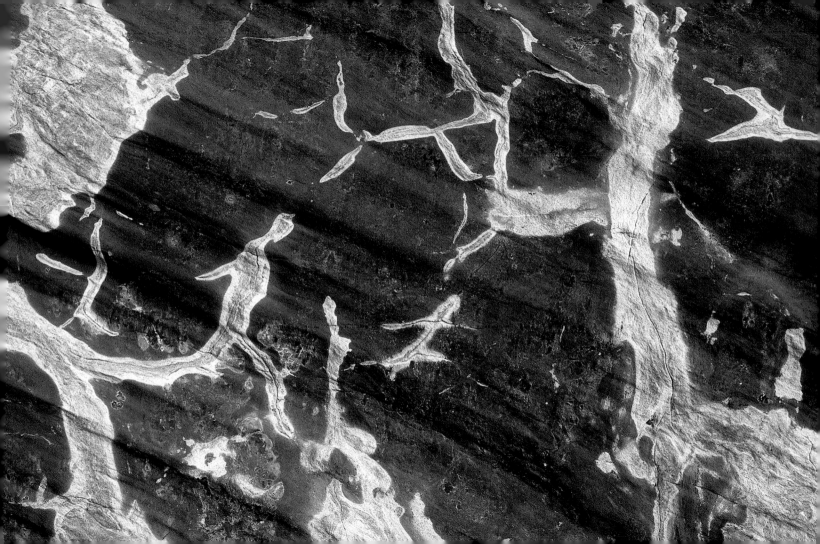

Be careful where you smoke.

In 2007 a wildfire destroyed more than 270,000 hectares of farmland, homes, and protected forests in Greece. Several of the series of wildfires were started by humans. One out of every 10 wildfires is caused by a careless smoker. In persistent hot and dry weather (which has increased greatly in many regions of the world), a simple brush fire can quickly grow into a major disaster that burns for days, destroys habitats and homes, and costs billions in resources.

Do not smoke when walking in woods, forests, or dry grasslands, and never throw cigarette butts out of your car window, even if you think you have stubbed them out. Even if you think it isn't dry enough to cause a fire, cigarette butts are not biodegradable, contain toxins, and are easily swallowed by wild animals.

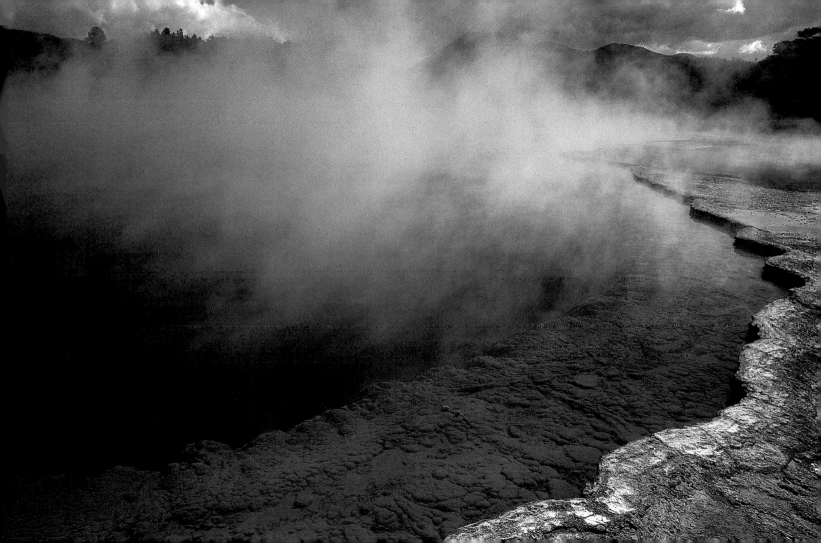

Cool off without resorting to air-conditioning.

In the United Kingdom and Europe, the use of air-conditioning is on the rise, despite our generally temperate climate. Yet artificially cooling air is one of the most energy intensive systems you can use—and although our climate may be getting hotter as a result of global warming, there are many simpler and more energy efficient ways of keeping cool.

A ceiling fan uses one-tenth of the energy of an air-conditioning unit; window shades, blinds, shutters, and opening windows to circulate air costs no energy at all. Having trees around your home can reduce air-conditioning use so much it can cut cooling-related energy costs by up to 75%. Consider carefully before having air-conditioning installed; it can double your electricity bill.

Dunes, Algeria

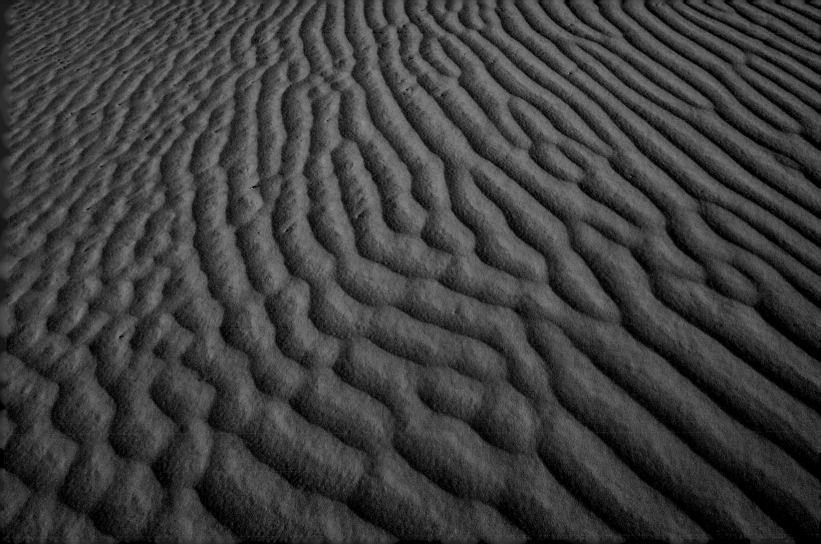

Learn to spot 'greenwashing'.

Now that eco-chic has become profitable, some manufacturers are cashing in on consumers' desire for green goods by 'greenwashing'—spinning unsustainable products as eco-friendly. The worst offenders, at least when it comes to consumer goods, are makers of cars, cosmetics, electronics, and cleaning supplies. Since even the oil companies are becoming quite adept at presenting themselves as part of the solution, consumers have to be vigilant when sifting through the mountain of available green products.

Ask yourself the following questions: Is there a trade-off that negates the so-called positive effects of the environmental element the product is touting? Is the language too vague? 'Earth-friendly' and 'eco-friendly' mean virtually nothing unless those claims are spelled out by the company and backed up by third-party certification. Is 'eco' even being used correctly? Many tourism programmes claim to be 'eco' simply because they operate out in the wilderness, but in actuality they've taken no measures to ensure that they minimize their impact on the environment. Similarly, products may be mislabelled 'eco' if they contain any natural ingredients.

Pink flamingoes, Kenya

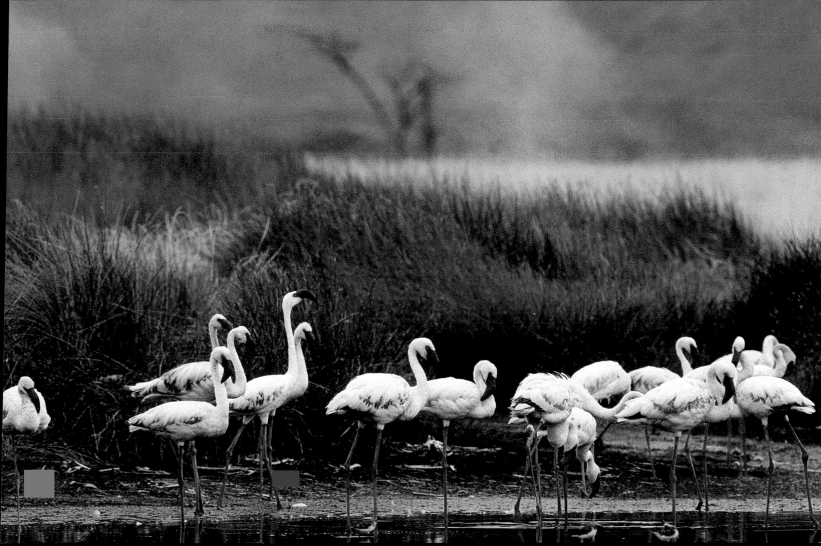

Recycle your old fridge.

A 3.2 kilometre-deep ice core sample taken from Antarctica has shown that the levels of heat-trapping greenhouse gases are higher now than at any time in the last 420,000 years. The heat these gases trap will cause sea levels to rise by about 90 centimetres, among other things. The agents responsible include coolant gases such as Freon (a trade name of the infamous CFCs, or chlorofluorocarbons), which are contained in the cooling circuits of old refrigerators, freezers, and air-conditioners. The formidable greenhouse gases are released into the atmosphere when those appliances leak, or are dumped.

More than 3 million domestic refrigeration (fridges, fridge-freezers, and freezers) units are disposed of in the United Kingdom each year. Take your old fridge to a facility where it will be dealt with properly, or ask your local authority recycling department how to dispose of it correctly.

Namib Desert, Namibia

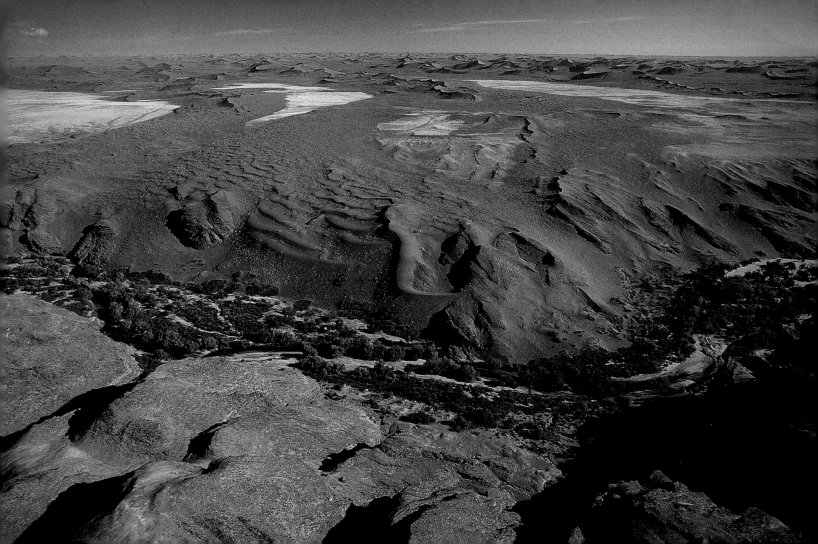

Say 'no' to individual portion packs.

Each person in the United Kingdom generates about 512 kilograms of rubbish every year. By the end of our lifetimes, we will have each created about 40 tonnes of rubbish. The fashion for prepackaged miniportions — of cheese, yoghurt, biscuits, and snacks — is no more than a marketing strategy. Take the time to create your own portions.

Stop buying preportioned food and drink for children's meals or mid-morning snacks. Instead, you can buy in bulk and invest in reusable plastic containers and drinking bottles. And make your children more aware of the waste in packaging by explaining why you've changed.

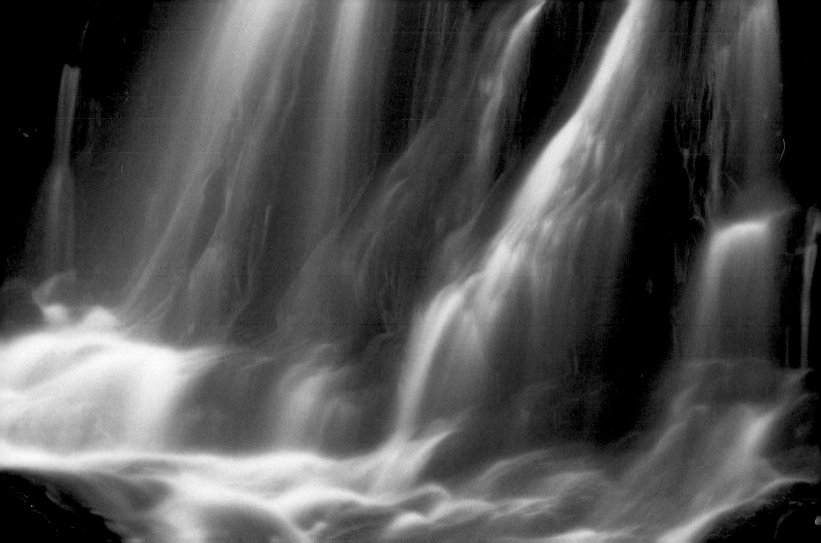

Buy in bulk when possible.

For every black bag of rubbish placed on the pavement, the equivalent of 71 bags of waste are created in the course of the production, transportation, and industrial processes used to convert raw materials into finished products and their packaging.

Limiting the amount of waste for disposal inevitably involves reducing the volume of packaging. For cheese, ham, pulses, and rice, buy food in bulk, by weight, or cut to your needs, rather than in prepackaged sizes. This also benefits your kitchen, since you will be able to find ingredients for your next meal instead of heading for the store every time you prepare a meal.

Swans, Japan

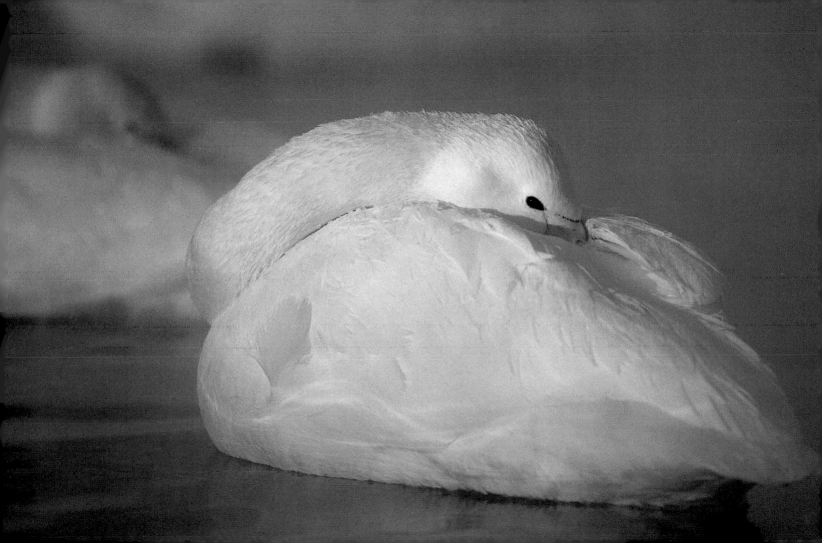

Eat fruits and vegetables in season.

How do shops obtain fruits and vegetables out of season? Most produce is from specially grown crops (using soil-less cultivation or heated greenhouses) that use large amounts of water, energy, and raw materials or are from distant countries where the climate is more favourable. In the latter case, transporting this produce uses considerable amounts of energy (especially if the produce travels by air), increases pollution, and contributes to climate change. A meal from a conventional supermarket uses 4 to 17 times more oil for transport than the same meal using local ingredients.

Eat fruit and vegetables in season: They are higher quality, healthier, and taste better, and their cultivation has far less impact on the environment.

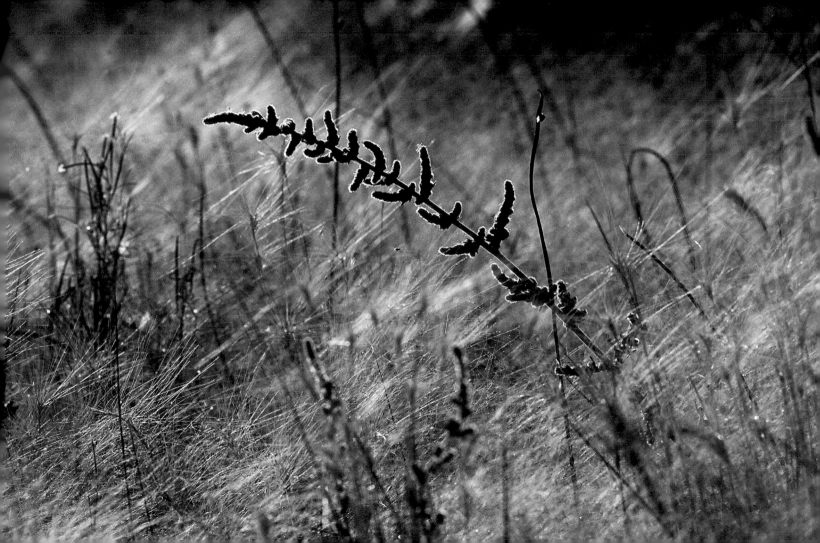

Do not drive your car on very hot days.

Poor air quality in many European cities is caused by polluting gases, such as tropospheric ozone, the main ingredient of photochemical smog, which can cause breathing difficulties. It is formed at ground level from car exhaust gases reacting under sunlight and heat, so it gets much worse when the weather is warm.

On very hot days, drive more slowly. Or, better yet, leave the car in the garage on most days. Invest the money you save in maintaining your bicycle or buying a nice pair of running shoes.

Cactus flower, Mexico

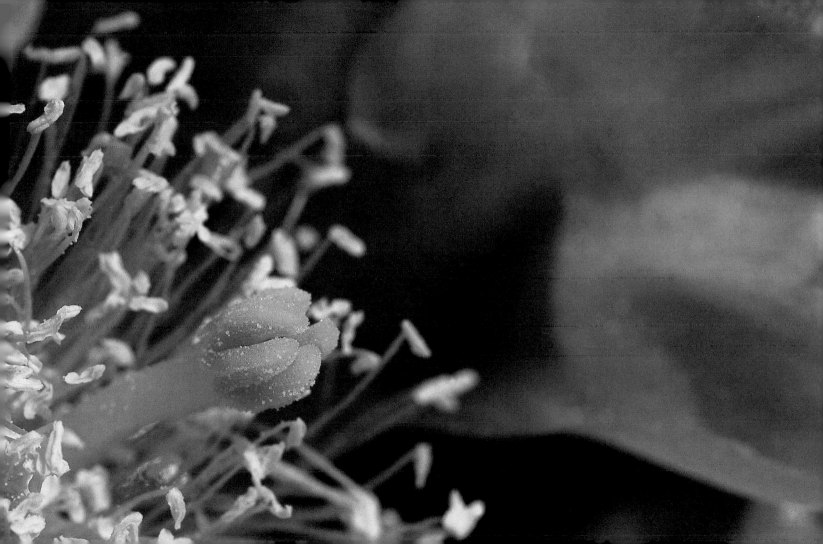

Mow the lawn at reasonable times.

If you need to do something noisy at home, think of your neighbours first. A drill can produce between 90 and 100 decibels; the threshold of discomfort is 60 decibels.

We all contribute to the audible environment. Be aware of the time of day that you run a lawn mower, or go back to using a manual mower. Rake leaves instead of investing in a leaf blower. Enjoy the time in your garden with the sounds of birds and the wind in the leaves, not your machinery.

Cherry trees in bloom, Japan

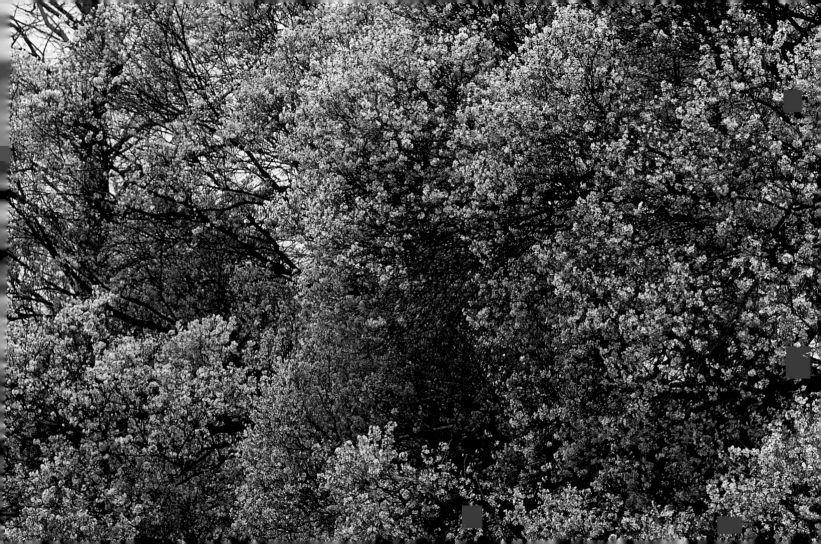

Help to clean up a river.

Local nature conservation organisations regularly organise river cleanup operations. These involve removing the waste that pollutes a watercourse and clearing riverbanks of the detritus of human life. Excessively dense vegetation creates a closed habitat that does not favour aquatic life. This maintenance and clearing is beneficial even if the water is not polluted, because it preserves the ecosystem and its biodiversity.

These operations always need volunteers. Do not be afraid to join one: It is an opportunity to learn more about the stream, its banks, and the fauna and flora that live there.

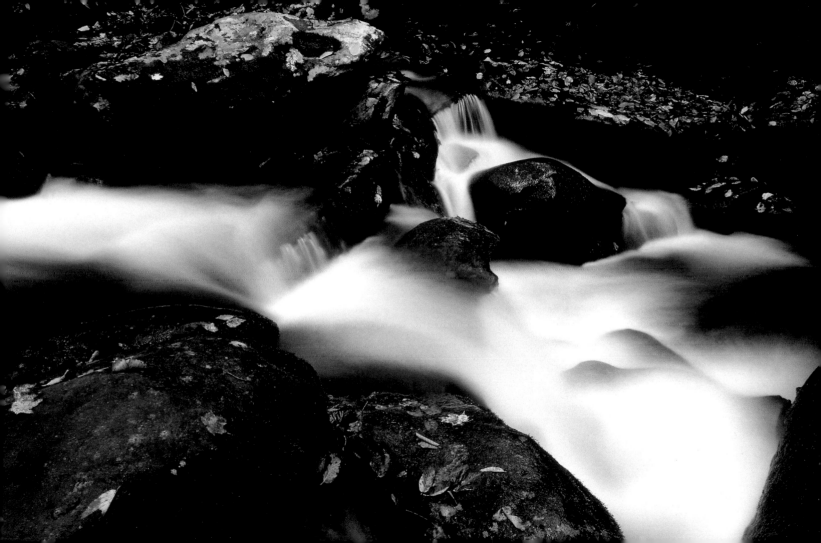

Start a community garden.

Whatever the purpose of a community garden—whether to grow flowers or food for sale or for charity, to beautify and reduce pollution in urban areas, or to offer pleasant waiting areas near institutional buildings like hospitals—getting involved with one in your town will help you connect with your neighbours, get outside, and learn about local plants and produce.

Community gardens and city farms can raise property values, reduce crime, and provide outdoor classrooms for local schools. Contact the Federation of City Farms & Community Gardens in the United Kingdom as they can give advice on how to get involved or even create a new garden. If gardens already exist in your neighbourhood, find out if they need volunteers and sign up; and if they are threatened—even established and well-known urban gardens get destroyed by developers—find out how you can advocate for them.

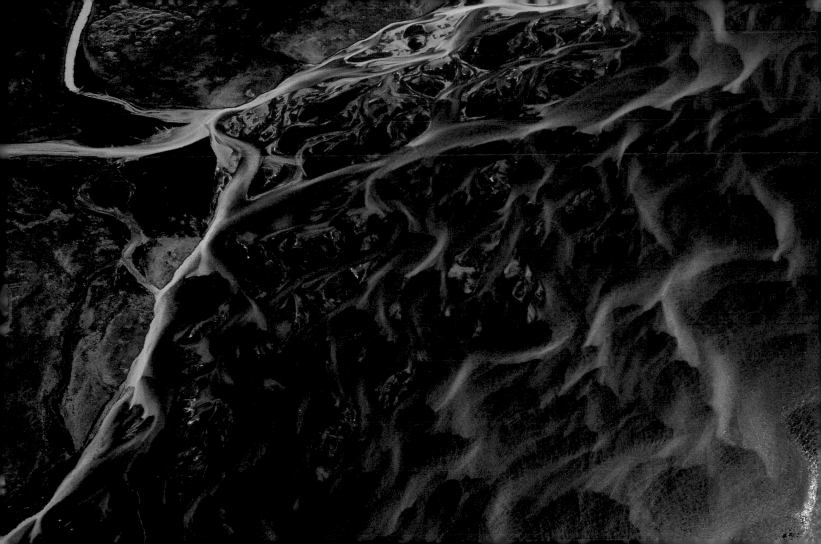

Think before you DIY.

Standard chipboard and plywood often contain formaldehyde, a chemical that can aggravate or even cause respiratory ailments along with a slew of other medical conditions. Laminates may prevent some formaldehyde gases from escaping particleboard furniture, but they can't contain them all.

Look for formaldehyde-free boards instead of plywood — such products are often made from recycled wood or plant fibre waste. The Forest Stewardship Council (FSC) certifies and catalogues formaldehyde-free pressed-wood products. Buying furniture from hardwoods that have been sustainably harvested is always a good way to go.

Mehedjibat *erg* (sand desert), Algeria

Help preserve our coastlines.

The world's oceans play an important role in counteracting the greenhouse effect: They are the biggest producer of oxygen (via plankton) and the biggest carbon sink (carbon is dissolved in water) on the planet. Of the 6.3 billion metric tonnes of carbon dioxide produced by human activity every year, the seas absorb 1.8 billion. They also interact with the atmosphere, a process that governs currents, winds, clouds, and climate. Rich in fish, geological resources (oil, and minerals at great depths), and energy (ocean currents and tides), as long as the seas are in good health they are utterly vital to human beings.

If you live near the sea, contact a local charity to become a volunteer and help monitor the health of our coasts. Activities may include collecting water samples, organising beach cleanups, or monitoring the ecologies and wildlife that exist at the water's edge.

Cuttlefish, Australia

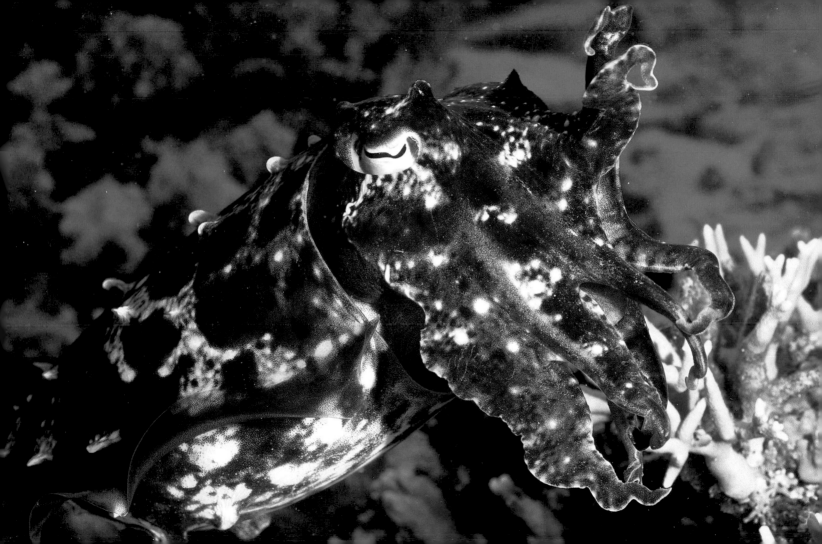

Choose sustainable school supplies.

The return to school in the autumn provides an opportunity to choose sustainable items for your children. More than half of a family's substantial budget for school supplies at the beginning of the school year consists of paper products. Make sure all of those notebooks contain a high percentage of recycled paper.

Choose pencil sharpeners and rulers in metal or wood (not coloured or varnished). These will last longer and produce less pollution than their plastic equivalents. Buy pencils made from 100% recycled materials and refillable pens. Choose a solar-powered calculator rather than a battery-powered one. Above all, sift through last year's stationery supplies and reuse as much as possible to avoid buying the same reusable product again. Encourage your child to trade supplies with friends to learn the habit of reuse.

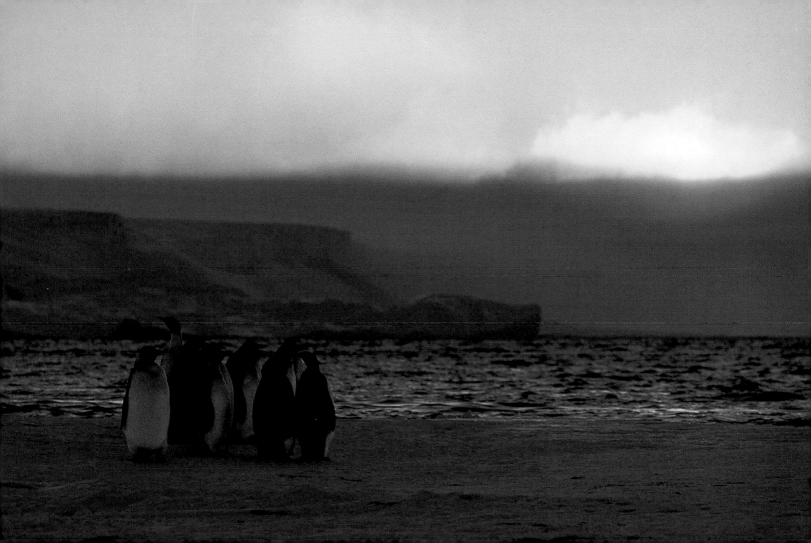

Avoid burning fuel for fun.

Some leisure activities seem far from appealing in light of their impact on the environment and landscape. These include off-road driving, hunting, golfing (whose landscaping demands excessive fertilizer and watering), and skiing, the infrastructure of which permanently blots the landscape.

We burn enough oil in our everyday activities — when you are relaxing, try not to burn more. And if you do take part, avoid noisy motorized activities (such as jet skis, 4 x 4 vehicles, trail bikes, and snowmobiles) that disturb plants and animals outside the areas set aside for them. Never drive an off-road vehicle on a beach, in a marsh, or anywhere near birds' nests.

Clouds, United States

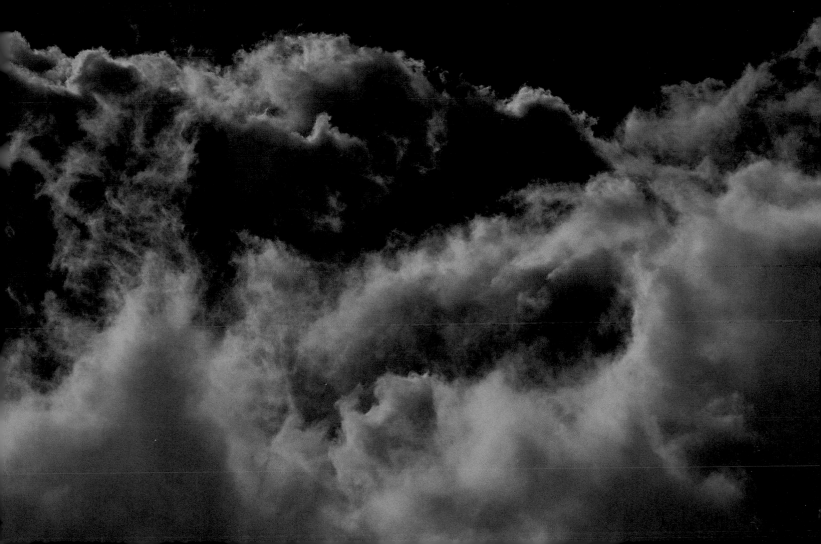

Choose reusable cleaning cloths.

Most single-use cloths are made from nonbiodegradable synthetics and soaked in toxic cleaning agents. Although paper towels come in recycled form and are easily recyclable or compostable, they still require resources to create and their manufacture emits pollution.

Replace single-use, prepackaged wipes and paper towels with a few cloth towels. Microfibre wipes that are handy for cleaning and polishing can be washed and reused hundreds of times and come in organic, biodegradable styles. Biodegradable scouring pads made from a variety of materials like palm fibres or fine-grit sandpaper are less abrasive than steel wool and contain no detergents or plastics.

Grasses, Iceland

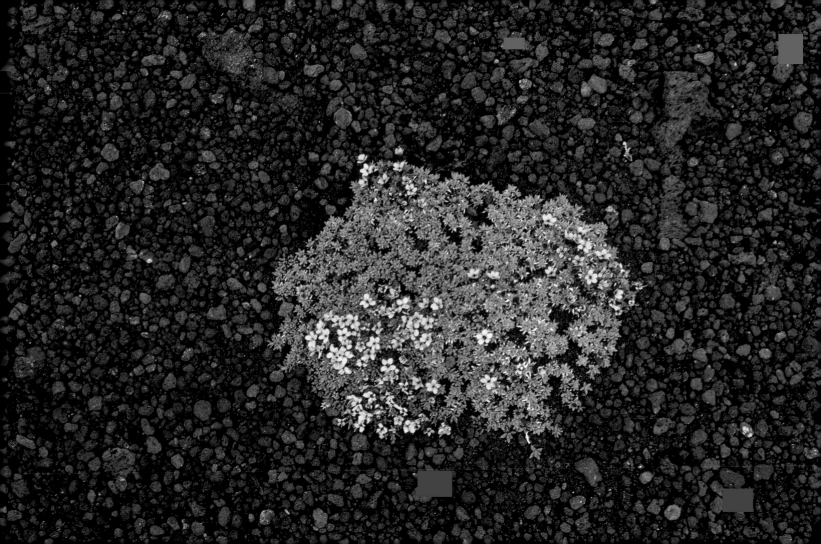

Choose furniture made of SmartWood or FSC-certified wood.

During the last century, half the world's tropical forests disappeared. Tropical forest uses are all around us — from wood furniture, to insulation, rope, and medicine. Indonesia loses 2.1 million hectares of forest each year and 75% of its wood products are harvested illegally. When you buy FSC- (Forest Stewardship Council) or SmartWood-certified products, you can be sure that they come from a sustainable, managed forest where strict environmental, social, and economic standards are observed and that they have not contributed to the worldwide plundering of tropical forests.

Before buying any piece of furniture, ask where the materials come from, especially where exotic woods are concerned: Mahogany, teak, ipe, and ebony are examples of popular exotic wood types. By buying furniture made from sustainable, local timber, you will be supporting the local economy in a place where it can be properly controlled.

Icebergs, Greenland

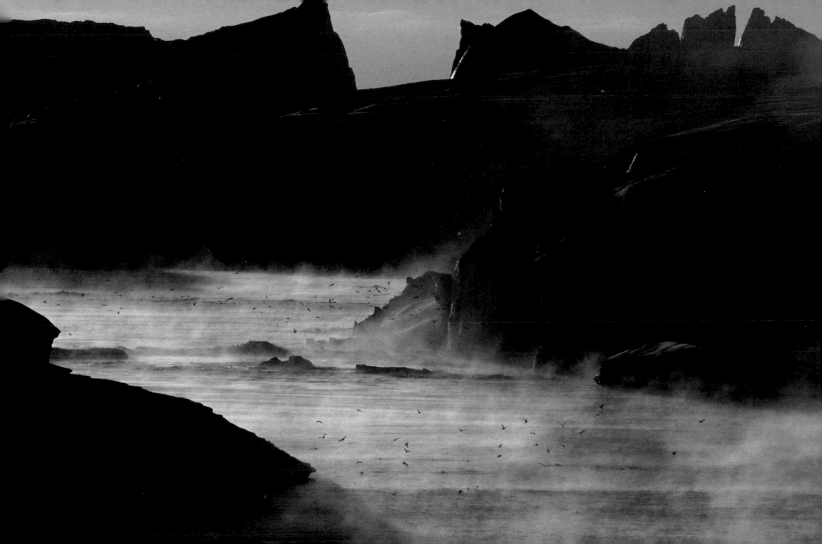

Buy fair-trade coffee.

Fair trade endeavours to establish equitable commercial relations between rich and poor countries so that underprivileged workers and farmers can live and work with dignity. Workers on conventional farms must often meet harvesting quotas in order to receive a daily wage, forcing them to enlist their families to help them make their quota. Technically, their children are not employees and thus are not protected by any laws. Fair-trade coffee sets a minimum fair price for coffee, meaning that workers' earnings are unaffected by market fluctuations, thus eliminating the need for unfair quotas. In addition, fair-trade coffee is usually grown on small farms that cultivate under the rain forest canopy and without the use of pesticides.

More than 100 brands of fair-trade coffee are now available in more than 35,000 markets worldwide. Make a commitment to only buy fair-trade coffee.

Lake Titicaca, Bolivia

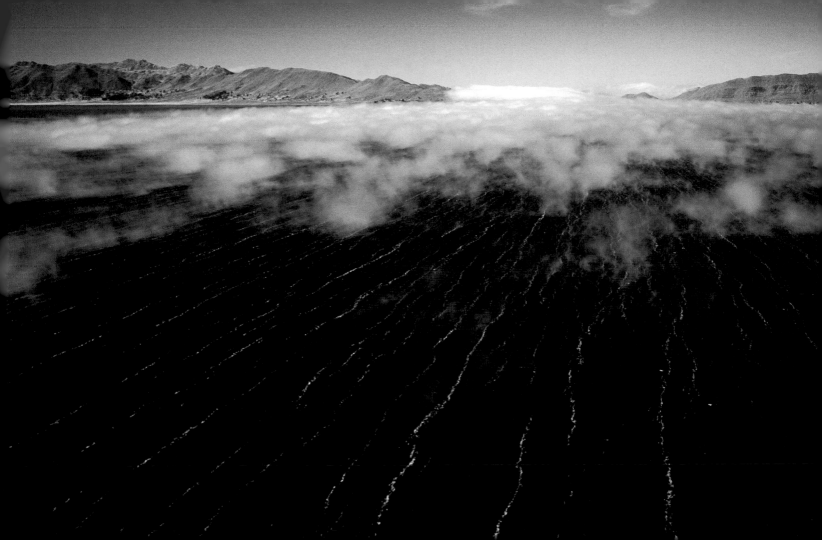

Cook with gas rather than electricity.

The 1,500 researchers of the United Nations Intergovernmental Panel on Climate Change (IPCC) set up jointly by the UN Environment Program (UNEP) and the World Meteorological Organization now agree that human activity is affecting the world's climate: Every year, human beings emit more than 27 billion metric tonnes of greenhouse gases as they meet their energy needs in transportation, heating, air-conditioning, agriculture, industry, and so forth.

We should be equally aware of this when dealing with the little, day-to-day things in life. On average, a gas cooker uses half the energy of an electric cooker, as long as the burners are regularly cleaned. A clogged burner can use up to 10% more energy than a clean one.

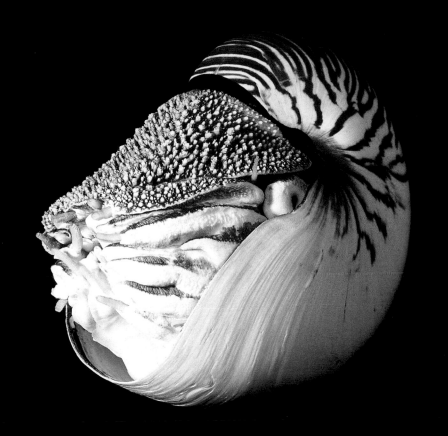

When travelling, take your polluting waste home with you.

In many developing countries you may visit, waste is not collected, disposed of, and treated in safe or environmentally responsible ways. Often such countries cannot afford to establish the necessary infrastructure, and have huge problems with disease, pollution, and contamination of soils and drinking water as a result.

Take your most polluting waste, such as batteries and plastic bags, home in your luggage, so that they can be disposed of properly when you return. And try not to buy excessively packaged products when abroad, to avoid increasing their waste problems.

Detail of scorpion fish, Australia

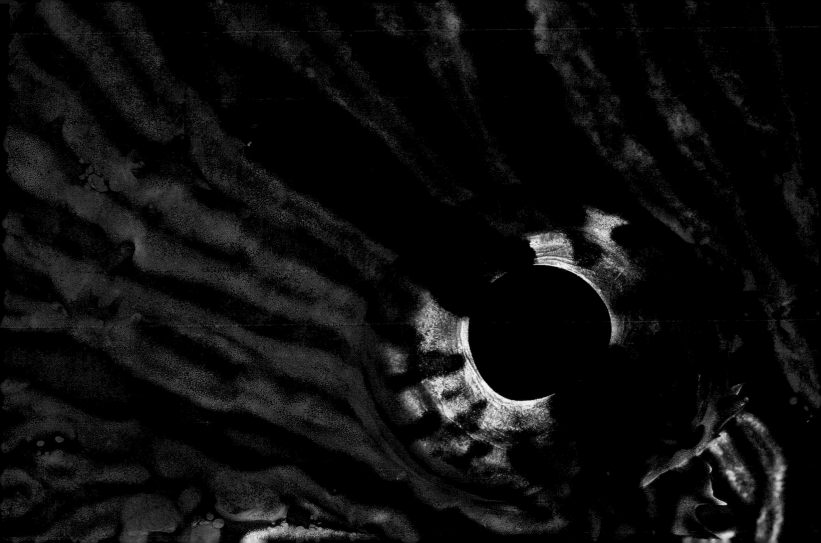

Wear less makeup.

Cosmetics often contain potentially harmful ingredients like formaldehyde, phthalates, and lead acetate—and many of them contain petroleum derivatives as well. The average woman is exposed to up to 200 chemicals through daily use of makeup and skin products. Makeup is also highly disposable, as trends change from season to season and some products—like mascara, which goes bad after about 4 months—have very short shelf lives. Most discarded makeup ends up in landfills or incinerators, where their toxic components can contaminate groundwater or the air.

The simplest beauty regime is the best one for both you and the environment. When it's time to throw away old cosmetics check with manufacturers to see if they accept old containers for recycling. Since 2004 the EU Cosmetics Directive bans specific toxic chemicals in cosmetic and personal care products sold in the European Union and requires that all companies reformulate their products for the European Union market.

Coral reef, Australia

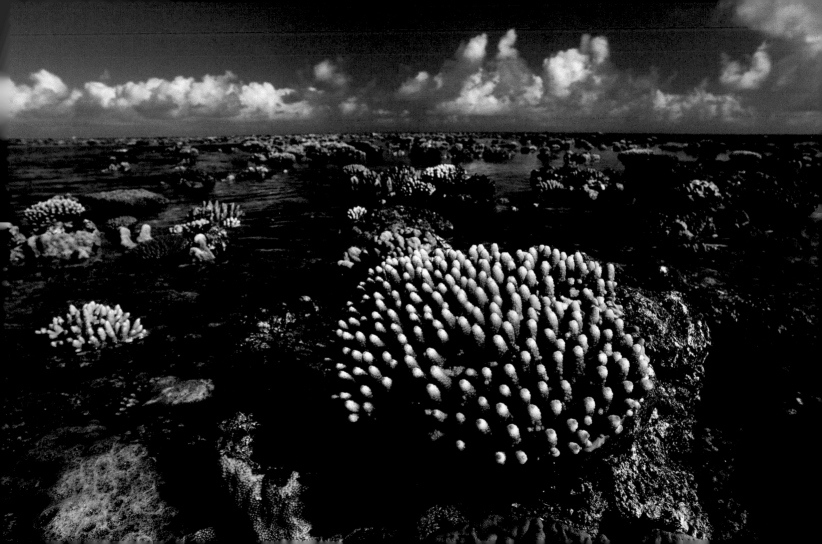

Buy refillable products.

A quarter of the household waste generated in the United Kingdom is packaging. Plastic accounts for 53% of all goods that are packaged. By definition packaging is disposable—you open the package, remove the product, and discard the container.

Reducing packaging enables raw materials to be saved, pollution to be reduced, and needless transportation to be avoided. To cut the volumes of single-use packaging choose refillable products—soap, liquid detergent containers, coffee cans, rechargeable batteries, pens, and so forth.

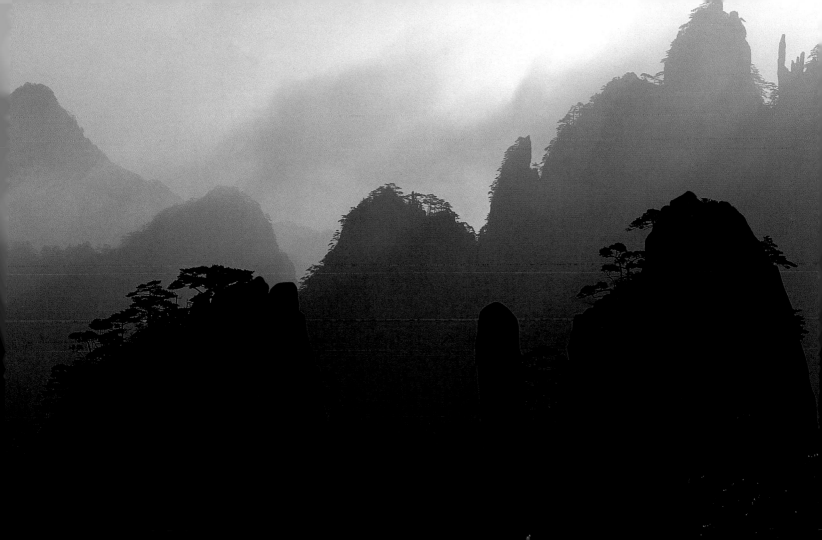

Read and know your poultry labels.

By choosing the breeds that produce the highest yields, farmers have succeeded in reducing the average time it takes to raise a 2 kg chicken from 84 days in 1950 to 45 days today. Living conditions for these animals are grim, and their controlled grain-heavy diets (as opposed to a natural diet that would include foraged plants and insects) lead to nutrient deficits in the meat and eggs we consume. Free-range and organic chicken and eggs have become widely available as an alternative. In the United Kingdom there is a legal definition for using the label 'free-range', which requires that hens have access to an outside area, and stipulates a maximum number of hens per meters squared. This applies to 'free-range' eggs as well. Organic certification stipulates that organic feed is used, antibiotics and hormones are not added, and adequate freedom of movement is provided. The Soil Association organic symbol is the United Kingdom's main certification mark, and appears on approximately 70% of organic food produced in the United Kingdom.

Choose free-range or organic chicken to help stamp out battery farming. And get to know your producers: Buy directly from small, local farms that meet the national standards.

Maple, United States

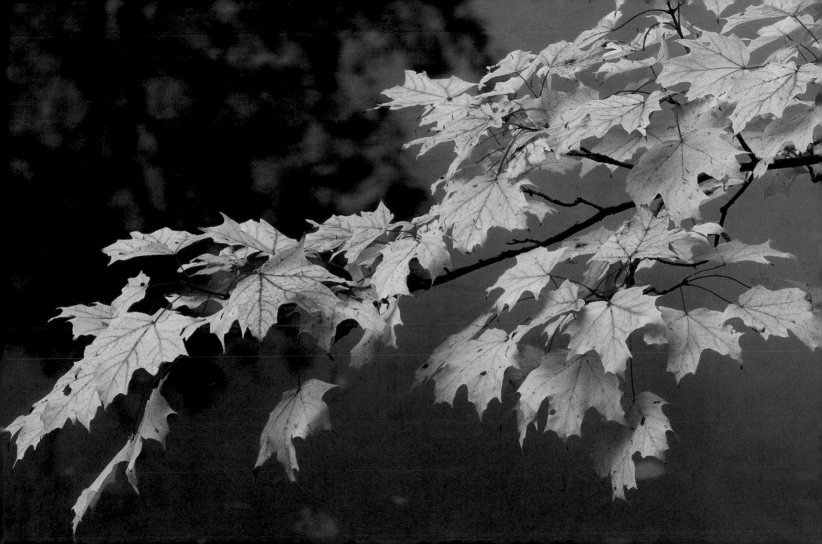

Know which companies are actually 'all natural'.

It's easier than ever to find 'all natural' products touting organic ingredients on supermarket shelves. However, big conglomerates are increasingly buying up former family-owned businesses, a fact that is often not advertised on the packaging. Though the quality may continue to be high despite their new affiliations, you have to ask yourself if you want to support their parent companies, which also manufacture many products that are harmful to the environment or act in unethical ways. In addition, many food conglomerates and supermarket chains have created their own organic brands and ranges while still supporting intensive agriculture and other energy-intensive processes.

When buying so-called organic or all natural products look closely at the label. Some products may be exactly what they claim to be while others may only include a few organic ingredients and a slew of unwanted others. Trace your favourite brands back to their parent companies so you know exactly who is making your whole-grain cereal or organic yoghurt.

Altiplano, Bolivia

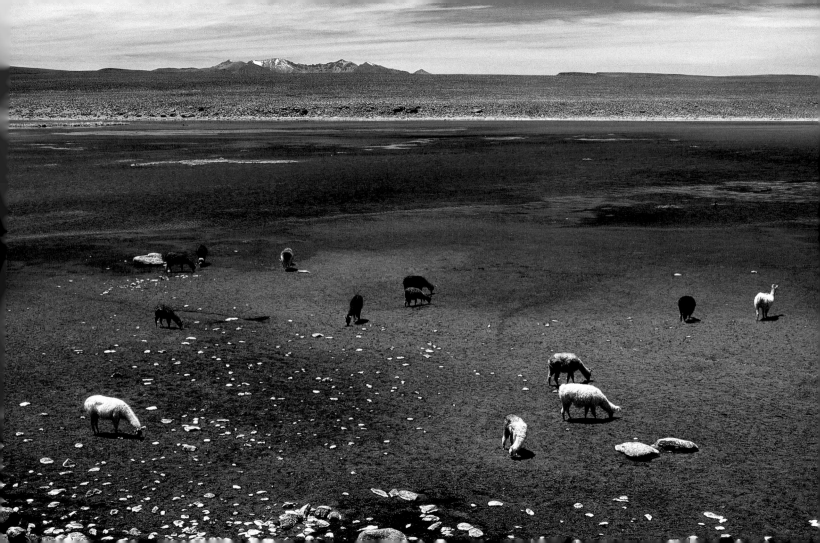

Give a struggling entrepreneur a small business loan.

Microfinance is the antithesis of writing anonymous checks to large NGOs. Through a third-party nonprofit organisation you can provide a loan to help an underserved person in a developing nation start a business or grow a current one. (The recipients often lack access to banks and traditional lending schemes.) Organisations like Kiva provide profiles of entrepreneurs in need; you choose which business receives your loan. Requests rarely exceed £500, but you can give partial loans, and as the sums are repaid, so are you.

Microfinance fosters positive connections between donors and recipients: You know exactly where your money goes and get regular updates as real people transform their businesses and their lives. And because recipients must usually present cohesive business plans before being able to request loans, the system ensures self-sufficiency.

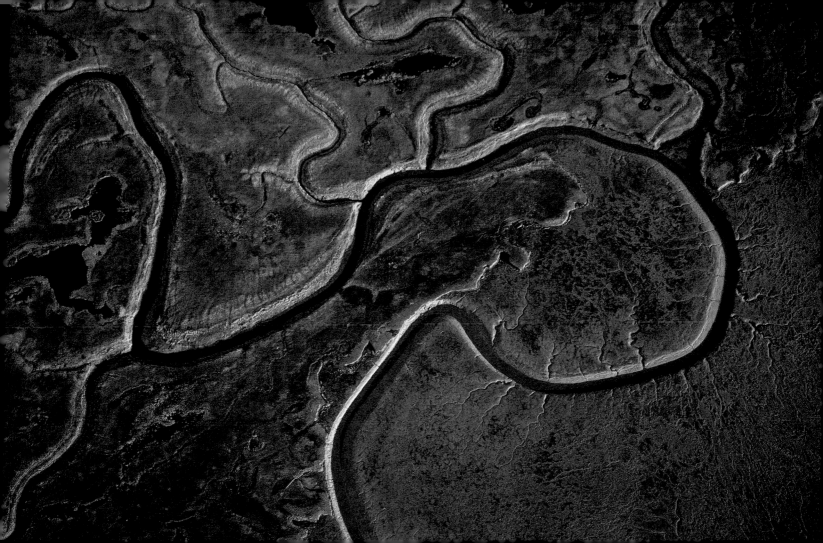

Eat local food on holiday.

One study of loss of tourism revenue in Thailand estimated that 70% of the money spent by tourists eventually left the country through hotel chains, tour operators, airlines, and the import of foods and drinks. To make sure that your money stays in the local economy, it is best to choose small, local hotels, local transport, and services that earn money for local people, such as guides, cooks, mule drivers, porters, and domestic servants.

When you are thousands of miles from home, don't go for the familiar fast-food brand names or search for tastes of home on the menu. Those tasteless apples that travelled halfway around the planet, producing pollution in the process, will never be as good as the local mangos. Try local specialities, fruits, and vegetables, and discover new dishes in the process.

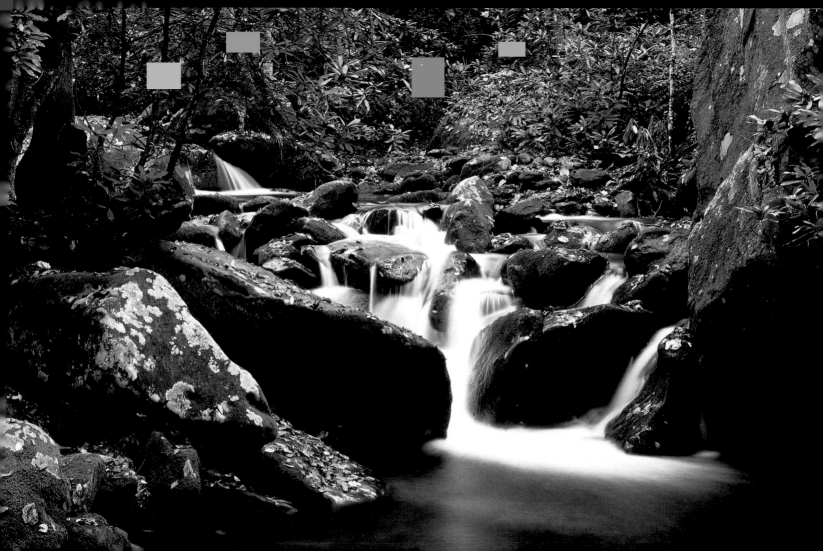

When travelling abroad, look for local ecological labels.

The EU eco-label (a dandelion with a green E in the centre) identifies accommodations that respect certain environmental criteria, such as water consumption, use of renewable energy, waste management, and environmental education. The label encourages those who run tourist facilities to adopt good environmental practises, and promotes sustainable tourism initiatives. There are other, equivalent international certification programs for other areas of the world that you can investigate when planning your next trip abroad.

Take a holiday where the attention is paid to the environment on a daily basis, just as you do at home.

Shark, Australia

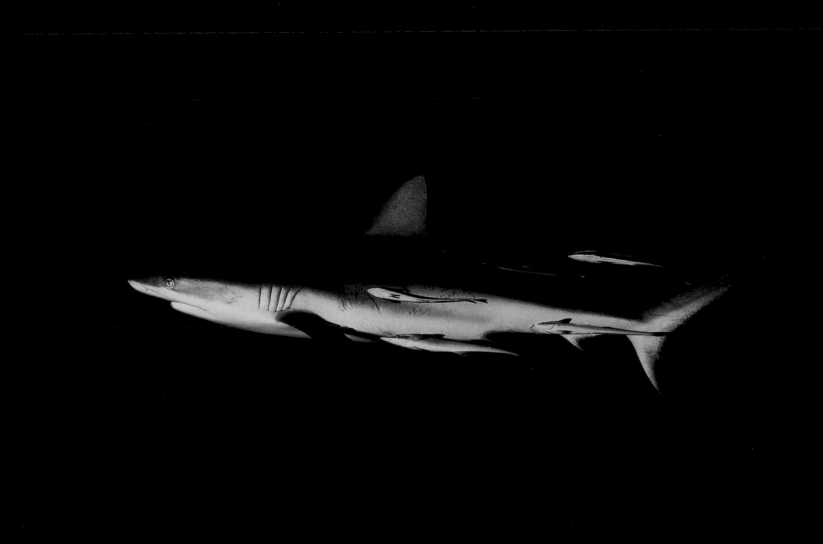

Switch to rechargeable batteries.

The manufacture of a battery uses 50 times as much energy as the battery itself will produce during its life. The only exception is rechargeable batteries. A personal stereo battery lasts 6 days; if you use a rechargeable battery, it can last up to 4 years. Like disposable batteries, some rechargeable ones contain cadmium, but since they can be recharged between 400 and 1,000 times, their impact on the environment is considerably reduced (if they are properly disposed of at the end of their life).

The best alternative for most portable electronics is nickel-metal hydride (NiMH), as these batteries are rechargeable and contain no cadmium. The upfront expense of these and their charger is soon recovered: Their lifetime cost is 3% of the comparable amount of disposable battery power.

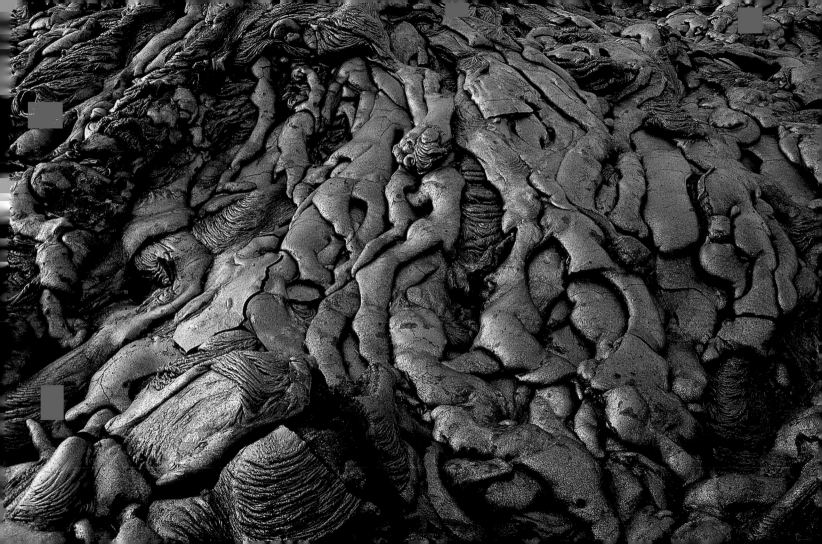

Take your children to school on foot.

Cars already produce a fifth of worldwide carbon-dioxide emissions, and their numbers will increase considerably over the coming decades to meet growing demand in developing countries. Twenty percent of cars on the roads at 8.50 am in the United Kingdom are solely used for taking children to school, yet over 80% of primary age children live less than 2 miles from their school. Less than half of all children walk to school regularly.

Instead of taking your children to school by car, send them by public transport or school bus, or accompany them on foot or by bike.

Bristlecone pine, United States

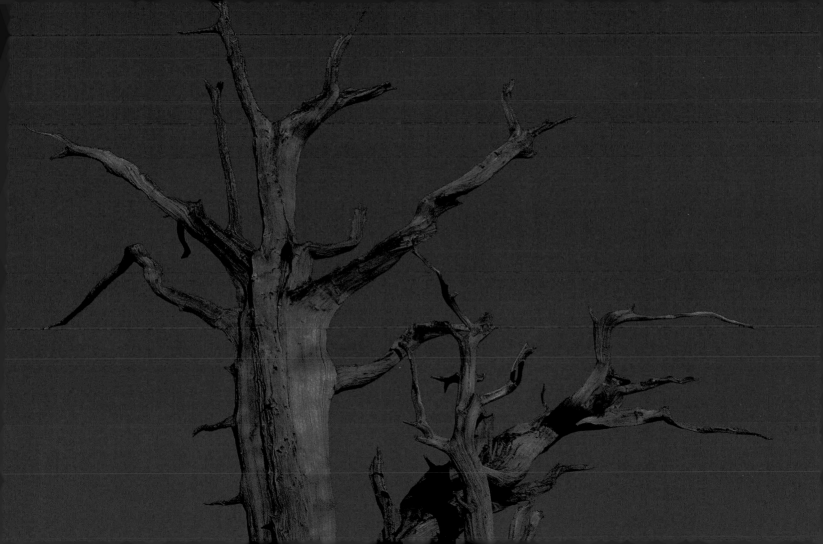

Replace paper and plastic with real cups and glasses.

For the past 20 years our way of living has demanded too much of the earth, which can no longer absorb the pressure humanity is placing upon it. Human use of biological resources exceeded the earth's natural capacity by 23% in 2006. This figure is expected to rise to between 80% and 120% in 2050.

Many workplaces provide plastic cups for water and coffee. These are in our hands just a few minutes before they are thrown away. To stop this needless waste, take your own cup to work and encourage your colleagues to do the same. Saving the cost of the disposable cups will also up your company's profit, so encourage your workplace to stop using disposable cups as a matter of policy.

Yellowstone National Park,
United States

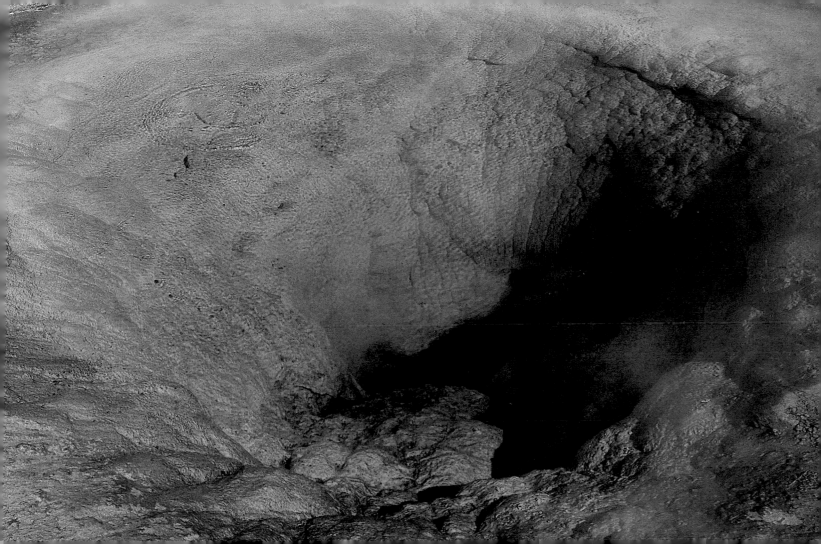

Control the temperature in your home.

Home heating is a huge energy drain, but it doesn't take much to regulate the temperature according to each room's use, the outside temperature, and the times when you are not there.

Install a digital thermostat system that will allow you to set the heating as you desire, room by room, according to the time of day or night and use up to 25% less energy than if your heating were not regulated. And if you can't install a thermostat system, simply turn your heating down by 1°C — this can save up to 10% of your energy bill.

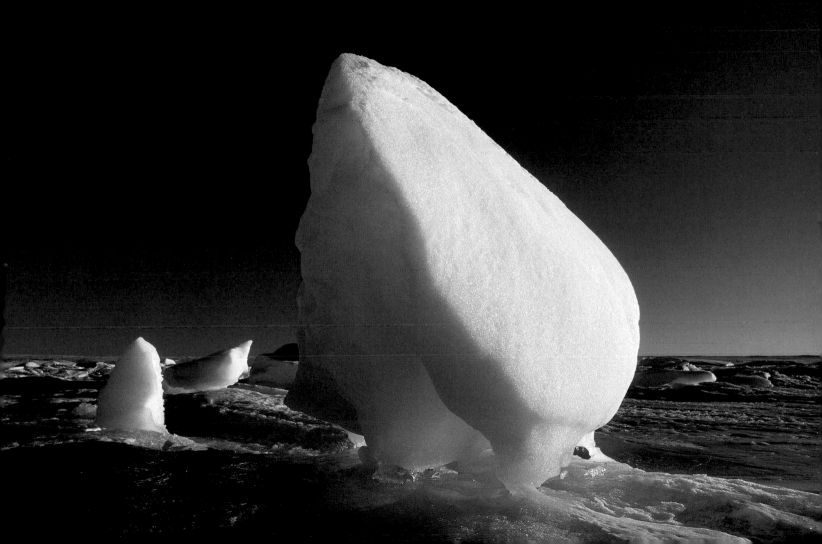

Reject junk mail.

We are producing ever-greater quantities of waste. Our letterboxes are clogged with catalogues and advertising: Every year in Britain, we receive more than 21 billion items, which weigh up to 550,000 tonnes and consume nearly 3 million trees. This mail, 40% of which is unread, goes directly to swell the volume of household waste, and is costly in terms of local taxes spent on collecting and treating. Certain adhesives used can contaminate the recycling process and as a result make recycling difficult and expensive.

When dealing with a company or an organisation that knows your address, always tell them to keep your address private. This will prevent them from selling it to other organisations and exposing you to unwanted junk mail. Register with the Mailing Preference Service to stop unsolicited mail — and if you continue to get junk mail, contact the companies to request to be taken off their mailing list.

Prairie, Mount Rainier National Park, United States

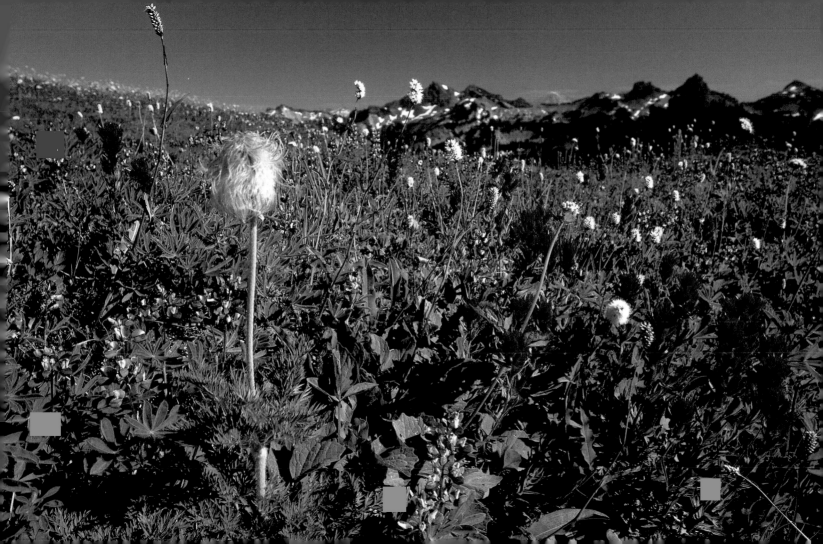

Follow the rules in parks and nature reserves.

About 34,000 plant species throughout the world, or a quarter of the total species of flora on the planet, face extinction in the coming years. Many of these were once considered common—and many species that you might consider common now are actually under threat, such as the corn buttercup and corn cockle.

Observe the instructions displayed at the entrances to parks—they are there for a reason. You will not disturb the wildlife if you keep your dog on a leash, and by following the marked trails you can avoid accidentally stepping on protected plants.

Pink flamingoes, Kenya

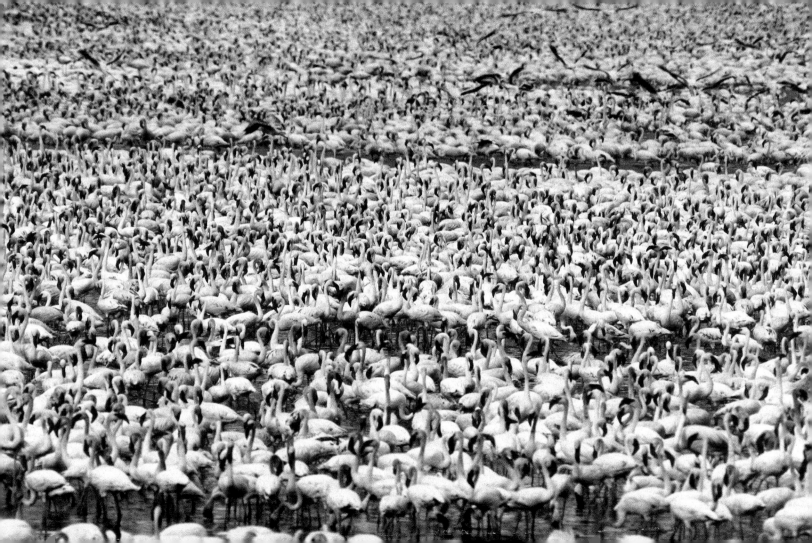

Find a greener dry cleaner.

Traditional dry cleaning uses a solvent called perchloroethylene, which is toxic enough to be treated as hazardous waste. Millions of tonnes of this chemical are used every year. It can cause allergic reactions among customers, and far more serious health problems for workers who are constantly exposed to it. Small amounts of perchloroethylene can seriously contaminate groundwater.

Look for cleaning firms that offer either 'wet cleaning' or a system that uses liquid carbon dioxide, both of which are safer treatments, and remember that in fact you can generally hand-wash silk, wool, and linen clothes that are tagged 'dry-clean only'. And of course, try not to buy clothes that require dry cleaning.

Crater Lake, United States

Borrow or lend your power tools.

Power tools are necessary for solid, reliable craftsmanship, but homeowners often invest in these tools without considering how often they may use them. How many hours a year will you use an electric drill? What about the power saw, the nail gun, the chainsaw, and the carpet shampoo machine? Our cupboards and garages are cluttered with equipment and tools that we use very rarely, if at all.

Rather than investing in new tools, try another approach. Why not borrow them from a neighbour or family member, or buy them together and take turns using them? Tools can often be easily mended — ask a local hardware shop or builder how to do so. There are also tool-sharing initiatives in some areas — if there isn't one near you, why not start your own? Learn your neighbours needs and interests — it's a great way to build community.

Rock, Malaysia

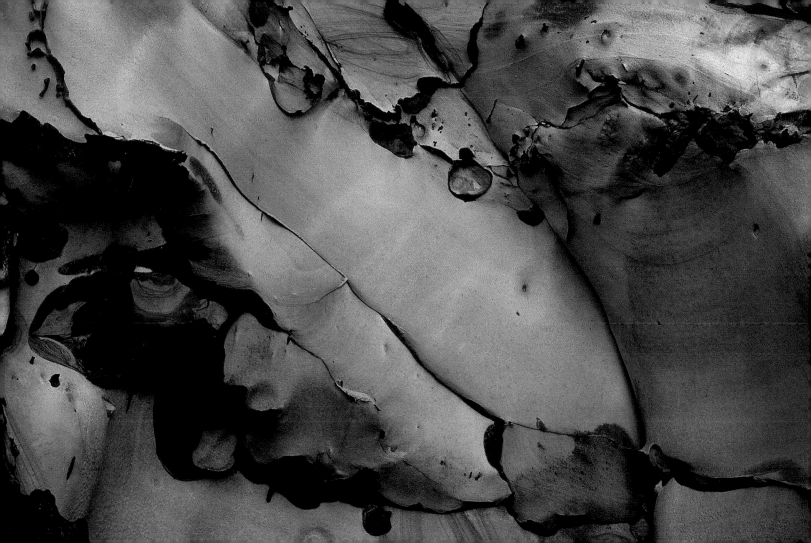

Take your old engine oil to the dump.

Engine oil contains substances—especially heavy metals (lead, nickel, and cadmium)—that are toxic to our health and the environment. A third of used engine oil is refined to make new lubricants, and the remaining two-thirds is used as fuel, chiefly in cement works. Most of us dump our used oil into the gutter or into storm drains when we change our oil, wasting over 120 million gallons of reusable oil per year. The leftover oil from one oil change can pollute 1 million gallons of water.

Recycling old oil saves raw materials and energy, and spares the environment. It also reduces our dependence on the ever-vanishing hydrocarbon: A barrel of crude oil can yield 2.5 litres of virgin motor oil. It takes only one litre of used motor oil to get the same amount of high-quality motor oil. Engine oil is collected at dumps and garages. Always bring your old oil there.

Red ibises, Venezuela

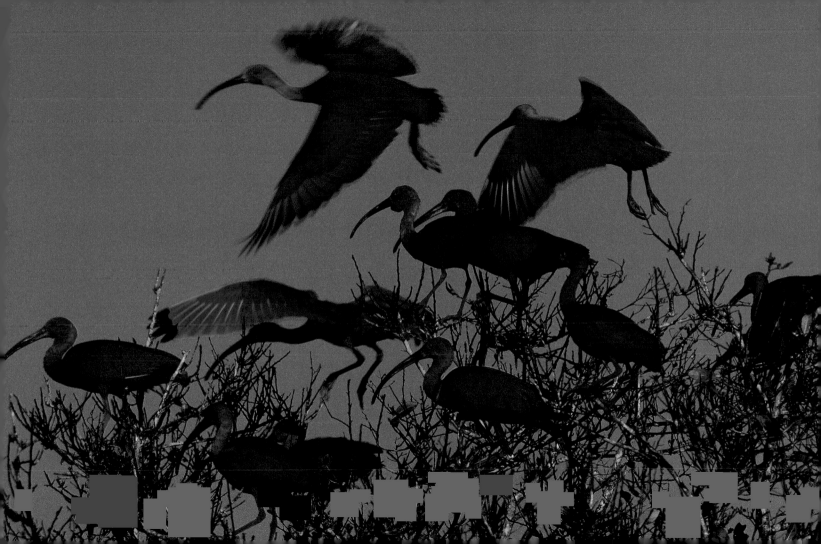

Don't burn the midnight oil.

Long exposure to artificial light at night can affect the body's ability to produce mela-
tonin, which helps to regulate sleep. It can also weaken the immune system and disrupt
hormone production. In addition to the detrimental effects routinely staying up late has
on our bodies, it also increases the amount of energy our homes use.

**So, unless you work the night shift, try to maintain reasonable sleep patterns.
You'll feel better and you'll save energy in more ways than one.**

Lake, Chad

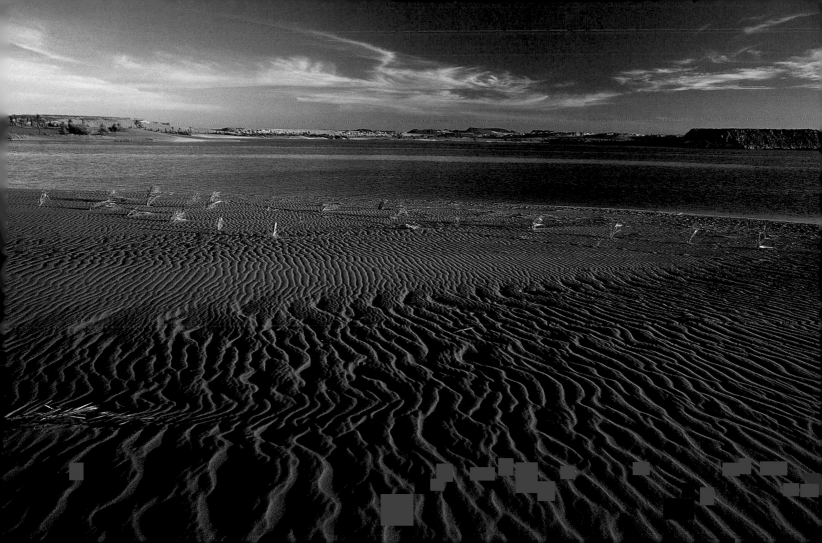

Do not use chemicals near water.

A garden is like a miniature field; even on this very small scale, it is essential not to contribute to water and soil pollution by using too many chemicals. Homeowners have been found to be much more lavish in the application of pesticides than other users. They apply 1.5 to 4.5 kilograms of lawn pesticides per 0.4 hectares; agricultural land generally receives 1.2 kilograms of pesticides per 0.4 hectares.

Do not use fertilizers, pesticides, or herbicides if you are near water, such as a well, stream, pool, or marsh. After each application, these products soak into the soil, sometimes permanently polluting aquifers.

Emperor penguins, Antarctica

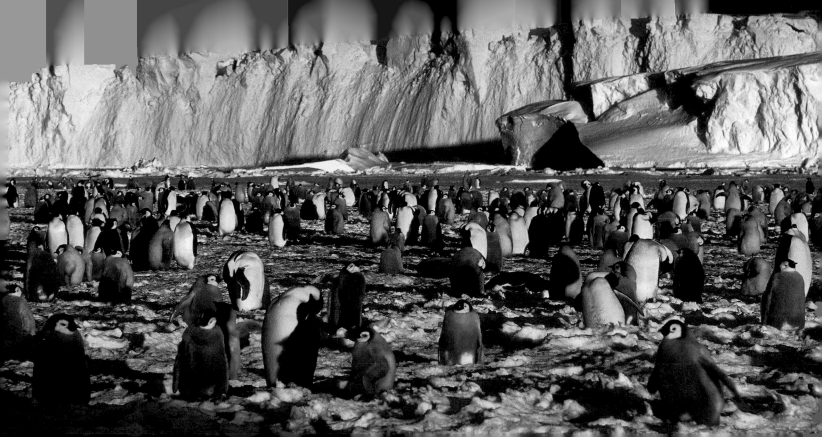

Adopt a pet from your local animal shelter.

The RSPCA in the United Kingdom takes in nearly 10,000 unwanted pets each year, and it is only one of the charities that shelters animals in need. By adopting a dog or cat from a shelter, you're giving a homeless pet a new chance at life.

Read up on the RSPCA's guidelines for adopting a pet, or the equivalent in your country. If you decide that you and your family are ready to make this commitment, don't spend money needlessly in a pet shop, thus encouraging even more pets to be raised. Find your next family member at the local animal shelter, instead.

Yosemite National Park,
United States

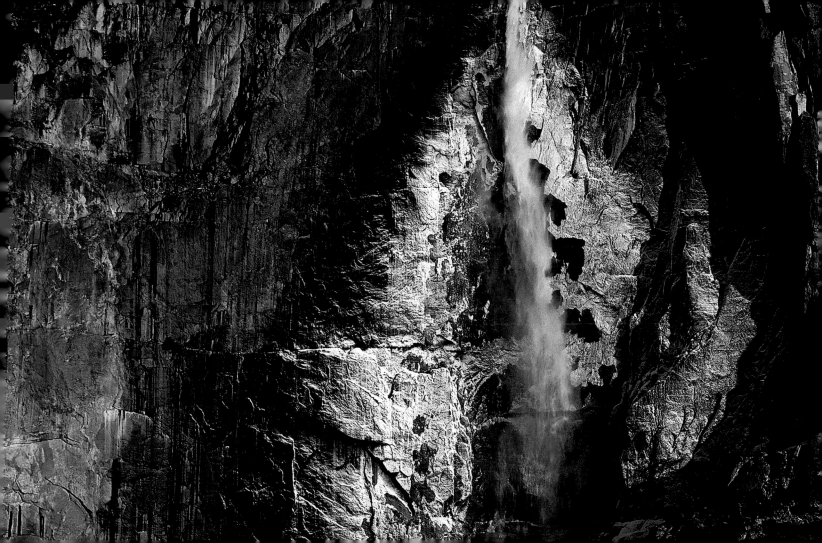

Install energy-efficient lighting.

Energy-saving compact fluorescent (CF) lightbulbs now come in a range of sizes, shapes, and colour tones, and use up to 80% less energy and last 10 times as long as an old-fashioned incandescent lightbulb—a technology that hasn't changed for over 100 years. If households in the United Kingdom replaced 3 incandescent bulbs with energy-saving lightbulbs, the energy saved would be sufficient to power all the country's street lighting for a year.

LEDs (light emitting diodes) are even more efficient and long lasting—they use up to 90% less energy than incandescents. Though not as widely available (or as affordable) as CFLs, LEDs come as standard bulbs as well as built into lamps and Christmas lights.

Make the switch in your home to energy-efficient lightbulbs and see your electricity bills dramatically decrease—a single bulb could save its owner up to £100 over its lifetime. Then encourage your workplace or school to do the same.

Dunes, Libya

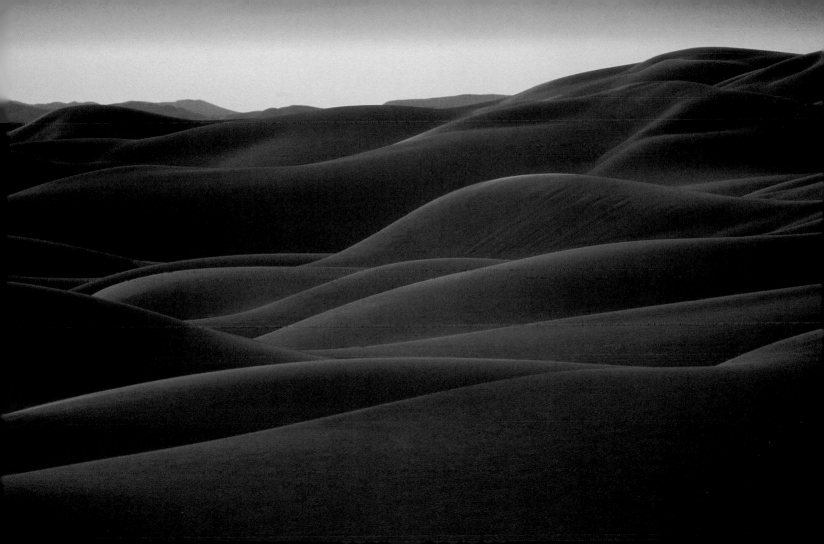

Refuse to accept paper telephone directories.

Every year, telephone companies automatically distribute directories in several volumes. About 55,000 tonnes of telephone books are produced each year in the United Kingdom, equivalent to nearly a million trees. While most are recycled, and recycling is much better than throwing them away, it is even better not to accept them to begin with. Putting something in the recycling bin, while better than the rubbish bag, always results in the use of some kind of resource to get the recycling done.

How many times have you looked in your telephone directories this year? If you do not use them, call the distributor's freephone number and opt out. Use the Internet to look up phone numbers instead. The Internet is also good for finding maps or looking up foreign numbers.

Niger River, Mali

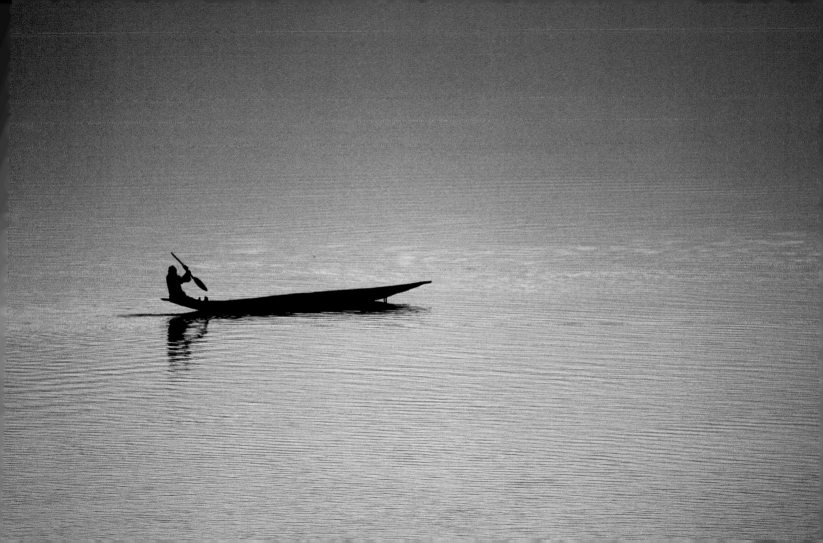

Recycle your computer.

Computers help us to be greener in some areas—they reduce our dependency on paper and allow us to telecommute—but wreak havoc on the environment in other ways. They contribute greatly to electronic waste, which accounts for 70% of hazardous waste worldwide.

The race is on to build the greenest computer. The European Union has devised strict regulations (RoHS) designed to phase out the toxic components of PCs, standards that are becoming more universally applied. Prototypes with bamboo casings and built-in solar panels promise that computers will continue to get greener, but these are not likely to be on the market soon.

For now, when you need a new computer, make sure you recycle your old one. Charities nationwide can put old computers to good use, either by reselling them to individuals and organisations that can't afford a new computer and don't need the latest, fastest machine, or by sending them to developing nations where computers are unaffordable but can make a huge difference, allowing people to trade, access information, and educate their children.

Puffin, United States

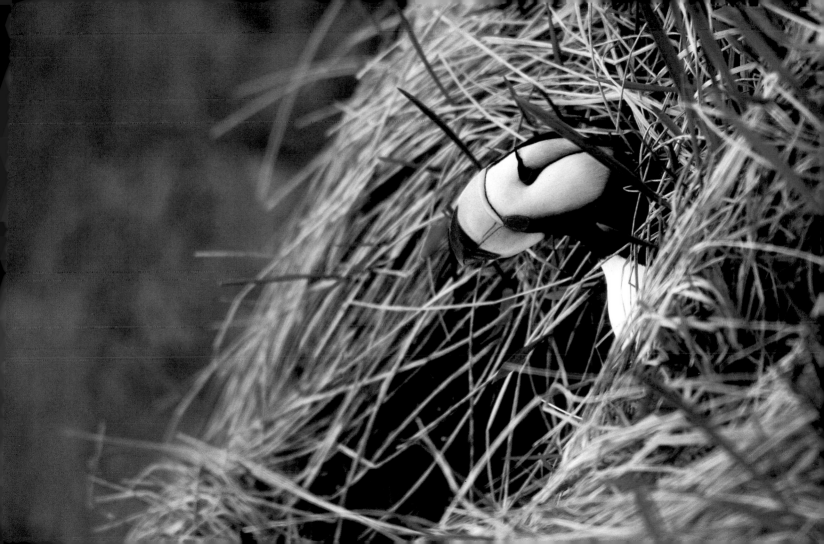

Plant a tree.

Eight thousand years ago, when human beings settled and began to grow crops,
half the planet's land mass was covered in thick forest. Today, less than a third is still
forested. Worldwide, over the last 10 years, forest cover has been reduced by some
7.3 million hectares. In order to live, all plants on the planet release oxygen and absorb
carbon dioxide. One hectare of mature forest absorbs the equivalent of the carbon
emissions from 100 midsize cars over a period of a year.

Plant a tree: You will be joining the fight against global warming.

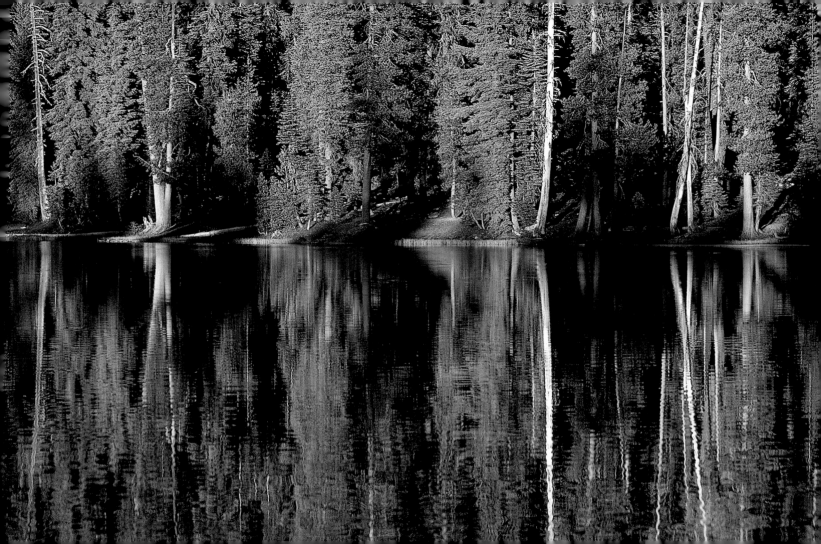

Pick up 1 piece of litter every day.

Even though we throw away so much, our everyday surroundings are not free of litter—and the waste that remains presents a danger to wildlife and children as well as an incentive for others to add to the mess.

If each UK resident bent down once a day to pick up a piece of litter, we would remove over 60 million pieces of rubbish from the streets and sidewalks every day.

Laguna Verde, Bolivia

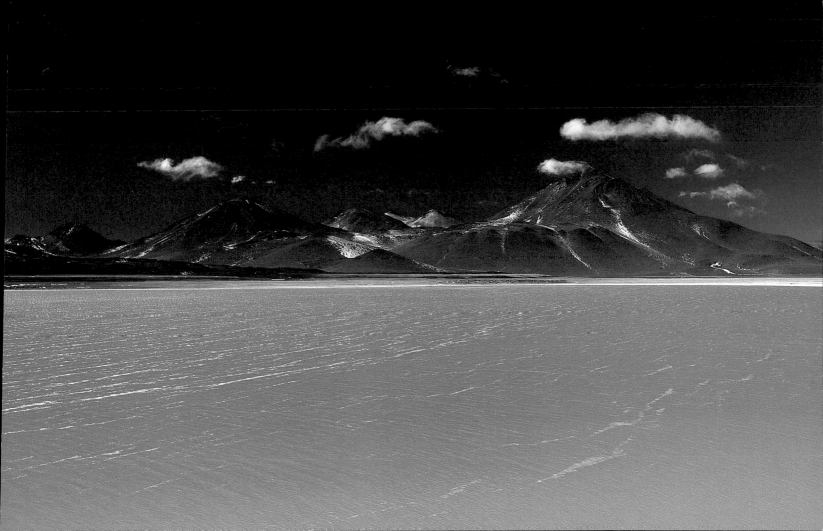

Lend your blog to a greater cause.

On 15 October 2007 more than 20,000 bloggers participated in Blog Action Day, devoting their daily posts to environmental stories. Lifestyle sites offered better recycling tips while techno geeks discussed how optimizing code could save energy, and the event garnered a great deal of international (print) press. Organisers intend to make this a yearly event.

On your blog, website, or social networking profile, be proud to write about your environmental convictions and discuss how you are trying to lessen your impact on the planet. You could also join environmentally themed online groups and forums, where you can share tips and learn more about how other people and communities are tackling the issues you face. Share the message online — use your Web space to help make a better world.

Laguna, Bolivia

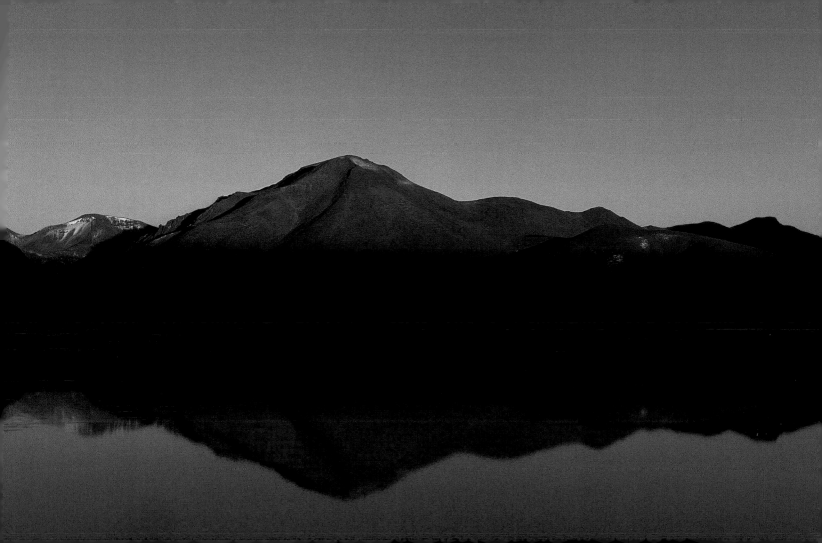

Optimize your computer.

Only 15% of the energy spent to power a computer is used during actual work time—the other 85% is wasted while the unit idles. The average desktop uses 70 watts of power when on standby, while the average laptop uses 20 watts.

Always use the sleep mode instead of screen savers (screen savers don't actually reduce energy use and they can prevent the CPU from going to sleep). Setting your computer to go to sleep after 10 to 15 minutes of inactivity can help one person cut their annual carbon-dioxide emissions by up to 0.5 tonnes. Don't leave your computer on when you've finished working—always shut it down completely and make sure laptop-charging adapters are fully unplugged. And consider buying a laptop—they use one-fifth of the power of a desktop computer.

Um el Ma Lake, Libya

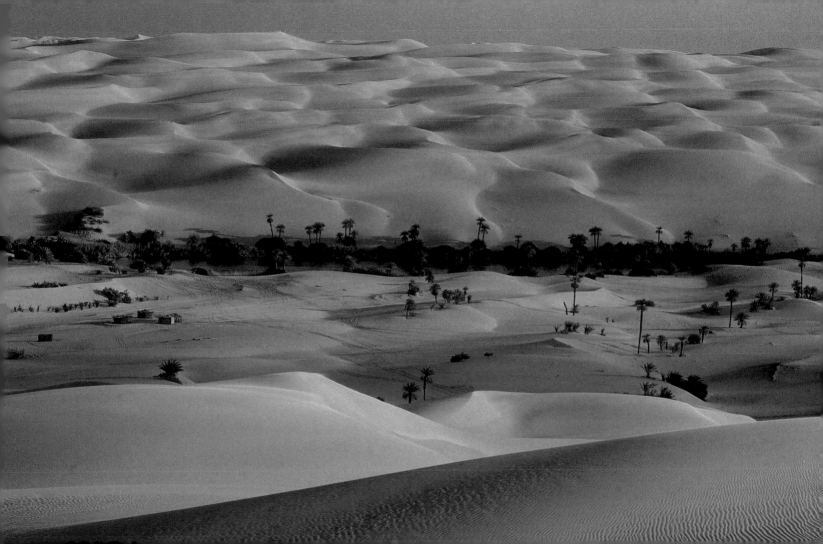

Do laundry at lower temperatures.

If we reduce the energy used in the home for lighting, heating, cooking, and so on, we can reduce energy demand. Less electricity needs to be produced by power stations, which means less global warming, and less development of new power stations including nuclear. Wherever we look, energy savings are possible. About 90% of the energy used by washing machines goes into heating the water. Washing and rinsing your clothes on the hot-water cycle uses 3.5 times more energy than washing in warm water and rinsing in cold. Using only cold water saves even more energy.

Modern washing machines, with modern washing powders, are just as effective at 30 or 40 degrees as they are at higher temperatures, so make sure you run your machine on low or an 'eco' setting; and don't use the prewash, leave clothes to soak if they have particularly bad stains.

Weddell seals, Antarctica

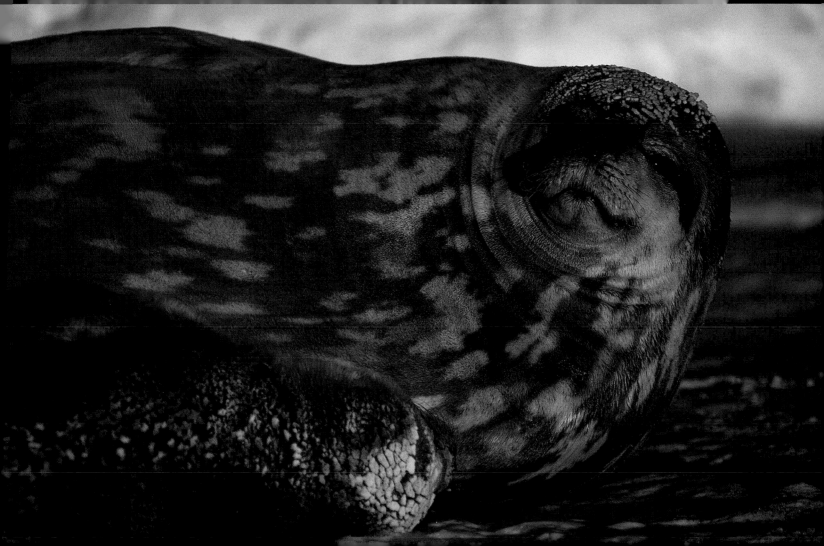

Drive smoothly.

Today the world burns as much oil in 6 weeks as it did over the course of a year in 1950. Oil reserves are running out and, at current rates of consumption, will be exhausted in less than 50 years. Transport alone accounts for half the world's oil consumption.

In cities, try to avoid accelerating and braking too hard and too frequently. Driving in this way increases fuel consumption by 40%, which means spending money needlessly and aggravating urban air pollution.

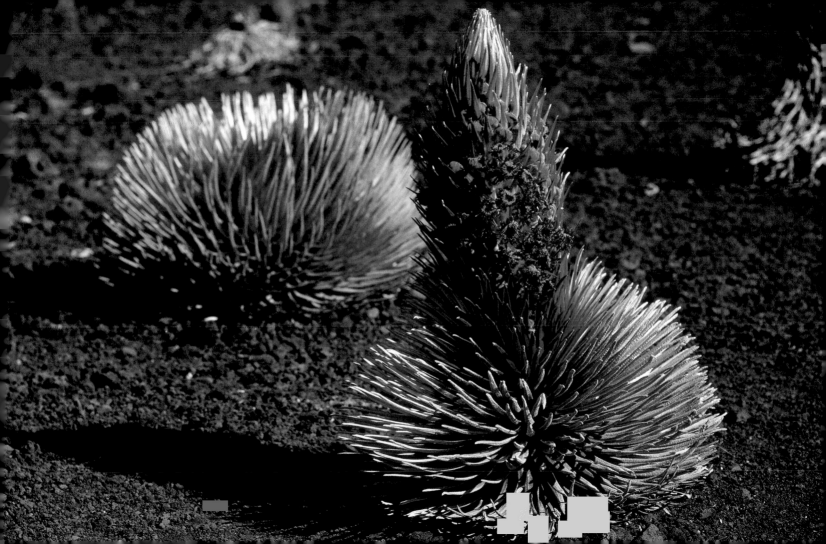

Choose appliances that use less water.

Water use increases as wealth increases. Greater purchasing power encourages household comforts and water use increases, despite the ever-shrinking supply of fresh water that we have.

If you are planning to replace your household washing appliances, allow your choice to be guided by the amount of water they use. Efficient dishwashers can use about 10 litres of water per load — half the volume used by conventional dishwashers.

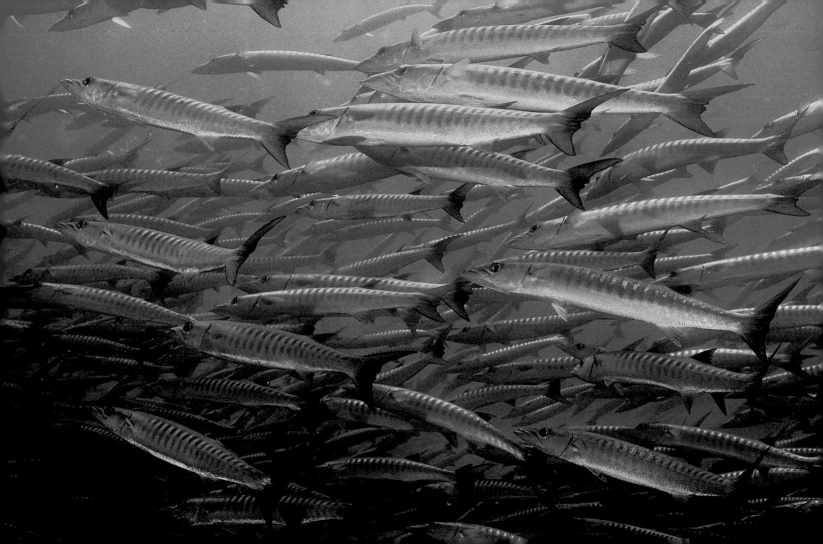

Recycle plastic.

Most plastic bottles today are made of PET (polyethylene terephthalate), which is easy to recycle. The PET symbol, which is marked on the bottom of plastic containers, consists of a triangle of arrows surrounding the number 1. Plastic packaging that has been sorted and recycled is reborn as fleece garments, tubes, watering cans, flowerpots, floor coverings, water bottles, carpets, car parts, phone cards, and more. Every tonne of recycled PET saves an energy equivalent of 11 barrels of oil.

At home, in the office, or when travelling, make sure you recycle plastic bottles. Encourage your office to start a recycling program if it doesn't have one. Recycling a single plastic bottle saves enough energy to keep a 60-watt bulb lit for 6 hours.

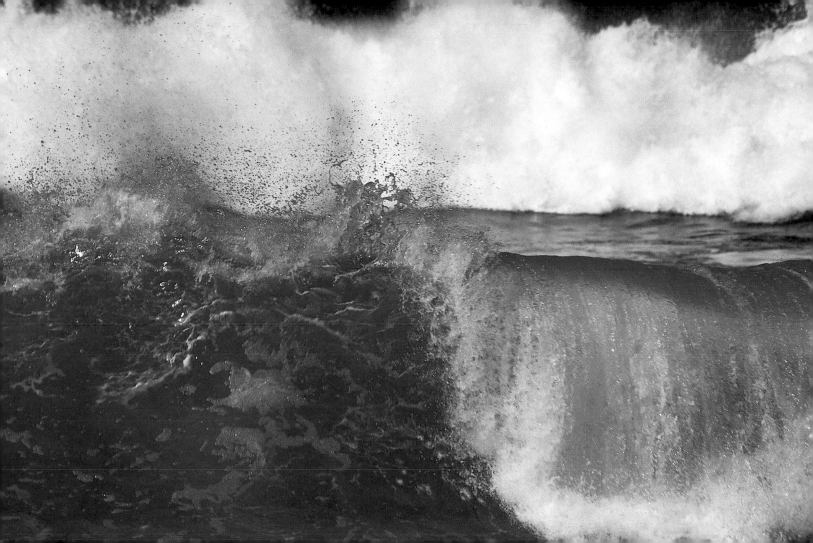

Join your residents or tenants association.

In our day-to-day social lives, we regularly take part in groups whose decisions may have a strong impact on the environment. Meetings of residents associations are an example. Every measure that is voted on can contribute to preserving the planet's natural resources, limiting pollution, and reducing water use. Your power to create change is greater if you act as a group.

Empower yourself and your neighbours to create a greener environment for you all to live in. In meetings, speak out in defence of environmental measures, such as low-energy heating, sorting of waste, low-consumption lighting in common areas, creation of drought-resistant, absorbent, green spaces or shared gardens, and maintenance of the plumbing system.

Wreck, Mexico

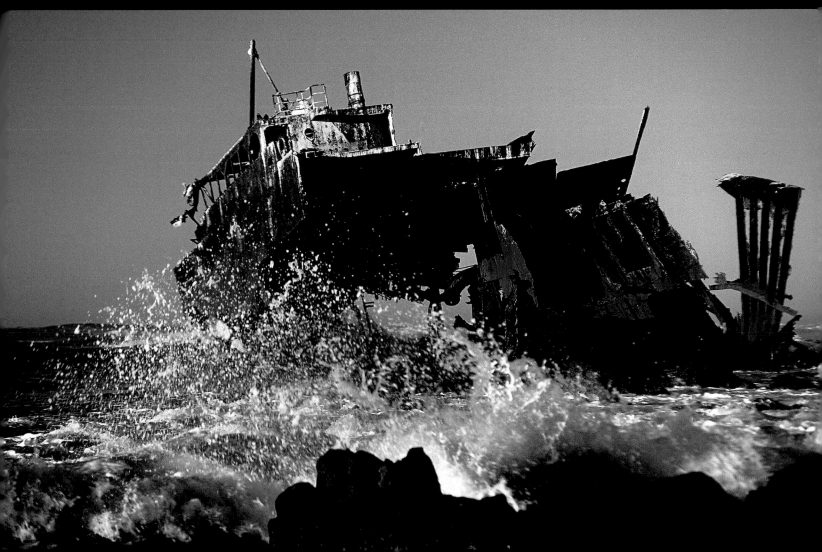

Downsize your life.

The average house in Japan is roughly half the size of the average house in North America (the size of which is constantly increasing). Small homes with smaller individual rooms are easier to heat and cool. They're also cheaper to maintain and to decorate. Before investing in a bigger house, ask yourself if you're really going to use all of that space. If you're about to buy a new SUV or people carrier, ask yourself if you really need such a big car for everyday tasks. Your TV can use up more electricity than a computer and washing machine combined, so ask yourself if you really need a screen so large it dwarfs your living room.

Think small and live within your means, not beyond them.

Crabs, Galápagos Islands

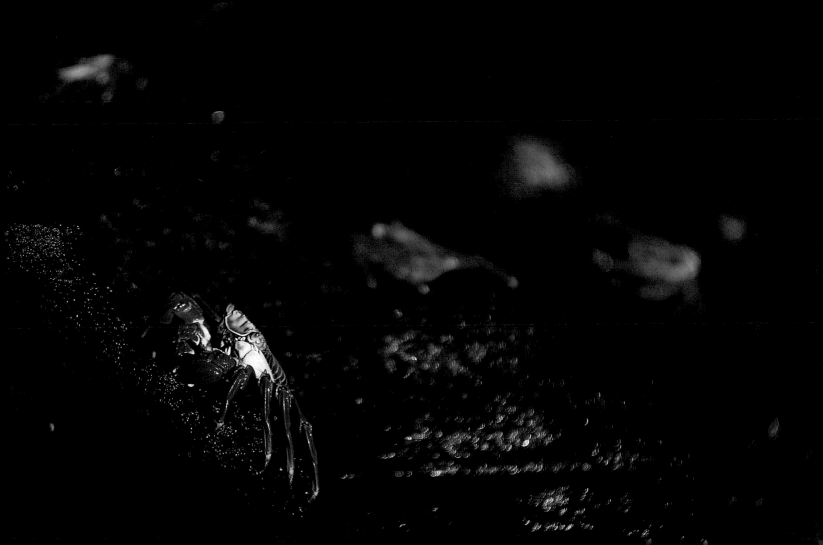

Buy greener soaps and detergents.

Phosphorus is one of the principal ingredients in conventional soaps, detergents, and washing powders. Increased phosphorus concentrations cause excessive algae growth in water bodies. Though algae are the basis of life for many ecosystems, an overabundance causes lower levels of dissolved oxygen in the waters, which in turn disrupts ecosystems and causes fish kills. Algae blooms also result in decreased aesthetic and recreational values.

You can choose low-phosphate or phosphate-free soaps and dishwashing liquids. Many popular brands, now widely available, have low phosphate levels and are harmless to the environment.

White Sands National Monument, United States

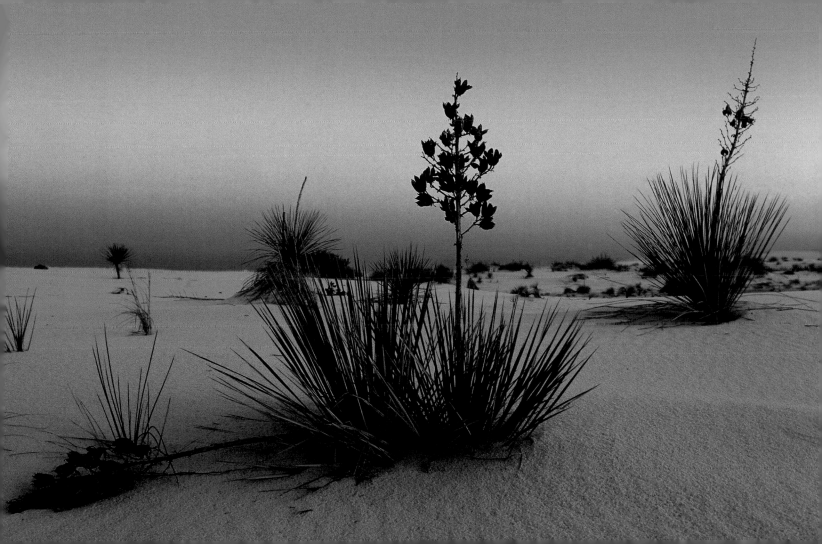

At the supermarket, question the true price of 'convenience'.

Packaging from processed foods contributes 30 million tonnes of waste each year. We buy many of these overly packaged products because they seem more convenient than their natural or bulk equivalents. But is it really so hard to make a sauce while the pasta cooks, rather than using a ready-made one? Is spooning a condiment or spread out of a glass jar, which you know will be recycled, so much of a hassle that we need all those plastic squeeze bottles?

Avoid packaging that contains unnecessary pollutants.

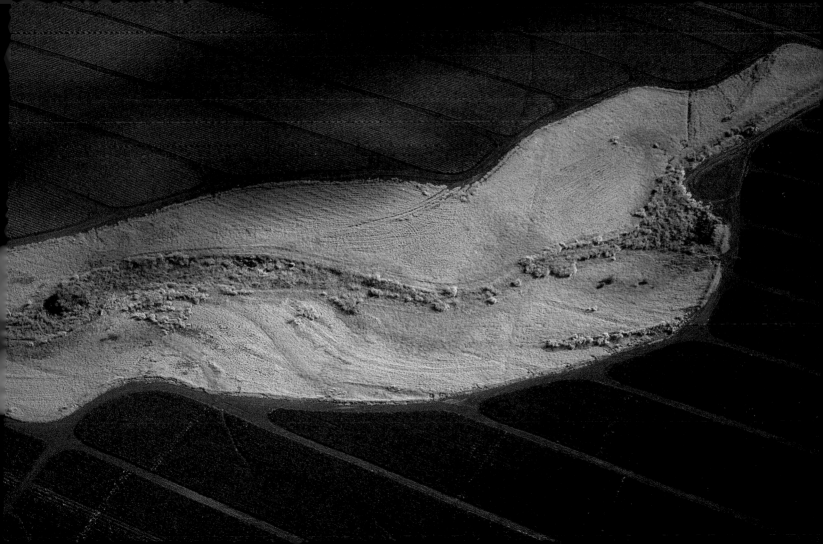

Choose jewellery with care.

In war-torn regions of Africa, the diamond industry is one of the biggest funders of armed conflict. 'Blood diamonds' or 'conflict diamonds' are mined in dire conditions and the profits are used by warlords to purchase more weapons. According to Amnesty International, diamond-funded wars have killed more than 4 million people. In answer to this, more than 70 countries now participate in the Kimberley Process, which tracks diamonds from the mines to the stores. But the trouble with jewellery doesn't end with diamonds. Gold mining has many detrimental effects on mining communities: Chemicals used during the extraction process contaminate groundwater, and swaths of wilderness are being destroyed for new mining operations even though there is enough gold already mined to supply the jewellery industry for the next 50 years.

When shopping for a precious stone, make sure it is 'conflict free' — demand to see certification. Search out eco-friendly jewellers who use recycled metals. Better still, buy rings from vintage shops that sell estate jewellery or recycle those old pieces gathering dust in safety deposit boxes — jewellers can reset stones and metalsmiths can melt down the rest so that they may be reshaped into new bands.

Kap Farvel region, Greenland

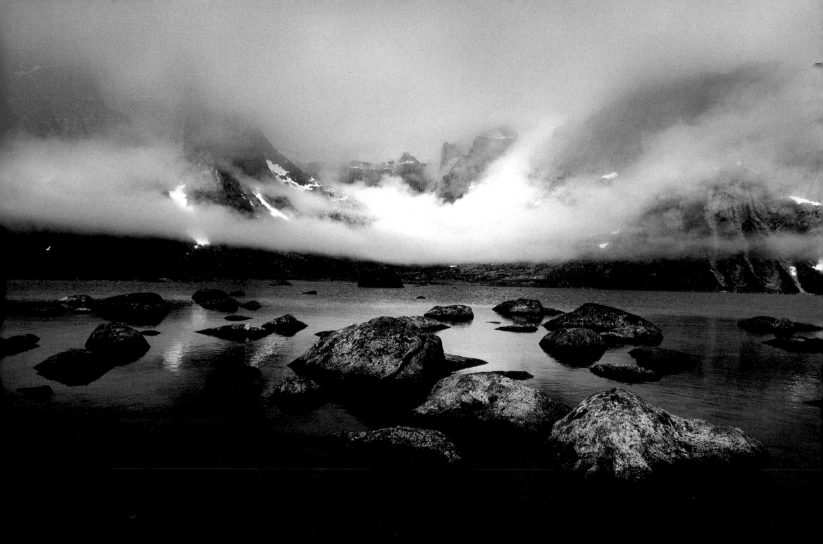

Don't waste residual heat.

All the small habitual changes we collectively make to our energy consumption will make a difference to the planet. At home, many household items give off enough residual heat to pull the plug a few minutes early.

Turn the oven off 10 minutes sooner, and electric hobs 5 minutes before you finish cooking. Unplug the iron when only 1 or 2 garments remain to be ironed. And throw the second load of clothes into the dryer before the heat from the first cycle has dissipated.

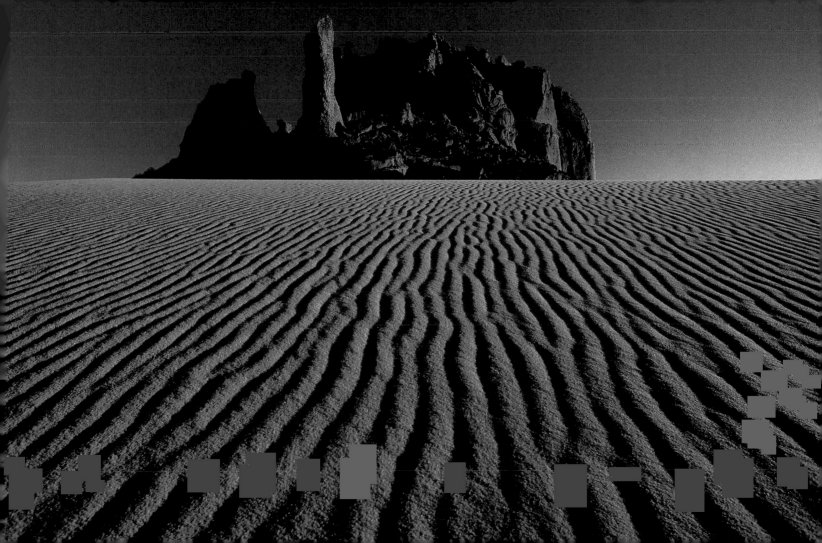

Install double-glazing.

Windows are a major source of heat loss, wasting up to 20% of the heat in your home. Yet they are one of the easiest and most cost-effective changes to your house's fabric that you can make, and they can cut the heat loss by half, saving around £100 a year for an average British home. They also insulate against noise, and can reduce draughts.

To reduce your consumption of energy for heating and the polluting emissions thus produced, consider replacing your single-glazed windows with double-glazing, preferably in wooden frames rather than uPVC or aluminium, both of which are highly energy-intensive to produce and often have short life spans. In the United Kingdom, look for the Energy Saving Recommended logo on windows to ensure you are getting the most efficient product. And remember to close the curtains at night, to keep your precious heat inside.

Thaw, Greenland

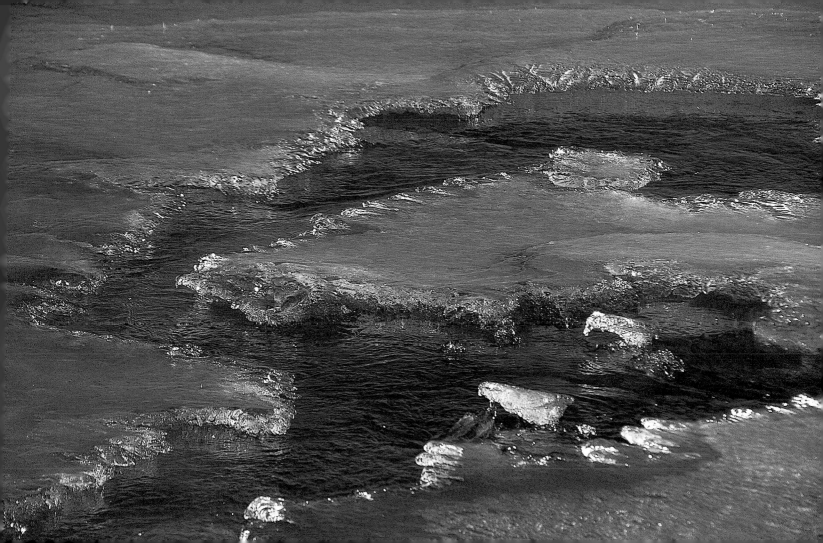

Join a car-sharing scheme.

Signs of climate change can already be observed—our planet's ecology is changing, and we must act now to slow this process down. Since 1989 Mount Kilimanjaro has lost a third of its snow and the mountain could be completely devoid of snow within 15 years. The spring ice thaw in the Northern Hemisphere happens 9 days earlier than it did 150 years ago, and the first freeze of autumn happens 10 days later. These facts have intense effects on bird migration and crop production.

In cities, more than 80% of cars carry just one person, and almost a third of all fuel is burned standing still in traffic. Consider joining a car-sharing program like Zipcar or Streetcar that enables you to rent cars by the hour, picking them up at any designated point in your city. You can also share a ride with others by registering on the national car-share database. Since you don't pay for petrol or insurance, car-sharing is often cheaper than owning.

Erosion, Theodore Roosevelt
National Park, United States

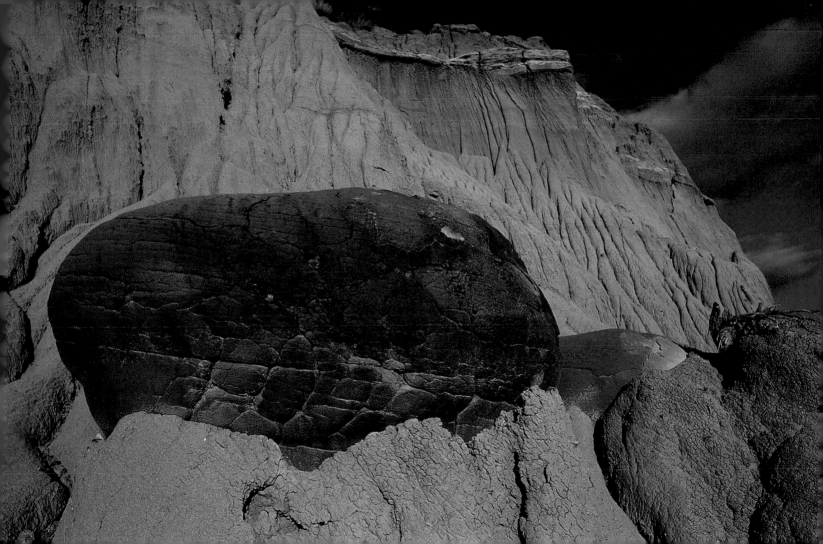

Choose solvents made from plants.

Solvents are powerful enough to dissolve other substances: They attack fats and keep certain products that contain them, such as glues and paints, liquid. Most solvents are organic (acetone, ether, white spirit) and belong to the family of volatile organic compounds (VOCs). White spirit is one of the most deadly solvents: It is harmful if touched or inhaled.

For decorating, maintenance, or hobbies, use plant-based solvents, which are less harmful to the environment—orange-based solvents that contain turpene are usually fairly potent.

Rocks, Seychelles

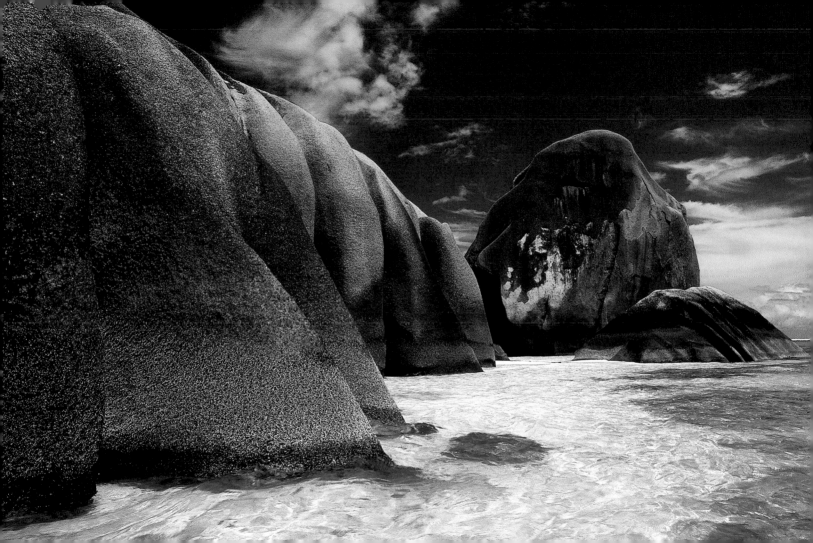

Report any unusual pollution.

In developed countries, polluting freshwater sources such as rivers, streams, lakes, and ponds is illegal, but still common practice for those who wish to avoid costly treatment of toxic waste. Pollution from sewage or farm waste can cause excess algae growth, starving the water of oxygen and causing fish and other species to die off. Pollution from chemical sources such as factories can cause the death of whole ecosystems very quickly. Oil spills stop light and oxygen getting into water, killing plants, and can cover the feathers of birds, causing them to be unable to fly.

If you notice an instance of freshwater pollution, such as froth, a brown trail, or the smell of sewage, alert your local environmental agency or council. If you notice pollution, such as waste or oil, while at the beach, notify a city or town official at once.

Scorpion fish, Australia

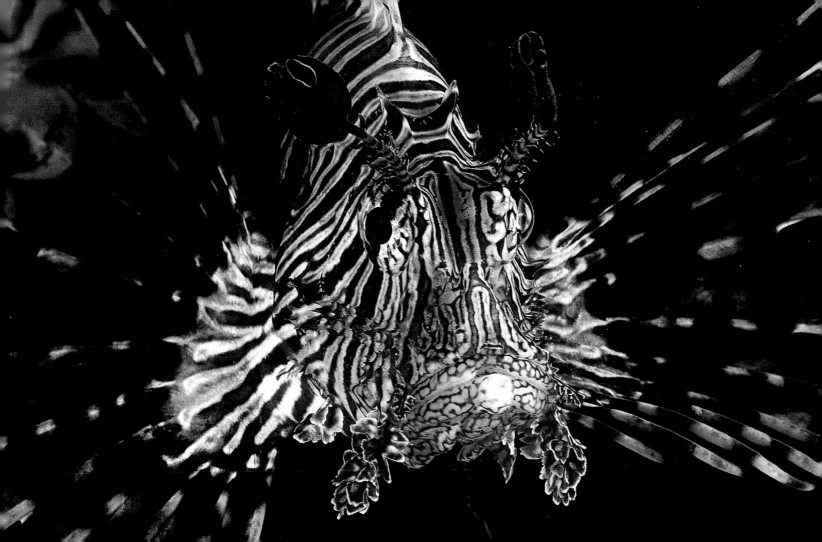

Buy recycled paper.

Recycling paper, while important, is only one part of the lifecycle of paper. We must also look at consumption of paper. Recycled paper products are widely available, and are considerably less damaging to the environment in production. Producing 1 tonne of uncoated virgin printing and office paper uses 24 trees and 98 tonnes of various resources (water, trees, energy), and manufacturing it produces toxic air pollutants such as VOCs, sulfur, chloroform, dioxins, and furans. Making paper from recycled materials results in 95% less air pollution and less water pollution as recycled paper is not usually bleached, which reduces the amounts of dioxins released into the environment.

Choose paper, box files, folders, envelopes, cards, toilet paper, and paper towels made from recycled paper and cardboard. Be sure to look for a high percentage of 'post-consumer' waste — paper that has been used in the home and office and recycled — otherwise a product may simply contain scraps left over from paper manufacturing and is not stopping our used paper from heading to the landfill.

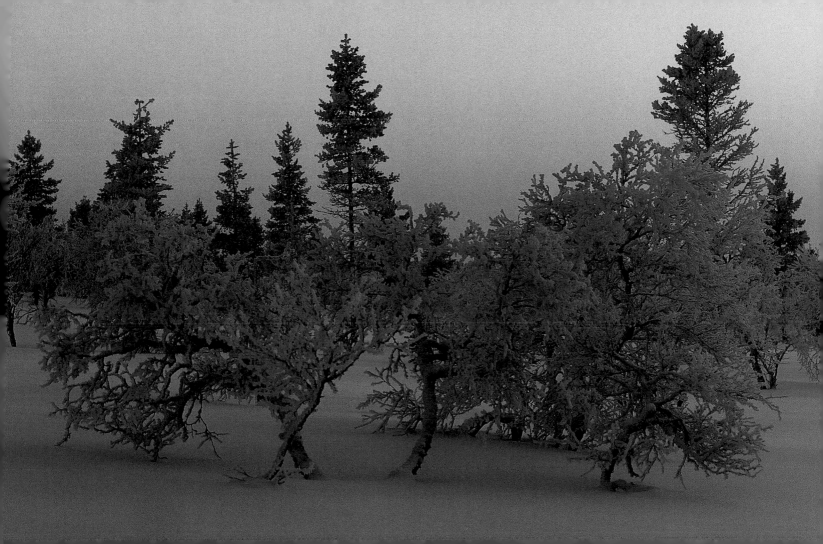

Dig a vegetable garden.

Growing your own vegetables is easy, satisfying, and healthier—in our temperate climate, you could be self-sufficient in many things with even a small amount of space. Salads, beans, herbs, tomatoes, and root vegetables such as carrots, beetroot, and turnips are easy to grow in almost any kind of soil—and if you have more space, potatoes, onions, sweet corn, and many other vegetables take minimal effort.

Autumn is a great time to prepare the ground for a vegetable patch. Dig the soil thoroughly and add compost, manure, fallen leaves, and other organic matter, which will be broken down over the winter and fertilise the soil. And on a winter's evening, you can plan your planting and order seeds, ready for the spring.

Krakatau volcano, Indonesia

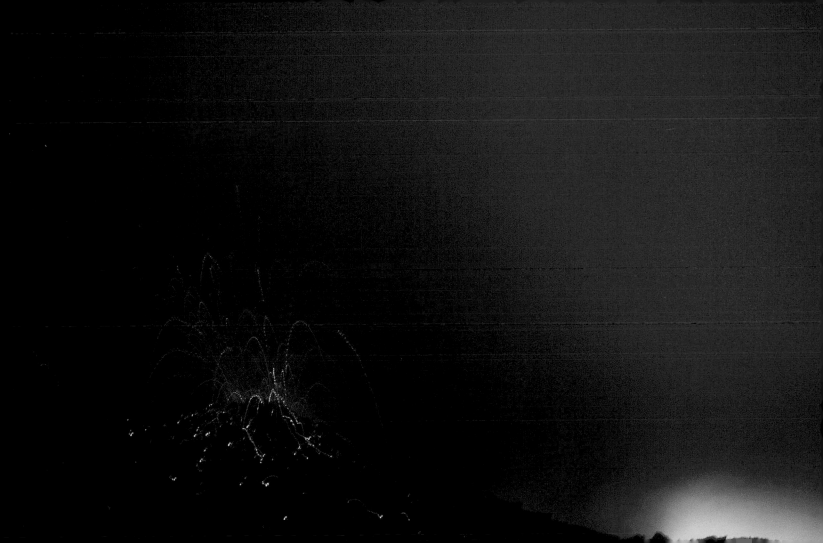

Settle for slower deliveries when shopping online.

A one-quarter-metre rise in sea level causes coasts to recede by 30 metres. Scientists expect the sea level to rise approximately 1 metre over the next 100 years. This scenario, which the world's climate change experts believe is likely to become reality within less than a century, would completely redraw the world's coastlines, without considering which regions currently are inhabited: 6% of the Netherlands, 17% of Bangladesh, and most of the Maldives could be submerged.

Transportation is the biggest contributor to global warming. If distributors are allowed more flexible delivery times, they can make full use of their trucking capacity, or use less polluting modes of shipping such as rail and canal barges. The demand for guaranteed delivery within 48 hours requires the use of more trucks. Is it really so urgent?

Humpback whale, Polynesia

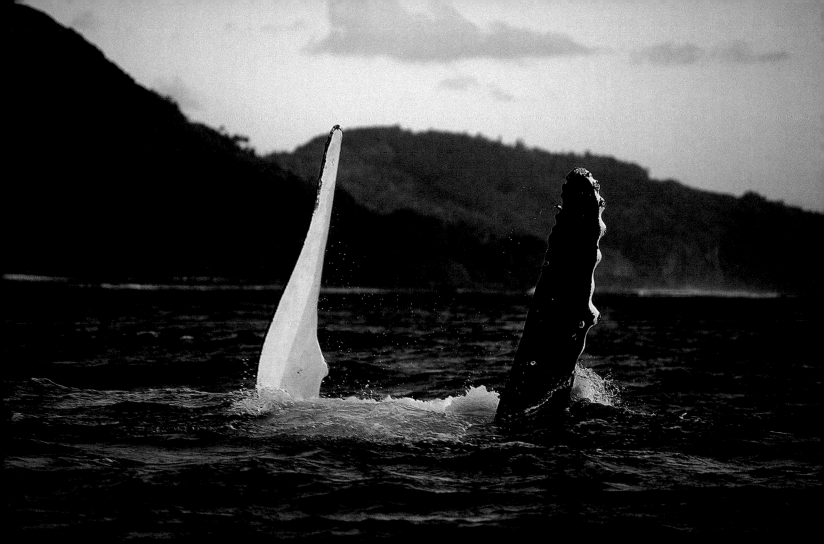

Don't burn or throw out fallen leaves.

Autumn leaves make excellent, micronutrient-packed mulch. Some local authorities collect leaves along with other garden waste to be sent to a composting centre, but if no such facility exists, your leaf pile just gets sent to the landfill.

Instead of throwing away or burning fallen leaves, make them into compost, either in a pile in a corner of your garden, or by filling black bags, sealing them tightly and leaving them to rot inside — the black material absorbs the sun's heat and speeds up the composting process. If you can't use them, ask around, as anyone who composts might have a use for them (community gardens are a good place to start). Whatever you do, don't burn leaf piles, as doing so releases carbon monoxide and particulate matter that can cause respiratory problems.

Mount Rainier National Park,
United States

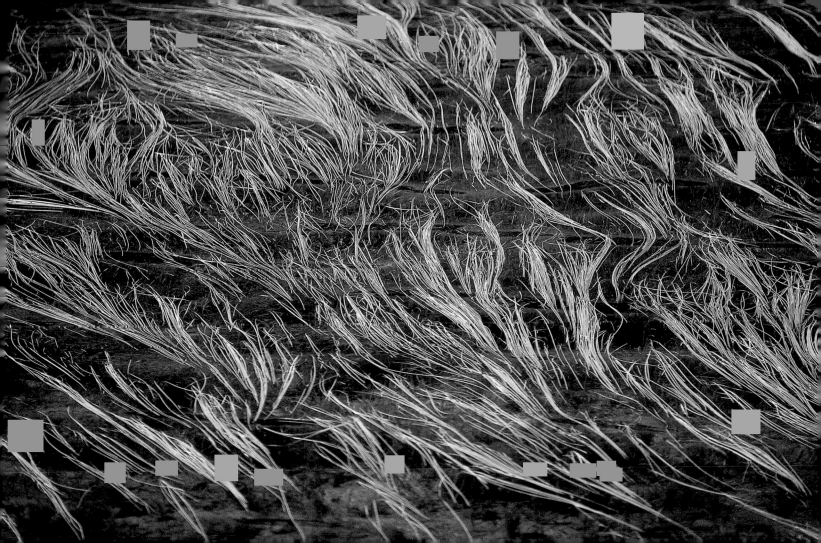

Find out what happens to your wastewater.

Water is the source of all life. We depend upon it completely. It is also the chief constituent of all living things: 65% of our bodies and 75% of our brains are water. It plays a crucial part in the economy, and allows the irrigation of cultivated land, the manufacture of industrial products, and the production of electricity. It provides superb leisure facilities. It is irreplaceable, and also guarantees hygiene and the comfort of our day-to-day lives.

Once it is dirty, water vanishes down the drain. Where does it go? Find out where your wastewater goes, how your local treatment plant works, and what happens to the sediment it produces. Let your vision of water see beyond the drain's vanishing act.

End of glacier, Greenland

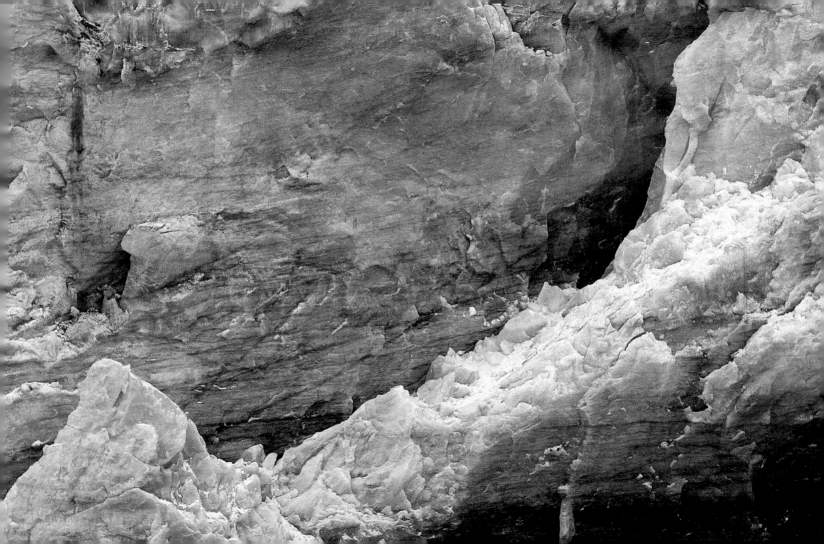

Buy juice in bulk.

Two of the world's largest landfills, now closed, are set to become symbols of restoration and environmental health over the next 30 years. The Paterson landfill site in Glasgow, Scotland, and the Fresh Kills landfill on Staten Island, in New York, are both slated for ambitious urban environmental renewal projects. In Glasgow, 1 million trees will be planted over 93 hectares of landfill over the next 12 years, making it the largest urban forest in the United Kingdom. Once the largest landfill in the world, Staten Island's Fresh Kills landfill is poised to become New York City's newest parkland. Its 890 hectares will be developed into a park 3 times as large as Central Park over the next 30 years.

Help reduce the need for huge landfills like Paterson and Fresh Kills. A household of 4 people can drink more than 170 litres of orange juice a year. Buy juice in the largest container possible and you will cut down on the amount of packaging waste that goes to the landfill. Most recycling centres accept large plastic juice containers; some will accept wax-coated paper containers. Always check before adding it to your recycling bin.

Swans, Japan

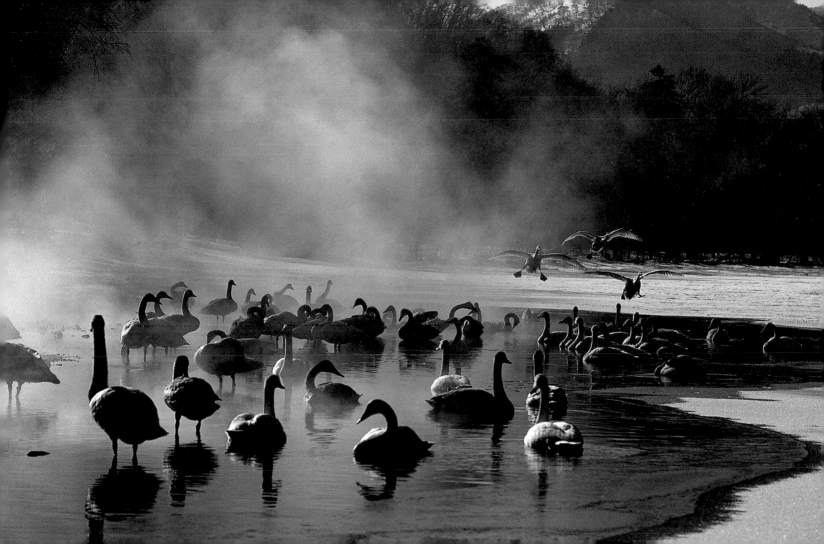

Sustainable development is about sustainable choices.

Reducing our environmental impact and slowing down climate change is not just about buying less and changing the products we buy to less energy-intensive ones, but also about lifestyle changes. Sustainable development is not just about how we develop land, but also about where and how people demand to live. Reducing the use of oil is most effectively done by changing your lifestyle so that you don't need to travel for your everyday business.

Think about living a truly local lifestyle — living close to where you work, shopping and socialising locally, taking your children to school locally rather than competing for school places far away, where they will have less chance to make friends who live nearby. Commit to using public transport and rediscover the character of your local community — its shops, leisure facilities, parks, and people.

Autumn, United States

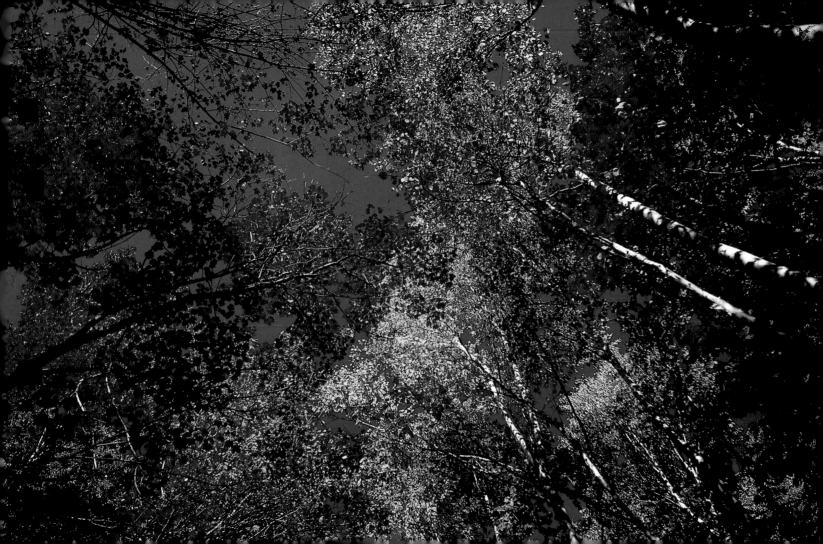

Ask for a home-energy audit.

In the United Kingdom, homes account for over a third of the total national energy load; they use the equivalent of 50 million tonnes of oil each year to heat, cool, and light. There are many simple things that can reduce the amount of energy you use in your home—from insulation, double glazing, draught excluders, or more efficient hot water systems—but it can be hard to know where to start without some advice.

Ask your energy supplier, or the government-run Energy Saving Trust, about receiving a home-energy audit—many offer the service for free. A professional will come to your house, assess your cooling and heating systems and structural issues (draughts, insufficient insulation), and offer specific advice on how to make your house more energy efficient. In the United Kingdom, you must now have an Energy Performance Certificate when you sell your home, so finding out how efficient your property is in advance makes sense—you can then make the changes and see the value of your house rise.

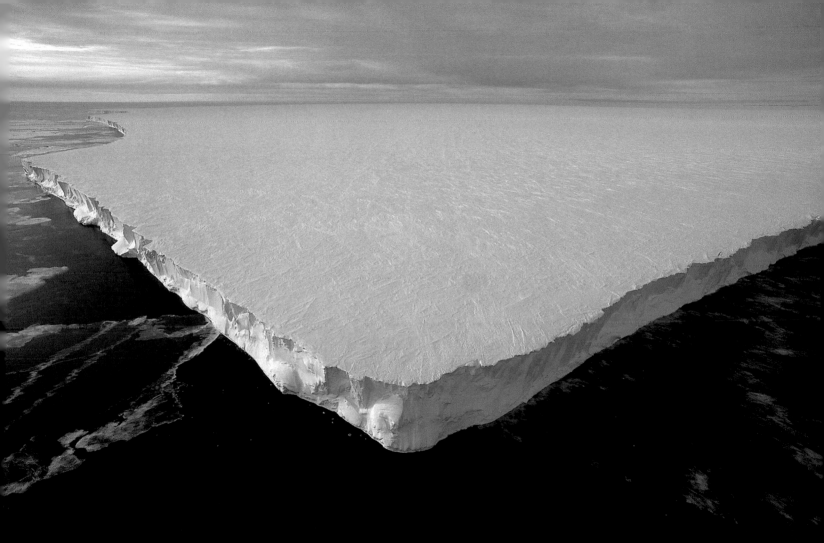

Print on both sides of the paper.

Human beings exploit forests to produce wood for industries, including construction, carpentry, and the manufacture of paper and cardboard. The paper industry uses 40% of commercially produced wood, and 17% of the wood used to produce printing or writing paper comes from virgin forest that contains centuries-old trees.

Almost all photocopiers and printers now print on both sides of the paper. Change your computer settings so that 'duplex' is the default, and encourage your company to adopt this as a policy. If your printer doesn't print on both sides, save waste paper to use for drafts by printing on the other side.

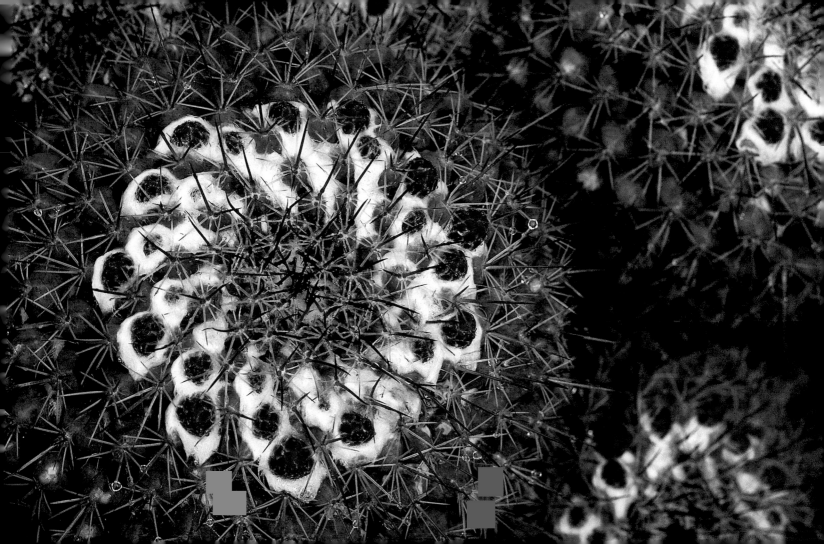

Recycle old tyres.

An old tyre, replaced by a new one, still has several centuries of life left in it: It takes 400 years for a tyre dumped in a landfill site to start to decompose. In 2005, 47.9 million tyres were discarded in Britain. These are a threat to the environment, because of the pollution their storage and disposal create. Alternatives exist, however; specialized companies can grind them up, melt them down, and convert them into material used by industry. Some companies also incinerate tyres, providing the same energy production as coal incineration does.

It takes about 26.5 litres of crude oil to produce 1 new car tyre. Recycle your old tyres, and buy your new tyres from dealers who take part in tyre collection programs.

Bison, Yellowstone National Park, United States

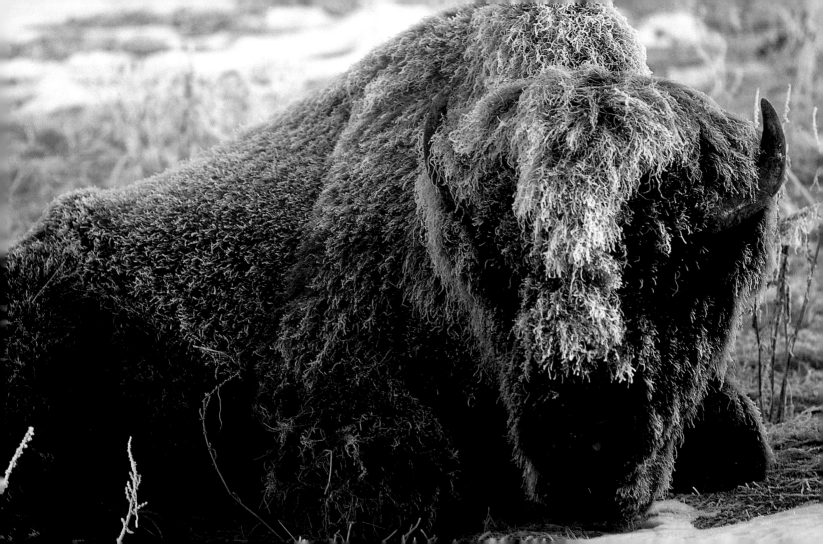

Extend the life of computers.

Computers are built with obsolescence in mind. Manufacturers expect their products to last only a year or two before the next best thing hits the market. But you can extend the life of your computer by upgrading it and adding peripherals like external hard drives (to increase memory) and replacing components like video drivers (to keep up with multimedia demands).

Maintain your computer the way you would your car. Keep it clean (dust free) and take it in for a tune-up every year — having an expert do a simple check can identify computer-killing problems. Temperature control is important for most electronics as heat and humidity can wreak havoc on components; it's particularly important for extending the life of laptop batteries. Sometimes buying a newer system that's more energy efficient is actually the better choice, but before you throw away your old computer make sure that it cannot be saved with a few simple upgrades.

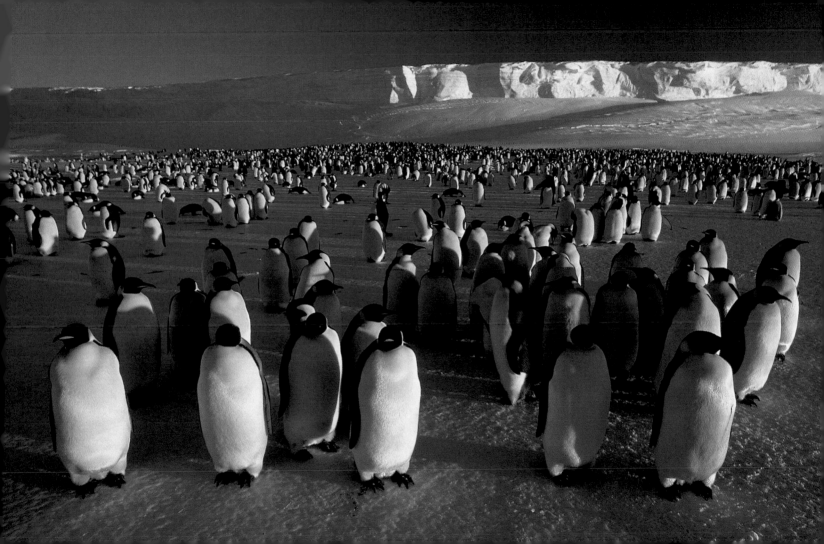

Have your home fitted with thermostatic valves.

Water is essential to the survival of all living things, making it all the more precious. If no wide-ranging action is taken, within 50 years about 3 billion people in the world will suffer from water shortages. Human beings can go without food for several weeks, but without water they die in 3 to 4 days. Access to freshwater has already become a vital issue of the twenty-first century.

To reduce water consumption, have your showers and taps fitted with thermostatic valves that help keep the water at a constant preset temperature. Your water heater will not work overtime by overheating water past the desired temperature, nor will you have to continually add cold water to balance the temperature, thereby wasting water.

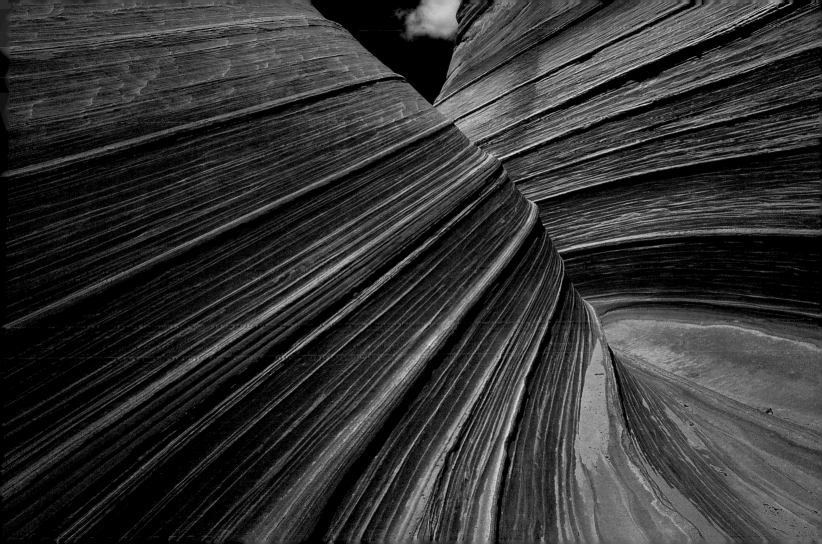

Wash your windows with vinegar.

Most of the world's pollution comes from developed countries, which produce more than 95% of dangerous pollution. However, in these countries the regulations governing the disposal of dangerous industrial waste have become so strict and involve so much expense that companies have turned to developing countries to take their waste. And industry is not the only area in which chemical products proliferate.

Most window-cleaning fluids contain synthetic compounds that are harmful to rivers and the marine environment. Replace them with 4 litres of water to which you have added a few spoonfuls of vinegar. Apply this with a cloth or newspaper rather than with a paper towel.

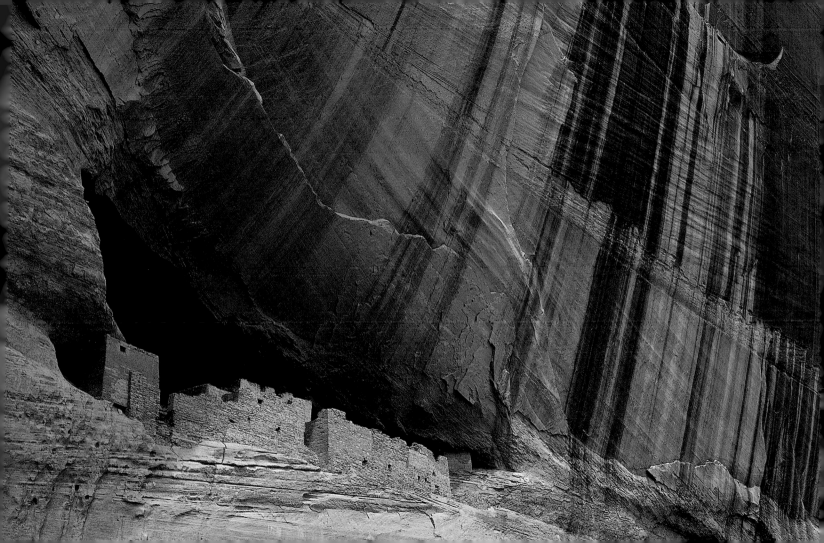

Recycle aluminium.

Aluminium is extracted from bauxite in the form of alumina. Opencast bauxite mining is one of the most destructive forms of mining, causing deforestation and destroying ecosystems. The conversion of alumina into aluminium also pollutes water and air, and consumes enormous amounts of energy. Producing recycled aluminium, however, saves 90% to 95% of the energy needed to produce new aluminium.

Take care to recycle your aluminium cans: They will reappear as aircraft and car parts, as well as new cans. Five billion drink cans are thrown away by the United Kingdom alone each year — think before you buy them, and think before you throw them away.

Yellowstone National Park,
United States

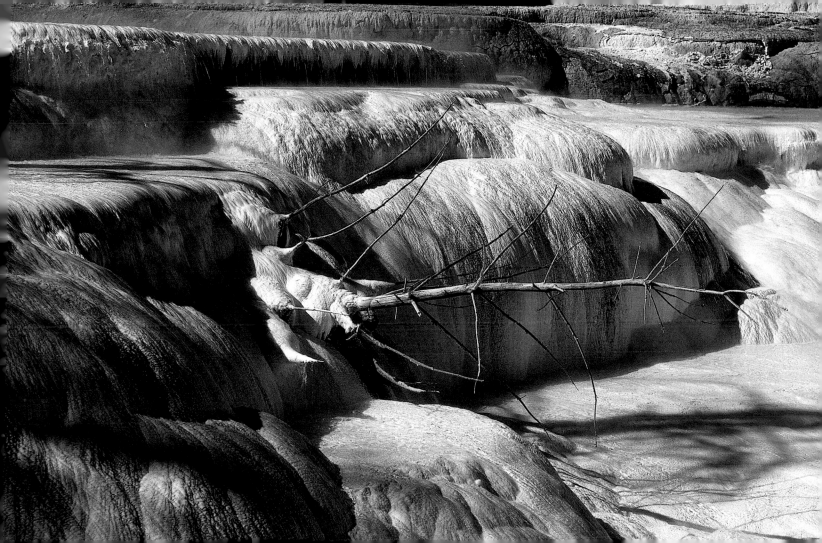

Switch to natural hair care products.

Many popular shampoos include a phalanx of harmful chemicals including methyliso-
thiazolinone, which may cause neurological damage, and formaldehyde, phthalates,
and coal tar, which are all carcinogenic. Almost all contain petroleum products and
synthetic fragrances. These chemicals do double the damage as they go down the
drain and end up in groundwater.

**Look for shampoos and conditioners that use organic and natural ingredients like
plant extracts, but read labels carefully and be on the lookout for parabens and
sulphates. Choose brands that use recycled materials in their packaging — some
shampoos even come in bar form, doing away with the need for another
plastic bottle.**

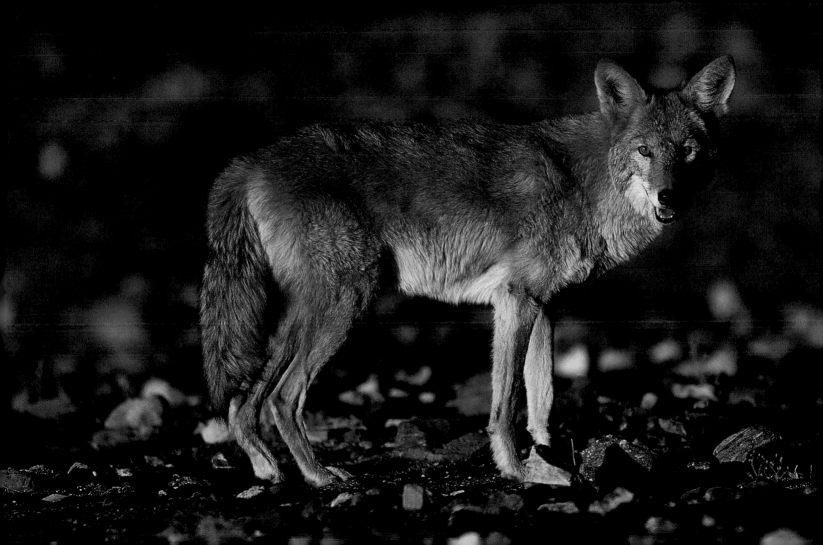

Don't use the prewash on your washing machine.

Worldwide, 80% of the energy we consume comes from the burning of fossil fuels—oil, coal, and natural gas—which emit polluting gases and increases the greenhouse effect. Renewable energy, which comes from natural sources, only accounts for a small fraction of the energy used, even though it is inexhaustible and nonpolluting: One wind turbine saves 1,000 tonnes of greenhouse gases per year. The European Union has announced that by 2020, 20% of its electricity must come from renewable sources, but it looks unlikely that this target will be met.

As we await the arrival of cleaner energy, we should not wait to start consuming less. Today's washing machines, which are highly efficient, allow you to bypass the prewash, thus saving 15% of the energy required for the full cycle.

Macaque, Japan

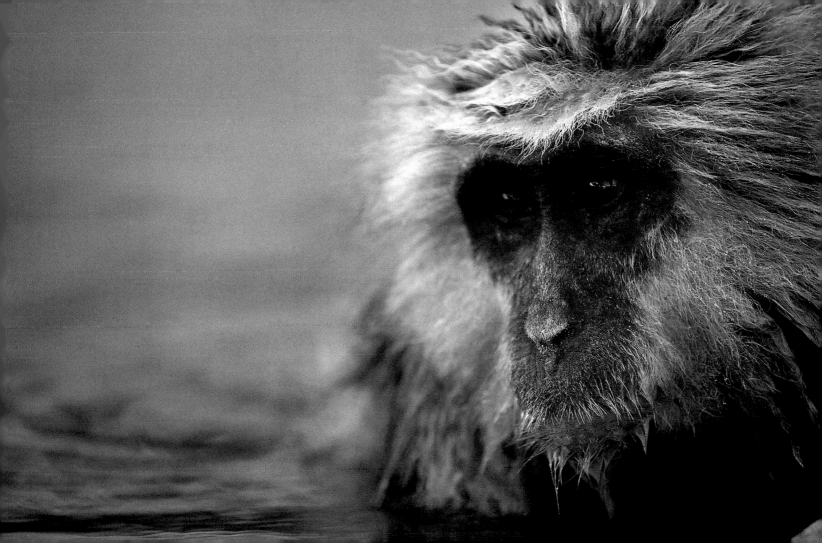

Buy used, sell used.

In 2050 there will be almost 3 billion more people on Earth than there are today. Many will be living in developing countries, and what will happen when the inhabitants of these countries want to live more comfortably, buy their own cars, and use more water or more electricity? The earth's resources cannot be increased at will, and we don't have a spare planet at our disposal.

Rediscover the joy of vintage goods, secondhand shops, garage sales, and bargaining to buy or sell used items.

Namib Desert, Namibia

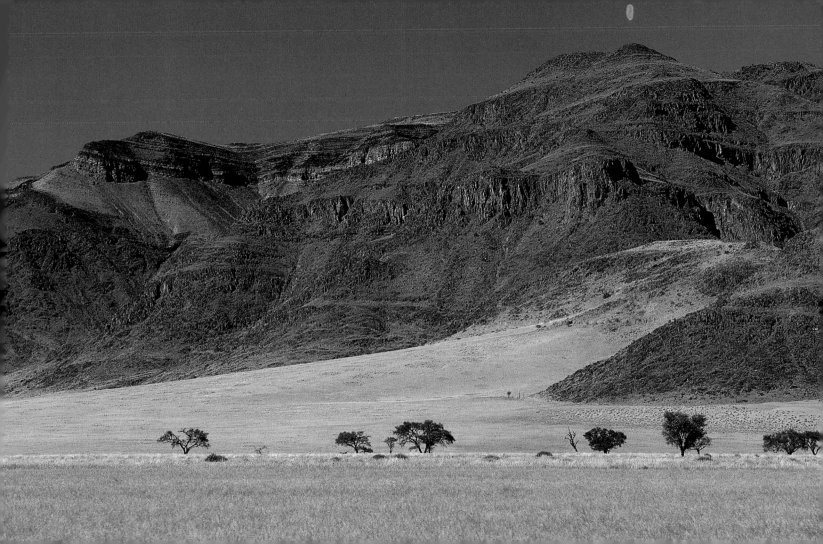

Replace disposable paper towels with washable ones.

In our throwaway world, 90% of the materials used for the production of consumer goods and their containers enter the sanitation system less than 6 weeks after the product was sold. Do not encourage this waste of natural resources.

Are disposable paper towels used in the WCs at your place of work? Why not suggest that washable towels replace them? And although they require electricity to run, hand dryers on average use fewer resources than paper towels.

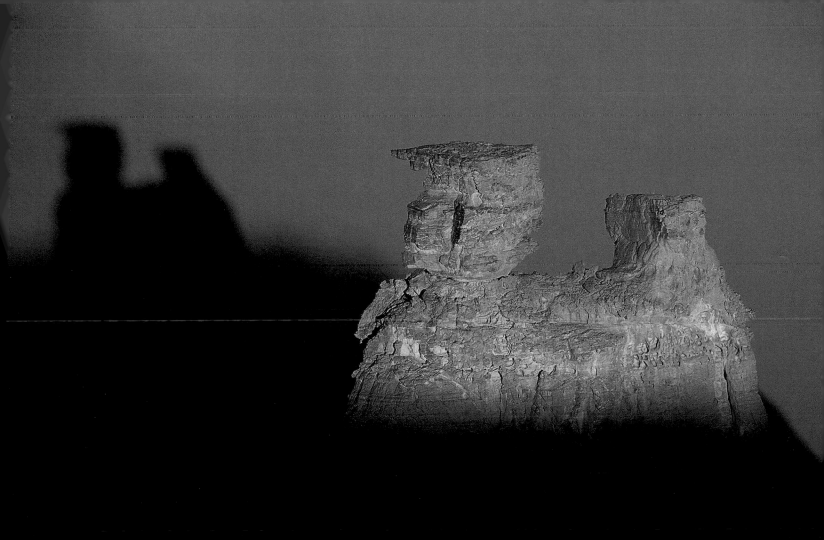

Do not use chemicals to unblock drains.

Chemicals affect our health—causing asthma, allergies, cancers, and reduced fertility—and the health of the environment. They disturb the reproduction of certain species, kill aquatic life, make wastewater even more difficult and expensive to treat, and pollute air and soil. Despite all this, human beings continue to come up with about 1,000 new substances every year, which are added to the 70,000 chemical products already on the market.

Most of the toxic chemicals used to unblock pipes contain lye or sulphuric acid. They are highly corrosive and extremely dangerous. Instead, use a mixture of boiling water, baking soda, and a plunger.

River, Iceland

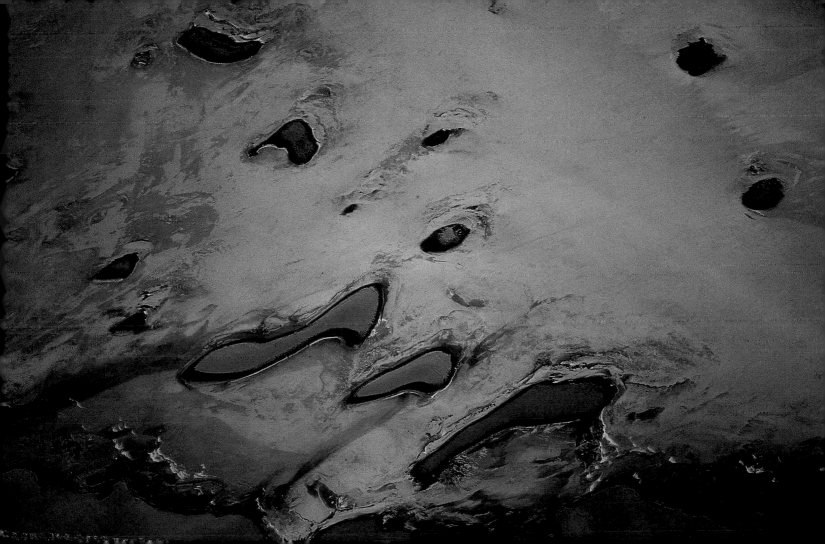

Choose petroleum-free cosmetics.

Many of us grew up thinking of petroleum jelly (Vaseline) as a personal care cure-all—used for everything from easing minor burns to removing eye makeup to moisturizing the face and lips. But petroleum derivatives in personal care are more hurtful than helpful (mineral oil, for example, may lock in moisture but blocks pores in the process; propylene glycol, another common additive, has been linked to liver and kidney damage and weakens cellular structure). You'll find these additives in most cosmetics, and hair- and skin-care products. The EU's Cosmetics Directive, which requires European manufacturers to rid their products of chemicals that are carcinogenic, mutagenic, or toxic, has included many petroleum-based additives on its list of banned substances. In addition to its possible toxic effects, petroleum is a nonrenewable resource and ridding our personal care items of it is significant—Europeans buy over 5 billion cosmetic products each year.

Check labels carefully for mineral oil, petrolatum, paraffin, and propylene glycol. Don't automatically trust 'organic' brands—some use parabens, which are petroleum-derived preservatives. When choosing lip care products, opt for beeswax.

Emperor penguin, Antarctica

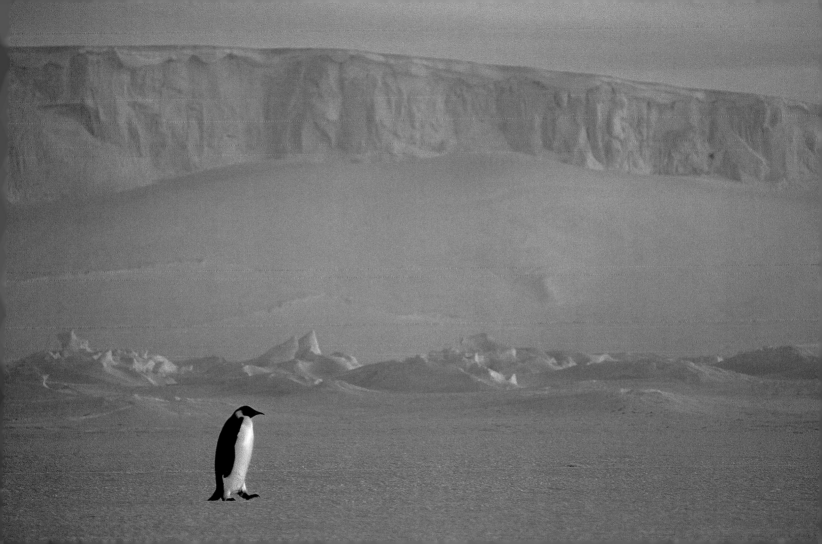

Learn where your paper products originate.

Less than 3 percent of the virgin forests in Europe remain intact. More than 150 square kilometres of intact forest landscapes fall victim to the chainsaw every year, and the intact boreal forests in Russia are shrinking rapidly. Only 20% of the world's ancient forests remain large enough to maintain their biodiversity.

Consider switching to alternative fibres for your paper products, including 100% post-consumer recycled paper, or paper made with agricultural residue. There are hundreds of alternative paper companies from which to choose.

Nyiragongo Volcano, Congo

Discover the wetlands in your area.

Wetlands — the collective term for marshes, peat bogs, ponds, wet grasslands, and estuaries — account for 6% of the earth's land mass. They are some of the richest and most valuable natural environments, filtering out pollution and purifying the waters that are seeping toward rivers and underground reservoirs, and at the same time acting as sponges to guard against both flooding and drought. Despite this vital ecological role, they are constantly receding in the face of encroaching human activity: urban expansion, development along rivers and coasts, and agriculture. This is a heritage in danger: Since 1900 half of the world's wetlands have disappeared.

Wetlands have inspired the creative talents of humans from the earliest times in all climatic zones, producing a great wealth of songs, music, dance, art, literature, stories, and rituals. It is likely that wetlands exist close to where you live. Find out where the nearest are, and visit them; learn what you can do to protect them from development.

Arches National Park,
United States

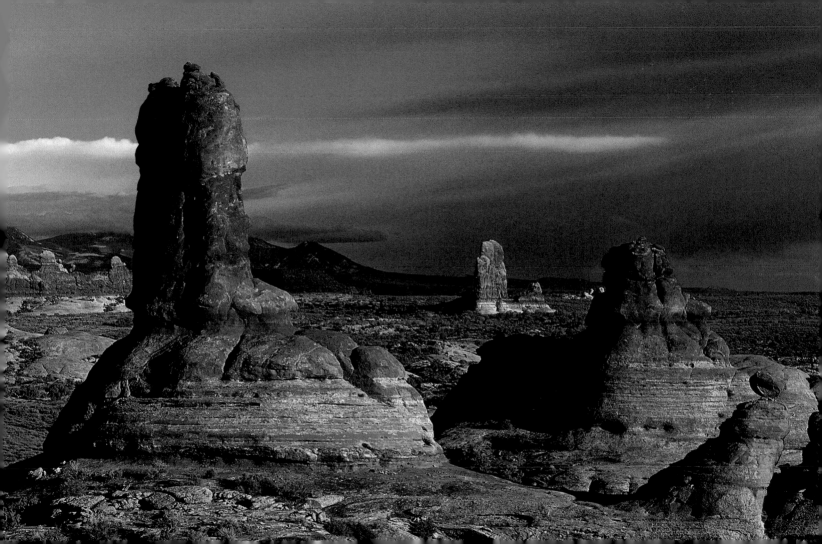

Use reusable shopping bags.

Each year, the United Kingdom uses an estimated 17.5 billion plastic carrier bags; only 7% of total plastic waste is recycled. If dropped in nature, a plastic bag will last for over 200 years. If incinerated, they produce pollutants. In the sea, they prove fatal for crustaceans, which swallow them, mistaking them for jellyfish. And they are not biodegradable in the ocean. Almost half a square kilometer of ocean may be contaminated by as many as 46,000 pieces of plastic.

Rediscover your trusty old shopping bags, baskets, and boxes, and bring them with you to the supermarket. Keep bags on a hook by the front door so you can grab them on your way out to the store.

Sequoias, United States

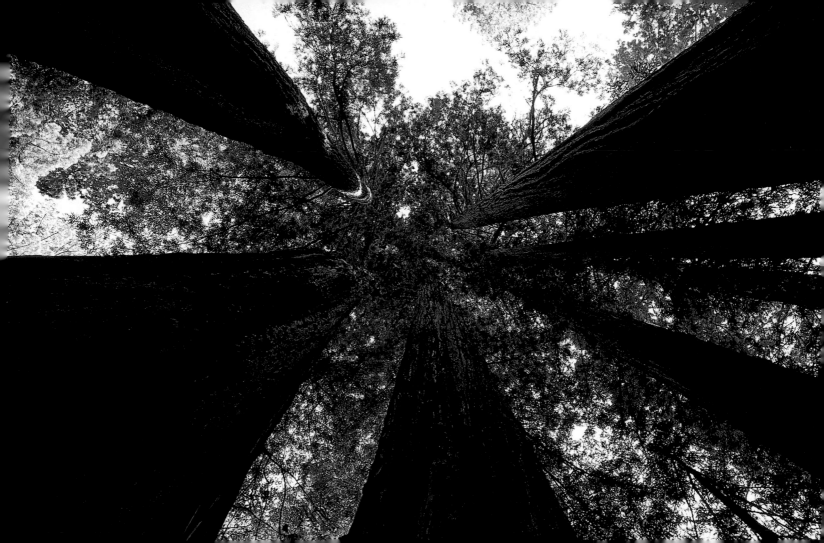

Have your engine serviced and tuned.

The decade of the 1990s was the warmest ever recorded, particularly the end of the decade. By 2100, global warming will have brought major changes. The earth's average temperature will have risen by between 1.1°C and 6.4°C.

To avoid contributing to global warming, have your engine regularly serviced (carburettor, ignition, air filter) by a professional. With a properly tuned engine, you will reduce your vehicle's polluting emissions by 20% and save up to 10% on petrol.

Dallol Volcano, Ethiopia

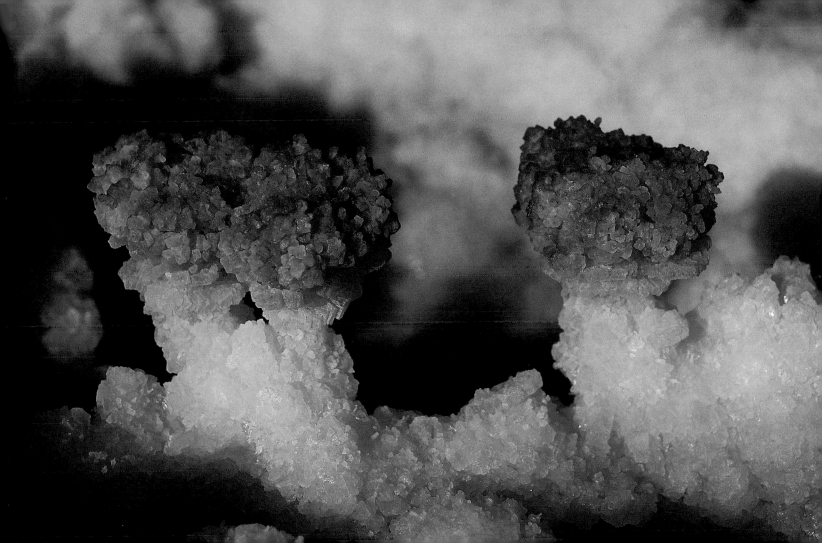

Don't think of sustainability in terms of sacrifice.

So many green living tips speak of cutting back—conserving water and energy, driving less, reducing your personal waste stream—that it's easy to dwell on what we think we're giving up, instead of what we're gaining. The environmental movement is not anti-technology or anti-progress: Many of the world's problems will in fact be solved by cutting-edge design and technology. And the goods and experiences that replace our unsustainable practises will be of much higher quality than any of the things we're so attached to today.

Don't dwell on perceived losses. Think of the exercise you've taken while walking or biking instead of driving; the greater health you're promoting by eating fewer processed foods; or the better connections you're fostering with other cultures when you travel responsibly.

Lake Natron, Tanzania

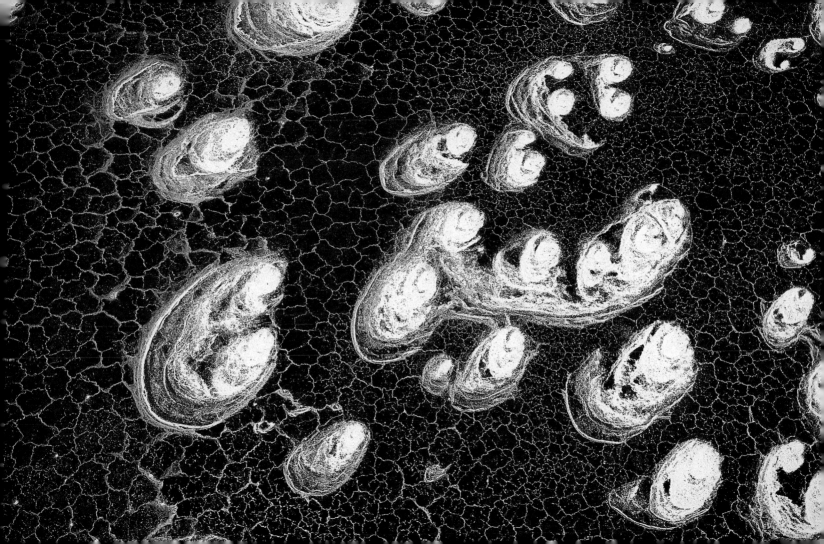

Buy local, and not just your food.

The abundance of cheap oil has made the world a small place. Products from around the world crowd our grocery store shelves. Plastic toys hail from a multitude of Asian countries, such as China, India, and Thailand, and every year world transportation statistics rise.

Think of the waste of resources, the pollution, and the contribution to the greenhouse effect from cargo aircraft and trucks. Do not encourage the transport of goods over long distances: Seek out locally made products. This will help create jobs by stimulating economic activity, and encourage the development of shorter, less polluting delivery routes.

Rain forest, Malaysia

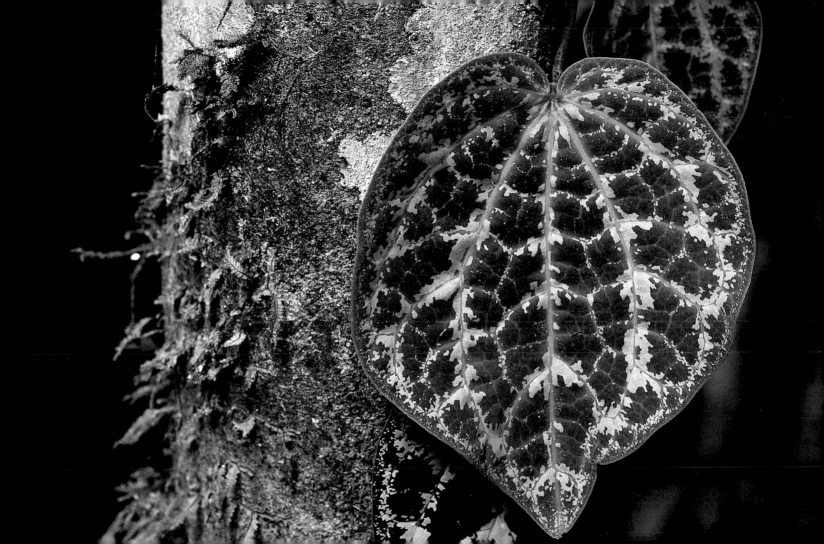

Green your Halloween.

As Halloween becomes ever more widely celebrated, think about the impact of your ghoulish revels. Most costumes are made of plastic or PVC, and are thrown away after one use—and there are many other aspects of Halloween that celebrate consumerism rather than the ancient marking of All Soul's Day.

Rent a costume or invest in a better quality one made of natural fibres that can be worn year after year. Secondhand shops are great sources for retro costumes and most of the materials can be resold or donated. Get a locally sourced, pesticide-free pumpkin and use the carvings to make soup or dessert. Light up your jack-o'-lantern with nontoxic candles made from soy or beeswax and remember to throw old jack in the compost bin.

Ice, Iceland

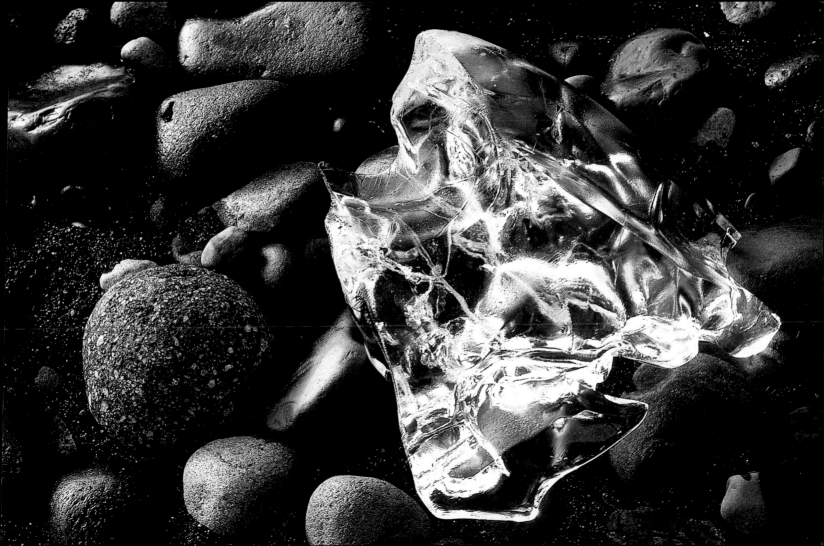

Save the trees, but see the forest.

So much of the language of sustainability focuses on the state of our natural world that it's easy to compartmentalise our efforts, focusing solely on habitat and wildlife conservation. However, we can't forget that sustainability is about social equality as well. Social inequalities, human rights violations, corrupt or inefficient governance — all of these things make our world harder to live in, our species unsustainable.

We need to keep planting trees and saving energy, yet there are many more ways to encourage a sustainable future that cannot be measured in kilowatt-hours — it may be campaigning for freedom of the press in a country where information is heavily censored; working to ensure for basic education — a right and not a commodity; or puzzling out better methods of conflict resolution.

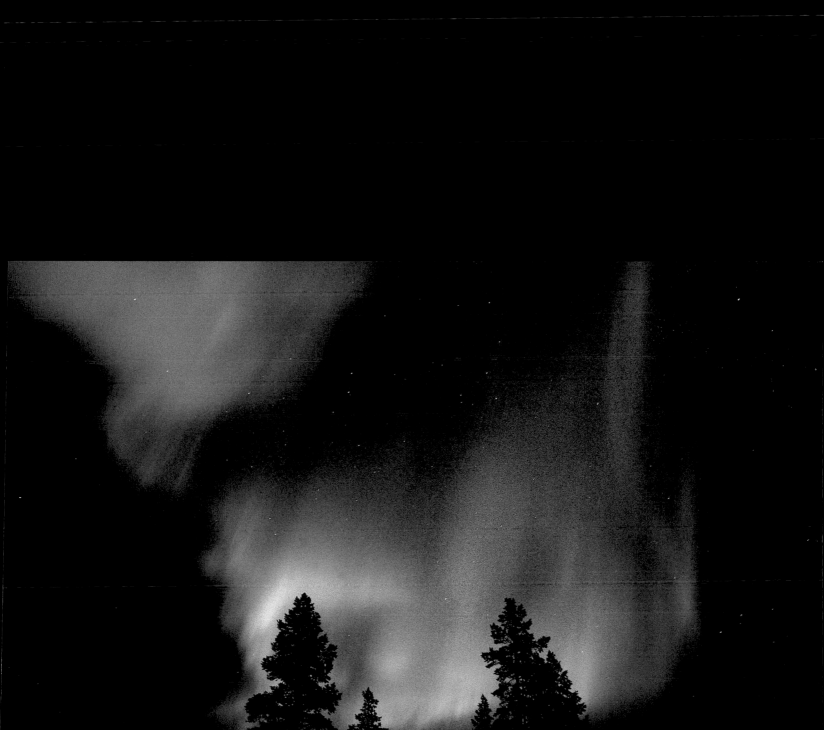

Drive an electric car.

Electric cars are well suited to city use. They are powered by batteries, which are recharged from the main supply via a charger and a plug similar to that of a washing machine. Electric vehicles emit no pollutants and are silent in operation, and are therefore effective in reducing urban air pollution. Moreover, the cost of the electricity needed to travel 97 kilometres is a fifth of that of petrol, and an electric car's maintenance costs are 40% lower (there is no need to change the oil), insurance and car tax is cheaper, and parking is free in some cities.

If you need a car in a city for short- or medium-length journeys, think about buying an electric car — and buy your electricity from a green provider to complete the virtuous circle.

Talkeetna Mountains,
United States

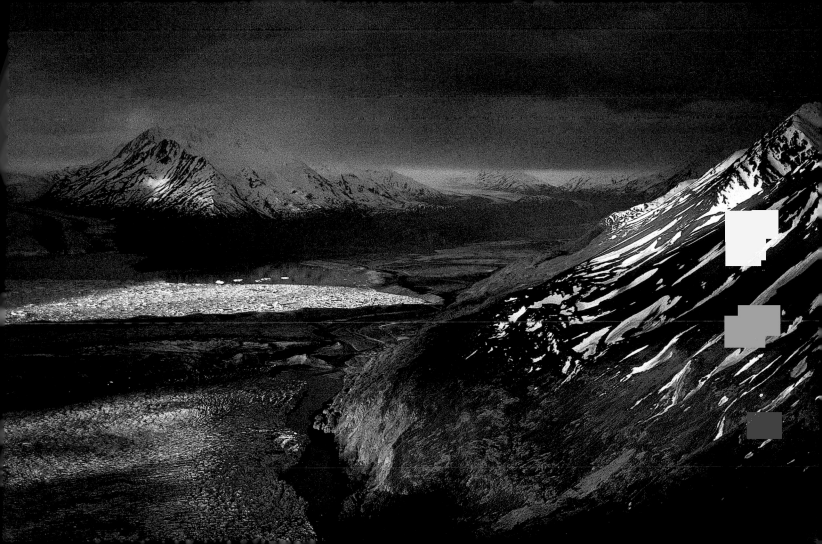

Take action through committees at work.

In your workplace, various measures can be taken to make room for the environment in day-to-day life. These include an employee travel plan, use of clean vehicles, adoption of nonpolluting and energy-efficient technologies, waste recycling, and purchase of recycled, organic, and fair-trade products.

Talk to your colleagues about these choices. Discuss them with those responsible for purchasing, with members of your workplace committee, with the cafeteria chef, and with management, to come up with appropriate plans.

Water lilies, Venezuela

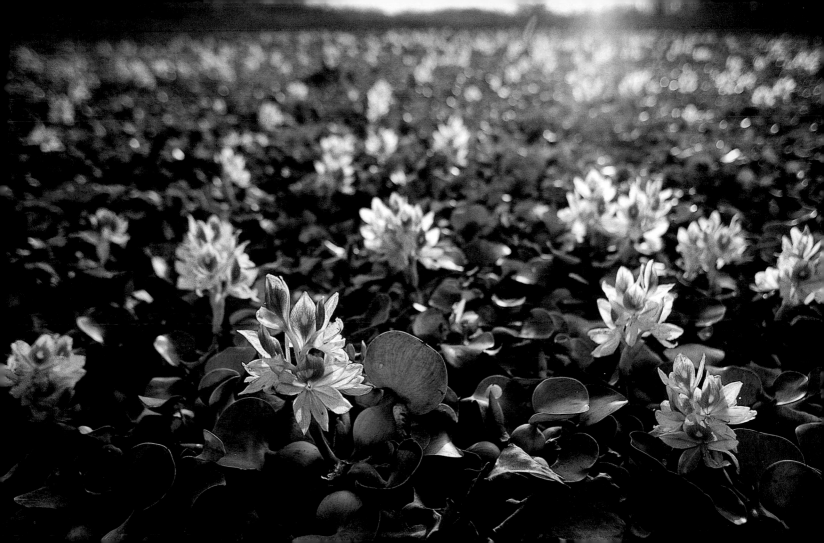

Use your vote.

Voting is the best way to make your hopes and needs known. Our power as citizens includes the election of people who represent us, and whose job it is, in theory, to set an example. Find out the environmental policies of all the political parties, and vote accordingly. It is both simple and essential.

———————————————

Do not forget that you also cast votes several times each day by what you buy, and by your choices as a consumer. These choices influence, sometimes even more than elections do, means of production and the way the economy is organised, and they contribute to the way in which society develops.

Northern forests, Russia

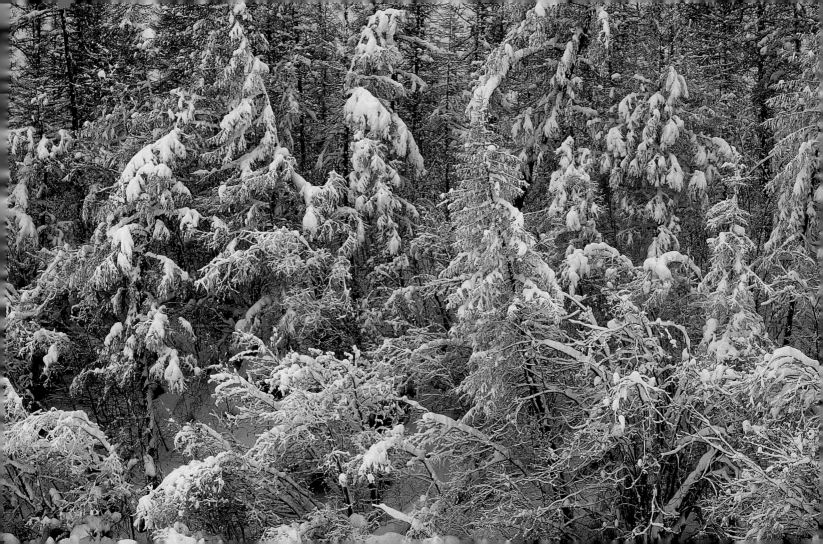

Be green about Guy Fawkes.

On Bonfire Night, we burn tonnes of fireworks that create huge amounts of smoke pollution along with the excitement. The bonfires themselves also pollute, and many people are less than careful about adding toxic materials to the fire. Approximately 14% of the UK's dioxins — highly toxic particles linked to cancer — are produced around Bonfire Night, mostly from bonfires.

Instead of having a bonfire celebration at home, get together with your neighbours to organise a joint party, or go to your local municipal firework display — that way you can have all the fun with a fraction of the environmental cost.

Yellowstone National Park,
United States

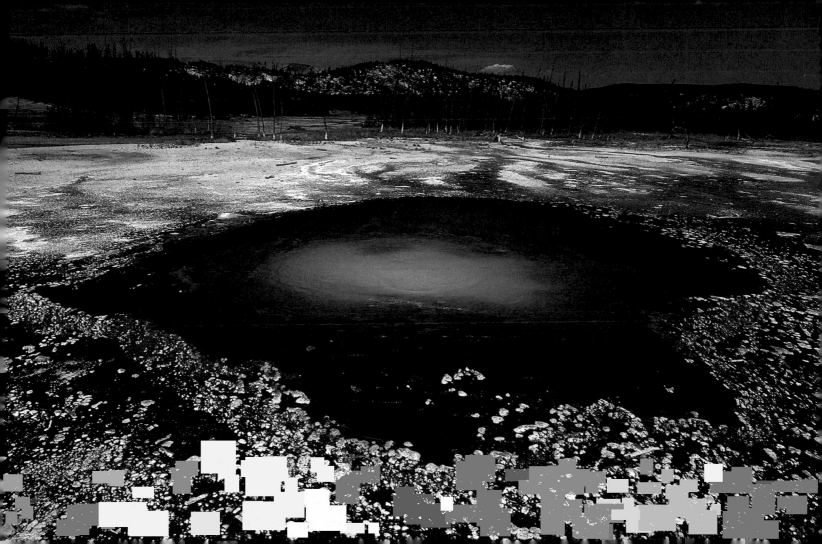

Choose renewable energy for your home.

There are many ways that you can make your home closer to the zero-carbon ideal. Solar energy, which is free, easily accessible, and easily converted, can help to heat water and the rest of the house, without producing pollution or greenhouse gases. Geothermal heat pumps that use the energy calories stored in the ground (also free, renewable, and nonpolluting) can provide part of your heating and reduce your electricity bill. Most of these installations qualify for grants and financial aid.

Find out more. Your local authorities and a number of organisations like the Energy Savings Trust provide free practical advice on energy use and renewable energy, which will reduce your bills while protecting the planet.

Ripples in the sand, Algeria

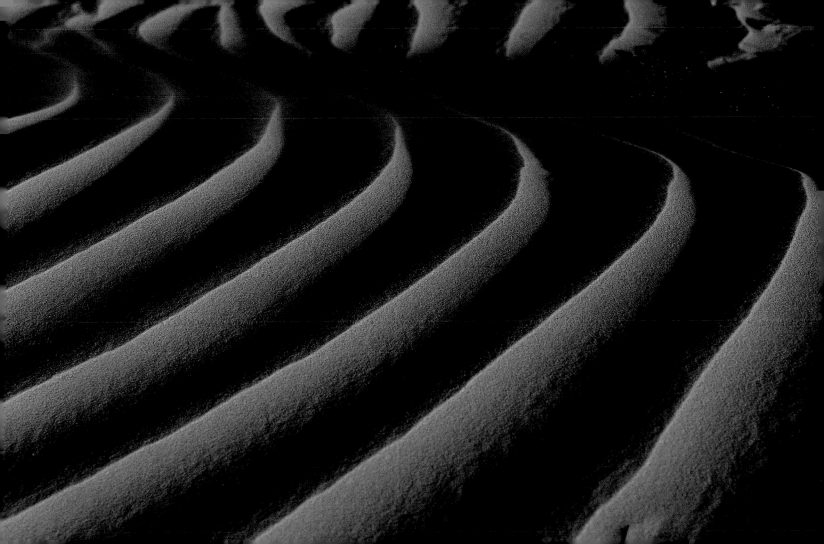

Give away your old furniture and household appliances.

There are charitable organisations that collect unwanted furniture and old appliances and will repair and sell them, either intact or for parts. At last report, there were over 400 organisations in the United Kingdom diverting over 2.5 million items from the waste stream. Many of these will collect items from your home for free, recondition them, and resell or donate them to businesses, charities, and low-income families for another useful life. In the United Kingdom over 700,000 low-income households have been helped in this way—yet over 4 million children live in households that cannot afford to replace broken furniture.

Rather than throwing out unwanted goods, find a reuse centre in your area—you can help more than the environment.

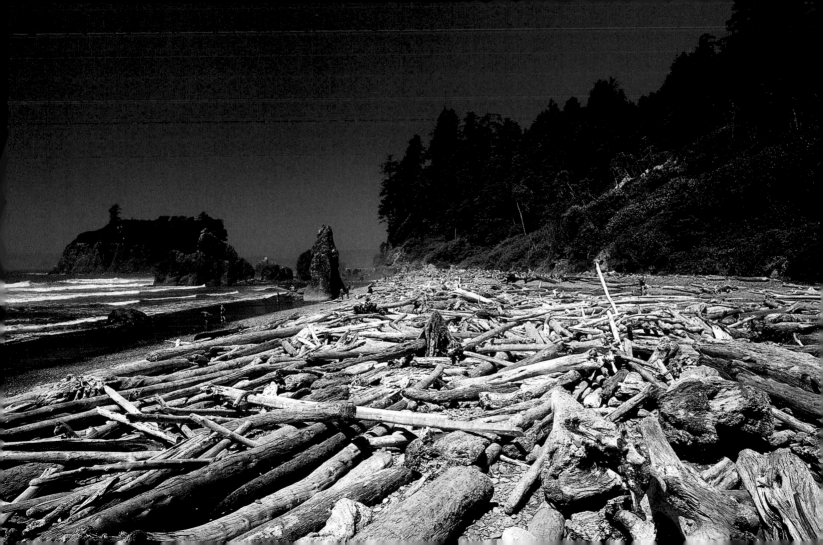

Buy in bulk.

The United Kingdom alone produces over 3 million tonnes of plastic waste every year. Not all of those discarded plastic bottles held drinks or bottled water. Tonnes of plastic shampoo, conditioner, washing-up liquid, and cleaning product bottles get tossed every year, many before the contents are fully used up.

Some shops now offer the facility to refill bottles of detergent or beauty projects. Alternatively, buy in a bulk size from a beauty-supply store using the extra-large container to refill one smaller, reusable bottle. If you buy lotions from a specialized retail store, ask if they'll refill your empty containers.

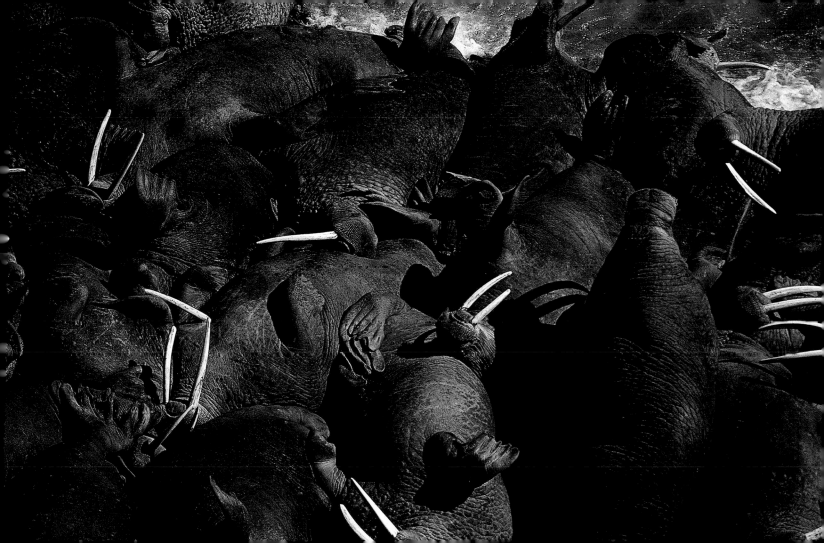

Buy A-rated household appliances.

Every product comes with an ecological footprint. Everything we buy draws on natural resources for raw materials and for the energy needed for its manufacture, and releases the waste and pollution it generates into the environment. Our present mode of consumption is therefore one of the biggest reasons for the rapid degradation of the environment that we are experiencing on a global scale.

All new appliances in the European Union now carry an easy-to-read energy label indicating their energy efficiency. Make sure you always buy A-rated.

Dunes, Chad

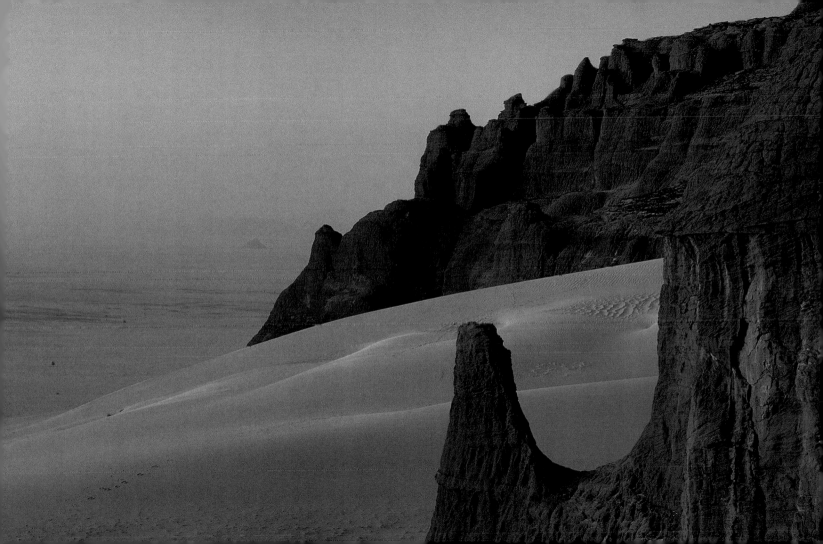

Make better coffee.

If you've gone to the trouble of buying fair-trade coffee, you don't want to offset the good you've done by brewing your coffee in a machine that wastes energy and natural resources. Don't be fooled by the 'efficiency' of 1-cup coffeemakers that brew individual pods of prepackaged coffee—the waste caused by all the excess packaging (especially if the pods are made of plastics) isn't worth the energy you save by quickly heating a very small amount of water. Filterless coffeepots, like French presses, cut down or eliminate paper waste and use no electricity. If you like filter coffee, don't use an electric one, but make a tastier, better cup using a traditional filter and unbleached papers.

Make a pot of coffee in the time-honoured, traditional way, and pour any leftovers into a thermos to keep it hot.

Inlandsis, Greenland

Reduce the noise you make in your neighbourhood.

Noise is part of our environment and plays a part in our quality of life. Noise pollution has clear effects on our bodies — it can cause irritability, indigestion, high blood pressure, and lack of sleep. In all developed countries, there are set standards for the level of noise that is defined as reasonable, but these are often poorly enforced.

Contribute to a happier neighbourhood, and be considerate of the noise that you make. Be aware of the noise level in your home and work environments and try to eliminate as much noise as possible — it will be better for you, and for your neighbours.

Huangshan Mountains, China

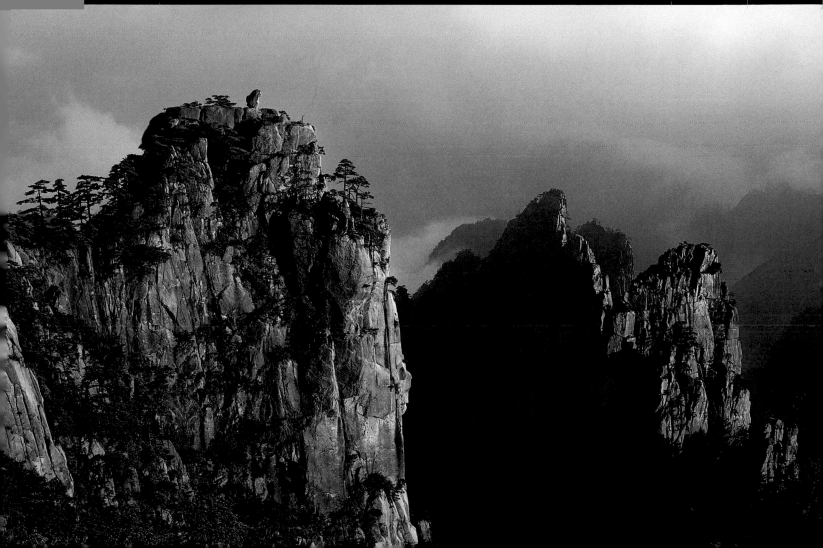

Choose greener, safer paints.

Paints used inside the home may contain up to 50% organic solvents. These render them more liquid and easier to apply. However, they emit volatile organic compounds (VOCs) that are diffused in the air and are a threat to health. Inhalation and absorption through the skin can affect the nervous system and internal organs, as well as irritate the eyes, nose, and throat.

Choose paints that do not contain harmful solvents, heavy metals, or synthetic binders. Replace them with natural paints made from plants that have a mineral base, such as vegetable oils (linseed, castor oil, rosemary, or lavender), beeswax, natural resins (such as pine), casein, or chalk as binders; balsamic oil of turpentine, or citrus distillates as solvents; and vegetable pigments (valerian, tea, onion), or mineral ones (sienna, iron oxides). They have minimum impact on the environment and on your health, and their quality is just as good.

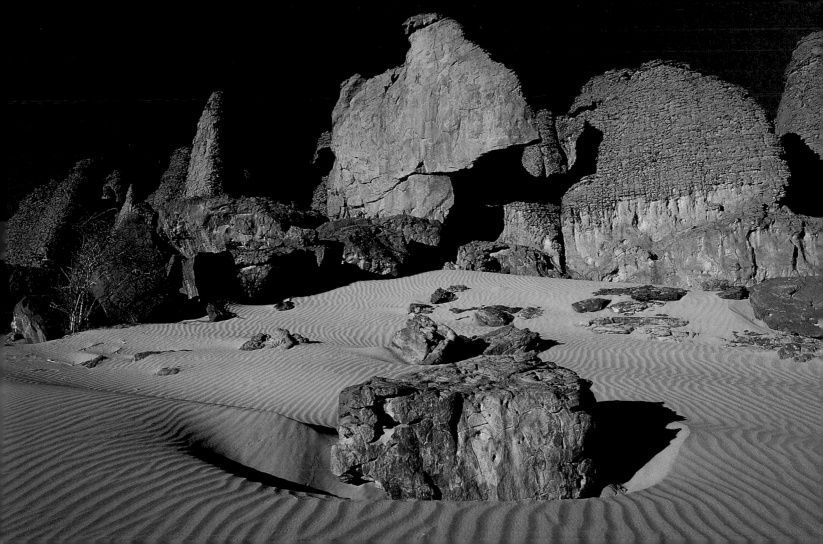

Make socially and environmentally responsible investments.

Some banks contribute to increasing the debt burdens of developing countries; favour the manufacture or sale of arms; or support dictatorial regimes through trade associations. Socially Responsible Investing (SRI) on the other hand, not only looks at the bottom line, but also at the environmental and social impact of where your money goes. SRI seeks out companies that demonstrate that they have obligations toward the environment and society, and not just to the consumer; companies that develop collaborative relationships with employees and investors; and finally, businesses that are honest and transparent in their reporting processes.

Make ethical investments. Show business that there is more to the bottom line — that improving the conditions of the planet and our societies is just as important as making money.

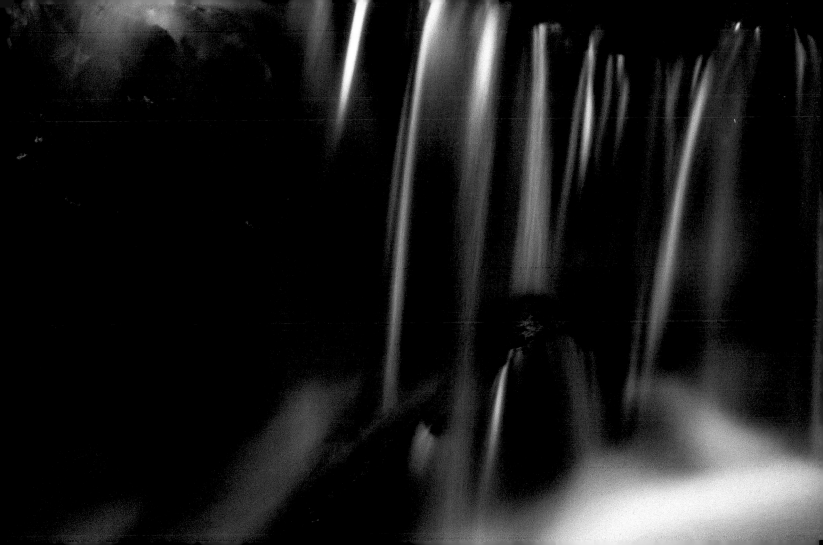

Feed energy back into the grid.

Installing a wind turbine or another renewable energy system can significantly reduce your personal energy bill. And if you produce more energy than you use, several countries in Europe now offer a system called net-metering that feed the excess power back into the national grid. This means that you would be paid the same price for surplus electricity exported to the national grid during daylight hours, as you pay for any conventional electricity imported at night. This also helps energy suppliers to distribute more alternative power produced using clean methods.

Think about installing renewable power generation equipment, if you have the right kind of home. You might be able to make your home carbon neutral, and even have clean energy to spare.

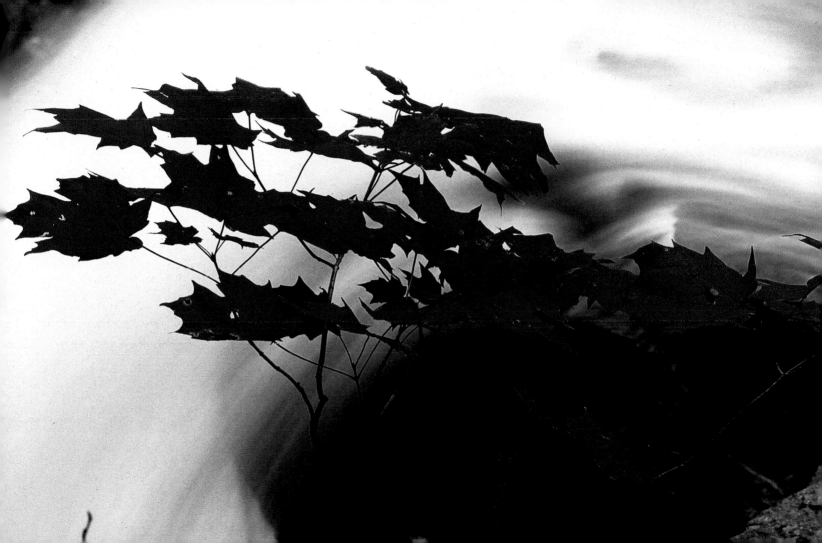

Dust your lightbulbs.

You can cut your electricity consumption by using less light and heating at home. If everyone does the same, global electricity demand will go down, and so will the use of coal, gas, and oil, along with the corresponding carbon-dioxide emissions that contribute to climate change. Conservation is also cheaper and more efficient than technological fixes—that is, changing to an energy-efficient compact fluorescent bulb (CFL) is very good, but turning off the lamp with a CFL in it is even better.

Remember to wipe the dust off your lightbulbs; this increases the amount of light they give off by 40% to 50% and provides better lighting for the same cost.

Acid lake, Waiotapu,
New Zealand

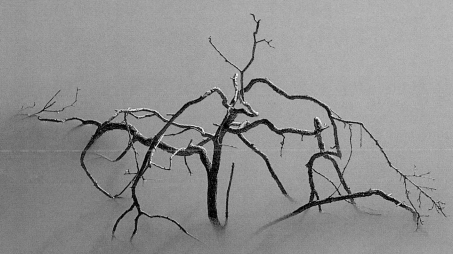

Defrost your freezer.

Our refrigeration appliances use a lot of energy. They use even more if we do not look after them. When the layer of ice inside a freezer is thicker than 5 millimetres, it is time to defrost it. Any thicker and the ice acts as an insulating layer that can increase electricity consumption by up to 30%.

Take care when defrosting: Do not try to save time by using a sharp object to break the ice. You risk making a hole in the cooling system, which would release polluting gases into the atmosphere, as well as damaging your appliance.

Orinoco Basin, Venezuela

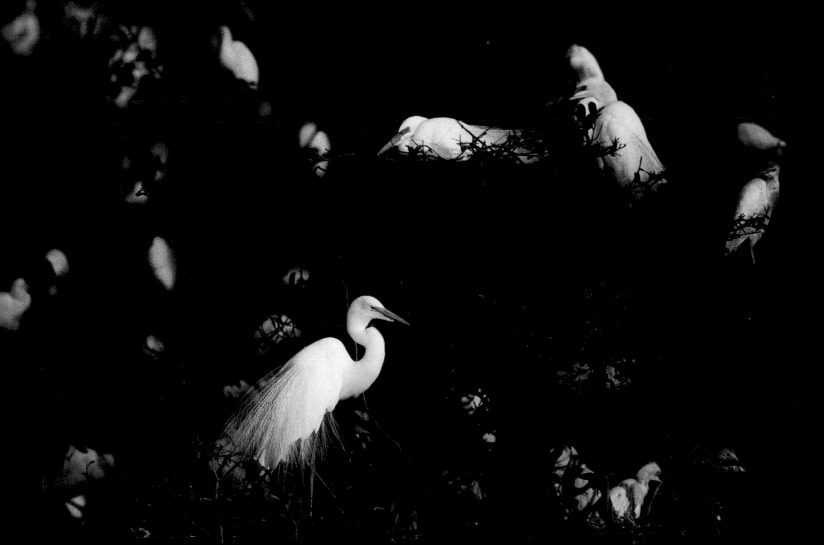

Buy less meat.

Our choices of food can encourage sustainable farming practices and contribute to solving food shortages in developing countries. Raising animals for meat uses large amounts of grain, and the huge growth in global demand for meat is resulting in food shortages in many less wealthy countries. Farmers now use 250 million tonnes more grain to feed animals than they did 20 years ago. We eat more meat than ever before, and have forgotten how to make best use of the cheaper cuts and leftovers, or that a slow-cooked stew full of vegetables can be far more delicious than a huge, bland steak from an intensively reared cow.

Decide not to eat meat for 3 days a week — it is healthier, and will contribute to a more equitable food economy. And when you do buy meat, only buy organic and from local producers — and make the most of what you buy when you cook, by reducing portion sizes for meat and including more vegetables.

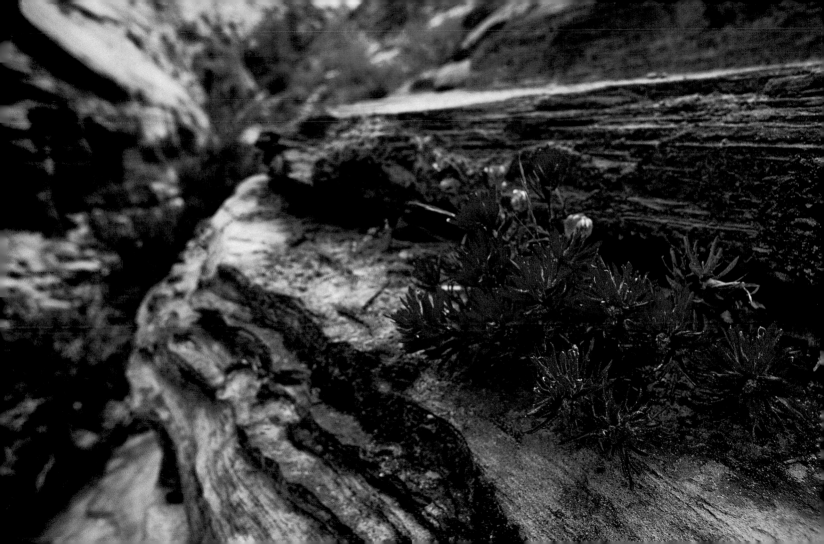

Choose your heating apparatus carefully: Consult a specialist.

Electric heating uses a lot of energy and is expensive: This is apparent on your bill in the winter, especially if rooms are not well insulated. If you are having building or renovation work done, now is the time to choose a heating system that uses renewable energy, such as wood-pellet cookers or solar heating. Among fossil-fuel energy sources, natural-gas heating is the least polluting. Pellet stoves are the cleanest of solid fuel-burning appliances. They can burn a variety of organic waste—pellets can contain wood scraps, corn kernels, and other corn by-products, pits, and nutshells—and are direct-vented and airtight, so you don't lose the hot air generated through an open flue.

To choose the most energy-efficient and least-polluting heating system, consult a specialist, who will be able to advise on the best energy options for your home and your needs.

Gray whales, Mexico

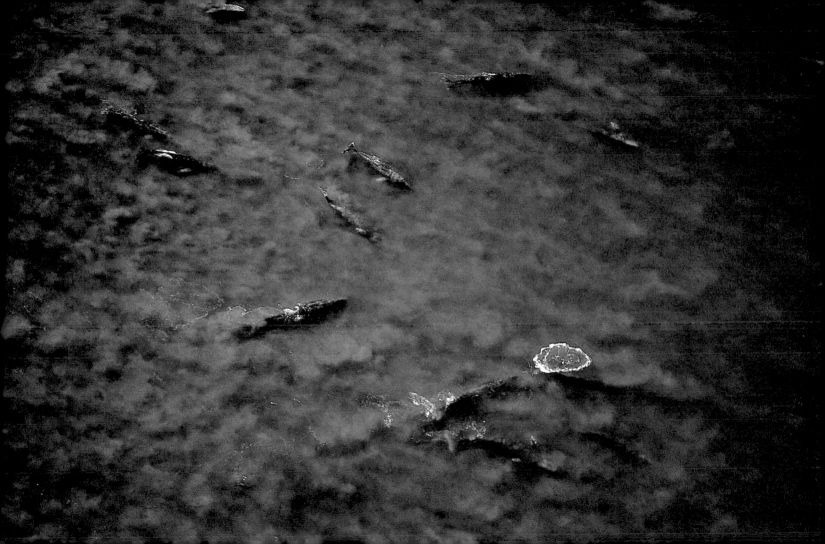

Buy energy-efficient Christmas lights.

If left on from dusk until dawn, 10 strings of standard Christmas lights produce roughly 136 kilograms of carbon dioxide. The same number of light-emitting diodes (LEDs), on the other hand, generates only 13.6 kilograms. By switching the lights on its iconic Rockefeller Centre Christmas tree to LEDs, the City of New York cut the tree's energy use in half, saving, each day, the equivalent of the amount of energy used by an entire family in a 185-square-metre home each month.

Replace incandescent lights with LEDs. Some manufacturers make lights that come with a small solar panel for recharging. LEDs don't overheat so they are safe to use on trees, and if one light burns out, it doesn't affect the rest of the strand. Even if you use only LEDs, control them with a timer to limit the number of hours you run your holiday lights — don't leave them on all night.

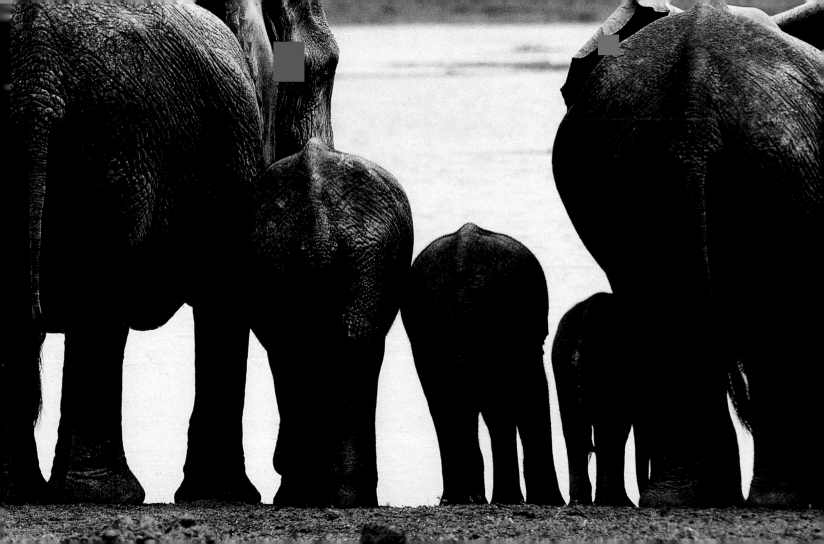

Find out about the decisions made by your local authorities.

Information is indispensable if we are to understand what is truly at stake in environmental issues, and how to take action. Local authorities are required to release information about their environmental policies, initiatives, and the impact of their activities. Look online or ask your local councillors how they are prioritising environmental issues in your area. Are there decisions in keeping with sustainable development, respect for the environment, and a fair society?

Look for information and demand it if you can't easily find it. Your local authorities and government agencies are accountable to you as voting, tax-paying citizens, so make sure that they take account of your principles and concerns.

Ray, Australia

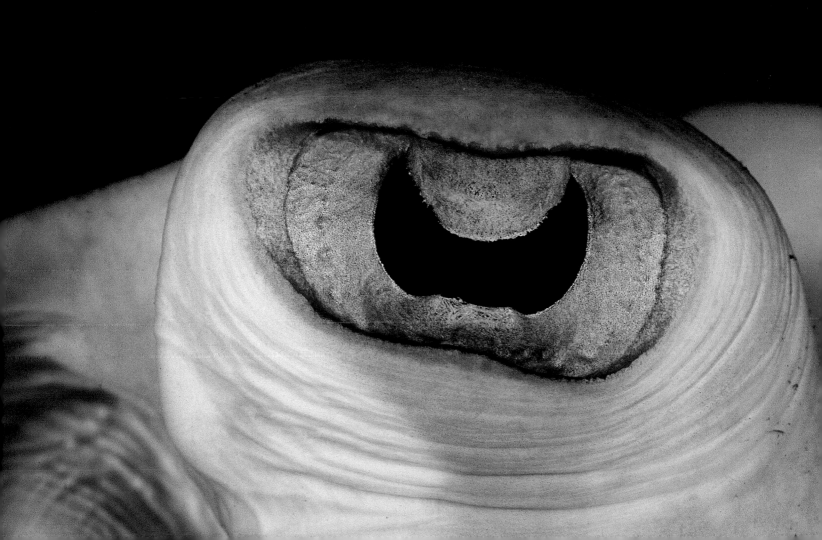

Your saucepans can save energy, too.

Putting a saucepan on the cooker is an utterly commonplace act, yet by paying attention to small details you can use less heat and save energy without changing the way you cook.

Use pots and pans with flat bottoms. Do not place a pot on too big a ring if using an electric cooker; if you are cooking on gas, turn the flame down so that the contents do not boil over and spill around the sides. This wastes the energy that was used to heat the liquid. When boiling food in water, use just enough water to cover it — it is pointless to boil twice what you need.

Atacama Desert, Bolivia

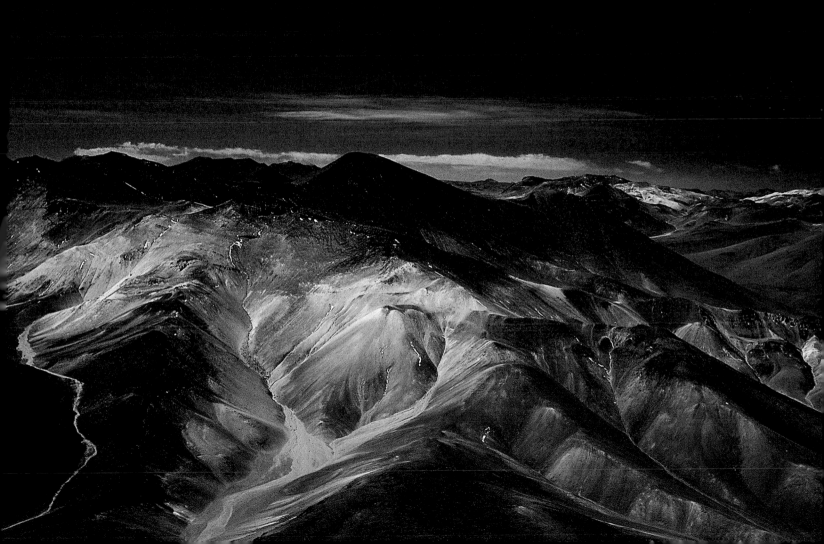

Lobby for better cycling provision.

Using a bicycle to commute to work 4 out of 5 days a week for an 8-mile round trip would save 54 gallons of gas annually. If every worker did this, our demand for and reliance on oil would plummet. However, high-speed traffic, dangerous junctions, and distracted drivers are enough reason to keep many people from riding on city streets. Even those who make the switch to cycling are frustrated by the lack of secure bike parking and ways to link bike trips with public transport.

Demand that your city provide a greater infrastructure for cyclists — one that goes beyond painting a few narrow bike lanes on already congested streets. Organisations such as Critical Mass hold rallies in support of cycling, and when your local authority publishes plans for road alterations or relandscaping in your area, demand that they include dedicated cycle paths or lanes that are physically separate from motor traffic, and separate signals for bikes.

Rain forest, Malaysia

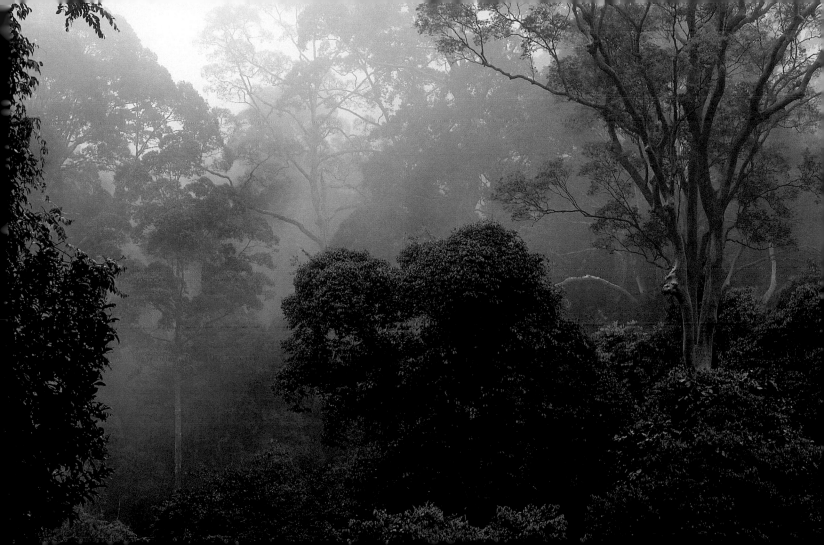

Say 'no' to disposable nappies.

It takes 4.5 trees to produce the pulp needed for the 4,600 disposable nappies an average baby needs. A glassful of crude oil is needed to make the plastic found in a single disposable diaper. The nappy is worn only a few hours, but will take about 400 years to decompose in the waste dump. There has always been an alternative: washable 'real' nappies. Absorbent, effective, and comfortable, reusable modern nappies can be very different from the old, folding variety. A single washable layer can be used for several years. When it is finally thrown out, it decomposes in 6 months, without producing any pollution.

Choose the economical, and ecological, nappy: Cover your baby's bottom in cloth.

Stalactites, Greenland

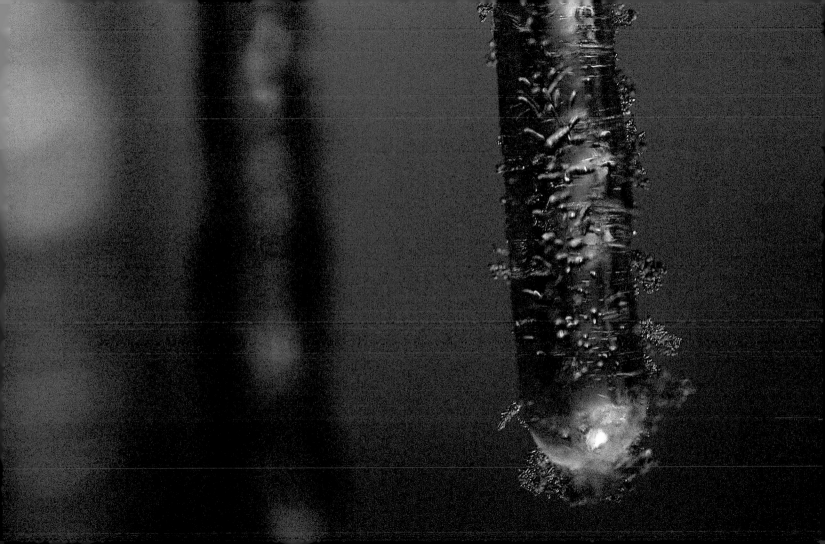

When you fly, pack lightly.

The white plumes of exhaust that fan out from airplanes are called contrails, essentially water vapour given off by jet engines as they burn fuel. Contrails can condense and linger in the air, trapping heat and thereby worsening global warming. Airplanes generally fly at higher altitudes to conserve fuel—the air is thinner, so there's less resistance. However, it's at these higher altitudes that contrails form.

Some 747s burn 4 litres of fuel each second. The heavier the aircraft, the more fuel it burns. Pack only the essentials and use lightweight luggage.

Yellowstone National Park, United States

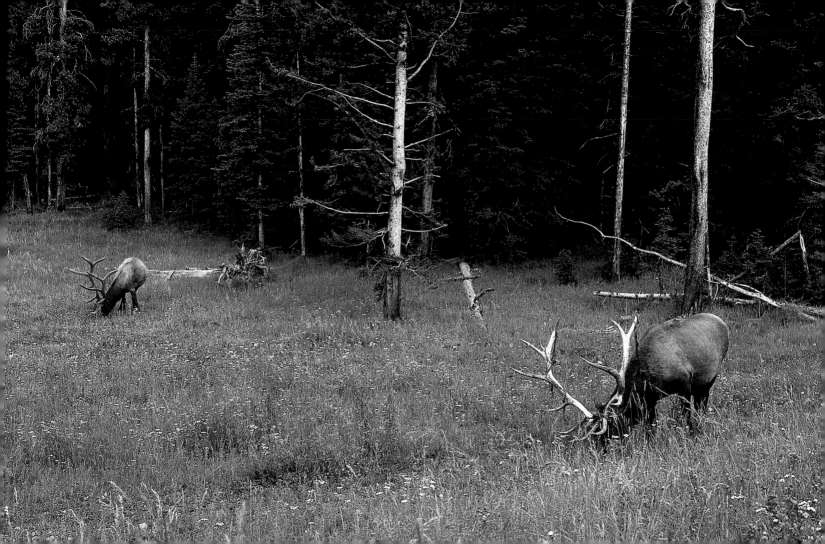

Use organic methods of control rather than pesticides.

Chemical insecticides for garden use have several drawbacks: They harm all insect life, including beneficial species that prey on pests, such as greenflies, caterpillars, and arachnids; and they pollute the land and water. Living biological controls are an alternative; they are the natural enemies of pests and can be used to keep pest populations below destructive levels. They allow the population of an undesirable organism to be reduced by being devoured by its natural predator.

There are simple ways of encouraging the natural predators of pests to flourish in your garden. Companion planting of certain species, such as marigolds, attract insect predators, and you can also plant species that attract pests next to the species that attract their predators, to lure the pests away from other vulnerable plants. And if you need to use a spray, a simple solution of washing-up liquid and water, with the addition of some garlic, is highly effective at killing aphids and other pests.

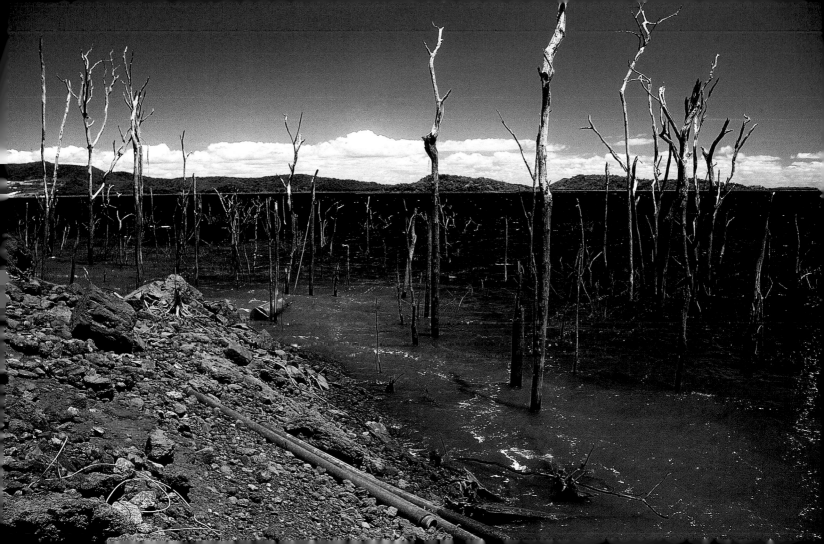

Take part in Buy Nothing Day.

Since 1970, world production of goods and services has multiplied sevenfold. The earth lost a third of its natural resources over the same period.

If you are weary of our overconsuming society, don't miss Buy Nothing Day at the end of November. It provides an opportunity to think about the social, economic, and ecological impact of global consumption. If you feel particularly resourceful, promote a local Buy Nothing Day once a month, or even once a week.

Rain forest, Malaysia

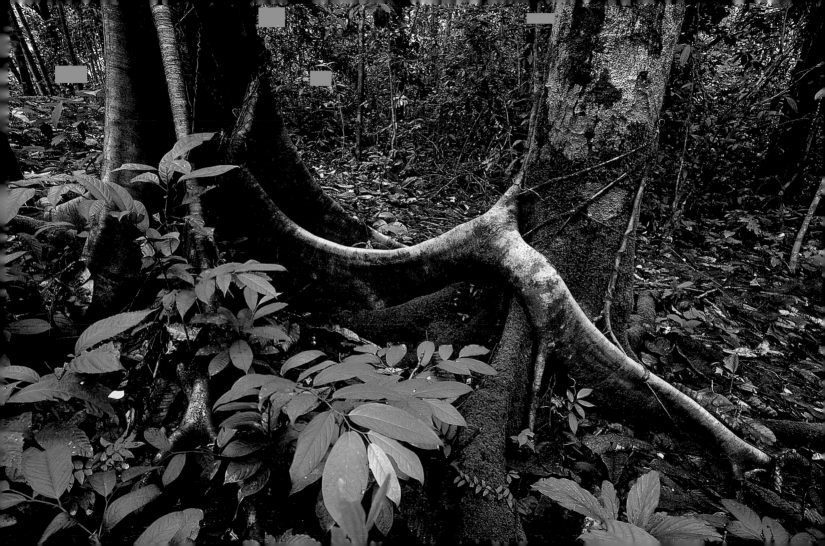

Take the bus.

Global pollution, such as greenhouse-gas emissions, is worrying because of its impact on the balance of the planet's climate. Local pollution directly damages health and well-being, especially in big cities. Over 300,000 deaths in Europe each year are attributed to the effects of air pollution. Cars are the biggest source of urban air pollution: Each car emits, on average, 3 times its own weight—that is, several tonnes—in various pollutants.

Fight air pollution by using your car less often. And take the bus: A fully loaded bus can keep as many as 40 drivers off the streets.

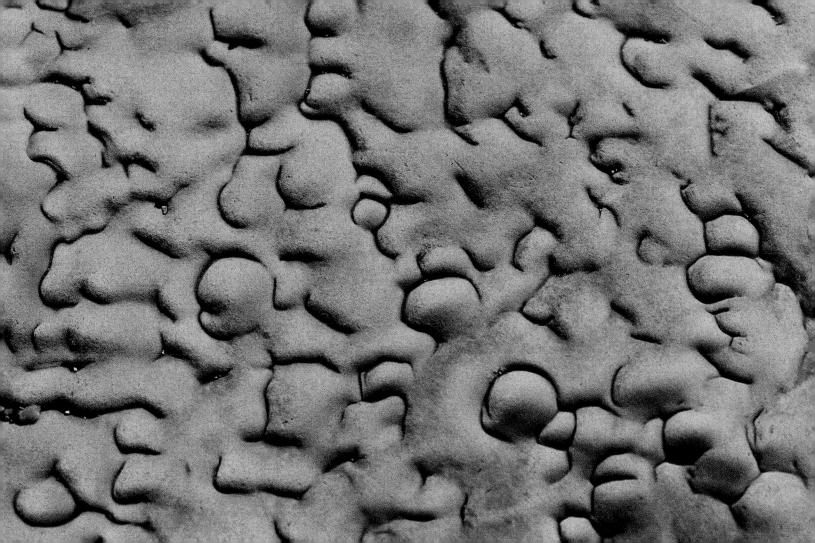

Recycle ink cartridges.

Every year 350 million laser printer and inkjet cartridges end up in our landfills. These are made of plastic, iron, and aluminium, none of which is biodegradable—yet these cartridges can be reused up to 50 times. It takes up to 3.5 litres of oil to make a single new cartridge. Recycling cartridges seems like common sense, yet 90% of the 60 million cartridges used each year in the United Kingdom end up in landfills.

Contribute to the growth of recycling by handing in used cartridges and asking your employer to do the same. There are also organisations that collect them and use the proceeds for humanitarian or educational purposes. You can also buy refilled inkjet cartridges online and from retail stores.

Starfish, United States

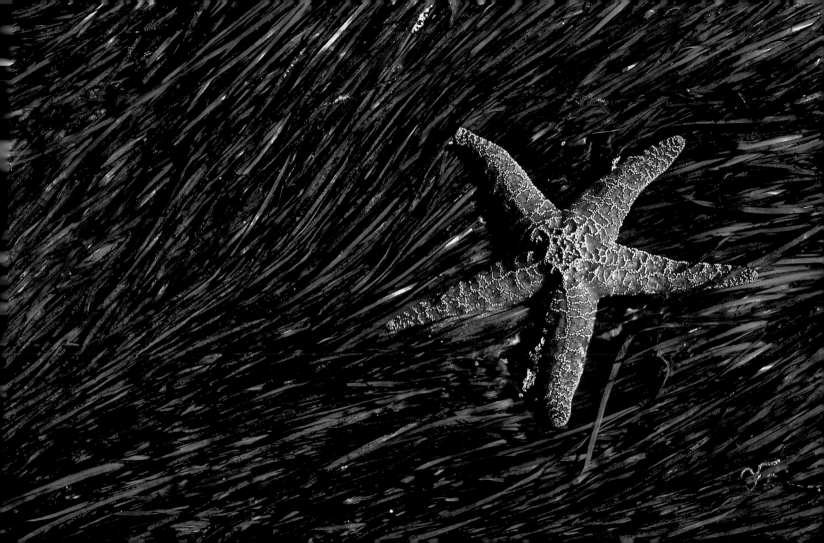

Donate your spectacles for recycling.

In developing countries, 1 billion people need glasses but can't afford them. Meanwhile, nearly 4 million pairs of perfectly good spectacles are thrown out annually.

The next time you replace your specs, donate your old pair, and any unused cases, to an organisation that collects and distributes them where they can be reused. Some opticians take part in collection programs. Every year more than 100,000 pairs of glasses find a new pair of eyes that they can help.

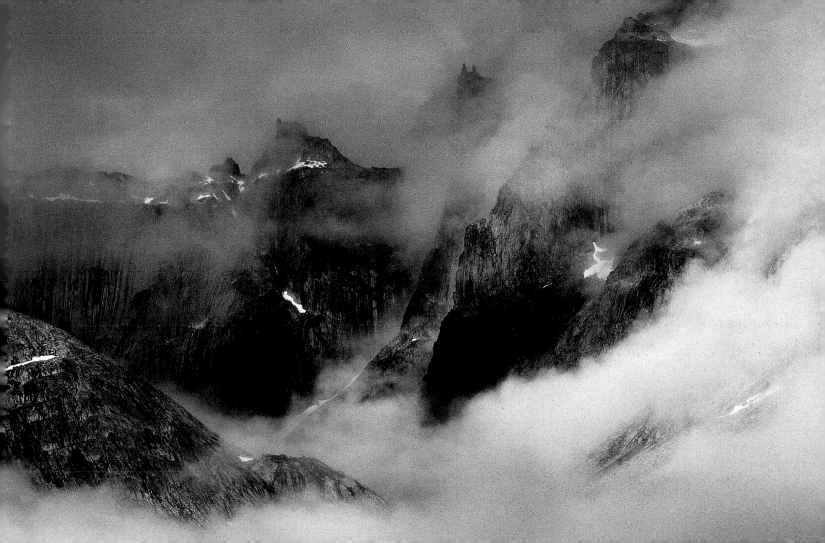

Be prepared to pay more for quality.

The combination of globalization and consumerism often leads us to buy irresponsibly. Cut-rate prices are tempting, but products are often made as cheaply as possible on the other side of the world, in countries devoid of environmental legislation. Often of poor quality, these products quickly break down, break apart, or stop working, and are soon discarded.

Choose the alternative that is locally made and of better quality, even though it may be more expensive. It will last longer and break the cycle of consumerism into which it is too easy to fall.

Lava, Kilauea Volcano, United States

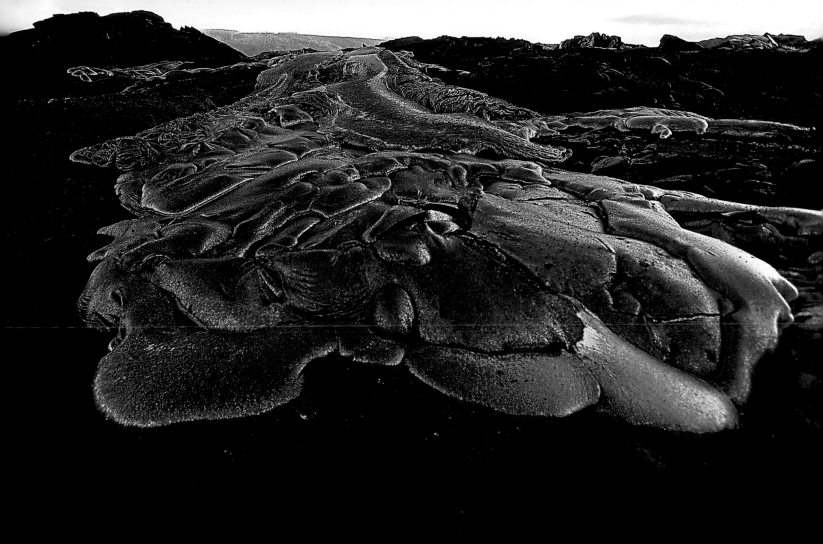

Do not use your car for short journeys.

Every large city on the planet is suffocating because of car traffic. The car is the dominant means of travel in the United Kingdom yet the Energy Savings Trust estimates that half of us use our cars for trips we could easily make by other means at least once a week.

Avoid using your car for short trips. A vehicle produces the most pollution when being started from a cold engine. Moreover, the catalytic converter is fully efficient only when it reaches a certain temperature, which happens after a few kilometres have been covered.

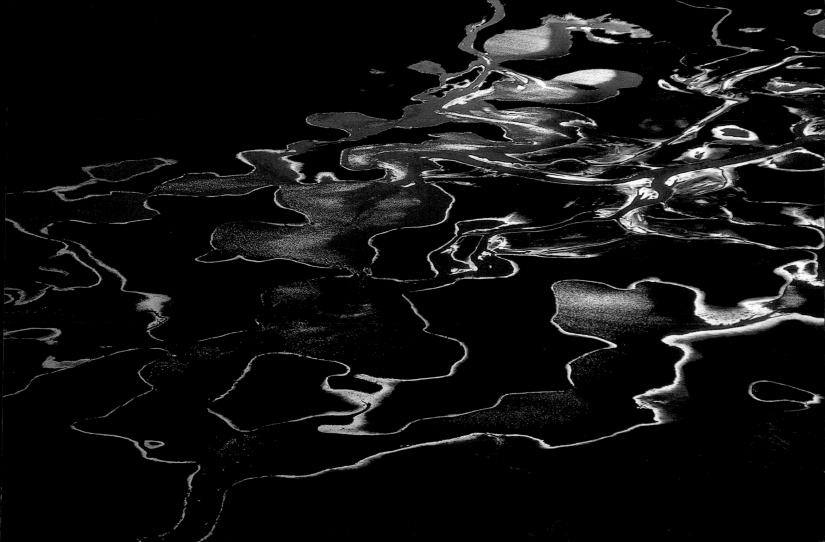

Use baking soda to clean the cooker.

Between 1940 and 1982, production of synthetic substances increased by 350 times. Since 1970, world sales of chemical products have risen from £87 billion to £759 billion. This vast market leads to the release into the environment of millions of tonnes of different chemical compounds. This pollution is widely implicated in the increase in cancer rates, loss of biodiversity, and destruction of the earth's ozone layer.

Household cooker cleaners contain corrosive and toxic substances. You can replace them with a solution of water and baking soda, which is less damaging and just as effective.

Arches National Park,
United States

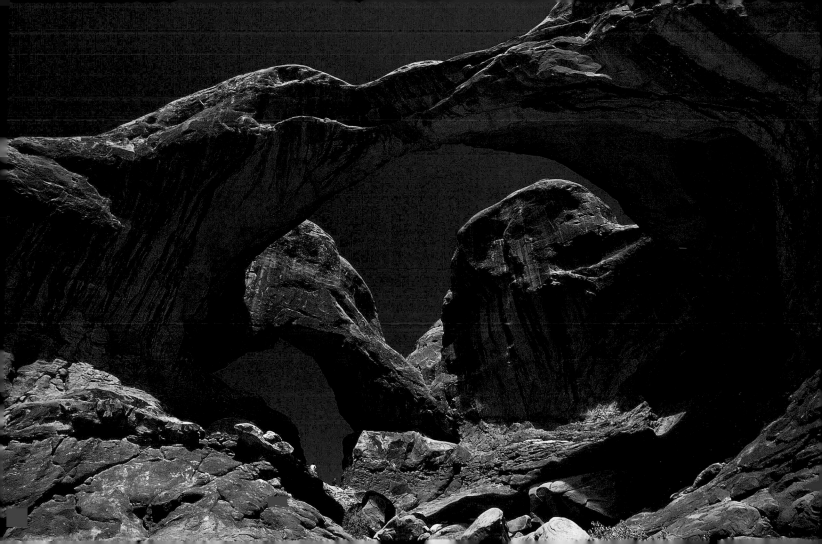

Persuade your workplace to buy fair-trade coffee and tea.

In many regions of the developing world, earnings are too low for farmers to support their families. Unable to make a decent living from the land, they are sometimes forced to leave it and join the swelling ranks of the urban poor. In some regions, they yield to the temptation to grow coca (from which cocaine is produced) or poppies (which produce opium), both of which will earn them more money.

By building more equitable commercial relations, fair trade ensures a decent wage for craftsmen and farmers, who can then live in dignity from their work. Tell your colleagues about fair-trade coffee and tea, and urge your employer to buy them.

Patagonia, Argentina

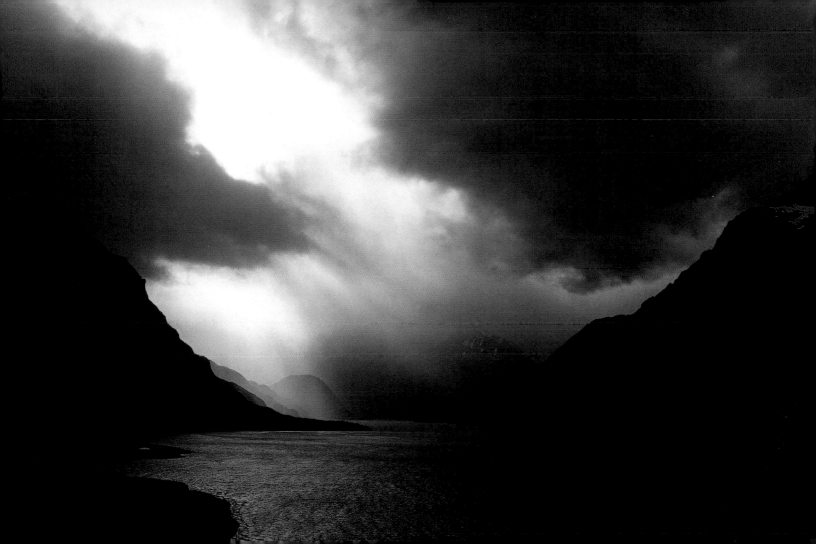

Take biodegradable waste to the compost centre.

Composting is nature's way of recycling its own waste. Dead leaves, branches, and plant debris fall to the ground and are digested by bacteria and microscopic fungi. As weeks pass, humus—the natural compost produced by this process—is formed. Composting in specialised facilities gets rid of our biodegradable waste (fruit and vegetable peelings, garden waste) using the same process. This natural fertiliser, which can restore degraded soil to a condition in which plants thrive, is the reason that community composting is so important, particularly given current agricultural practices.

If your local council does not collect biodegradable waste and you don't have a garden, find a compost centre nearby. Boroughs and councils in the United Kingdom, recognize that the reduction of solid waste in landfill benefits everyone, and that individual households can help reach this target by either making their own compost or by participating in a centralised community scheme through instituted kerbside compost pickup. Encourage your local legislators to consider the option of municipal composting.

Autumn, Canada

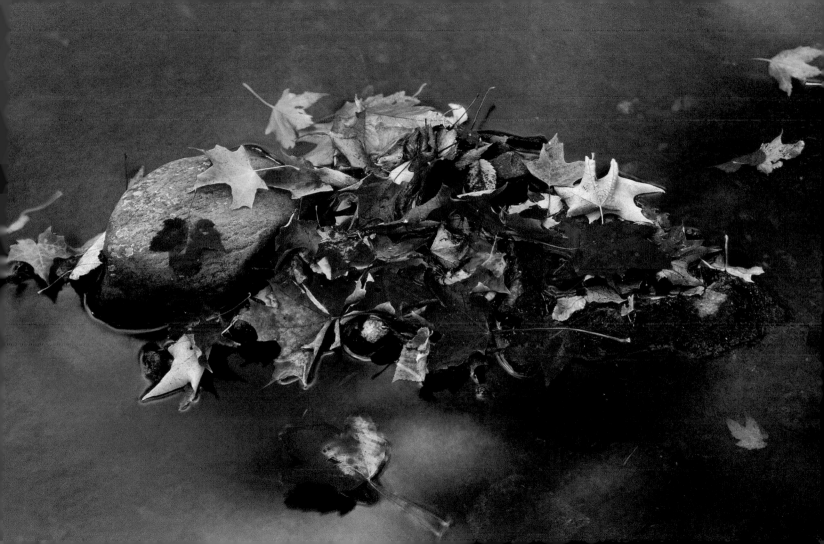

Set your refrigerator to 4.5°C.

In industrialised countries, electricity generation produces half of all carbon-dioxide emissions. The comfort of our day-to-day life consumes vast amounts of electricity, and sometimes wastes vast amounts, as well.

The ideal temperature for the inside of the refrigerator is 4.5°C. Similarly, the freezer should be set to -15°C. Any setting below these temperatures does not affect how well food keeps, but it does increase energy consumption by at least 5%. Keep a thermometer in the refrigerator and freezer to check the temperature.

Icebergs, Antarctica

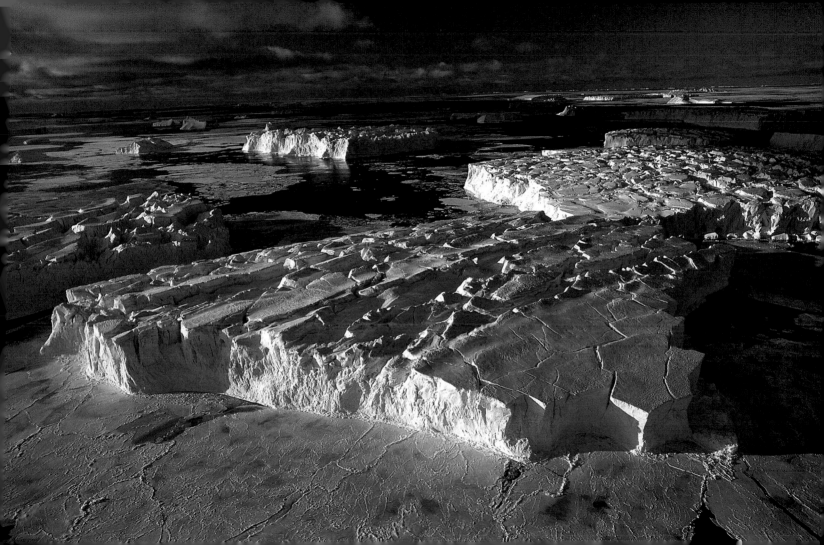

Choose the best TV.

TVs account for about 10% of a home's energy bill. Some plasma TVs consume up to 500 kilowatt hours per year—as much as a new fridge, traditionally the biggest energy user in the house. Traditional cathode ray TVs on average still use the least power. LCD flat-panel screens also use less power than plasma screens; however, the bigger the screen gets, the more power it needs, so a 50-inch TV in any format will never be energy efficient.

When buying a TV, always check the wattage it uses, including how many watts are drained when the set is in standby mode. Look for an energy-saving label, as those sets are up to 30% more efficient than their uncertified counterparts. To further optimize your TV, turn down the brightness or backlight (particularly on superbright LCDs) and utilise any built-in power-saving modes. Of course, the less TV you watch, the less power you use.

Emperor penguins, Antarctica

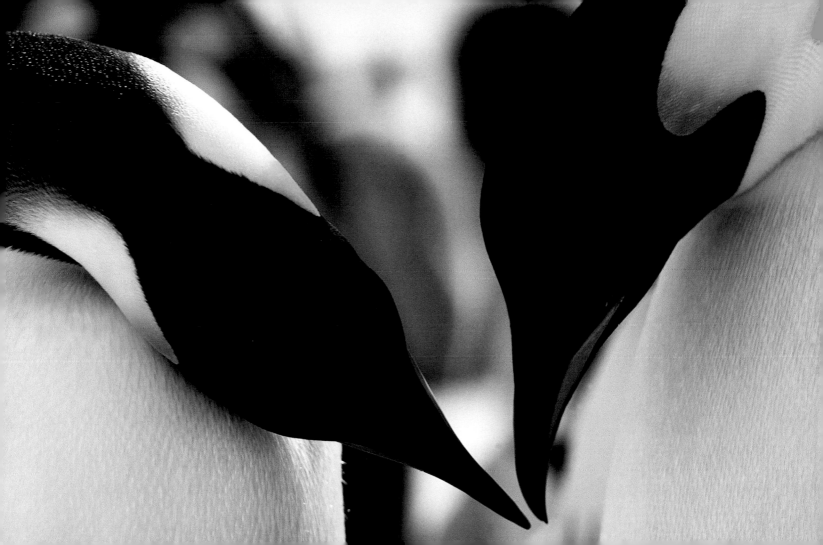

Reduce noise pollution to make our cities more liveable.

Compact communities are good for the planet—when we build up instead of out we protect undeveloped habitats and watersheds. However, city living is not always easy and many people leave cities for the suburbs to escape the bustle and noise of urban areas. Three-quarters of the noise in cities comes from motor vehicles. It is so pervasive that we no longer even notice it. A typical van passing at 80 kilometres per hour is 4 times as loud as an air-conditioner and 8 times as loud as a refrigerator. And then there's the noise inside our apartments. A recent British research paper found that 21% of people questioned felt their home lives were disrupted by noise. Too much noise causes fatigue and stress, and affects our nervous system.

For cities to remain liveable, it is essential to keep noise pollution to a minimum. Car exhausts must be fitted with a muffler. Have yours changed when it becomes too noisy. Carpeting is the best way to soundproof the floor in your apartment. If you have a tiled or hardwood floor, consider putting padded blocks under the feet of furniture, placing electrical appliances on shock-absorbing pads to reduce the vibrations transmitted through the floor, and putting down rugs to dampen the sound of footsteps.

Red ibises, Venezuela

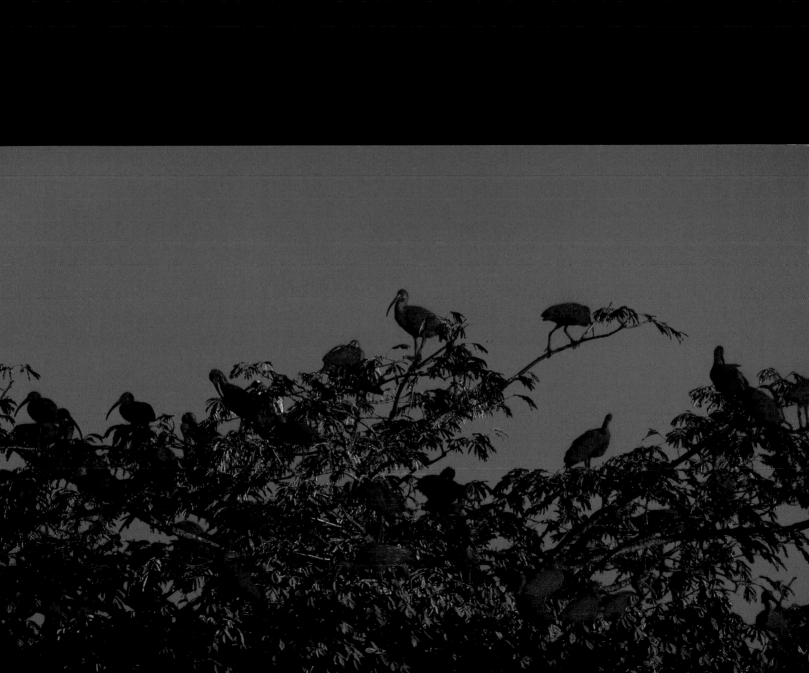

Replace your old domestic appliances.

Recent years have seen a considerable reduction in the amount of water and energy used by domestic appliances. Some dishwashers are at least 13% more energy efficient than standard models, and save water, as well. An energy-efficient dishwasher saves approximately 4,540 litres of water a year, which is equivalent to the amount of water that 6 people can drink in a year. By law, the European Community Energy Label must be displayed on all new household products to indicate the level of energy efficiency the appliance has. If in addition it has the European Eco-label (the flower), this certifies that consumers are investing wisely. The Eco-label indicates that a product has been independently assessed and meets strict environmental criteria (considering more than just energy consumption), putting it among the best in its class.

Your appliances may have served you faithfully for years, but if they use much more water and energy than newer models it is better to replace them — especially if they are used frequently. Energy- and water-efficient models may require greater initial investment, but you will continue to see the benefits over the life of the machine.

Erg (sand desert), Mauritania

Encourage your employer to invest in an environmental audit.

Not surprisingly, companies, institutions, and schools have a larger impact on the environment than the individual, and thus, when these entities choose to act sustainably, their potential for influence is much greater. There are numerous ways for companies and institutions to assess their footprint on the earth in a quantifiable and productive way. Environmental audits are accompanied by individualised, self-proposed goals and improvements for the short- and long-term that are made by organisations to become more ecologically sound in their operations.

You can encourage your employer to invest in an environmental audit. The goal-making process that follows—where the company or institution decides how best to reduce its environmental footprint—can be a motivational, team-building experience for all involved.

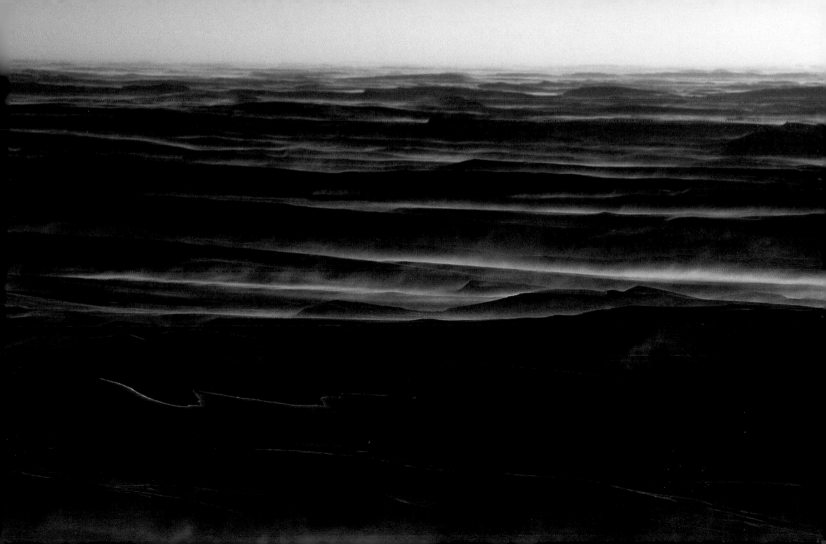

Ask for a matching donation the next time you support an environmental cause.

Many companies offer to match any donations their employees make to registered charities. This year ask your company to double your support of an environmental cause. And know that such giving doesn't begin and end with Greenpeace — providing solar power to a community that lacks the infrastructure to have electricity or constructing eco-friendly temporary housing for climate refugees are just a few of the tangible things your donations can help accomplish.

Instead of having everyone waste £5 on a Secret Santa gift, pick a worthy cause or two, pool all of that money and ask your company to match the donation.

Malachite, Zaire

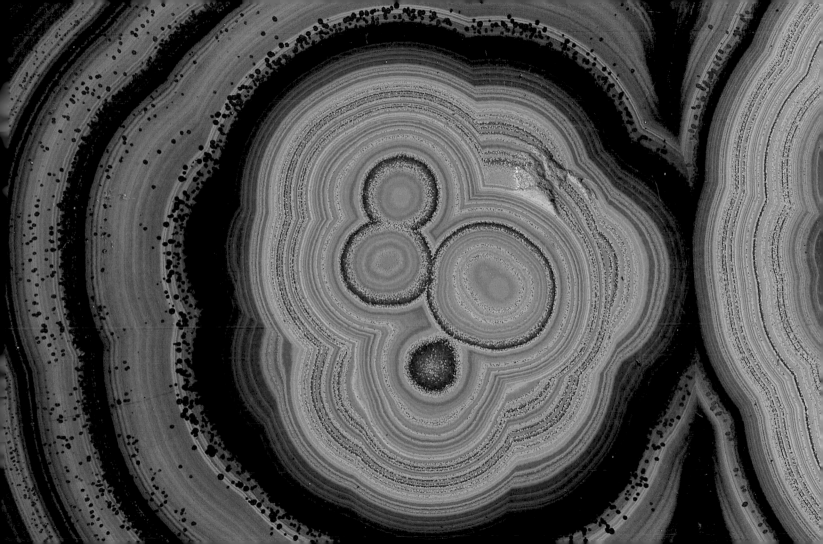

In winter, turn nighttime heating down to the minimum.

Eighty percent of the energy the world uses comes from nonrenewable fossil-fuel resources, the combustion of which produces greenhouse gases. Oil, natural gas, and coal reserves are replaced at 1/100,000th of the speed at which we are now using them up. The exhaustion of these resources within a few decades will probably herald the rise of renewable, nonpolluting energy sources. We may yet have cause to regret not having developed them earlier.

To moderate your energy consumption (and reduce your bills), remember that a temperature of 16 to 18°C is enough in a bedroom at night. For a healthy, economical, and ecological night's sleep turn your heating down and sleep under a good soft blanket or a duvet.

Atacama Desert, Bolivia

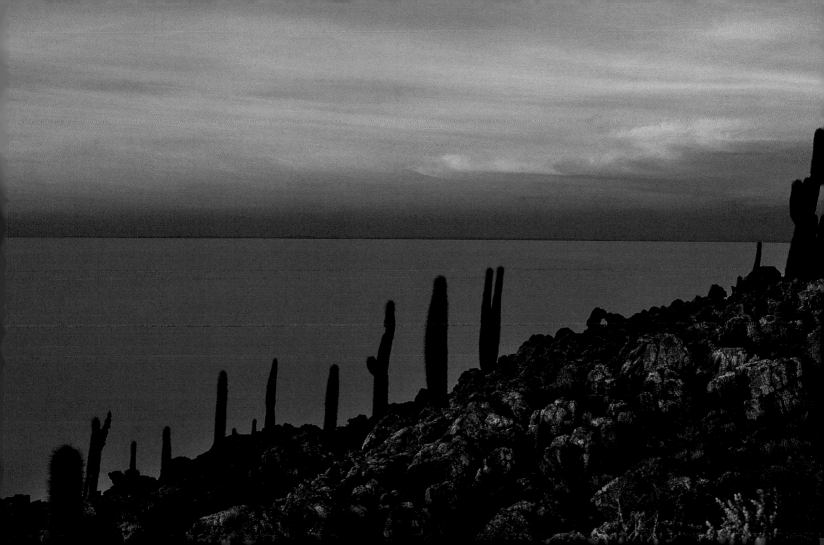

Give a waste-free gift.

Christmas is a time for celebration but also a feast for waste that results in an estimated 3 million tonnes of waste in Britain. Instead of purchasing an item of dubious quality that may have been manufactured under unfair working conditions and transported thousands of kilometres to the store at the cost of burning fuel, concentrate on giving people experiences.

Tickets to music, theatre, or sporting events; restaurant vouchers at restaurants that support local resources and use organic ingredients; lessons to help discover new hobbies or further existing ones. These are just a few examples of gifts that won't get sent directly to the landfill along with a heap of wrapping paper.

Glacier, New Zealand

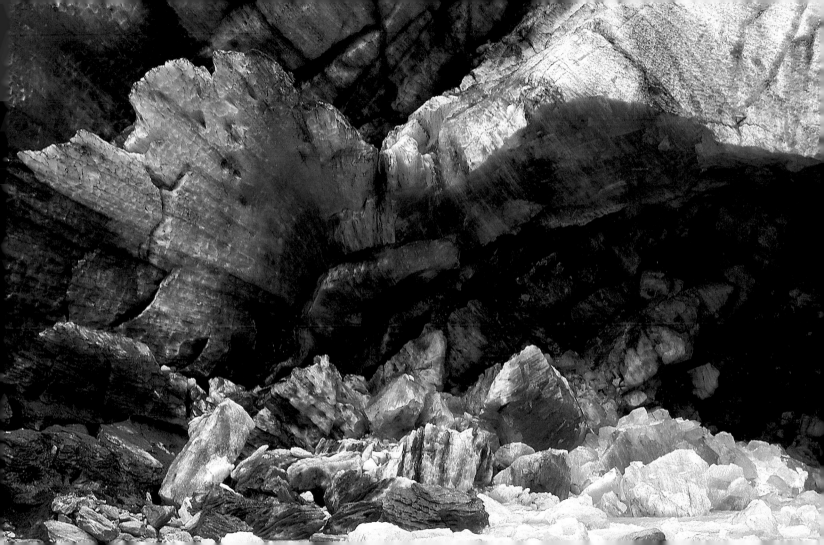

Avoid total treatments in the garden.

Many chemicals regarded as too dangerous are now banned in industrialized countries, yet they are still on the market in developing countries, where 30% of the pesticides sold do not comply with international standards.

If you must use a chemical treatment in your garden, avoid total treatments: lindane and atrazine kill indiscriminately, eliminating earthworms, which aerate the soil, and beneficial insects, as well as harming birds and the health of the user. Read the information on the packaging, and choose products described as authorised for garden use: They have less impact on the environment. Whatever treatment you use, if you must throw out what is left over, remember that the place for toxic substances is the hazardous-waste disposal facility, not the rubbish bin.

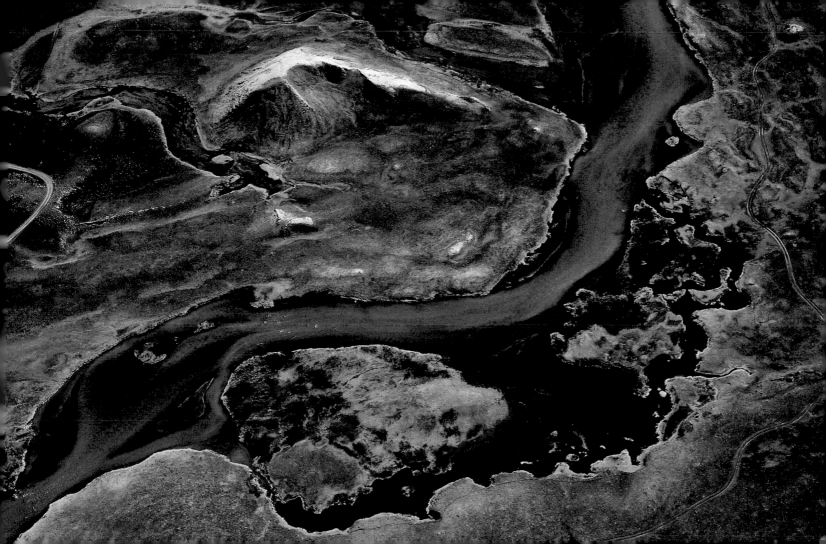

Keep warmth in by insulating your home.

Most of our homes were not built to modern standards of energy efficiency, and old homes are likely to have little or no insulation. Yet the potential energy savings through insulating your home can have a huge impact on your carbon footprint and your heating bills. Cavity wall insulation could save 750 kilograms of carbon dioxide a year, and if all UK homes with unfilled cavity walls were insulated, the energy saved would heat a staggering 1.4 million homes. Loft insulation could save even more — up to 1 tonne of carbon dioxide a year and over £100 on your annual heating bill.

Insulating your home is the cheapest and most effective way to reduce the emissions you produce through heating – it is a step that everyone should take. And simple steps like installing draught strips to your windows, and tightly closing curtains at night can save even more.

Kilauea Volcano, United States

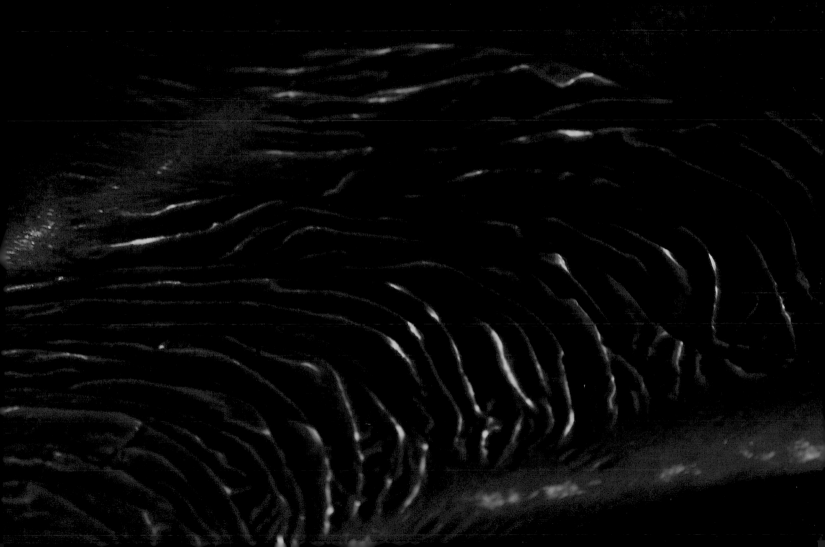

Educate your children.

Indiscriminate use of new technologies, private and state economic interests looking for short-term gain, and disregard for both the common good and for the consequences for future generations are at the foundation of the dangerous situation facing the earth today. We cannot shrug off our responsibility as consumers and as citizens.

Explain to your children that the Western model of consumption has limits. Teach them to have concern for the environment. Be firm about saving electricity, turning off faucets, and turning off the computer when it is not being used. Set an example! When education succeeds, it is often a result of having a model to follow every day.

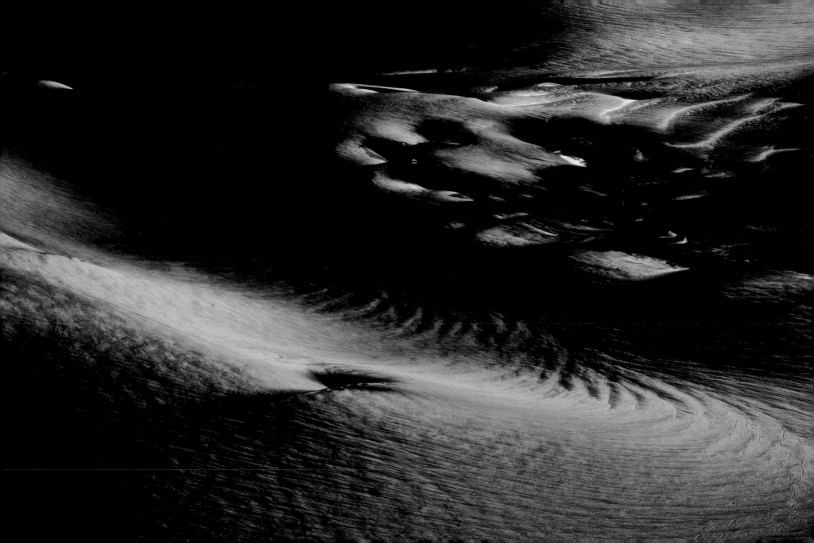

Choose the right Christmas tree.

Christmas tree farms typically use tonnes of pesticides, and although the trees capture carbon dioxide as they grow, some farms may replace areas of hardwood trees that are better at capturing carbon dioxide than pines. Not to mention that we've created an entire industry—one that requires land—so we can have a few weeks of holiday decoration. Plastic trees, on the other hand, though they are reused for years and years, are not biodegradable and require petroleum to create and to ship from overseas factories and may contain toxics like PVC and lead.

So, which is the more sustainable choice? The best traditional Christmas decoration would be a plant, evergreen or other, that has a life beyond the holiday—you can get a UK-grown real tree with roots that can be kept in a pot for next year or be planted outside, whether in your backyard or in another spot in the community. If you're not a traditionalist, you can decorate citrus trees or any sturdy plant. Beyond that, buying a farmed tree from a small grower that uses few pesticides is the best you can do. Or forget the tree and get creative—you'd be surprised at how many household items can do double duty as trees when strung with lights and ornaments.

Parinacota Volcano, Chile

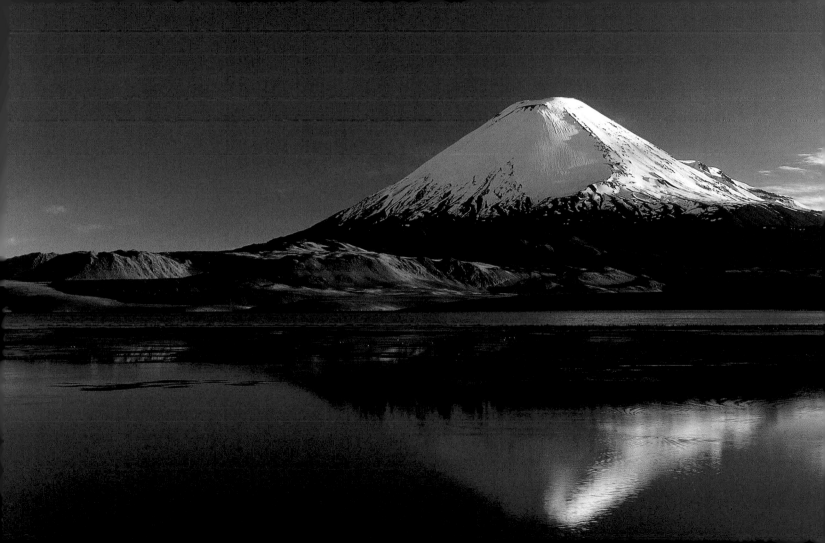

Use wood for heating.

Contrary to what many people think, burning wood can be environmentally beneficial. Much of the woodland in the United Kingdom is seminatural woodland and benefits from being managed. The ecosystems that exist in those woods today depend on continuing management to sustain their survival. As a source of energy, wood does not contribute to global warming. Although burning it releases carbon dioxide, a greenhouse gas, the amount given off is the same as the amount absorbed while the tree was growing.

Wood heating is more environmentally friendly than electric or gas, and modern wood-burning cookers are highly efficient, producing virtually no smoke and using few logs to produce a lot of heat. Consider using it for your home, particularly if you live in a more rural area where transport costs from forest to fire will be lower.

Geyser Valley, Kamchatka, Russia

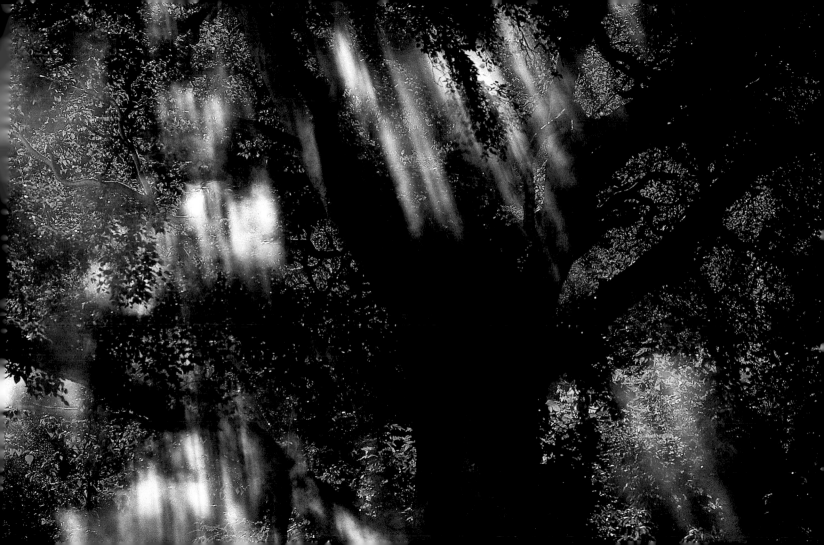

Invest in a solar charger.

Outfitting your home with solar panels isn't a viable option for most people, especially those who rent. But everyone can generate a little bit of green power with a small solar charger that's capable of powering laptops, MP3 players, cell phones, and all the other gadgets that require constant recharging.

Solar chargers are portable and affordable. Not only can they reduce your power load at home, they can be of great use when travelling abroad, especially if you are in an area where electricity is a luxury or where there are frequent surges that could harm some electronics.

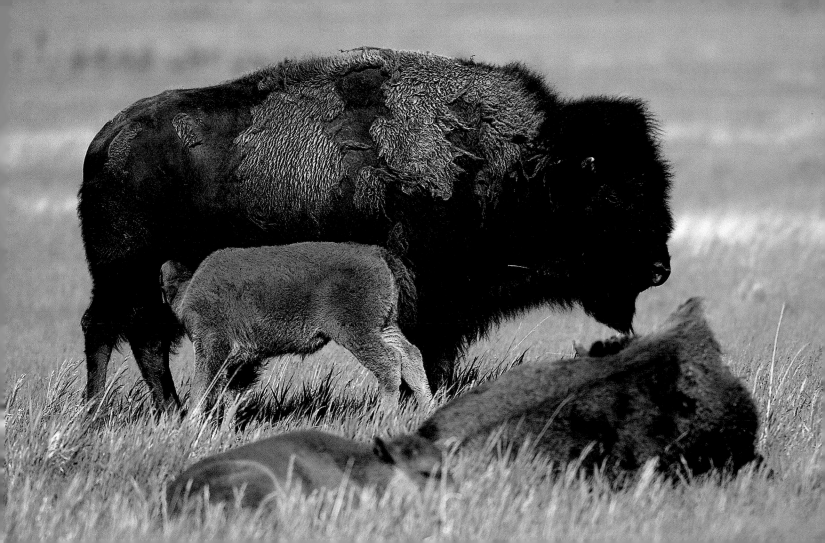

Run the washing machine only when it is full.

Although intolerable inequality still exists in the world, the quality of life is improving for a growing proportion of humanity. The more our standard of living rises, however, the more water each person uses. Indeed, our modern lifestyle is very greedy for water.

An average washing machine uses between 38 and 75 litres of water per cycle. To cut your water consumption, take care not to use the washing machine unless you have a full load of laundry to do. When looking to replace your washing machine, invest in a front-loading machine: They generally use 40% less water than top-loading machines.

Ol Doinyo Lengai Volcano,
Tanzania

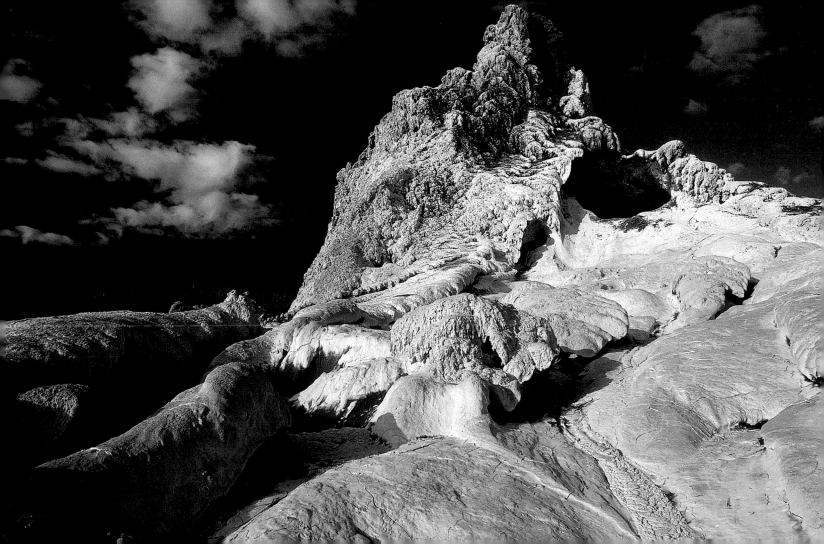

Choose organic cotton.

Cotton accounts for only 3% of the world's farmed land, but it uses 25% of the world's pesticides, making it the most pollution-causing crop. In order to grow the pound of cotton needed for the average T-shirt the conventional cotton farmer uses about one-third of a pound of hazardous chemical pesticides and fertilizers. Industrial processing of the raw fibres is equally harmful to the environment; it involves chlorine bleaching and the use of dyes made with heavy metals that are harmful to people and the environment. When grown without the use of pesticides, organic cotton restores soil fertility and preserves the balance of ecosystems.

Choosing organic cotton contributes to your well-being as well as that of those who grow it, and safeguards the health of humans and the environment.

Sequoias, United States

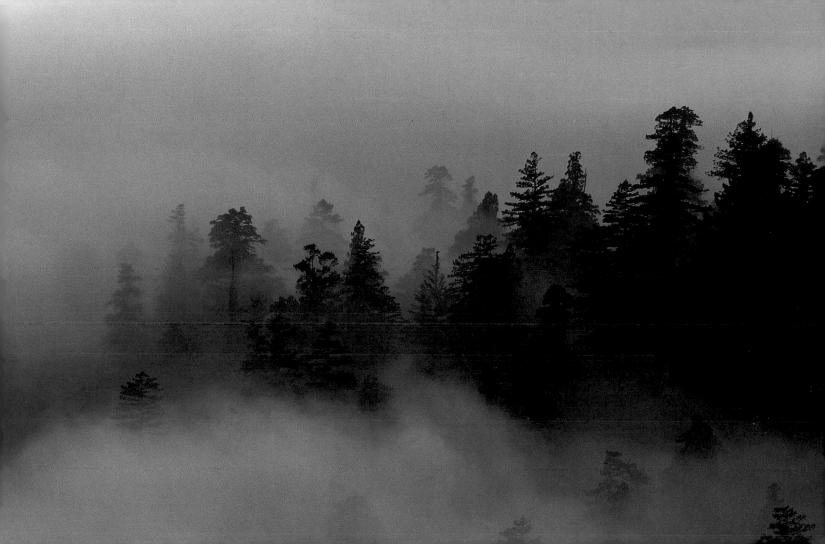

Make your own greeting cards.

To date, scientists have counted 1.5 million plant and animal species on earth and estimate there are 15 million in all. Every day, however, several species disappear before we have even recorded their existence. Deforestation is thought to be causing the extinction of 27,000 diverse rain forest species—especially plants and insects—every year. Since making just 1 tonne of paper requires 2 tonnes of wood, the amount of deforestation required is almost unimaginable.

When you need to send greetings, choose an e-card (a card sent by e-mail), or one that is printed on recycled paper. Better still, be creative and make your own greeting card from recycled or recovered paper and materials.

Lava, Kilauea Volcano,
United States

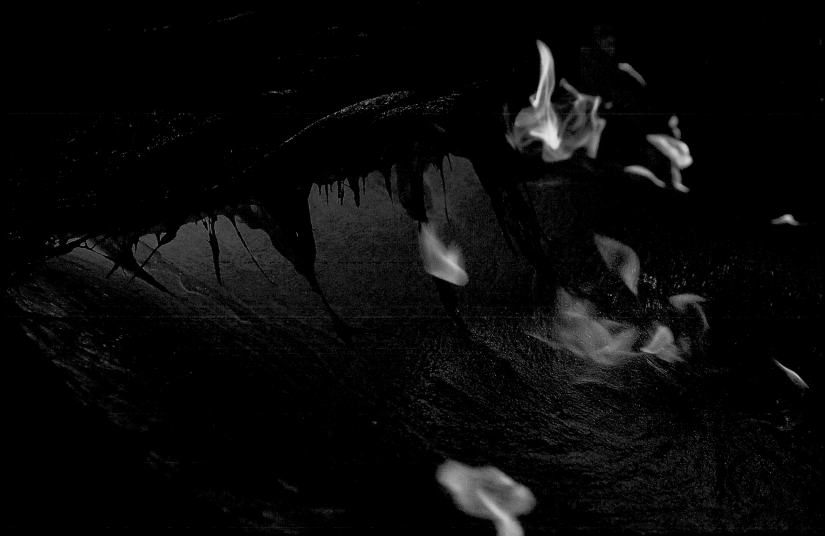

Use less wrapping paper.

Every second an area of tropical forest the size of a football field vanishes from the planet. Every year 13 million hectares of rain forest are destroyed, including the extinction of 137 plant and animal species every day. Tropical forests are home to more than half the world's biodiversity.

Millions of these trees end up as wrapping paper each year. Use fabric ribbon or cord, instead of sticky tape, to fasten your gift wrappings: Then you can reuse the ribbons and wrapping paper instead of tearing it up and throwing it out. If you buy new paper, look for products made from post-consumer recycled material (or hemp blends), printed with vegetable inks. Some types of wrapping paper are recyclable, but what's accepted varies greatly from town to town, and paper with metallic or foil prints is not recyclable (neither is cellophane or any of those manufactured ribbons and bows).

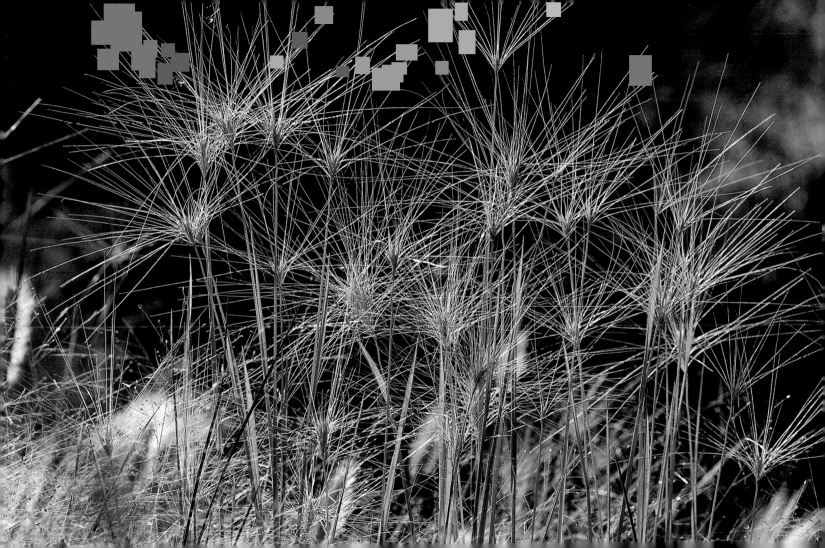

Give fair-trade toys as presents.

At a time when half of humanity lives on less than £1 a day, the average UK shopper spends nearly £400 on Christmas presents alone. Eighty-five percent of toys sold in the United Kingdom are made in China, sometimes by children and with no regard for the social rights of workers, in order to meet demand from wealthy countries.

If you have had enough of receiving useless gifts, gadgets that soon break and are eventually discarded, plastic toys that pollute, and packaging that contributes to producing more waste, then give fair-trade toys and waste-free presents, or buy from charity Christmas shops. Pay more attention to the social and environmental quality of your purchases and ask those who are buying for you to do the same.

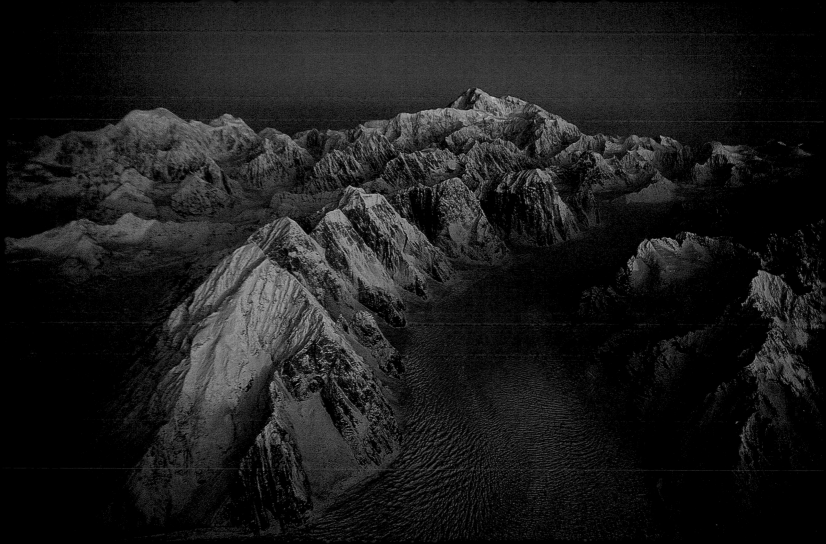

Support green schemes through gift giving.

Sometimes, people who may be open-minded toward supporting green services may be hesitant to try them out if there is an initial cost. Once they experience the benefits for themselves, they're likely to be willing to keep paying for themselves.

If friends or colleagues have expressed interest in car- or bike-sharing programs; allotment gardening; environmental charities; or any other projects that have membership fees, offer to help them get started by paying annual fees or buying a trial subscription. You can also offer to purchase carbon credits for people who are travelling long distances for the holidays.

Celebrate Christmas sustainably.

When Christmas approaches, the developed world becomes gripped by a frenzy of consumption, and good environmental resolutions are temporarily forgotten. A fifth more rubbish is thrown out at Christmas than during the rest of the year.

You can be creative and make your own Christmas tree decorations rather than buying a plastic angel that was manufactured on the other side of the world and will perch at the top of the tree for just a few days before being thrown out. Make a donation or give your time to a charity.

Glacier National Park,
United States

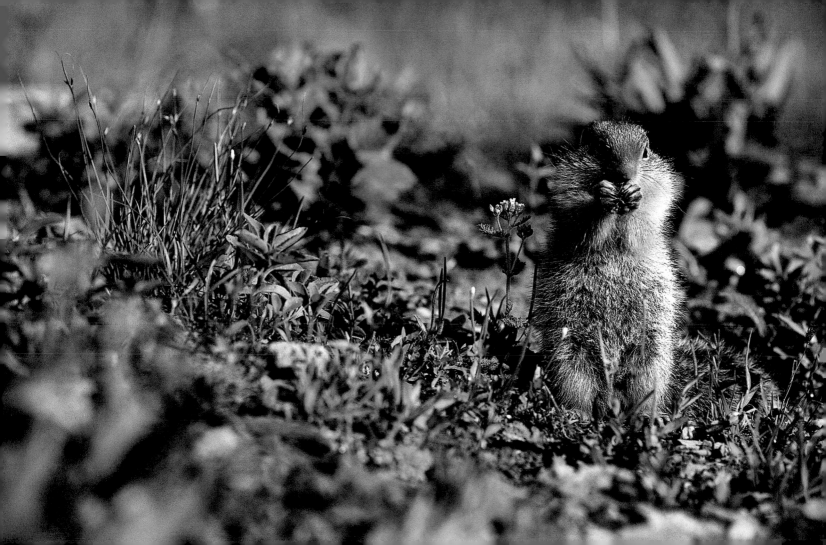

When travelling, respect the environment as you do at home.

In developing countries, the conditions under which tourists live, with swimming pools, air-conditioning, and excessive living areas, often divert natural resources at the expense of the people who live there, or the ecosystem at large. For example, a single cruise ship produces 6,350 tonnes of waste every year. However, some tourist destinations are attempting to reverse this trend. The Seychelles, a group of islands northeast of Madagascar in the Indian Ocean, introduced a £45 tax on travellers entering the islands. Revenue will be used to preserve the environment and improve tourism facilities.

Abroad, as at home, respect the environment and its resources: do not waste water; switch off the light and television before leaving your hotel room; do not drop your litter indiscriminately; and use public transport.

Namib Desert, Namibia

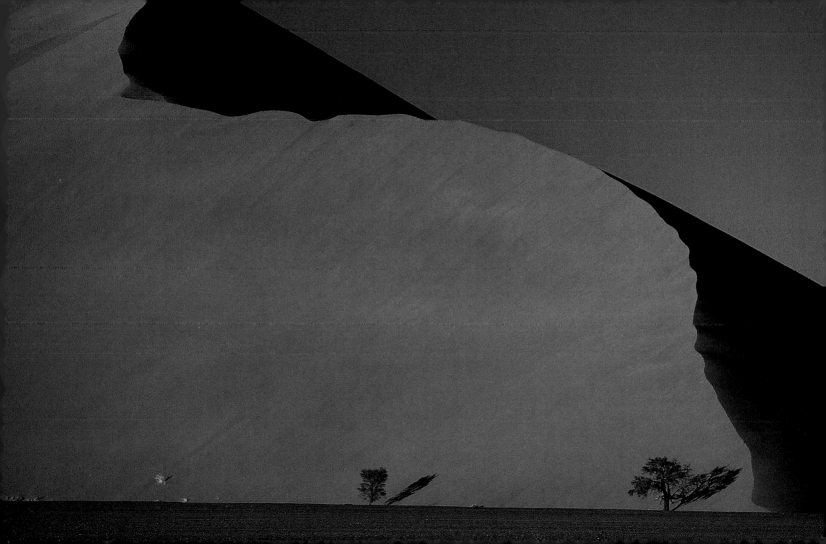

Learn to understand logos on packaging.

A wide range of different eco-labels are used throughout Europe and the United Kingdom. The European Eco-label is a label that indicates that a product or service meets strict criteria limiting the impact on the environment from the manufacturing process through disposal and recycling. However, the criteria differs between the different labels and it can be confusing to know how environmentally friendly a product's packaging is.

The difference between recyclable and recycled — that is, between what is possible and what actually happens — may depend on you and whether you sort your waste To avoid misunderstandings, learn to decipher the array of marks and logos on packaging, particularly plastic, and ask your local recycling centre what they will accept.

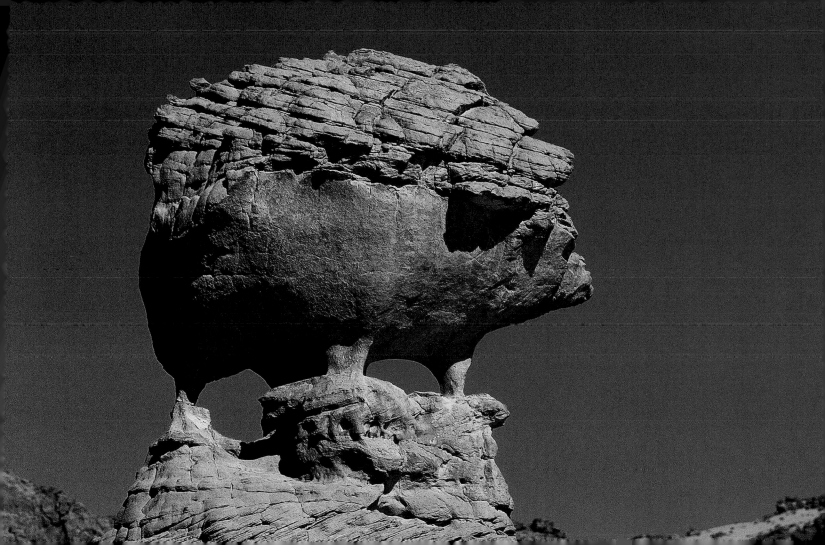

Turn down the heat when you are away from home.

Contrary to what is widely believed, lowering the temperature setting of heating does not cause extra consumption when the system is turned up again. For every degree you turn down your heat, you will save 5% on your heating bill.

Don't wait to turn down the thermostat. During the working day and when you are away for the weekend, turn the heating down 10 degrees below the temperature you usually find comfortable. When you are away for longer, set it just high enough to avoid freezing. On a daily basis, lower the temperature by 1°C: You will be doing your heating bill and the environment a lot of good.

Waterfall, Costa Rica

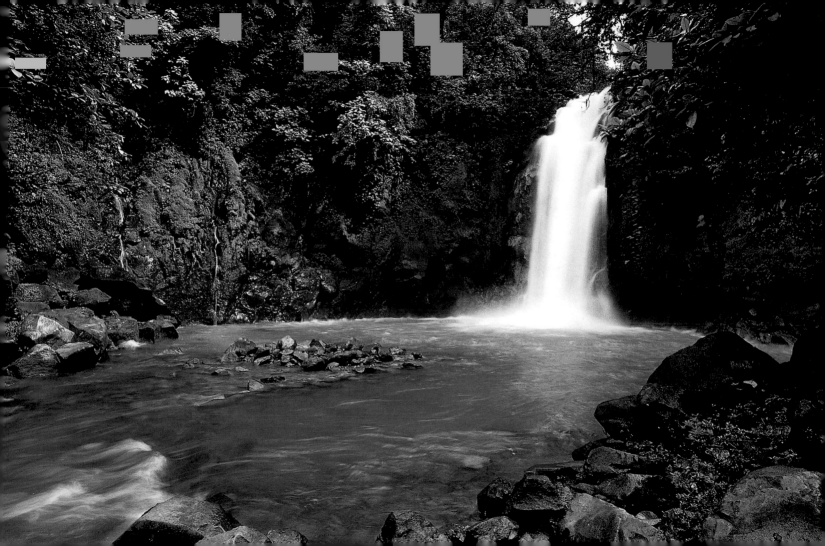

Understand the 'water footprint' of soft drinks.

One litre of a fizzy drink requires about 2.7 litres of water to make — this number increases to 250 litres if you factor in the water needed to produce the sugar in that litre of drink. Coca-Cola uses on average more than 290 billion litres of water per year. Although some Coca-Cola plants have started to use rainwater-recycling schemes, the company has come under constant attack in the past few years for the stress its bottling plants put on already scarce water supplies around the world. In India, villagers from several drought-stricken states have called for the closing of several plants, alleging that water table levels have dropped significantly since the company started bottling operations. The bottling practices of major soft drink manufacturers affect local water supplies, too, by drawing from often scarce groundwater supplies.

Reduce your consumption of soft drinks and buy only from those companies that have made documented efforts to address their impact on one of our most-endangered resources. Find out what measures local bottling companies are taking to decrease their water use and campaign for more responsible water use by industry.

Rock painting, Australia

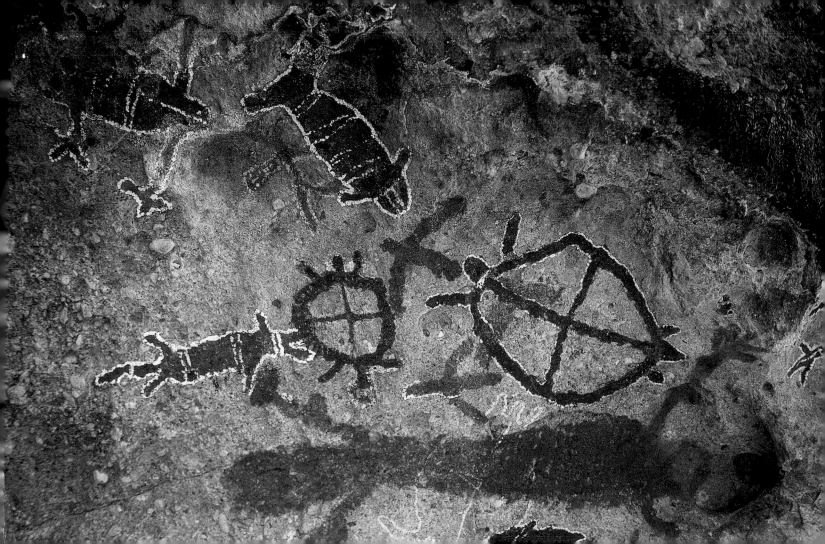

If you move house, think green.

The environmental standards to which our homes are built increases all the time, but there is still a long way to go. If you have to move house, think about what home you buy. If you are buying a newly built home, ask about the Ecohomes standards or the Code for Sustainable Homes, both of which specify levels of energy efficiency. Ask about where the materials come from — are they locally sourced, recycled, recyclable? And if you buy an older home, the new Home Information Packs in the United Kingdom have to include information on energy use and aim to buy the most highly rated home you can afford. And think beyond just what's in the house. If it's part of a new development that encroaches on previously undeveloped land, or if it is too far from local services and public transport connections, is it really that green? In addition, no matter how many energy-efficient features it contains, if a house is oversized (a family of 4 does not need 4 bathrooms) then it's not a sustainable property.

If you move house next year, make sure you move to a house that is better for the environment than the one that you sell, and support the efforts of those homebuilders who are genuinely trying to build better homes for you and the environment.

Atacama Desert, Bolivia

Be positive.

To fully implement every change detailed in this book could take far longer than a year. And the suggestions here are just the tip of the (vanishing) iceberg. Pondering the state of our planet, our role in its degradation, and the sheer number of changes big and small that we have yet to enact is, to put it very mildly, overwhelming. But pessimism isn't going to solve any of our problems: While sorting through the cold, hard facts, we must also take the time to recognize the enduring beauty of the earth and the resilience and creativity of the people who inhabit it.

Stay positive. Stay motivated. Do your best every day and focus not on the damage already done but on the achievable goal of a sustainable future.

Gray whale, Mexico

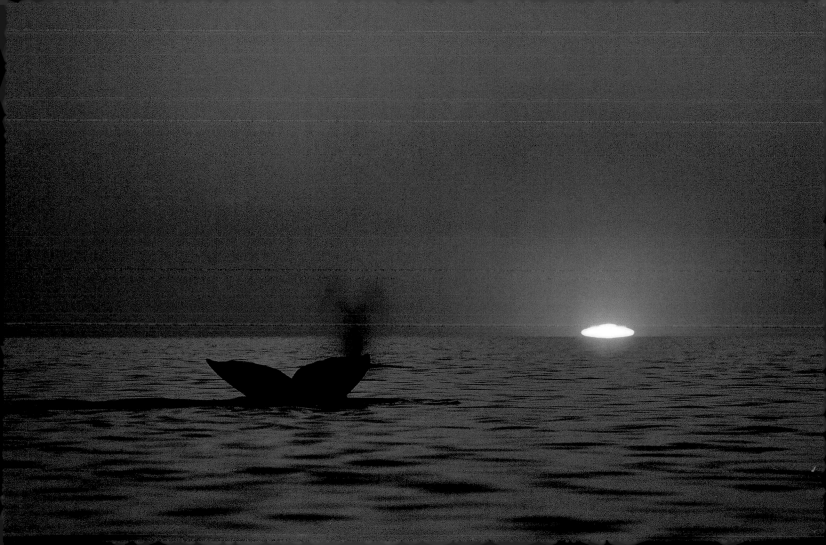

WEBSITES

Climate Change Information

www.climatenetwork.org (Climate Action Network)

www.climatecrisis.net (informational website for Al Gore's *An Inconvenient Truth*)

www.ipcc.ch (Intergovernmental Panel on Climate Change)

www.tyndall.ac.uk (Tyndall Centre for Climate Change Research)

www.ukcip.org.uk (UK Climate Impacts Programme)

www.realclimate.org (ten scientists blogging about climate change)

www.unfccc.int (United Nations Framework Convention on Climate Change; link to Kyoto Protocol)

www.climatechallenge.gov.uk (UK government resources on climate change)

www.sternreview.org.uk (Stern Review website)

General Sustainability Resources

www.earthday.net/footprint (calculate your ecological footprint)

www.unep.org (The United Nations Environment Program)

www.defra.gov.uk (UK Department for the Environment, Food and Rural Affairs, responsible for environmental policy in the UK)

www.sd-commission.org.uk (UK Sustainable Development Commission)

www.bbcgreen.com (BBC Green)

www.grist.org (environmental news and humour)

www.sustainablog.org (environmental and economic sustainability blog)

www.treehugger.com (environmental news website)

www.worldchanging.com (Worldchanging online magazine)

Banking and Investing

www.uksif.org (UK Social Investment Forum)

www.ethicalinvestment.org.uk (The Ethical Investment Association)

www.grameenfoundation.org (microfinance nonprofit)

www.ethicalperformance.com (news on ethical investing worldwide)

www.European-microfinance.org (European Microfinance Network)

www.microfinanceclubuk.co.uk (UK Microfinance Association)

http://uk.zopa.com (lending and loans community)

www.cooperativebank.co.uk (Cooperative Bank)

Business

www.carbontrust.co.uk (UK Carbon Trust)

www.environment-agency.gov.uk/business/ (the UK Environment Agency business website)

www.envirowise.gov.uk (practical environmental advice for business)

www.netregs.gov.uk (information on environmental legislation)

www.wrap.org.uk (resources on waste reduction for businesses)

www.businessgreen.com (resources for greening business in the UK)

www.sustainableworkplace.co.uk (resource and pilot projects)

www.environmentawards.net (environmental awards)

www.nisp.org.uk (National Industrial Symbiosis Programme)

www.telework.org.uk (The Telework Association)

www.workwiseuk.org (Work Wise UK)

Carbon Offsetting

www.carbonfund.org

www.climatecare.com

www.terrapass.com

Consumer Choice and Green Labels

www.carbontrust.co.uk/carbon/briefing/carbon_label.htm (information on the UK Carbon Trust labeling scheme) *www.defra.gov.uk/Environment/consumerprod/glc/index.htm* (information of the different green labels used in the UK)

www.brookes.ac.uk/eie/ecolabels.htm (resource on a variety of eco-labels)

www.energysavingtrust.org.uk/compare_and_buy_products (product comparison for the UK)

www.climatecounts.org/scorecard.php (scorecard that rates corporate responsibility)

www.greenconsumerguide.com (independant media company)

www.terrachoice.com/files/6_sins.pdf (document explaining the basics of greenwashing)

Energy Saving and Carbon Reduction

www.energysavingtrust.org.uk (UK Energy Saving Trust)

http://actonco2.direct.gov.uk (carbon footprint calculator)

www.nef.org.uk (UK National Energy Foundation)

www.carbonrationing.org.uk (Carbon Rationing Action Groups network)

www.cred-uk.org (Community Carbon Reduction Programme)

www.biggreenswitch.co.uk (tips on carbon reduction and environmental awareness)

www.earthhour.org (international energy awareness campaign)

www.diykyoto.com (Wattson energy-conservation device)

www.p3international.com (Kill a Watt energy-conservation device)

Fair Trade

www.fairtrade.org.uk (Fairtrade Foundation)

www.fairtradeuk.org (online fair trade shop)

www.bafts.org.uk (British Association of Fair Trade Shops)

Fashion and Style

www.conflictfreediamonds.org (The Conflict-Free Diamond Council)

www.ecofabulous.blogs.com (green goods and design blog)

www.inhabitat.com (stories and links to sustainable fashion)

www.nodirtygold.org (campaign to make gold industry more sustainable; links to responsible retailers)

www.stylewillsaveus.com (e-zine on sustainable fashion)

www.sustainablecotton.org (information on organic cotton)

www.sustainablestyle.org (Sustainable Style Foundation)

Food and Farming

www.soilassociation.org (The Soil Association)

www.whyorganic.org (information on organic issues)

www.foodforlife.org.uk (Food for Life)

www.farmersmarkets.net (directory of farmers' markets)

www.localfoodweb.co.uk (information on local food producers and shops)

www.bigbarn.co.uk (find local food producers)

www.sustainweb.org (Sustain – the alliance for better food and farming)

www.localfoodgrants.org (UK local food grants programme)

www.cuco.org.uk (Cultivating Communities, community supported agriculture programme)

www.foodaware.org.uk (Foodaware: the Consumers Food Group)

www.foodfacts.info/blog (blog with fast food nutrition information)

www.msc.org (Marine Stewardship Council)

www.responsibletechnology.org/GMFree (Institute for Responsible Technology; information on GMO-Free food)

www.seaweb.org/resources/aquaculturecenter (SeaWeb's page on sustainable aquaculture)

www.slowfood.com (Slow Food Movement)

www.actiononadditives.com (list of products that contain suspect additives)

www.veriflora.com (eco-label for sustainably grown flowers and plants)

Gardening and Composting

www.allotment.org.uk (information on allotment gardening)

www.gardenorganic.org.uk/hsl/index.php (Heritage Seed Library)

www.farmgarden.org.uk (Federation of City Farms and Community Gardens UK)

www.nsalg.org.uk (National Society of Allotment and Leisure Gardeners)

www.thegreengarden.co.uk (The Green Garden resources)

www.gardenorganic.org.uk (information on organic gardening)
www.rhs.org.uk (Royal Horticultural Association)
www.compost.org.uk (the Compost Association)
www.compostguide.com (online composting guide)
www.howtocompost.org (online guide on composting)
www.wrap.org.uk/composting/index.html (compost suppliers)
www.pan-uk.org (Pesticides Action Network UK)

Green Building

www.bre.co.uk (the Building Research Establishment)
www.breeam.org (Building Research Establishment Environmental Assessment Method)
www.newbuilder.co.uk (resources and news on green building)
www.greenbuildingforum.co.uk (forum for green building)
www.sustainable-construction.org.uk (practical guidance for planners and developers)
www.sustainablebuild.co.uk (eco-friendly building tips and advice)
www.fscus.org (Forest Stewardship Council; label for sustainably harvested wood products)
www.greenbuildingstore.co.uk (online store for green building products)
www.constructionresources.com (sustainable building products outlet)
www.cat.org.uk (Centre for Alternative Technology)
www.ukgbc.org (UK Green Building Council)

Green Energy Generation

www.energywatch.org.uk (UK energy watchdog)
www.energysavingtrust.org.uk/generate_your_own_energy (advice from the Energy Saving Trust)
www.bwea.com (British Wind Energy Association)
www.r-e-a.net (Renewable Energy Association)
www.restats.org.uk (Renewable Energy Statistics for the UK)
www.reuk.co.uk (Renewable Energy UK)

Health and Beauty

www2.btcv.org.uk/display/greengym (information on starting a green gym program)
www.cosmeticsdatabase.com (Cosmetics Safety Database)
www.colipa.com (European Cosmetic Toiletry and Perfumery Association)
www.eartheasy.com/live_nontoxic_solutions.htm (online guide to nontoxic cleaning alternatives)
www.greenlivingideas.com/household-cleaning/index.php (suggestions for making your own nontoxic cleaners)
www.leapingbunny.org (Coalition for Consumer Information on Cosmetics)
www.redcross.org (for information on donating medication)
www.safecosmetics.org (Campaign for Safe Cosmetics)
www.uniteforsight.org/donate_eyeglasses.php (for information on donating eyeglasses)
www.neweyesfortheneedy.org (for information on donating eyeglasses)
www.greenpeople.co.uk (certified organic beauty ranges)
www2.btcv.org.uk/display/greengym (information on Green Gyms in the UK)

Politics and Activism

http://petitions.pm.gov.uk (e-petitions site for the UK Prime Minister)
www.mysociety.org (online tools for activism and political engagement)
www.actionnetwork.org (Action Network)
www.oneplanetliving.org (WWF sustainability initiative)
www.buynothingday.co.uk (information about Buy Nothing Day)
www.blogactionday.org (Blog Action Day information)
www.which.co.uk (consumer action campaigns)
www.globalpolicy.org (monitors policy making at the United Nations)
www.greenpeace.org (Greenpeace, wildlife conservation activism)
www.hrw.org (Human Rights Watch)

Recycling and Waste Management

www.recyclenow.com (general recycling resources)
www.wrap.org.uk (Waste and Recycling Action Programme)

www.crn.org.uk (Community Recycling Network)
www.frn.org.uk (Furniture Reuse Network)
www.recycle.co.uk (free giveaway network)
www.actionaidrecycling.org.uk (printer cartridge and mobile phone recycling)
www.ban.org (Basel Action Network; monitors e-waste recycling programs)
www.wasteonline.org.uk (waste information resources)
www.environment-agency.gov.uk/subjects/waste/ (UK Environment Agency waste information)
www.wastewatch.org.uk (WasteWatch UK)
www.freecycle.org (reuse and resource sharing organisation)
www.mpsonline.org.uk (Mail Preference Service to reduce your junk mail)
www.readymademag.com (DIY magazine featuring inventive reuse projects)

Schools and Children
www.eco-schools.org (International EcoSchools initiative)
www.eco-schools.org.uk (EcoSchools in the UK)
www.saferoutestoschools.org.uk (Safe Routes to School)
www.schoolfoodtrust.org.uk (School Food Trust)
www.cee.org.uk (Council for Environmental Education)
www.rhs.org.uk/schoolgardening (School Gardening initiative)
www.teachernet.gov.uk/growingschools (Growing Schools gardening resource)

Transport
www.sustrans.org.uk (Sustrans, the sustainable transport charity)
www.whatgreencar.com (ratings for cars based on their environmental credentials)
www.critical-mass.info (Critical Mass bike rides worldwide)
www.dft.gov.uk/pgr/sustainable/ (UK government resources on transport)
www.walktoschool.org.uk (UK campaign for walking to school)
www.bike-sharing.blogspot.com (blog about worldwide bike-sharing schemes)
www.liftshare.org (carsharing network)
www.freewheelers.co.uk (international carsharing network)
www.dailyfueleconomytip.com (tips for more efficient driving)

www.hybridcars.com (reviews of hybrid vehicles)
www.nearbio.com (resource for finding biodiesel stations)
www.raileurope.com (information on traveling Europe by train)
www.dft.gov.uk/ActOnCO2 (UK government advice on better driving)
www.streetcar.co.uk (national car-sharing company)

Tourism
www.blueflag.org (eco-label for international beaches and marinas)
www.eco-label.com (eco-label for European products, including tourism facilities)
www.ecovoluteer.org (Eco-volunteer Nature Travel)
www.ethicaltraveler.org (responsible travel blog)
www.globalvolunteers.org (voluntourism site)
www.green-business.co.uk (sustainable tourism certification scheme in the UK)
www.greenglobe21.com (sustainable travel and tourism information)
www.greenhotels.com (Green Hotels Association)
www.green-key.org (international eco-label for tourism facilities)
www.lonelyplanet.com/responsibletravel (tips on responsible travel from Lonely Planet)
www.nationalgeographic.com/travel/sustainable (Center for Sustainable Destinations links and articles)
www.touringnature.com (green tourism guide for Europe)
www.sustainabletravelinternational.org (directory of eco-friendly operators, resources on responsible travel)
www.treadlightly.org (tips on sustainable recreation)
www.voluntourism.org (information on voluntourism)
http://whc.unesco.org (information on UNESCO World Heritage Sites)
www.worldwildlife.org/buyerbeware (tips to avoid buying souvenirs made from endangered species)

Water
www.defra.gov.uk/ENVIRONMENT/water/index.htm (UK government water policy)
www.environment-agency.gov.uk/savewater (tips on saving water)
www.eca-water.gov.uk (business savings on water reduction equipment)

www.water-guide.org.uk (information on UK water industry)

www.ukrivers.net (UK Rivers Network)

www.foodandwaterwatch.org (resources on how to test and filter tap water)

www.h2ouse.org (guide to making your home water efficient)

www.irn.org (International Rivers Network; information on conservation campaigns)

www.rain-barrel.net (guide to collecting rainwater)

www.waterfootprint.org (tool to calculate the water footprint of your lifestyle and certain consumer practices)

www.wateruseitwisely.com (water conservation tips, regional news, and links)

www.worldwaterday.org (information on worldwide water and sanitation issues)

Wildlife and Habitat Conservation

www.defra.gov.uk/wildlife-countryside/ewd/index.htm (information on UK wildlife and habitat conservation)

www.naturalengland.org.uk (Natural England)

www.rspb.org.uk/birdwatch (RSPB Big Garden Birdwatch)

www.treeforall.org.uk (Woodland Trust Tree For All campaign)

www.treesforcities.org (Trees for Cities)

www.coralreefalliance.org (international reef conservation foundation)

www.citizensci.com (general resource and networking site for citizen science projects)

www.rspca.org.uk (Royal Society for the Protection of Animals — advice on rehoming pets and animal care)

www.mangroveactionproject.org (restoration project for mangrove forests worldwide)

www.oceanconservancy.org (The Ocean Conservancy)

www.saveourseas.org (Save Our Seas)

www.surfrider.org (Surfrider Foundation; advocacy against ocean and beach pollution)

www.traffic.org (Traffic, illegal wildlife-trade monitoring organisation)

www.wetlands.org (Wetlands International)

www.worldwildlife.org (World Wildlife Foundation; info on endangered species and conservation projects)

BIBLIOGRAPHY

Bartillat, Laurent de and Simon Retallack. *Stop.* Paris: Éditions du Seuil, 2003.

Bouttier-Guérivé, Gaëlle and Thierry Thouvenot. *Planète attitude,* les gestes écologiques au quotidian. Paris: Éditions du Seuil, 2004.

Callard, Sarah and Diane Millis. *Le Grand guide de l'écologie.* Paris: J'ai lu, 2003.

Carson, Rachel. *Silent Spring.* New York: Mariner Books, 2002.

Chagnoleau, Serge. *L'écologie au bureau.* Paris: Maxima, 1992.

Desai, Pooran. *One Planet Living.* Bristol, U.K.: Alistar Sawday's, 2006.

Dubois, Philippe J. *Un nouveau climat.* Paris: Éditions de La Martinière, 2003.

Dubois, Philippe J. *Vers l'ultime extinction? la biodiversité en danger.* Paris: Éditions de La Martinière, 2004.

Dupuis, Marie-France and Bernard Fischesser. *Guide illustré de l'écologie.* Paris: Éditions de La Martinière, 2000.

Glocheux, Dominique. *Sauver la planète, mode d'emploi.* Paris: Éditions J. C. Lattès, 2004.

Hillman, Mayer. *How We Can Save the Planet.* New York: St. Martin's Griffin, 2008.

Matagne, Patrick. *Comprendre l'écologie et son histoire.* Paris: Delachaux et Niestlé, 2002.

Ramade, François. *Dictionnaire encyclopédique de l'écologie et des sciences de l'environnement.* Paris: Dunod, 2002.

Steffen, Alex. *Worldchanging.* New York: Harry N. Abrams, 2006.

ACKNOWLEDGMENTS

I would like to particularly thank:

My editor Hervé de La Martinière for his loyalty.

Benoît Nacci for his attentive photographic selection.

Anne Jankéliowitch for the quality of her research and her work on the 365 texts that accompany my photographs.

Catherine Guigon and Emmanuelle Halkin for their thoughtful arrangement of the texts.

The team at Éditions de La Martinière: Dominique Escartin, Sophie Giraud, Audrey Hette, Marianne Lassandro, Valérie Roland, Isabelle Perrod, Sophie Postollec, Cécile Vanderbroucque.

Thanks to:

Everyone who participated in these trips at close quarters or from a distance:

Claude Arié, Yann Arthus-Bertrand, Jean-Philippe Astruc, Jacques Bardot, Allain Bougrain Dubourg, Jean-Marc Bour, Monique Brandily, Yves Carmagnolles, Sylvie Carpentier, Jean-François Chaix, Carolina Codo, Richard Fitzpatrick, Alain Gerente, Patrice Godon, Robert Guillard, Nathalie Hoizey, Gérard Jugie, Janot and Janine Lamberton and the Inlandsis expedition team, Monique Mathews, Frédéric and Mimi Neema, Stephan Peyron, Philippe Poissonier, Gloria Raad, Le Raie Manta club, Margot Reynes, Hoa and Jean Rossi, John and Linda Rumney and the Undersea Explorer team, Diane Sacco, Hervé Saliou, Vincent Steiger, Sally Zalewski…

Gero Furcheim, Gaelle Guoinguené, Jean-Jacques Viau at Leica, who have been loyal followers for so long. I worked with excellent Leica R9 and M7 cameras and 19 mm to 280 mm lenses that are reliable in any circumstance.

Marc Héraud and Bruno Baudry at Fujifilm for their help and support. All the photos were shot on Fujichrome Velvia (50 Asa) films.

Olivier Bigot, Denis Cuisy de Rush Labo, Jean-François Gallois de Central Color, and Stephan Ledoux at cité de l'Image.

The Richard Lippman team at Quadrilaser.

My apologies to all those I have forgotten to name and who helped me in this work.

I am sincerely sorry and thank them wholeheartedly.